"For many centuries Europe was the citadel of the Christian faith, resisting attempts to dislodge it and taking steps to extend it more broadly. Here is a set of chapters that outline, thematically as well as chronologically, the main features of its historical experience. They reveal both why the continent's Christian strength survived so long and why it has been sapped in the recent past."

—DAVID BEBBINGTON, professor emeritus of history, University of Stirling

"Looking for a current and accessible book on the story of Christianity in Europe? Search no longer! This lucid and engaging picture of European Christianity from the early church to the present day offers an excellent resource for scholars, students, and general readers. Congratulations to Alec Ryrie and his team of contributors for this outstanding volume."

—KARIN MAAG, director, Meeter Center for Calvin Studies

"A superb historical overview of European Christianity. The contributors have done a masterful job in their short chapters of summarizing the subject assigned to each; the net effect is an incisive treatment of the complex history of the Christian church in Europe."

—DAVID TRIM, professor of church history, Seventh-day Adventist Theological Seminary

"This excellent collection by leading scholars redefines the way historians tell the story of European Christianity by integrating it into a global framework. While remaining attentive to classical themes and periodization, the chapters draw out the European Church's reciprocal relations with faith communities across the world established by mission, empire, and trade. *Entangling Web* is a most welcome addition to scholarship on the history of Christianity."

—DAVID MAXWELL, professor of ecclesiastical history, Emmanuel College, University of Cambridge

"Christianity did not begin in Europe, and today its most vibrant forms may be found on other continents. And yet, from the rise of the papacy to the upheaval of the Reformation, it is in Europe that much of Christian history and development has played out. This excellent collection explores that story without Eurocentrism or knee-jerk revisionism. It will help readers understand the events and forces that have shaped both contemporary Europe and world Christianity."

—JAMES WALTERS, professor in practice, London School of Economics and Political Science

"This collection of essays illustrates clearly and succinctly how Europe became a 'Christian' continent, while demonstrating the enormous divergences within this progression, its expansion into other parts of the world, and European Christianity's current decline. An essential read for understanding this essential part of the history of world Christianity."

—ALLAN H. ANDERSON, professor emeritus of mission and Pentecostal studies, University of Birmingham, UK

"Boldly conceived and argued, these essays not only overturn the tables of the familiar history but offer a vision for the story of Christianity in its proper global context. Innovative and provocative history writing at its best."

—BRUCE GORDON, professor of ecclesiastical history, Yale Divinity School

"*Entangling Web* is a magisterial refutation of the notion that the growth of Christianity in the Global South is a corrective to the historically 'European' character of Christianity. Instead, the volume skillfully shows that the story of Christianity in Europe is complex and endlessly diverse. Masterfully outlining how multiple players constructed the idea of Europe as a Christian entity, the volume shows us that historic centers of Christian faith—Rome, Canterbury, Geneva—continue to be relevant today as in the past."

—JOEL CABRITA, associate professor of history, Stanford University

"For better or worse, European Christianity has played a significant role in the resurgence of the phenomenon of world Christianity since the late twentieth century. This book impressively captures the major features of European Christianity that are pertinent to the study of the transmission of the Christian faith within the diverse context of Europe. It is a welcome contribution to the discourse on world Christianity."

—VICTOR I. EZIGBO, professor of theology and world Christianity, Bethel University

"The historical narratives in the book expose the hypocrisy of disowning the role of Christianity in the formation of European culture and identity. Simultaneously, it skillfully avoids projecting an imagined homogenous European Christian identity as the normative standard for the many Christianities worldwide, especially of the Global South. This highly thought-provoking work arrives at a critical juncture as Europe transits from secularism to nihilism. A refreshing approach makes it a compelling read."

—FELIX WILFRED, professor emeritus of philosophy and religious thought, State University of Madras

"With accessible language and appealing narratives, Ryrie and Lamport bring together a collection of essays with a fresh interpretation of European Christianity. *Entangling Web* is a pedagogical resource to help the student of Christian history re-imagine European Christianity as a world religion rather than the normative standard for other expressions of Christianity."

—CARLOS F. CARDOZA, professor of world Christianity, Baylor University

Entangling Web

The Global Story of Christianity Series
History, Context, and Communities

Seven One-Volume Books

SERIES EDITORS
Emma Wild-Wood & Mark A. Lamport

SERIES ASSISTANT EDITOR
Gina A. Zurlo

SERIES INTRODUCTION
Dana L. Robert

BOOK EDITORS
Mitri Raheb *(Middle East)* | Amos Yong *(Asia)* | Wanjiru Gitau *(Africa)*
Alex Ryrie *(Europe)* | Raimundo Barreto *(Latin America)*
Upolu Lumā Vaai *(Oceania)* | Christopher Evans *(North America)*

SERIES EDITORIAL ADVISORY BOARD
Edwin Aponte *(Louisville Institute)*
Elias Bongmba *(Rice University)*
Arun Jones *(Candler School of Theology/Emory University)*
Brett Knowles *(University of Otago)*
David Maxwell *(University of Cambridge, UK)*
Elizabeth Monier *(University of Cambridge, UK)*
Dana L. Robert *(Center for Global Christianity
and Mission/Boston University)*
Nelly van Doorn-Harder *(Wake Forest University)*
Stephanie Wong *(Valparaiso University)*

SENIOR EDITORIAL CONSULTANT
Joshua Erb

Series Concept

The Global Story of Christianity Series is designed as a set of accessible introductions for those who wish to understand the emergence of the Christian faith and its global church presence today. The concept of "story" will be the featured motif and is reflected in fifteen chapters spread over three main subheadings in each book:

Section One: The Story of Christianity Narrated
 in Historical Context

Section Two: The Story of Christianity Expressed
 in a Grand Church Family Mosaic

Section Three: The Story of Christianity Encounters
 Twenty-First Century Issues

The Global Story of Christianity Series

Book Title	Year of Release	Editors
Surviving Jewel: The Enduring Story of Christianity in the Middle East	Book 1: 2022	Mitri Raheb *(Dar al-Kalima University College, Bethlehem)* & Mark A. Lamport
Uncovering the Pearl: The Hidden Story of Christianity in Asia	Book 2: 2023	Amos Yong *(Fuller Theological Seminary)* & Mark A. Lamport
Globalizing Legacies: The Intermingling Story of Christianity in Africa	Book 3: 2024	Wanjiru M. Gitau *(Palm Beach Atlantic University, Florida)* & Mark A. Lamport
Entangling Web: The Fractious Story of Christianity in Europe	Book 4: 2024	Alec Ryrie *(University of Durham, UK)* & Mark A. Lamport
Engaging Coloniality: The Liberative Story of Christianity in Latin America	Book 5: 2024	Raimundo César Barreto Jr. *(Princeton Theological Seminary)* & Mark A. Lamport
Restoring Identities: The Contextualizing Story of Christianity in Oceania	Book 6: 2023	Upolu Vaai *(Pacific Theological College, Fiji)* & Mark A. Lamport
Expanding Energy: The Dynamic Story of Christianity in North America	Book 7: 2024	Christopher H. Evans *(Boston University)* & Mark A. Lamport

Entangling Web

The Fractious Story of Christianity in Europe

EDITED BY
Alec Ryrie
AND
Mark A. Lamport

Introductions by Dana L. Robert and Brian Stanley

CASCADE *Books* • Eugene, Oregon

ENTANGLING WEB
The Fractious Story of Christianity in Europe

Copyright © 2024 Wipf and Stock Publishers. All rights reserved. Except for brief quotations in critical publications or reviews, no part of this book may be reproduced in any manner without prior written permission from the publisher. Write: Permissions, Wipf and Stock Publishers, 199 W. 8th Ave., Suite 3, Eugene, OR 97401.

Cascade Books
An Imprint of Wipf and Stock Publishers
199 W. 8th Ave., Suite 3
Eugene, OR 97401

www.wipfandstock.com

PAPERBACK ISBN: 978-1-6667-3002-9
HARDCOVER ISBN: 978-1-6667-2102-7
EBOOK ISBN: 978-1-6667-2103-4

Cataloguing-in-Publication data:

Names: Ryrie, Alec, editor. | Lamport, Mark A., editor.

Title: Entangling web : the fractious story of Christianity in Europe / edited by Alec Ryrie and Mark A. Lamport.

Description: Eugene, OR: Cascade Books, 2024. | The Global Story of Christianity Series. | Includes bibliographical references and index.

Identifiers: ISBN 978-1-6667-3002-9 (paperback). | ISBN 978-1-6667-2102-7 (hardcover). | ISBN 978-1-6667-2103-4 (ebook).

Subjects: LCSH: Christianity—Europe—History. | Europe—Church history.

Classification: BR252 E57 2024 (print). | BR252 (epub).

03/15/24

Scripture quotations marked KJV are from the King James or Authorized Version.

Scripture quotations marked NIV are from the Holy Bible, New International Version®, copyright ©1973, 1978, 1984, 2011 by Biblica, Inc.® Used by permission. All rights reserved worldwide.

For *Alec*—To *William L. Wizeman, SJ* (1964-2010), who would have enjoyed arguing with this book

For *Mark*—To *Bede* (English church historian, 673-735), *Peter Waldo* (1140-1205) and the Proto-Protestant *Waldensians*, *Conrad Grebel* (1498-1526) and the *Anabaptists* (from whom my Swiss Brethren ancestors emerged), *John Wesley* (1703-1791) and the *Methodists* (from whom my English ancestors emerged), *John R. Mott* (1865-1955) and the *Edinburgh World Missionary Conference* (1910), and *John Stott* (1921-2011) and the *Lausanne Congress on World Evangelization* (1974)

Contents

Series Introduction: The Global Story of Christianity: History, Contexts, and Communities—Dana L. Robert | xi
Editors | xxi
Preface—Gina A. Zurlo and Mark A. Lamport | xxiii
Acknowledgments | xxxi
About the Contributors | xxxiii
Abbreviations | xxxvii
Book Introduction—Brian Stanley | xxxix

Section One
The Story of Christianity Narrated in Historical Context

1. Christianity Emerges in the Era of Late Antiquity—Christine Shepardson | 3
2. Christianity Negotiates the Western Middle Ages—Peter Sherlock | 18
3. Christianity Transforms in the Reformation—Alec Ryrie | 32
4. Christianity Navigates the Enlightenment and the Age of Empire—Ambrogio A. Caiani | 47

Section Two

The Story of Christianity Adapts to the European Context

5. The Orthodox Story of Christianity in Europe—ANDREW LOUTH | 65
6. The Catholic Story—SHAUN BLANCHARD | 80
7. The Protestant Story: National and Territorial Churches—CHARLOTTE METHUEN | 97
8. The Protestant Story: Nonconformists, Radicals, and Sects—MARK W. LEE | 114
9. The Story of Christianity and Other Religions—MARK R. LINDSAY | 130

Section Three

The Story of Christianity Encounters Modernity and Postmodernity

10. Industry, Economic Transformation, and European Christianity—JAMES KENNEDY | 149
11. Empire and European Christianity—DARIN D. LENZ | 166
12. War and European Christianity—MICHAEL SNAPE | 182
13. Communism and European Christianity—KATHARINA KUNTER | 196
14. Social Transformation, Gender, and European Christianity—LAURA RAMSAY | 213
15. Diaspora and the Redefinition of European Christianity in the Twenty-First Century—DARRELL JACKSON | 230

Time Line: Europe—BRETT KNOWLES | 249

Index | 285

Series Introduction

The Global Story of Christianity

History, Contexts, and Communities

DANA L. ROBERT

WHAT DOES IT MEAN *to tell the story* of global Christianity? Storytelling is important for personal identity, for community life, and for shared humanity. When people tell their own stories, both individually and as communities of faith, they share who they are and who they hope to become. When people make friends, they swap stories. They introduce themselves. They discuss their work, or where they went to school. They might talk about the sports teams they support, or what activities they enjoy. As people get to know each other better, they exchange stories about their families, or politics, or other important issues. Friends do things together—and the being together creates memories that launch new stories they recall when they see each other again. In listening to each other, people's stories merge and create a common basis for relationships—even across boundaries or divisions.

Global Christianity is the story of a huge extended family. Christians are rooted in a common ancestor, Jesus Christ. For two thousand years, the followers of Jesus of Nazareth have traced their spiritual lineage through him to the God of ancient Israel, as spoken through the prophets and written in the Bible and celebrated in worship and outreach. Christianity is now the world's largest religion, encompassing one-third of the world's peoples. During the twentieth century, the family of faith burst out of European frameworks and began growing rapidly in Africa, Asia, and Latin America. By 2018, Africa had become the continent with the largest number of Christians, followed by Latin America, and Europe, with Asia soon to become second in numbers.[1] Christianity as a global story reminds me of the chatter at a giant family reunion, where the relatives get together and reminisce about their distant family history, and the departed saints that

---

1. Zurlo, "Who Owns Global Christianity?"

they remember—and the old family arguments that never seem to end. For better or worse, whether or not they know each other personally, the people who call themselves Christians are spiritual brothers, sisters, and long-lost cousins. Shared family history connects them.

And yet, nobody has only *one* story. This book series on the global story of Christianity embodies many stories that have unfolded across two thousand years of time, and which inhabit wide-ranging geographic and cultural spaces. The sheer size and complexity of the global Christian family means that a shared history is composed of multiple memories, from thousands of contexts. Being part of a community means organizing the stories into a convincing whole and claiming a common identity through them. Communities can be direct sets of relationships, such as families, neighborhoods, sports clubs, therapy groups, and local churches. They can also be "imagined" and thus composed of people who may never meet in person, but whose groups—including ethnicities, cities, political parties, and even nations—share common interpretations of experiences. For Christians, both personal and imagined faith communities use shared narratives to organize their spiritual realities. And yet, the meaning and identity of faith communities also changes over time, depending on the context. Depending on one's purpose or needs, different parts of one's story become more important than others. I am reminded of a friend who was the new pastor of a small church. Each week, no matter how hard he tried to get the old-timers to move, nobody would sit in the front section of the church. Finally, in frustration he asked one old man why he wouldn't move toward the front of the church. "I've been sitting in this pew for forty years," he replied. "It is not my fault that the people who used to sit in front of me have died or moved away." In his mind, the old man was still sitting in his imagined community made up of previous generations of friends and neighbors who had composed his church. But the new minister, looking out every week, saw nothing but empty front pews, waiting to be filled with new faces and new stories. Because the context had changed, the church community had changed; and because the community had changed, the context had changed—even though the old man had not moved anywhere at all. And yet, until the old man shared his story, the history of his community, the new minister couldn't understand the old man's resistance to his request.

History, contexts, and communities—all these pieces are important frameworks for organizing the many stories that together paint a global picture of Christianity. The connection among history, contexts, and communities was beautifully expressed by the late Andrew Walls, Scottish historian and expert on African Christianity, and a founder of the field of "world

Christianity."[2] Walls asked his readers to imagine a visitor from outer space, a professor of comparative religions, who visits Earth for fieldwork every few centuries, to observe the practices and beliefs of representative Christians. First the space man visits the original Christians in Jerusalem, a few years after the death of Jesus. He finds that they are Jewish and follow Jewish customs, including offering animal sacrifices, worshiping on the seventh day, and reading old scrolls in Hebrew. They identify the Messiah, Son of Man and Suffering Servant, with their teacher who just died, Jesus of Nazareth. They live in close-knit families and eat meals together in each other's homes. When the visitor from space next returns to earth, he observes a big church meeting of church leaders around 325 CE, in Nicaea (now in Turkey). Hardly any are Jewish and most are unmarried. To them, sacrifice means a ritual meal of bread and wine and they worship God on the first day of the week, not the seventh. They talk about Jesus, but they are debating whether the Greek words *homoousios* or *homoiousios* better characterize his nature. They argue a lot about theology.

Walls goes on to describe the space visitor's next field visit, Ireland in the 600s. There monks are gathered on a rocky coastline reciting the psalms. Some are going into a small boat with a box of beautiful manuscripts heading toward nearby islands to ask the inhabitants to give up worship of multiple nature divinities. Other monks sit alone in caves, denying themselves food. Upon examining the manuscripts, he finds they are the same writings he saw on his last visit, and he hears the monks recite the same basic statement of belief or creed he heard at Nicaea in 325. Yet these monks seem much more interested in being holy than in debating theology.

Next the space visitor returns to earth in 1840s London. He finds a convention of mostly white Christians hearing speeches about the desirability of promoting Christianity and trade in Africa. To eliminate the slave trade, they are planning to send missionaries, lobby the government, and promote the education of black Africans. He sees many people carrying printed Bibles and finds out they accept the creed of Nicaea. They talk about holiness but would be shocked at the thought of praying alone in a cave. Rather, they are well fed and committed to political activism.

Finally, the space visitor returns in the 1980s to Lagos, Nigeria, in time to see a white-robed procession of people dancing and chanting through the streets. They are inviting people to come with them and experience the power of God. They talk about healing and driving out evil

---

2. Walls preferred the term *world Christianity* to what this book series is calling *global Christianity*. On the use of the terms *world* versus *global*, see Robert, "World Christianity"; Sanneh and McClymond, "Introduction," 4–6; Johnson and Kim, "Describing the Worldwide Christian Phenomenon."

spirits. They say they accept the creed of Nicaea, but they are not really interested in theological creeds or in political activism. They do care passionately about personal empowerment through prayer, preaching, and healing. Back on his own planet, the professor must figure out what it all means. He notes that the location of the Christian heartland has shifted each time he has visited. How does he conclude what it means to be a Christian? Is there any coherence across time? What do Christians around the world have in common, despite the visible differences in culture, race, locations, ethnicities, and practices that he observed?

Andrew Walls's fantasy about the space visitor illustrates the complexities of telling the global story of Christianity. What each era had in common was its historical connection. Like links in a chain, history connected the different communities to each other. Jews from Jerusalem preached to Greeks and led to the events of Nicaea in 325. Emissaries from the Mediterranean planted the seeds that became Irish Christianity. Celtic missionaries launched what became the religion of London in the 1840s, and the British evangelical lobby sent the messengers who energized churches in Africa. To bring the story up to the present, today Nigerian churches send missionaries around the world, including to London. In fact, some of the largest churches in Europe have African pastors. Other historical connections involve a "continuity of consciousness" across time.[3] In each group's story, Jesus Christ "has ultimate significance." They use the "same sacred writings," though in different formats and languages. Writes Walls, "Each group thinks of itself as having some community with the others," continuous with ancient Israel, even though they are no longer Jews.[4] These elements of continuity, however, are embedded in very different contexts, ranging from the Middle East to West Asia, to Europe, Africa, and beyond. In each context, the space visitor found worshipping communities, ranging in form from house churches to bishops' gatherings, from monasteries to conferences and popular processions. The shape of the Christian communities and what they do differs according to their local cultures, politics, and historical period. And yet, taken together, the many stories echo the shared memory of Jesus Christ, passed down through the ages.

About This Book Series

To tell the global story of Christianity, each book in this series is organized into a common format. If we think about what goes into telling our stories,

3. Walls, "Gospel as Prisoner," 6.
4. Walls, "Gospel as Prisoner," 6–7.

the elements are common to the books in the series. The *first* thing to notice is that the books each cover a different *geographic region*. In other words, they are organized by "neighborhood." This organization allows the editors, who come from each region, to explore the "historical context" and to answer the questions: Where are we from and how did we get here? Who are the people who brought Christianity? How did the Christian story change in each part of the globe, and what difference did it make? How are the followers of Jesus in that region anchored in his heritage? What is the testimony of the people of each region about their Christian identity, and how did they become part of the global story of Christianity? There are a range of answers to questions like "Where are we from and how did we get here?," including stories of migration and mission, slavery and coercion, violence and resistance, joy and struggle. Analyzing where they have come from also allows the editors to build toward where they think their region might be going.

The *second* section of each book in the series talks about the kind of *faith communities* found in each geographic region, and the issues they face. Communities reflect group identities shaped by such factors as theology, ethnicity, language, or persecution. In the case of the volume on Asia, a vast continent with thousands of different ethnic groups, the communities described are organized by subregion. The North America volume discusses some of the fundamental theological and organizational issues behind different groups of North American Christians. In Christian parlance, faith communities shaped by shared theologies and histories are often called "denominations," organized groups of Christians that recognize each other as brothers and sisters but have different stories to tell about how they got to be where they are today. Some faith communities are rather like private clubs, with high membership fees and strict rules as to who can belong. Others are more like groups of sports fans, open to anyone who feels like supporting the team and participating in its activities. In all cases, the discussion of different communities shows how their identity reflects both its local context and its participation in the global story of Christianity. Communities each have their own special saints, prophets, and leaders—people who have guided them and symbolize their identity to the world. They have their own favorite religious practices. Conversations internal to each community spill into the outside world, and sometimes attract others to join them. Contexts shape communities, and communities shape contexts. Faith communities are where the global story of Christianity forms church families and creates spaces in which they build a home.

The *third* section of each volume discusses *global issues* that are important to each region today. This is where the urgency behind each volume becomes clear. What are the passions that drive the communities in context?

What problems do they face? What political and social issues are vital to their well-being? Some of the volumes explicitly discuss what churches call "ecumenism," churches cooperating and joining together to pursue shared ideals and common goals. Important twenty-first-century issues such as climate change, racism, interfaith relations, war and peace, gender, church-state relations, and religious persecution are global issues that affect people on every continent. It is often these pressing issues that connect Christians in solidarity with others across geographic boundaries.

Elements of a Global Story

Although each book in the series stands alone, putting them into dialogue with each other paints a bigger picture of what is called "global (or world) Christianity." As already mentioned, Christianity in the twenty-first century has become a multicultural religion practiced by one third of the world. The fact that it exists nearly everywhere means that to tell the story of Christianity in one region affects the story of Christianity in another region. To think of Christianity as a global story requires seeing each region as connected. In scholarly terms, this idea is called "entanglement," an important concept in global history. The idea of historical entanglement means that each region is shaped by its relationship to the others. To think of Christianity as a global story means looking for ways in which the local and the global are entangled—all mixed up together, influencing each other, and not easily separated. As people in each region embrace what they see as the universal story of Jesus Christ, the way they practice their faith affects the nature of the religion as a whole. To be "global" means that regional stories are linked, with and through their Christian faiths.

Looking for interconnections among the regions is a way to trace how the assumption of entanglement creates a global story out of what are usually thought of as separate stories. As you read the different books in this series, also zoom out and look for common themes that bind the regions together to create a global story, though from different perspectives and angles. What follows are three major themes that intersect all the volumes—movement, translation, and public theologies:

- *Movement* is central to the global story of Christianity. Without new people entering old spaces, or people on the move, Christianity could not spread from one place to another. The New Testament journeys of Paul throughout the Mediterranean modeled how Christians moved from place to place in spreading their faith. Migration and "global diaspora" are features of the global Christian story, especially today when more people are on the move than ever before. When people deliberately cross boundaries to spread their faith, they are often called missionaries. During the era of colonialism, Europeans sent missionaries around the world. Today missionaries go from everywhere to everywhere, including especially from Korea, Brazil, Nigeria, and North America.[5] Sometimes movement to new areas causes migrants to embrace Christianity as a new way of life. Although migrants typically seek economic security over religious change, sometimes the act of moving to a new place can inspire them to launch missions of their own: Central Americans moving to North American cities, and Africans moving to Eastern Europe, have started numerous churches. Forced migration can also spread Christianity. In a monstrous crime against humanity, over ten million Africans were sent to the Americas as slaves. Many of their descendants became Christians and reshaped the faith into a vehicle of resistance. Migrating people—whether forced or by choice—bind together their places of origin with their destinations and change both places in the process.[6]

- *Translation* is another theme that makes Christianity a global story. In literal terms, translation of the Bible into thousands of languages has been the foundation of Protestant missions for centuries, and the basis for faith-sharing across linguistic and cultural boundaries. Once people have the Bible in their own language, they interpret it according to their own cultural norms and needs.[7] During the twentieth century, many indigenous prophets—equipped with the Bible in their own language and inspired by dreams and visions—launched new Christian movements in Africa, Asia, and Latin America. Studies of conversion show how new Christians translate the Christian faith into their own personal contexts, or use it to revitalize their surroundings.[8] At a more theoretical level, translation can refer to cultural processes of hybridization, of adopting the Christian message and reframing it to fit new contexts and to energize Christian communities.[9] Since all commu-

5. Robert, *Christian Mission*.
6. See Frederiks and Nagy, *Religion, Migration, and Identity*; see also Hanciles, *Migration and the Making*, and Hanciles, *Beyond Christendom*.
7. Sanneh, *Translating the Message*.
8. Kling, *History of Christian Conversion*.
9. For a postcolonial analysis and typology of historical religious encounters, including syncretism and selection, see Lindenfeld, *World Christianity and Indigenous Experience*, 1–30. See also Jones, *Christian Interculture*, and Gruber, *Intercultural Theology*.

nication comes packaged in particular cultural forms, the process of translation is necessary for sharing the Christian faith across all kinds of ethnic, cultural, and geographic barriers. As Christians encounter other cultures and live alongside persons of other religions, their faith is often stimulated into renewed life. The translation process, both on personal and social levels, is an endlessly rich source of innovation that feeds into the global story of Christianity.

- *Public theologies* also shape the global story of Christianity. In the modern West, people often think of faith as a private matter, separate from politics or social life. But the idea that religion is a matter of personal choice, irrelevant to community life, is a fairly recent cultural innovation that itself assumes a public theology of secularism.[10] In most of the world, in most periods of history, religion carries practical implications for how people live in community. Christianity shapes people's attitudes toward authority, power, nature, gender relations, and human rights. Such ideas as "the doctrine of discovery," or the "priesthood of all believers," or "one nation under God" express the relationship of Christianity to peoples, politics, and land. The global story of Christianity consists of theological flows that spread around the world through migration and social media.[11] Public theologies require analyzing flows of power, including the supernatural and spiritual power embedded in Christian belief itself, the unequal political and economic power of Christians who use faith to justify control of others, and the tenacious power of resilience by Christians who are suffering or persecuted. By the late 1900s, evangelicalism, liberation theologies, and Pentecostal practices were all vehicles for political power, especially in Africa and the Americas. Christian charitable outreach through nongovernmental organizations remains a major social factor throughout the world, especially in poor communities. Half of all Christians are Roman Catholics, a worldwide faith network with a central teaching authority lodged in the pope and the Vatican. Public theologies—the globalization of religious ideas, institutions, power, and practices—are a key feature of Christianity as a world religion.

---

10. Casanova, *Public Religions in the Modern World*.
11. Schreiter, *New Catholicity*.

Conclusion: From Local Stories to Global Story and Back Again

To tell the global story of Christianity requires reconstructing the entangled histories of communities down through the ages, in different regions. It requires retracing their historical contexts and learning how communities respond to the urgent issues of the day. As this series shows, only as different Christian communities tell their own stories—and listen to the stories of others—can the global story of Christianity be glimpsed in all its fullness.

For Further Reading

Casanova, José. *Public Religions in the Modern World*. Chicago: University of Chicago Press, 2011.

Frederiks, Martha, and Dorottya Nagy, eds. *Religion, Migration, and Identity: Methodological and Theological Explorations*. Theology and Mission in World Christianity 2. Leiden: Brill, 2016.

Gruber, Judith. *Intercultural Theology: Exploring World Christianity after the Cultural Turn*. Göttingen: Vandenhoeck & Ruprecht, 2018.

Hanciles, Jehu J. *Beyond Christendom: Globalization, African Migration, and the Transformation of the West*. Maryknoll, NY: Orbis, 2008.

———. *Migration and the Making of Global Christianity*. Grand Rapids: Eerdmans, 2021.

Johnson, Todd M., and Sandra S. Kim. "Describing the Worldwide Christian Phenomenon." *International Bulletin of Missionary Research* 29 (2005) 80–84.

Johnson, Todd M., and Gina A. Zurlo. *World Christian Encyclopedia*. 3rd ed. Edinburgh: Edinburgh University Press, 2019.

Jones, Arun, ed. *Christian Interculture: Texts and Voices from Colonial and Postcolonial Worlds*. University Park: Penn State University Press, 2021.

Kling, David. *A History of Christian Conversion*. New York: Oxford University Press, 2020.

Lindenfeld, David. *World Christianity and Indigenous Experience: A Global History, 1500–2000*. Cambridge: Cambridge University Press, 2021.

Robert, Dana L. *Christian Mission: How Christianity Became a World Religion*. Hoboken, NJ: Wiley-Blackwell, 2009.

———. "World Christianity as a Revitalization Movement." In *World Christianity: History, Methodologies, Horizons*, edited by Jehu Hanciles, 17–18. Maryknoll, NY: Orbis, 2021.

Sanneh, Lamin, and Michael J. McClymond. "Introduction." In *The Wiley Blackwell Companion to World Christianity*, edited by Lamin Sanneh and Michael McClymond, 1–18. Malden, MA: Wiley-Blackwell, 2016.

Sanneh, Lamin O. *Translating the Message: The Missionary Impact on Culture*. Maryknoll, NY: Orbis, 2009.

Schreiter, Robert J. *The New Catholicity: Theology between the Global and the Local*. Maryknoll, NY: Orbis, 2004.

Walls, Andrew. "The Gospel as Prisoner and Liberator of Culture." In *The Missionary Movement in Christian History Studies in the Transmission of Faith*, 3–15. Maryknoll, NY: Orbis, 1996.

Zurlo, Gina A. "Who Owns Global Christianity?" https://www.gordonconwell.edu/blog/who-owns-global-christianity/.

Editors

Alec Ryrie (DPhil, theology, St Cross College, University of Oxford) is Professor of the History of Christianity at Durham University, coeditor of the *Journal of Ecclesiastical History*, and a Fellow of the British Academy. He is Emeritus Professor of Divinity at Gresham College, London. His books include *Unbelievers: An Emotional History of Doubt* (2019); *Protestants: The Faith That Made the Modern World* (2017); *Being Protestant in Reformation Britain* (2013); and *The Sorcerer's Tale: Faith and Fraud in Tudor England* (2008).

Mark A. Lamport (PhD, Michigan State University) has been a professor for forty years at theological schools in the United States and Europe. He is coauthor of *Nurturing Faith: A Practical Theology for Educating Christians* (2021); and coeditor of *Emerging Theologies from the Global South* (2022); *Christianity in the Middle East* (2 vols., 2020); *Encyclopedia of Christianity in the Global South* (2 vols., 2018); *Encyclopedia of Martin Luther and the Reformation* (2 vols., 2017); *Encyclopedia of Christianity in the United States* (5 vols., 2016); and *Encyclopedia of Christian Education* (3 vols., 2015). He works from Grand Rapids and Fort Myers.

Series Introduction

Dana L. Robert (PhD, Yale University) is Truman Collins Professor of World Christianity and History of Mission, and Director of the Center for Global Christianity and Mission at Boston University School of Theology. She is a member of the American Academy of Arts and Sciences and in 2017, she received the Lifetime Achievement Award from the American Society of

Missiology. Recent books include *Faithful Friendships: Embracing Diversity in Christian Community* (2019) and *African Christian Biography: Stories, Lives, and Challenges* (2018). An active lay United Methodist, in 2019 Roberts spoke at the 150th anniversary of the United Methodist Women.

Book Introduction

Brian Stanley (PhD, University of Cambridge) has taught in theological colleges and universities in London, Bristol, and Cambridge, and from 1996 to 2001 was Director of the Currents in World Christianity Project at the University of Cambridge. He was a Fellow of St Edmund's College, Cambridge, from 1996 to 2008, and joined the University of Edinburgh in January 2009 as Professor of World Christianity and Director of the Centre for the Centre for the Study of World Christianity. He is now Professor Emeritus of World Christianity. His most recent book is *Christianity in the Twentieth Century: A World History* (2018); he has also edited for publication Andrew F. Walls's *The Missionary Movement from the West: A Biography from Birth to Old Age* (2023).

Preface

GINA A. ZURLO AND MARK A. LAMPORT

EUROPE HAS A TREMENDOUSLY important role in the history of Christianity and was the continent with the most Christians from roughly the year 900 to 1980. However, Europe is now home to only 22 percent of all Christians in the world, down from 68 percent in 1900. The major trend of European religion in the twentieth and twenty-first centuries has been secularization—disestablishment and decreased influence of state churches, lower importance of religion in the public sphere, decline of religious beliefs and practices, and individual religious switching from Christianity to atheism and agnosticism. The data presented in this preface are of religious affiliation, that is, self-identification as Christian by membership in an institutional church structure, *not* beliefs, attitudes, or practices. Christian self-identification in Europe remains high, but it is widely observed that most European Christians are nonpracticing. In Western and Northern Europe in particular, rates of belief in God, prayer, and church attendance are quite low. The situation is different for ethnic minority churches, however, which report much higher levels of belief and practices. Like everywhere else in the world, religion in Europe is complex.

Figure 1. North/South Distribution of Christianity, 33–2050 CE

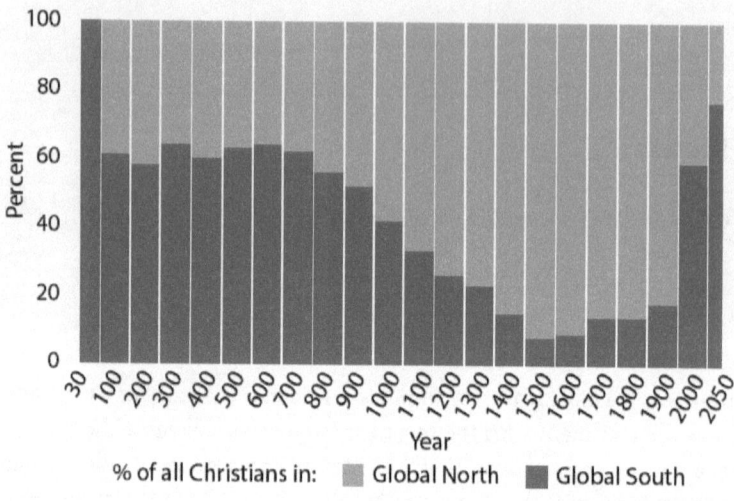

% of all Christians in: ▪ Global North ▪ Global South

Source: Todd M. Johnson and Gina A. Zurlo, *World Christian Encyclopedia*, 3rd ed. (Edinburgh: Edinburgh University Press, 2019), 4. Used by permission of the authors.

Table 1 shows trends in religion and nonreligion in Europe from 1900 to 2020, with projections to 2050. In 1900, Europe was nearly entirely religious in 1900 (99.6 percent), mostly Christian, but with small populations of Muslims and Jews (each 2 percent). By the turn of the twenty-first century, religious affiliation in Europe had dropped to 84 percent, coupled with an increase of atheists and agnostics, together with 16 percent of the population in 2000. Although still growing in absolute numbers from 381 million in 1900 to 561 million in 2000, the Christian share of Europe's population decreased to 77 percent by 2000 and continues its decline. Muslims grew substantially in the twentieth century, from 9 million in 1900 to 40 million in 2000, adding another 11 million between 2000 and 2020 to now represent nearly 7 percent of the population (51 million). Europe's Jewish communities suffered the most in the twentieth century due to the Shoah, with their population decimated from nearly 10 million in 1900 (2.4 percent) to just over 1 million today (<1 percent). Looking toward 2050, Europe is likely to be 70 percent Christian, 18 percent nonreligious, 10 percent Muslim, and less than 1 percent Jewish.

Table 1. Religions over 1 Percent in Europe, 1900–2050

Year	1900		2000		1900-2000 % p.a.	2020		2000-2020 % p.a.	2050	
Religious	400,854,000	99.6	608,587,000	83.9	0.42	631,160,000	84.4	0.18	580,223,000	81.7
Christians	380,647,000	94.5	560,871,000	77.3	0.39	572,603,000	76.6	0.10	496,682,000	69.9
Catholics	180,044,000	44.7	253,403,000	34.9	0.34	251,997,000	33.7	-0.03	211,164,000	29.7
Orthodox	104,557,000	26.0	195,001,000	26.9	0.63	205,608,000	27.5	0.27	183,176,000	25.8
Protestants	84,540,000	21.0	91,900,000	12.7	0.08	87,516,000	11.7	-0.24	76,981,000	10.8
Independents	185,000	0.0	9,368,000	1.3	4.00	11,792,000	1.6	1.16	15,624,000	2.2
doubly-affiliated	-529,000	-0.1	-6,751,000	-0.9	2.58	-6,909,000	-0.9	0.12	-7,550,000	-1.1
unaffiliated Christians	11,851,000	2.9	17,950,000	2.5	0.42	22,599,000	3.0	1.16	17,287,000	2.4
Muslims	9,365,000	2.3	40,493,000	5.6	1.47	50,647,000	6.8	1.13	73,792,000	10.4
Jews	9,786,000	2.4	1,614,000	0.2	-1.79	1,322,000	0.2	-0.99	1,146,000	0.2
Nonreligious	1,753,000	0.4	116,971,000	16.1	4.29	116,476,000	15.6	-0.02	130,263,000	18.3
Agnostics	1,548,000	0.4	99,393,000	13.7	4.25	101,371,000	13.6	0.10	112,774,000	15.9
Atheists	205,000	0.1	17,579,000	2.4	4.55	15,106,000	2.0	-0.76	17,489,000	2.5
Total population	402,607,000	100.0	725,558,000	100.0	0.59	747,636,000	100.0	0.15	710,486,000	100.0

Data source: Gina A. Zurlo and Todd M. Johnson, eds., *World Religion Database* (Leiden/Boston, Brill, accessed May 2023).

Within Christianity, Catholics were the largest tradition in 1900 (47 percent of all Christians), followed by Orthodox (27 percent of all Christians), then Protestants (22 percent of all Christians). The internal makeup of Christianity in Europe has changed only slightly since then: 44 percent Catholic, 36 percent Orthodox, 15 percent Protestant, and 2 percent independent in 2020. Orthodox Christianity is the only major Christian tradition that is a majority Global North faith—70 percent of all Orthodox in the world today live in Europe. The largest Orthodox populations in Europe are Russian Orthodox (111 million in Russia), Romanian Orthodox (17 million in Romania), and the Church of Greece (8 million in Greece). Before the Russian invasion of Ukraine in February 2022, Ukrainian Orthodox churches were the third-largest Orthodox population in Europe (31 million), but the ongoing war, massive internal and external displacement, and shifting ecclesial boundaries make it nearly impossible to know the state of the churches there.

Some of the largest independent denominations in Europe are the Jehovah's Witnesses, found in large numbers in Russia, Italy, Ukraine, and Germany. However, the increase of independents is partly due to migration of Christians from Pentecostal/charismatic churches in the Global South, primarily sub-Saharan Africa and Latin America. The Redeemed Christian Church of God, New Apostolic Church, and Church of Jesus Christ on Earth by His Special Envoy Simon Kimbangu, for example, experienced growth between 2000 and 2015. New churches have also begun from immigrant communities in the last few generations, such as Tamil Christian churches in Switzerland and the Kingsway International Christian Centre in London, with members mostly from West Africa. The Pentecostal/charismatic movement has not really taken off in Europe compared to other continents; Europe is only 3 percent Pentecostal/charismatic and home to just 3 percent of the world's Pentecostals/charismatics—compared to, for example, North America, which is 18 percent Pentecostal/charismatic and home to 11 percent of the world's Pentecostal/charismatic population. Nevertheless, some of the fastest-growing Christian movements in Europe are indeed Pentecostal/charismatic in nature, mostly populated by immigrants from the Global South.

Table 2. Christianity in Europe by Region, 1900–2050

Country	Pop. 1900	% Christian 1900	Pop. 2020	% Christian 2020	Pop. 2050	% Christian 2050
Eastern Europe	152,083,000	89.8	245,905,000	83.9	220,373,000	84.1
Northern Europe	56,893,000	98.1	74,919,000	70.5	68,689,000	59.8
Southern Europe	68,404,000	96.8	122,688,000	80.6	98,482,000	72.1
Western Europe	103,268,000	98.7	129,091,000	65.8	109,137,000	55.4
Europe	380,647,000	94.5	572,603,000	76.6	496,682,000	69.9

Data source: Todd M. Johnson and Gina A. Zurlo, eds., *World Christian Database* (Leiden/Boston: Brill, accessed May 2023).

Historical, geographic, political, and numerous other factors in Europe have shaped religious trends differently in each of its four regions—Eastern, Northern, Southern, and Western (table 2). Each region was majority Christian in 1900, though Eastern Europe was 4 percent Muslim and 5 percent Jewish. By 2020, all of these Christian figures had dropped substantially, especially Western Europe, which has experienced the greatest Christian losses (66 percent Christian in 2020). Eastern Europe had a particularly tumultuous twentieth century due to shifting boundaries, religious influences, and political powers during two World Wars. Its Christian population dropped from 90 percent in 1900 to 57 percent in 1970 at the height of Communism and its ideology of state-imposed atheism. With the breakup of the Soviet Union in 1991, however, Christianity rebounded in most of Eastern Europe, rising to 78 percent in 2000 and 84 percent today. However, Eastern Europe's Jewish population will never demographically recover from the Shoah, where it dropped from 8.5 million in 1900 to only 256,000 today, with continued expected decline to 179,000 by 2050. Europe's Christian decline trend is likely to continue in the future.

Table 3. Christianity in Europe by Country, 1900–2050

Country	Pop. 1900	% Christian 1900	Pop. 2020	% Christian 2020	Pop. 2050	% Christian 2050
Albania	250,000	31.3	1,082,000	37.6	1,055,000	43.5
Andorra	5,000	99.6	70,200	90.8	60,700	79.8
Austria	5,828,000	97.1	6,222,000	69.1	5,493,000	60.2
Belarus	6,048,000	86.6	7,351,000	77.8	7,242,000	83.9
Belgium	6,623,000	99.0	7,384,000	63.7	6,636,000	54.3
Bosnia-Herzegovina	684,000	60.1	1,614,000	49.2	1,322,000	49.3
Bulgaria	3,066,000	81.9	5,749,000	82.7	4,531,000	84.1
Channel Islands	82,200	99.0	148,000	85.2	163,000	81.8
Croatia	2,700,000	96.3	3,850,000	93.8	3,182,000	94.6
Czechia	7,848,000	96.9	3,746,000	35.0	3,564,000	33.8
Denmark	2,440,000	99.6	4,695,000	81.1	4,256,000	68.2
Estonia	637,000	98.4	495,000	37.3	433,000	37.4
Faeroe Islands	15,000	100.0	47,900	98.0	51,200	95.7
Finland	2,713,000	100.0	4,354,000	78.6	3,626,000	66.1
France	40,731,000	99.3	42,497,000	65.1	35,184,000	52.1
Germany	41,533,000	98.6	56,377,000	67.3	47,450,000	59.2
Gibraltar	19,500	96.4	29,900	88.6	29,300	86.5
Greece	2,599,000	85.2	9,338,000	89.6	7,465,000	82.7
Holy See	1,000	100.0	810	100.0	810	100.0
Hungary	6,411,000	93.5	8,429,000	87.3	7,426,000	87.7
Iceland	77,900	99.9	317,000	93.0	332,000	88.0
Ireland	3,227,000	99.9	4,550,000	92.2	4,818,000	84.9
Isle of Man	37,600	98.9	71,500	84.1	68,500	75.5
Italy	32,903,000	99.7	46,863,000	77.5	35,083,000	64.5
Kosovo	49,000	12.7	129,000	6.2	128,000	6.3
Latvia	1,200,000	99.5	1,529,000	81.1	1,356,000	91.7
Liechtenstein	9,400	99.8	33,900	88.8	32,500	80.5
Lithuania	2,054,000	99.7	2,426,000	89.1	1,929,000	90.9
Luxembourg	235,000	99.4	474,000	75.8	534,000	67.6
Malta	208,000	100.0	424,000	96.0	382,000	89.5
Moldova	1,310,000	99.1	3,920,000	97.2	3,298,000	98.1
Monaco	15,300	98.7	33,500	85.3	38,000	82.7
Montenegro	214,000	93.9	498,000	79.2	473,000	80.2
Netherlands	4,999,000	96.5	9,515,000	55.5	7,174,000	41.8
North Macedonia	400,000	67.1	1,332,000	64.0	1,203,000	64.8
Norway	2,208,000	99.4	4,685,000	86.4	4,986,000	75.5
Poland	22,050,000	91.1	36,184,000	95.6	32,050,000	96.3
Portugal	5,421,000	100.0	9,228,000	90.5	7,744,000	85.2
Romania	10,384,000	94.4	18,959,000	98.6	16,063,000	98.8
Russia	62,545,000	84.8	119,945,000	82.2	109,077,000	80.3
San Marino	8,000	100.0	31,100	91.5	29,800	88.6
Serbia	3,192,000	98.2	5,940,000	89.4	4,627,000	91.4
Slovakia	3,921,000	96.4	4,616,000	84.6	4,308,000	86.4
Slovenia	956,000	100.0	1,732,000	83.3	1,568,000	80.9
Spain	18,795,000	100.0	40,526,000	86.7	34,127,000	78.2
Sweden	5,077,000	98.9	5,857,000	58.0	5,182,000	45.5
Switzerland	3,295,000	99.4	6,555,000	75.7	6,596,000	67.2
Ukraine	28,501,000	97.2	37,005,000	84.6	32,814,000	93.2
United Kingdom	37,125,000	97.4	45,742,000	67.4	41,488,000	56.0
Europe	380,647,000	94.5	572,603,000	76.6	496,682,000	69.9

Data source: Todd M. Johnson and Gina A. Zurlo, eds., *World Christian Database* (Leiden/Boston: Brill, accessed May 2023).

The countries with the most Christians in Europe are Russia (120 million), Germany (56 million), and Italy (47 million) (table 3). Russia's largest denomination is the Russian Orthodox Church; Germany is nearly tied between the Evangelical Church in Germany (Protestant) and the Roman Catholic Church; and Italy's largest denomination is the Roman Catholic Church, headquartered at Vatican City, a microstate within Rome. Of the forty-nine countries in Europe, forty-four experienced proportional decline of their Christian populations between 1900 and 2020. The largest declines were in Czechia (97 percent Christian in 1900 vs. 35 percent in 2020), Estonia (98 percent vs. 37 percent), and the Netherlands (97 percent vs. 56 percent).

Figure 2. Christianity in Europe

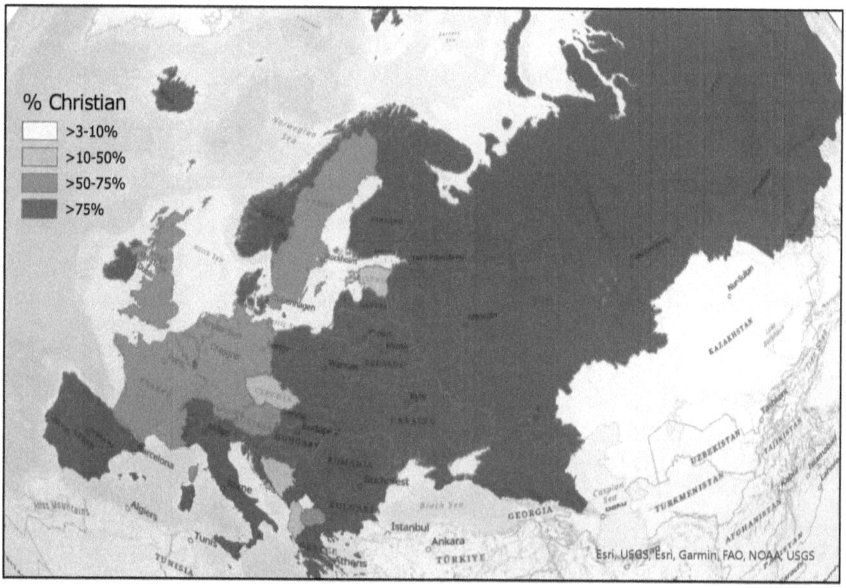

Data source: Todd M. Johnson and Gina A. Zurlo, eds., *World Christian Database* (Leiden/Boston: Brill, accessed May 2023).

One hundred years ago, it was true that the typical Christian in the world was a white European. Given current trends, however, Europe is clearly no longer the geographic nor demographic center of world Christianity. Yet, that does not mean Europe has no role in the future. It is still the home of major Christian communions, such as Catholics (Rome), Anglicans (Canterbury), Russian Orthodox (Moscow), and Lutherans (Geneva). European mission agencies are active throughout the world providing theological education, social welfare programs, combatting climate change, and advocating for gender equality. Immigration is changing the European Christian landscape with the increased prominence of ethnic minority congregations, and it does appear that the future of Christianity there is in the hands of migrants, largely from the Global South.

Acknowledgments

THE GERM OF AN idea pollinated into a book-length treatment of the history, plight, and experiences of the multifaceted expressions of Christianity celebrated in the church. We have been more than a little assisted by the comments, guidance, and perspective of sensational scholars Philip Jenkins, Erica Hunter, Wafik Wahba, Harold Suerman, Akram Khater, Jonathan Swift, Deanna Ferree Womack, and Michael Ghiz. Thanks one and all for your friendship and collegiality in the spirit of collaboration. Thanks, too, to Michael Hahn for smoothing out the voices in the preface.

Conceptualizing on the angle for the book titles and their intended appealing splash came from the fertile minds of Rachel Baker, Jean Van Horn, Gary Camlin, Bill Engvall, Alayna Baker, Aaron Lamport, Jay Ellis, Amy Grubbs, Zachary Grubbs, and Michelle Lamport.

The following were instrumental in shepherding the contents of the book into production-worthy copy—Joshua Erb (senior editorial consultant) and Philip Bustrum and Mel Wilhoit for tremendous skill and detail in indexing the contents.

Further, we are beholden to Michael Thomson, acquisitions and development director for Wipf & Stock Publishers. Michael tracked Mark down in the produce aisle of a large grocery chain in Grand Rapids and proposed the first book in the series to him! Alec Ryrie filled out the team nicely. Soon thereafter Mark came back to Michael and pitched *this* book (and the remaining five) to fill out this seven-book series: to tell the global story of Christianity. Michael is at once analytical and spontaneous, perceptive and intelligent, exacting and gracious. We are pleased that an additional large, international, edited book is also in process under Michael's guidance describing emerging theologies from the Global South (Cascade, 2023). Thank you for cheering on our vision.

Finally, we feel great respect for Christians in Europe and wish to tell their historic, unique, and inspiring story of Christianity. We are most anxious to track the future trajectory of how the story of Christianity will emerge in Europe.

About the Contributors

Shaun Blanchard (PhD, Marquette University) is Lecturer in Theology at the University of Notre Dame, Australia. He coedited *The Catholic Enlightenment: A Global Anthology* (2021) and coauthored *Vatican II: A Very Short Introduction* (2023).

Ambrogio A. Caiani is Senior Lecturer in Modern European History at the University of Kent. His work focuses on the French Revolution and Napoleonic Empire. He is the author of *To Kidnap a Pope: Napoleon and Pius VII 1800–1815* (2021) and *Louis XVI and the French Revolution* (2012). His most recent book is *Losing a Kingdom, Gaining the World: The Catholic Church in the Age of Revolution and Democracy* (2023).

Darrell Jackson (ThD, University of Birmingham) is Director of Research and Associate Professor, Whitley College, University of Divinity, Melbourne. He has fifteen years' experience of researching migration and the Churches of Europe. He has recently published *Mapping Migration, Mapping Churches' Responses: "Being Church Together,"* 3rd revised and updated edition (2020).

James Kennedy (PhD, University of Iowa) is Professor of Modern Dutch History at the Universiteit Utrecht. He penned *Concise History of the Netherlands* (2017) and (with Mark Rutjes) a history of Dutch church-state relations titled *Gescheiden partners* (2022).

Brett Knowles (PhD, University of Otago) recently retired as Associate Professor of Church History at Sydney College of Divinity, Australia, and Teaching Fellow in Church History at the University of Otago, Dunedin, New Zealand. His most recent publication is *A Timeline of Global Christianity* (2020).

Katharina Kunter (PhD, University of Gießen) is Professor for Contemporary Church History in the Faculty of Theology at the University of Helsinki. She completed postdoctoral work (habilitation) at the University of Karlsruhe in 2016. Her most recent publication is *Es gibt keinen Gott! Kirchen und Kommunismus: Eine Konfliktgeschichte* (There is no God! Churches and Communism: A history of conflict) with Thomas Bremer and Nadezhda Beljakova.

Mark W. Lee (DPhil, Oxford University) is Assistant Professor of History at Crandall University. He is currently working on a book that explores madness, medicine, and religious identities in the Atlantic world, ca. 1760–1860.

Darin D. Lenz (PhD, FSA Scot) is Professor of History at Biola University in La Mirada, California. His research has been published in a variety of academic journals and edited volumes, and he has also contributed to and coedited *Civil Religion and American Christianity* (rev. ed., 2020).

Mark R. Lindsay (PhD, University of Western Australia) is a historical theologian, with particular expertise in the theologies of Karl and Markus Barth, Dietrich Bonhoeffer, and post-Holocaust studies. He is the Joan Munro Professor of Historical Theology at Trinity College Theological School, the University of Divinity, Australia. Lindsay's most recent book is *God Has Chosen: The Doctrine of Election through Christian History* (2020).

Andrew Louth (PhD, FBA University of Cambridge) is Professor Emeritus, University of Durham, and archpriest of the Moscow Patriarchate. A patristics scholar, his books include *The Origins of the Christian Mystical Tradition* (1981; 2007); *Denys the Areopagite* (1989); *Maximus the Confessor* (1996); *St John Damascene* (2002); and *Modern Orthodox Thinkers* (2015).

Charlotte Methuen (PhD, University of Edinburgh) is Professor of Ecclesiastical History at the University of Glasgow, having previously taught at the University of Hamburg, the Ruhr-University Bochum, and the University of Oxford. She has published widely on the German Reformation and its reception.

Laura Ramsay is Senior Lecturer in History, Bournemouth University, England. She has published articles and chapters on the modern history of Christianity, sexuality, and gender, and is completing a book based on her doctoral thesis entitled *Sexuality and the Church of England, 1918–1980*.

Christine Shepardson (PhD, Duke University) is Professor of Religious Studies at the University of Tennessee. She is the author and coeditor of several books on Greek and Syriac Christianity in late antiquity and has received national NEH and ACLS fellowships.

Peter Sherlock (DPhil, Oxford University) is Vice-Chancellor of the University of Divinity, Australia. He is the author of numerous publications on practices of remembering and forgetting, especially the commemoration of the dead in early modern Europe. His current project is a history of the monuments of Westminster Abbey.

Michael Snape (PhD, University of Birmingham) is the Michael Ramsey Professor of Anglican Studies at Durham University and an ecumenical lay canon of Durham Cathedral. His most recent publications include *Forgotten Warrior: The Life and Times of Major-General Merton Beckwith-Smith 1890–1942* (2023) and *A Church Militant: Anglicans and the Armed Forces from Queen Victoria to the Vietnam War* (2022).

Abbreviations

BEK	*Bund der Evangelischen Kirchen in der DDR*
CLWS	Church League for Women's Suffrage
CMS	Church Missionary Society
CWSS	Catholic Women's Suffrage Society
EKD	*Evangelische Kirche in Deutschland*
EU	European Union
EVS	European Values Survey
JAAR	*Journal of the American Academy of Religion*
JECS	*Journal of Early Christian Studies*
SCM	Student Christian Movement
SPCK	Society for Promoting Christian Knowledge
UNSD	United Nations, Department of Economic and Social Affairs, Statistics Division
WCD	World Christian Database

Book Introduction

BRIAN STANLEY

CHRISTIANITY DID NOT ORIGINATE in Europe, but rather on the eastern Mediterranean shores of the vast land mass that we know as Asia. Furthermore, its missionary progress into Europe was, at least until the end of the third century of the Common Era, less extensive than its progress southward into Egypt, Ethiopia, and North Africa, or eastward into Syria, Mesopotamia, and Persia, extending probably as far as India (and later into China). These truisms are worth restating, for in the present age of the globalization of the Christian faith, and the growth of a rich variety of confessedly "non-Western" expressions of Christian theology and worship, there is an understandable tendency to interpret these diverse cultural expressions of Christianity as corrective reactions to an originally "European" or "Western" religion that has been exported from Europe to the rest of the globe.

The fact that such confusion is so widespread may be explained in several ways. First, even before it left its Palestinian birthplace, Christian theology began to be Hellenized, a process that would flower most fully in the writings of the early church fathers and the decrees of the early ecumenical councils. Christian thought was expressed in the Greek language, the common tongue of the Roman Empire, and arrayed itself in a distinctively Greek set of philosophical categories that for centuries to come did much to conceal the originally Semitic and Judaic background of its teachings. The long and tragic history of European Christian anti-Semitism has reinforced the process of separating Christianity from its Jewish roots. Second, the Roman emperor Constantine's profession of Christianity in 313 CE and subsequent adoption of the Greek colony of Byzantion as his new capital made Constantinople, or the New Rome, the exemplar of an explicitly imperial form of Christianity that would later inspire imitations in the western half of the Roman Empire. Thus, the Frankish emperor Charlemagne (ca. 742–814) was remarkably successful in stamping his proprietary mark of ownership on Christianity as the official territorial religion of his own revived and expanding Roman Empire, denominated (to the obvious annoyance of the Byzantine emperor in Constantinople) the "Holy Roman Empire" in the West. Chapter 11 recounts the ensuing chapters in this narrative—how from the late fifteenth century onwards, first Catholic and later Protestant missionaries sallied forth from European Christendom under the protective, if leaky, canopies of the successive European maritime and global imperial powers, seeking to evangelize the benighted "heathen" peoples of Africa, Asia, the Americas, and finally Oceania. Whether Catholic or Protestant in their confession, they took with them the forms of the Christian religion that bore all the marks of the "Europeanness" it had progressively acquired during the first millennium of Christian history.

It is, therefore, unsurprising that adherents of other religions in the non-European world, and even many indigenous Christian converts, widely assumed that to be a Christian meant conformity to European habits and ways of thinking. This is sadly ironic, for a revolutionary feature of the early Jesus movement was its insistence that one did not have to share a ruler's religious affiliation to give him one's political obedience and loyalty.[12] Early Christianity divorced religion from ethnicity, but by the late medieval period Europe's religion and that of its overseas representatives had become, in Joyce Chaplin's words, "a form of ethnicity."[13] The frontier between Christianity and Islam or "heathen" territories had become the main boundary of inclusion within civilization or exclusion from it, since European Christians assumed that their territorial Christendom was the center of the cosmos. The ethnic term *Frank* thus assumed a religious meaning during the Crusades, delineating Christians from Jews or Muslims. Those looking at Europe from the outside made a similar equation. From the end of the sixteenth century onwards, the Persian *Farang*, deriving from Frank, entered into many South Asian languages as *Farangi*, *Parangi*, or *Pharangi*, to denote not simply a Portuguese Catholic but all Europeans, and by implication, all Christians.[14] Within Europe itself, the principle of one religion per territory largely survived the upheaval that we call the Reformation, and indeed became enshrined in 1555 in the slogan *cuius regio eius religio* (the religion of the territory is the religion of the ruler; see ch. 7).

How should we interpret this long narrative of the Europeanization of Christianity that this volume recounts? One influential view has in recent

---

12. Hurtado, *Destroyer of the Gods*, 103, 187.
13. Chaplin, "Race," 177.
14. Frykenberg, *Christianity in India*, x, 119–41.

times acquired particular renown—or, depending on one's standpoint, notoriety—through the writings of the late Pope Benedict XVI, Josef Ratzinger (1927-2022). Pope Benedict believed, with considerable justification, that the very notion of Europe was crafted in the early medieval period in response to the encircling threat of Islam. He rightly identified the reign of Charlemagne as the crucial period in which the classical term *Europe* was revived and infused with new meaning, grounded in a specifically religious identity (see ch. 2). His empire aspired to be a specifically "holy" reconstitution of the Roman Empire, but it was also a Western or Latin entity, clearly set apart both from the Eastern Byzantine Empire and from the Islamic territories beyond its borders. The eastern portion of Christian Europe represented by the Byzantine Empire collapsed when Constantinople fell to the Turks in 1453. Although a new embodiment of an Eastern Christian Empire in the East emerged in the Slav lands in the north in 1588 with the establishment of the patriarchate of Moscow and all Rus' (see ch. 5), with Moscow now claiming the status of a "third Rome," Benedict believed that it was the peculiar and even God-given responsibility of Western Europe, with its long Catholic heritage, to defend European Christian civilization. Christian values, he argued, were therefore integral to its continuing identity and future prospects. Instead, he found Europe at the beginning of the twenty-first century to be absorbed in a peculiar form of self-hatred, interpreting multiculturalism as necessitating secularism. Europeans, he lamented, seemed strangely and uniquely reluctant to give public acknowledgment to their own religious heritage of the sacred.[15]

Pope Benedict's equation of European and Christian values remains controversial today, yet similar beliefs had once been a virtual truism in the minds of European Christians. For example, the English Romantic poet and essayist Samuel Taylor Coleridge could refer in 1825 to "the standing miracle of a Christendom" that was "commensurate and almost synonymous with the civilized world."[16] Europe had indeed for long defined itself by Christianity. However, when from February 2002 to June 2004 the European Union eventually set about producing a constitution, it decided after lengthy debate to make no reference to Christianity, not even in the preamble to the constitution, which refers to the "common history" and "shared values" of Europe's peoples, without any indication that this common history and shared values owed more to Christianity than to any

---

15. Ratzinger and Pera, *Without Roots*, 54-80.

16. Coleridge, *Literary Remains*, 4:260-61, cited in Walls, *Missionary Movement from West*, 22-23.

other religion or ideology.[17] The advocates of a strict secularist separation between political and religious identities had won the day.

From a strictly historical point of view, the assertion by Christian conservatives such as Pope Benedict that Christianity has been at the heart of the European cultural heritage is undeniable. The problem arises when such assertions are given providential weight—"God has given Europe a particular commission to embody Christian values to the world"—or when they are used to imply that nations who have a different heritage are thereby less "civilized." In the multicultural and religiously pluriform context of most modern societies affirmations of the central of Christianity to European civilization can too easily be read as claims that Christianity has been uniquely formative of civilization per se, and on occasion such a reading may be justified. For example, one recent attempt, by the Oxford Christian ethicist Nigel Biggar to argue that the British Empire was not all bad—an unfashionable assertion for which there is in fact a good deal of evidence—is vitiated by statements that in the late nineteenth century there was "a vast disparity in cultural development" between Europeans and most of their African contemporaries.[18] Similarly, Biggar affirms that, as late as 1960, "Asian and African peoples had yet to acquire the virtues that make democratic politics work," implying that Western nations, through their Christian and classical heritage, had safely imbibed such virtues.[19]

In a cultural and political environment shaped by the postcolonial reaction it is not surprising that a radically different interpretation of the European Christian story than that expounded by Josef Ratzinger has gained widespread currency, especially, but not only, among Christians from outside Europe. In this view, European Christian history presents a chronologically elongated version of that "Babylonian captivity of the church" against which Martin Luther fulminated so powerfully in 1520.[20] Luther directed his unrivalled abilities of theological invective against the papacy and the Catholic sacramental doctrine of his day, which, he maintained, had imprisoned the laity within a system of monopolistic priestly power. The parallel accusation widely levelled against European Christianity in our own times is rather that its historical evolution has uprooted the Christian faith from its original roots in the soil of Palestinian peasant society and sent it into a new Babylonian exile, in which it is imprisoned within the dominant

---

17. See https://europeanconstitution.eu/wp-content/uploads/2019/05/European-Constitution-Full-Text.pdf. For the debate, see Schlesinger and Foret, "Political Roof."

18. Biggar, *Colonialism*, 159.

19. Biggar, *Colonialism*, 215.

20. Luther, *On the Babylonian Captivity*.

political institutions of Western nations and empires. It has thus been tragically complicit with long histories of colonial exploitation and enslavement, on grounds of both ethnicity and gender. Thus Peter Cruchley, a prominent British missiologist from the United Reformed Church, traces the roots of colonial Christianity to the Byzantine image of "Christ Pantocrator," Christ as triumphant ruler of all:

> There is no Emperor now but Christ. The officers of empire are empowered to prosecute and promulgate in his name. . . . The co-mingling of human and divine is not revealed in the flesh and blood and struggle of a carpenter's son, but in the pomp and glory and reign of the Divine Emperor's heir. This image has remained potent since. It shaped and empowered the spread of Christianity in Europe in the midst of the emerging nation states, and propelled Christianity to claim that it should stand in place of Rome at its fall. . . . Pantocrator permitted the Doctrine of Discovery and the colonial expansion of European nations and their claim for supremacy over "heathen" peoples and land. . . . European peoples could conquer in the name of such a God, colonize, enslave, capitalize, and so it was.[21]

A further, and potentially distinct, charge often associated with this narrative is that Christian faith has been stripped of its innate spiritual dynamism by its unwillingness to transcend the narrow epistemological horizons imposed on Christian faith by the European Enlightenment of the seventeenth and eighteenth centuries. Although the Enlightenment was by no means hostile to all religious faith, it undoubtedly led the European churches to prioritize "rational" theology and downgrade "conspicuous, mystical, and flamboyant devotion" (ch. 4). One recent introduction to what has become known as "world Christianity," by an author from the heavily Christianized region of northeast India, describes the Christianity of the Majority World as typified by its open defiance of the rationalistic ethos of the European Enlightenment and its "deep religiosity characterized by strong belief in the supernatural power of God."[22] The implication that such strong belief has long since disappeared from Europe is clear, and is not easily to be dismissed. The rapidly emptying churches of much of present-day Europe, in this account, are the inevitable consequence, not simply of the capitulation of Christianity to the false attractions of wealth and power, but also of Europe's ingrained skepticism about the reality of invisible spiritual powers, and its callous indifference to the cries of the poor who insist in

---

21. Cruchley, "Counter-Creating Mission," 130.
22. Pachuau, *World Christianity*, 28.

believing on a God who really does act within history in works of redemption and miracle—the liberating God of the biblical exodus and the return from Babylonian captivity. This thesis might help to explain why Pentecostal varieties of Christianity, currently so dominant in the non-European world, remain comparatively weak in Europe itself, although even there they are undoubtedly growing in extent and significance.

The chapters that follow seek to complicate, and at least in some cases, to subvert both of these rather monochromatic accounts of the history of European Christianity as a narrative of either cumulative civilizational virtue or creeping spiritual and moral corruption by its proximity to the corridors of power. While both these metanarratives have their considerable merits, they ultimately fail to persuade, because both ascribe to the geographical entity we have come to know as "Europe" a degree of homogeneity and uniqueness that it never possessed, and still does not possess. From ch. 1 onwards, with its emphasis on the diversity of Christianity in the late antique period, "diversity" is perhaps the recurring theme of this volume. The European Christian story cannot be adequately told without careful reference to the marked divergences of religious culture between Jewish and Gentile, Orthodox and Latin, Catholic and Protestant, magisterial Protestant and radical separatist, not to speak of the transverse differences of gender, locality, wealth, and social or educational background running through all these sectors of European Christianity.

In recent times, further lines of theological or political fission have opened up, effecting major shifts in the historic European map of ecclesiastical geography. First, as recounted in ch. 15, large movements of migration by refugees and the economically disadvantaged to Europe, especially across the Mediterranean from Africa and the Islamic world, have set Christian predispositions to welcome the stranger largely at odds with the anxiety of political leaders to placate the fears of their electorates, potentially leading to new clashes between church and state. They have also radically reshaped the religious panorama of European cities, transforming Christian relations with other world faiths from an academic question of theological debate into a matter of the daily experience and human relations of most European Christians. Migration to Europe has, moreover, made the indigenous churches of Africa and the Caribbean, many of them Pentecostal in character, some of the most prominent features of the Christian landscape, at least in cities.

Second, in a development that has not perhaps received the attention it deserves in this volume, from the 1960s onwards global movements of charismatic renewal began to redraw ecclesiastical contours in Britain and some other parts of Europe (notably the Netherlands, Germany, and

Scandinavia), throwing up intra-denominational antagonisms within both Catholic and Protestant congregations, but also forging unprecedented cross-confessional alliances between Catholic and Protestant charismatics. New networks of charismatic churches have emerged, with their own structures of apostolic authority and succession, and their own theological rationales undergirding these structures.[23] These are denominations in all but name, the largest of them now being transnational in their reach. In Britain, certainly, and probably in some other European nations also, the aggregate numbers of attenders of such churches easily dwarf in size the remaining adherents of the older Protestant dissenting churches, whose origins lie in renewal or primitivist movements such as the Radical Reformation, Elizabethan Puritan separatism, or the pietist and evangelical revival movements of the eighteenth century (see ch. 8).

Third, and more explosive still, fundamental theological disagreements over human sexuality and gender threaten to give birth to new denominations and rivals to historic global communions such as the Anglican communion; in North America they already have. Chapter 14 concludes by surveying the arguments within late twentieth-century European churches over the ordination of women, but these may be surpassed in both scale and heat by the contemporary arguments over gay marriage, gay ordination, and the relationship of gender to biological sex.

Finally, on the political front, the outbreak of war in Europe in 2022 following the Russian invasion of Ukraine has split the supposedly seamless robe of the Orthodox Church. The authority of the current Russian patriarch, Kirill, has been repudiated, not simply by large sectors within the Orthodox churches of Ukraine, Poland, and Georgia, but also by the ecumenical patriarch in Istanbul (the former Constantinople), on account of Kirill's unqualified support for Vladimir Putin's attempt to reconstitute by military force the *Ruskiy Mir* (Russian world) as a single political entity and reclaim Kyiv as "the baptismal font of Russian Orthodoxy" (see ch. 5).

Christianity in present-day Europe, therefore, may appear as fractious as ever. While Christians may deplore the continuing proliferation of divisions within their faith, at least their existence serves as evidence that Christianity is a religion in which disagreement is possible, perhaps even encouraged. Precisely because it is so strongly a textual faith, committed to obedience to one holy Scripture, the scope for various and conflicting interpretations of the Bible is endless.

---

23. Maiden, *Age of the Spirit*.

Bibliography

Biggar, Nigel. *Colonialism: A Moral Reckoning*. London: Collins, 2023.

Chaplin, Joyce E. "Race." In *The British Atlantic World, 1500–1800*, edited by David Armitage and Michael J. Braddick, 154–72. 2nd ed. Basingstoke, UK: Palgrave Macmillan, 2009.

Coleridge, Samuel Taylor. *Literary Remains of Samuel Taylor Coleridge*. Edited by Henry Nelson Coleridge. 4 vols. London: Pickering, 1836–39.

Cruchley, Peter. "Counter-Creating Mission *in* but Not *of* Empire." In *Mission and Context*, edited by Jione Havea, 125–38. Theology in the Age of Empire. Lanham, MD: Lexington, 2020.

Frykenberg, Robert Eric. *Christianity in India from Beginnings to the Present*. Oxford History of the Christian Church. Oxford: Oxford University Press, 2008.

Hurtado, Larry W. *Destroyer of the Gods: Early Christian Distinctiveness in the Roman World*. Waco, TX: Baylor University Press, 2016.

Luther, Martin. *On the Babylonian Captivity of the Church*. In *Word and Sacrament II*, edited by Abdel Ross Wentz and Helmut T. Lehmann, 3–126. Vol. 36 of *Luther's Works*. Philadelphia: Fortress, 1959.

Maiden, John. *Age of the Spirit: Charismatic Renewal, the Anglo-World, and Global Christianity, 1945–1980*. Oxford: Oxford University Press, 2023.

Pachuau, Lalsangkima. *World Christianity: A Historical and Theological Introduction*. Nashville: Abingdon, 2018.

Ratzinger, Josef [Benedict XVI], and Marcello Pera. *Without Roots: The West, Relativism, Christianity, Islam*. New York: Basic, 2006.

Schlesinger, Philip, and François Foret. "Political Roof and Sacred Canopy?" *European Journal of Social Theory* 9 (2006) 59–81.

Walls, Andrew F. *The Missionary Movement from the West: A Biography from Birth to Old Age*. Edited by Brian Stanley. Grand Rapids: Eerdmans, 2023.

----- Section One -----

The Story of Christianity Narrated in Historical Context

1

Christianity Emerges in the Era of Late Antiquity

CHRISTINE SHEPARDSON

THE HISTORY OF CHRISTIANITY is as diverse as the Christians who have embraced it around the globe for nearly two thousand years. The period of late antiquity is one in which that diversity is on full display, particularly because normative definitions of orthodoxy (Greek: "correct teaching"), orthopraxy (Greek: "correct practices"), and catholic (Latin, Greek: "universal") Christianity were still emerging. This era includes the fourth century when Christianity famously gained new political clout under the emperor Constantine and his successors; the fifth-century military conquests that left the Latin church in the West more isolated from the churches of the eastern Mediterranean; the hotly disputed fifth- and sixth-century church councils that led to schisms, or splits, in the church that remain to this day; and the shifts that followed the seventh-century rise of Islam. The history of Christianity in Europe in this early period is thus intimately tied to the history of the wider Mediterranean and sets the stage for the regionally different paths that Christianity would take in the centuries that followed.

From Apocalyptic Judaism to Roman Superstition: Christians in the First Three Centuries

When we realize that the Roman world in which Christianity developed differed significantly from our modern world, we start to see the rich textures of those early traditions before some pieces were later deemed "correct" and domesticated into our modern worldviews. Identifying John the Baptist, Jesus, and Paul as apocalyptic Jews places them more comfortably in their own context rather than in the later Christianized world that their teachings inspired. Highlighting the imminent eschatology of their teachings (that the end of an era was at hand) reminds us of their urgency, and helps make sense of the transformations that communities underwent when the end did not arrive. The Roman destruction of the Jewish temple in Jerusalem in 70 CE marked a turning point in all of the biblical traditions that reconstituted themselves afterward: Pauline and gnostic forms of gentile "Christianity" flourished in the aftermath, as did the newly developing rabbinic traditions of Judaism. Slavery was an integral part of the economic and social fabric of the Roman Empire. Romans understood women's bodies to be imperfect and inferior to male bodies, and gender to be affected by things such as age, diet, behavior, and health. The vast majority of the population had little formal education and could not read or write. The books of the Jewish Bible were not yet settled in Jesus's lifetime, and books that came to be the Christian New Testament were written decades after his death and not canonized for centuries, leaving early Christians without public church buildings or the Christian Bible as we know it; the doctrine of the Trinity and the nuances of the incarnation also were not yet clearly articulated. In other words, Christians grew increasingly easy to find, but a cohesive definition of "Christianity" remained elusive.

Teachings about Jesus are already diverse in our earliest accounts, the letters of the apostle Paul (e.g., 1 Cor 1:10–11; Gal 1:6–9). When Jesus died, he left behind numerous women and men who had heard his teachings, observed his life, and witnessed his death, and their numbers increased especially with Paul's missions to the gentiles (non-Jews). By the second century there were multiple varieties of Christians: those who for convenience scholars usually call "Jewish Christians," who believed Jesus was the adopted son of God and a fully human Jewish messiah foretold in biblical prophecy; "gnostic" Christians who believed Christ was a fully divine figure whose teachings helped souls return to God (who was not the creator god); and "Pauline" or "proto-orthodox" Christians who believed that Jesus was the uniquely human and divine Son of God whose teachings superseded earlier teachings to the Jews. Each had their own gospels attributed to Jesus's apostles and their own understanding of the relationship between Jesus and the God of Abraham. In the mid-second century to the mid-third century these were supplemented by the dualistic "Marcionites" following Marcion of Sinope; "Bardaisanites" following the Syriac scholar Bardaisan who integrated Christian and non-Christian cosmological ideas in ways that his opponents declared heretical; and "Manichees" following Mani's integration of Jewish, Pauline, gnostic, Zoroastrian, and Buddhist teachings. Thus by the end of the third century, the number of teachings, texts, and communities claiming to continue the Jesus teachings were numerous and varied.

In response to this proliferation of teachings, church leaders spent much of the second and third centuries working to define who in their view was (and was not) correctly Christian in their practices and beliefs; because one group became dominant in the Roman Empire in the early fourth century, the texts that survive primarily tell their story. Some Christian apologists (Greek: "defenders") like Minucius Felix wrote literary defenses of Christian behaviors and ideas, primarily to those who still respected the traditional gods and were suspicious of what they labeled a new *superstitio*, whose followers refused to safeguard the empire by honoring the gods and were rumored to practice cannibalism, a misunderstanding of the Eucharist in which Christians ritually ingest bread and wine as the body and blood of Christ. At the same time writers like Clement of Alexandria in Egypt and Tertullian of Carthage in North Africa encouraged upright behavior from their congregants so they would be seen as model citizens and neighbors. Such concerns often led to particularly sharp surveillance of women's bodies, which were held to a higher ideal of chastity and decorum, such as in Tertullian's treatise "On the Apparel of Women." Thus, while third-century congregants were Romans and Christians, attending municipal baths and theaters and participating in imperial systems like the court and military that included rituals to the gods, church leaders grew increasingly firm about which of these typical Roman behaviors compromised their identity as Christians.[1]

In addition to defending themselves, many of these same Christian leaders went on the offensive in heresiological writings against other Christians they considered heretics, that is, adhering to practices or beliefs that fell outside what the author considered acceptable. Several themes are common in heresiological writings. Most, like Irenaeus's "Against the Heresies" and the gnostic Coptic Apocalypse of Peter, argue that their opponents are foolish and blind and misunderstand Scripture and the significance of Jesus's life, death, and resurrection, often (they claim) because they did not receive their teachings from a legitimate apostolic source. Many underscored these allegations by accusing their opponents' leader of sexual promiscuity and magic (in contrast to miracles).[2] Christians who followed Paul's teachings criticized "gnostics" for being too much like traditional Greeks, and "Judaizers" (e.g., Christians who circumcised, abstained from pork, and performed ritual ablutions) like those described in the *Didascalia apostolorum* for being too much like Jews. Sharp anti-Jewish rhetoric developed in these early centuries as church leaders struggled to define and defend their understanding of Christianity.

1. Rebillard, *Christianities*.
2. Knust, *Abandoned to Lust*.

Early Christians also wrote to praise their heroes, and in the second and third century many of these were martyrs (Greek: "witnesses") who died at the hands of the Roman state. Some of the same misperceptions that led apologists to write defenses led to other Christians being arrested and sometimes killed. Roman leaders rarely cared what Christians believed; it was not illegal to be Christian, and the number of Christians who died as martyrs in the first two centuries of Christianity is relatively small, with arrests taking place only locally and sporadically. In fact, one of the earliest sources about Christians on trial in a Roman courtroom is an exchange of letters in the early second century between Pliny, the governor of Bythinia, and the emperor Trajan, that suggests the governor had little idea what it meant to be Christian or why Christians were on trial. Roman officials did care, though, what their citizens *did* (or refused to do). Pliny described Christians who refused three times to sacrifice to Rome's emperor and gods, writing that whatever it was these Christians believed, it was their stubbornness that he was punishing with execution. Emperor Nero scapegoated some local Christians for a destructive fire in Rome in 64; Bishop Polycarp of Smyrna was put to death in 156; forty-eight Christians were tortured and killed in Lyons in 177; and others like Perpetua were killed in the arena in Carthage in 203. There is no doubt that Christians were killed by the Roman state in what they perceived as persecution, but Roman officials perceived Christians as bad citizens and their behavior as potentially treasonous.

In fact, it takes work to turn a murdered congregant into a martyr, and Christian martyrologies (Greek: "stories of martyrs") and hagiographies (Greek: "stories of saints") are more than a historical record; the narratives themselves shape our memories in particular ways.[3] As the urgent messages of Jesus and Paul settled into a multigenerational church, some of the more radical aspects of their early teachings were overshadowed by societal norms, with consequences for all aspects of community life. Church leadership came to be limited to certain types of men (e.g., 1 Tim 3–4); rituals developed more specificity as seen in texts like the Didache; and the charismatic leaders of the first generations gave way to increasingly structured processes of ordination such as described by Ignatius of Antioch. As the types of people who qualified for ordained leadership dwindled, however, charismatic leadership took other forms, including those who achieved sainthood through martyrdom or ascetic vows of virginity, avenues that remained accessible to people of any gender, education, and social status. Thus we read the stories of Bishop Ignatius of Antioch who begged the Christians of Rome not to interfere in his opportunity to die for Christ; the

---

3. Castelli, *Martyrdom and Memory*.

eighty-six-year old Polycarp, bishop of Smyrna, who accepted death for refusing to renounce Christ; Eusebius of Caesarea's description of the martyrs of Lyons, including the enslaved woman Blandina; and the young North African mother Perpetua, who with the enslaved and pregnant Felicitas and others accepted death in a Roman arena. The stories that commemorate these saints emphasize their masculine strength and virtue as they moved closer toward spiritual perfection.

Throughout much of the third century, Roman leaders struggled against increasingly frequent raids along, and migrations across, their borders, and the empire had twenty-six emperors in just fifty years between 235 and Diocletian's accession to the throne in 284; with some exceptions, Christians were not much on emperors' minds in this tumultuous period. When the emperors Decius and then Valerian briefly required sacrifice to the gods in 250 and 257–58 respectively in an effort to bolster their struggling empire, some Christians who refused were arrested and some of those like Bishop Cyprian of Carthage joined the ranks of the martyrs. As the century came to a close, however, Diocletian established greater stability through the system known as the tetrarchy in which power was shared between an Eastern and a Western emperor, each with an appointed junior successor. It was in this period of the early fourth century that Diocletian started to legislate support for the Roman gods more specifically, instituting in the process the most severe persecution, which shapes general perceptions of early Christian history to this day.

Building a Christian Empire: Roman Christians in the Fourth Century

While Christians were not the only ones targeted by Diocletian's early fourth-century legislation, they nevertheless suffered significantly. In 303, Christian Scriptures were sought out and burned; before long, church leaders were subject to arrest; by 304/5 all Romans were expected to sacrifice to the gods like earlier under Decian;[4] and as writers like Lactantius and Eusebius recorded, for years Christians were subject to arrest and potential martyrdom. A new schism began in this period in North Africa between those who believed that rituals performed by a Christian leader who had handed over the Scriptures to be burned (a *traditor*) were not effective, and those who believed that God's Spirit made the rituals effective regardless. In 311, Caecilian was ordained bishop of Carthage, but he was not accepted by some who believed that the bishop who consecrated him was a *traditor*; within years there were "Caecilianists" who accepted Caecilian

4. Lee, *Pagans and Christians*, 64–79.

and "Donatists" who accepted his rival Donatus, and as this division spread across the region, the North African church found itself sharply divided for over a century. Also in 311 the Eastern emperor Galerius issued the Edict of Serdica, ending the persecution in the East a decade after King Tiridates III of Armenia became the first ruler to name Christianity as a kingdom's official religion.

In 312 Constantine conquered Maxentius at the Battle of the Milvian Bridge and entered Rome as its new Western emperor, thanks, as Christian authors like Lactantius and Eusebius claimed, to the Christian God. A new era was dawning.

While Constantine retained the imperial title *pontifex maximus* (Latin: "high priest") over the empire's temples, he also became the first Roman emperor to give significant legal, political, and financial support to Christian leaders, and was baptized on his deathbed in 337. As such, Constantine found himself drawn into the disagreements about which church leaders were orthodox, from the Donatist schism in North Africa, to conflicts with the Manichees, remaining gnostic communities such as those that buried their writings at Nag Hammadi in Egypt, Judaizers such as those criticized in the *Didascalia* and later writings by John Chrysostom of Antioch, and a developing Christological controversy between the Libyan priest Arius and Alexander the bishop of Alexandria (alongside his deacon and successor Athanasius). With the powerful benefaction of Constantine and his mother Helena at stake, it became more critical than ever to determine which church leaders were the rightful imperial beneficiaries, and when Constantine defeated the Eastern emperor Licinius in 324, he convened a council of the empire's bishops to codify some of the parameters of this imperial church. Thus in 325 Constantine presided over a council in Nicaea, across the Bosphorus from where he had recently established his new capital, soon to be renamed Constantinople, and with the Council of Nicaea, which came to be seen as the First Ecumenical (Greek: "worldwide") Council, certain Christians for the first time claimed the title of imperial orthodoxy.

The Christianity that the Council of Nicaea defined became the benchmark of orthodoxy ever since, but that was not immediately evident at the time, and debates about whether the Son was "begotten" and thus the same substance as God as Athanasius argued, or was instead God's first creation and thus of a similar but not identical substance as God, as Arius argued, continued for decades with imperial support vacillating among different factions. Those who supported the doctrine of Athanasius argued against those they called "Arians," "Eunomians," "Anomeans," and "Aetians" who supported some version of the Son's difference from God the Father in an effort to preserve their understanding of monotheism. Athanasius spent years in exile when emperors supported his opponents, and from 361 to 363 the short-lived emperor Julian renounced his Christian upbringing and embraced traditional worship of the gods, though he was soon killed in battle. In the end, though, those who supported Athanasius and other Nicene leaders like John Chrysostom, Basil of Caesarea, his younger brother Gregory of Nyssa, and their friend Gregory of Nazianzus succeeded in defining imperial orthodoxy by their terms. In 379, the Western emperor Gratian appointed Theodosius I as the Eastern emperor, and in 380 they co-issued the *cunctos populos* (Latin: "all people") edict that for the first time declared Nicene Christianity the religion of the empire, as recorded in the Theodosian Code (*CTh* 16.1.2). In 381, Theodosius convened the Council of Constantinople, the Second Ecumenical Council, where bishops affirmed and strengthened the decisions made at Nicaea, expanded the earlier creed to include more about the Holy Spirit, and condemned the teachings of Apollinaris of Laodicea. The Nicene Creed still read in many churches today is usually this later creed. In the meantime, however, many Goths, Vandals, and others who lived predominately (but not exclusively) outside Rome's borders had embraced a non-Nicene creed that originated in a Western council in 359. The fact that the empire's leaders rejected that creed as too similar to the teachings of Arius meant that in the fifth century when these communities gained control over previously Roman land, some Romans considered them not only military opponents but also Christian heretics.

Doctrine was far from the only form of diversity in fourth-century Christianity, however, as practices remained at the core of Roman understandings of the piety and devotion that today we associate with "religion."[5] As bishops struggled to define Christianity and claim control over the empire's multiplying church buildings (and growing congregations), other charismatic forms of authority also emerged, particularly through devotional acts known as asceticism. Asceticism, from the Greek term *askēsis* that referred to the training of athletes, focused on training for spiritual (rather than physical athletic) contests through a rigorous focus on prayer and devotion that included a life of celibacy and other forms of overcoming the desires of the body. Early Christian ascetic practices were enormously diverse—many of the most renowned ascetics like Anthony withdrew to a solitary cave or cell, such as in the Egyptian or Judean desert; others supported each other in urban settings; while others established loose collections of cells or more structured monastic communities like the Pachomian monastery in northern Egypt; the Red and White Monasteries of southern

---

5. On the Christian development of modern conceptions of "religion," see Barton and Boyarin, *Imagine No Religion*.

Egypt; the fourth-century monasteries founded by Paula and Jerome near Bethlehem, by Melania on the Mount of Olives, by Basil of Caesarea and his sister Macrina in Cappadocia, and by Martin in Tours; the fifth-century monasteries started by Augustine in North Africa and by Cassian in Gaul; the sixth-century monasteries of Benedict in Italy; and others in Spain, Syria, Sinai, Ethiopia, Armenia, Mesopotamia, South Asia, and everywhere else that Christianity flourished.

The most extraordinary early ascetic practices, however, were often found in solitary devotion. Athanasius commemorated Anthony for renouncing his wealth and conquering demons in the Egyptian desert; Symeon lived for forty years atop a stone pillar in the Syrian countryside; Pelagia's asceticism left a body so emaciated that the once-renowned and wealthy female sex worker lived their final years as a male eunuch. As much as they might withdraw from worldly distractions, however, ascetic heroes like these soon found themselves the center of others' devotional practices as Christian pilgrimage flourished from this period onward. Often ascetics' rigorous practices led to stories of their miraculous abilities, such as healing, foreseeing the future, and their more mundane ability to serve as impartial mediators. The fourth century also saw a rise in the role of relics, that is, objects associated with holy people or places. Constantine's mother Helena was said to have discovered the powerful relic of the true cross on which Jesus was crucified, and in the late fourth century, the embattled bishop Ambrose of Milan made a timely "discovery" (Latin: *inventio*) of what he claimed were the remains of two local martyrs and used their authority to overcome imperial resistance to his leadership, while John Chrysostom encouraged his Eastern congregations to visit martyrs' shrines. Under the emperor Constantine, Jerusalem started to develop into a Christian "Holy Land" with the new Church of the Holy Sepulchre, and in the early 380s, the adventurous Egeria wrote about her pilgrimage from the West to countless biblical sites. Throughout the fourth century, the empire's people and places were becoming more specifically Christian.

Plague, War, and Schism: The Tumultuous Fifth and Sixth Centuries

By the end of the fourth century, Christians who agreed with the Council of Nicaea held a great deal of authority in the Roman Empire, and Christianity in various forms continued to spread widely within the empire and the regions outside its borders. In 410, Gothic troops shook Rome's sense of stability through their military sack of the city of Rome. Although Western imperial focus had shifted to Ravenna, Rome's symbolism as well as its historic structures and wealthy elite families sent shock waves through the empire and wealthy refugees fleeing. The Goths, pushed further west by the migration of the Huns to their east, spent years in conversation and conflict with Roman leaders, including the powerful general Stilicho, on the northern border of the empire, and in the early fifth century moved into Italy under the new king of the western Goths (Visigoths), Alaric. This period saw waxing and waning conflicts with the Sasanian Empire on Rome's eastern border; periodic incursions from Huns, Goths, Suebi, Alans, and Vandals along its long northern edge; and increasing attacks from Vandals into North Africa, such as their siege of Bishop Augustine's city of Hippo in 430 and of Carthage in 439. In 476 Odoacer deposed the young Western emperor Romulus Augustulus, bringing an end in some ways to the Western Empire, although Eastern emperors still claimed the territory and Emperor Justinian's troops under Belisarius temporarily reclaimed significant parts of Italy and North Africa in the 530s–550s before much of Italy fell to the Lombards. Concurrently, in 536, 540, and 547, massive volcanic eruptions led to thick dust clouds that significantly affected the climate in what scientists today refer to as the Late Antique Little Ice Age.[6] This cooling lasted over a century, with severe effects on agriculture, including famines.[7] These conditions set the stage for the devastating outbreak of the bubonic plague in the eastern Mediterranean in 541, which surviving texts by Procopius and John of Ephesus claim decimated staggering numbers of the population.[8] Despite these wars, famine, plague, and human migrations, Christianity nevertheless flourished, although these centuries also saw the separation of several distinct churches as a result of ongoing debates to define Christian orthodoxy.

Debates within Christianity continued in writing campaigns, political interventions, and regional and imperial councils. The influential North African bishop and theologian Augustine of Hippo, for example, strongly denounced the teachings of the Donatists and Manichees as well as the followers of the British monk Pelagius, who was condemned by a council at Carthage in 418 in part for teaching that free will gave humans the ability to avoid sin. Another Latin scholar, Jerome, joined Augustine in condemning Pelagius and also denounced the teachings of Jovinian, whom Bishop Ambrose condemned at a council at Milan in 390 in part for arguing that all sins and all heavenly rewards were equal. The legacy of the third-century

---

6. See, e.g., McCormick et al., "Climate Change"; Buentgen et al., "Cooling and Societal Change."

7. McCormick et al., "Climate Change," 197.

8. Rosen, *Justinian's Flea*; Harper, *Fate of Rome*, esp. 199–287.

Christian intellectual Origen, translated into Latin by Rufinus of Aquileia, also played a prominent role in fifth- and sixth-century conversations, particularly through the late fourth-century influence of Evagrius of Pontus and accusations of "Origenism" that his teachings inspired. Although Emperor Justinian's Second Council of Constantinople in 553 anathematized many of the teachings of Evagrius (misattributed to Origen), they nevertheless still influenced monastic practices in the Latin West and further east in Syriac and Coptic churches.

This Second Council of Constantinople, in fact, marked the end of a century of fierce doctrinal conflict and formal schisms within the church. One thread of these disagreements took shape in the early fifth century as the West experienced the Gothic and Vandal incursions, when despite its growing popularity bishop Nestorius of Constantinople rejected the title *theotokos* (Greek: "God bearer") for Jesus's mother Mary. Grounded in his understanding that the Son of God had two distinct *hypostaseis* (Greek: "beings"), one human and one divine, Nestorius rejected the idea that Mary could contain the divine *hypostasis* in her womb. Opponents like the powerful bishop Cyril of Alexandria accused Nestorius of misrepresenting the incarnation and countered that the Son was already fully human and fully divine in a single being in Mary's womb. The conflict led Emperor Theodosius II to call the First Council of Ephesus in 431 (the Third Ecumenical Council), where—after a great deal of intrigue—Cyril's supporters condemned Nestorius before Nestorius's delayed supporters arrived, leading to competing emissaries to the emperor who, influenced by his older sister Pulcheria, supported Cyril's council's rejection of Nestorius's teachings. As the debates around the topic continued, some criticized the monastic leader Eutyches for taking the idea of the Son's singularity too far in the opposite direction of Nestorius, and Eutyches's teachings were condemned by Bishop Flavian of Constantinople at a council in 448. In response, Theodosius II convened the Second Council of Ephesus in 449 under Bishop Dioscorus of Alexandria, who accepted the teachings of Eutyches, rejected Bishop Flavian, and reiterated the orthodoxy of Cyril's teachings that had prevailed in 431 against Nestorius.

Bishop Leo I of Rome, who was influential in giving the Western episcopacy in Rome the authority we now associate with its title as the papacy,[9] condemned Dioscorus's 449 council as a "robber council" and when emperor Theodosius II died in 450, his sister Pulcheria made Marcian the new emperor by marrying him, and they called the Council of Chalcedon (the Fourth Ecumenical Council) in 451. This council rejected the outcome of the 449 council, accepted Bishop Leo of Rome's statement (*Tome*), and anathematized

---

9. Demacopoulos, *Invention of Peter*.

Dioscorus and Eutyches. At the same time, though, the 451 council affirmed Dioscorus's condemnation of Nestorius, his acceptance of Cyril, and the validity of the first Council of Ephesus, declaring that the Son was "one person in two natures." In the decades that followed, the West upheld this definition even as Eastern emperors vacillated between supporting or rejecting the definition of Chalcedon (or proposing a compromise such as Emperor Zeno's *Henotikon*) before Chalcedonian Christianity prevailed more permanently in the East under the emperor Justin I and his nephew and successor Justinian. Justinian's empress Theodora offered some of the last imperial support for those who rejected Chalcedon, and soon after her death in 548, Justinian called the Second Council of Constantinople in 553 (the Fifth Ecumenical Council) and affirmed the decisions of Chalcedon. In the meantime, however, some Christians who had never accepted the decision of the first Council of Ephesus in 431, today's Assyrian Church of the East, flourished in the Sasanian Empire. Likewise, Christians who argued against what they saw as the heretical *diphysite* (Greek: "two-nature") teachings of both Nestorius and the Council of Chalcedon supported a *miaphysite* (Greek: "one-nature") Christology that the Son had a single nature that was simultaneously fully human and fully divine, and their legacy survives in today's Syrian, Armenian, Coptic (Egyptian), and Ethiopian Orthodox Churches.

The late fourth through sixth centuries were also periods of significant change in how Roman Christians legislated about those whom they considered heretics, Jews, and pagans. Their increasing imperial power led to laws in the Theodosian Code that prohibited Jews from holding certain jobs, owning Christian slaves, or marrying Christian women. By the late fourth century, heretics were forbidden from controlling public worship spaces in the empire's cities, and Libanius of Antioch complained that Christian monks were destroying pagan temples. The fifth-century Coptic monk Shenoute claims to have destroyed neighbors' pagan "idols," and the destruction of the Serapion temple and early fifth-century murder of the mathematician Hypatia in Egypt further changed the landscape.[10] In Italy, the Christian emperor Gratian removed the altar of the goddess Victory from the Roman Senate in 382, and in 384 Bishop Ambrose of Milan prevailed against the pagan senator Symmachus in convincing the young emperor Valentinian II not to replace it. In 388 Ambrose persuaded Emperor Theodosius I not to require Christians to make restitution to Jews in Callinicum on the Euphrates River whose synagogue Christians had illegally destroyed. In 386–87 John Chrysostom preached a series of anti-Jewish sermons to his congregation in Antioch, warning them to stop going to the

10. Watts, *Riot in Alexandria*; Watts, *Hypatia*.

local synagogue. Claims to have discovered the remains of Saint Stephen (Acts 7) in 415 led to some of Stephen's relics arriving in 418 on Minorca where Bishop Severus claims to have used them to convert the Jewish population to Christianity after their synagogue burned.[11] Rabbis completed the Talmud of the Land of Israel ca. 400 and the Babylonian Talmud ca. 500, but Roman Jewish and pagan communities start to dwindle in our historical record as the empire's legal codes of Theodosius II and Justinian, and the empire's identity more generally, became more firmly Christian.[12]

Western Kingdoms and the Rise of Islam: Christians in the Seventh Century

In late antiquity the bishops of Constantinople, Rome, Alexandria, Antioch, and Jerusalem held the higher administrative title of patriarch and oversaw other bishops under their jurisdiction. As the new Eastern capital of Constantinople gained power through the fourth century, the bishop of that city grew increasingly influential, as did the bishop of Rome as the lone patriarch in the Latin West, particularly from the fifth century onward as imperial control in the West weakened and then failed. During this period, the Western imperial church continued to call itself the catholic (universal) church, today the Roman Catholic Church, and to look to the authority of the bishop of Rome, later called simply the pope (Latin, Greek: "father"), even as it remained in communion with the imperial churches of the Eastern Empire who referred to themselves as the orthodox (correct teaching) church, today the Eastern Orthodox Church, and looked to the church councils under the leadership of the five patriarchs for their decisions. It was not until centuries later in 1054 that these churches formally separated from each other through mutual excommunications. Meanwhile, as the territory that had made up the Western Roman Empire came under the control of Visigothic (western Goths), Vandal, Ostrogothic (eastern Goths), Lombard, and other emerging regional kings, the vast and sophisticated writings of Augustine served to guide the Latin churches long after Augustine's death in 430 as the Vandals laid siege to his city. The rise of the Merovingian kingdom of the Franks and then the success of Muhammad's followers would again reshape these religious and political landscapes in the centuries that followed.

It is difficult to overestimate Augustine's influence on the Western, Latin history of Christianity. The development of Western theology,

---

11. See Severus of Minorca, *Letter on the Conversion*, esp. chs. 4–5, 13, 16 (pp. 82–85, 92–101).

12. Kraemer, *Mediterranean Diaspora*.

preaching, monasticism, and daily living for clergy and laity alike were all deeply affected by Augustine's prolific writings. Augustine articulated, for example, Western ideas of "original sin," the innately sinful (and thus in need of baptism and salvation) state of humankind after Adam and Eve. In the *filioque* controversy that influenced the eleventh-century schism with the East, the Western church relied on Augustine's teachings that the Holy Spirit proceeds from the Father "and the Son" (Latin: *filioque*), a teaching that was confirmed by the Third Council of Toledo in 589, but was rejected by Eastern Church leaders who argued that the Second Council of Constantinople in 381 had concluded that the Holy Spirit proceeds only "from the Father." Eastern and Western bishops continued to meet together at the Third Council of Constantinople in 680–81 (the Sixth Ecumenical Council), although in small numbers, to reject monotheletism (Greek: "one will") and confirm that the Son has two wills, one human and one divine. The Second Council of Nicaea in 787 (the Seventh Ecumenical Council) was the last council accepted by both Latin and Greek church leaders. This council, called by Empress Irene as regent for her seven-year-old son Emperor Constantine VI, affirmed the veneration of sacred images (Greek: "icons") and decried the iconoclasm (Greek: "destruction of icons") being encouraged by some leaders. Apart from these councils, however, Latin churches increasingly turned for leadership to the bishop in Rome, their pope, and to the thriving monastic communities in their midst.

The shape of Christianity in Europe was significantly influenced by the unification of the Franks under the leadership of Clovis in the late fifth century, and his decision to follow his wife Clotilda into the Latin church of Rome rather than its non-Nicene Germanic counterpart. As commemorated by the sixth-century bishop Gregory of Tours, Clovis was king of the Franks at the beginning of the Merovingian Dynasty and was baptized on Christmas Day in 508 after more than a decade in the church. While his kingdom was divided at his death in 511, the Merovingian Dynasty and its relation with the papacy lasted for more than two centuries. Further east in northern Italy, Odoacer, who had deposed the last Western Roman emperor, was himself conquered by a combined Ostrogothic force under Theodoric, who centered his kingdom in Ravenna where his "Arian" baptistry survives today,[13] until Ravenna's capture by Emperor Justinian's general Belisarius in 540 and the end of the Ostrogothic kingdom in 553. As for the Nicene Latin church, the power of the papacy grew considerably under the renowned leadership of Gregory I (Gregory the Great, bishop of Rome, 590–604), who expanded the church with missions that saw many of the

---

13. See, for example, Cohen, "Religious Diversity," esp. 510–21.

Vandals, Visigoths, Lombards, and even Anglo-Saxons join the Franks under Rome's ecclesiastical authority. The region that would become Western Europe was becoming more cohesively Catholic.

As the political influence of the Catholic Church in the West waxed and waned in the centuries that followed, a new religious community was developing in the East that would again shift the political and religious makeup of the world. According to Muslim tradition, the prophet Muhammad was born in the Arabian Peninsula in 570, and received his first revelation from the angel Gabriel while fasting in a cave outside Mecca in the month of Ramadan in 610; the revelations that he continued to receive until his death in 632 are preserved in the Qur'an (Arabic: "recitation"). After Muhammad's death in 632, many of his followers moved north, taking territory away from the Eastern Roman (Byzantine) and Sasanian Empires that had suffered in the arduous Byzantine-Sasanian wars (602–28). Although Constantinople remained under Christian control until 1453, Muhammad's early followers captured much of Roman Egypt, Syria, and Palestine, along with much of Georgia, Armenia, and Persia within a decade of Muhammad's death. Because it took several decades for Islam to emerge as a religious presence in these regions, miaphysite Christians initially thrived more easily under this new regime than under the Byzantine Empire where they had been renounced as heretics. Once 'Abd al-Malik consolidated power under the Umayyad Caliphate in 690, however, there was an increasing coherence and visibility to the emerging religion, and after decades of Arab rule, Syriac-speaking Christians started to produce apocalyptic literature like the Apocalypse of Pseudo-Methodius in an effort to understand why God had allowed Christians to be subjugated to Muslim rule.

It was not only Christians in the Byzantine and Sasanian East who were encountering Islam, however, as Muslims quickly traveled west across North Africa and in 711 crossed into the Iberian Peninsula at what is today known as the Straits of Gibraltar, named for Jabal Tariq (Arabic: "mountain of Tariq") after Tariq ibn Ziyad who led the conquest. As these Muslims continued north through Vandal Christian territory, they were defeated in northern Aquitaine (western France) in 732 by the Catholic Frankish leader Charles Martel. While Muslim kingdoms remained in the Iberian Peninsula until 1492, to their north Charles Martel's son Pepin (Pépin le Bref) inaugurated the new Carolingian Dynasty and in 751, only months after the Abbasid Caliphate overthrew the eastern Umayyads, Pepin became the king of the Franks with the blessing of Rome's papacy. Pepin's son Charlemagne later famously persuaded Pope Leo III to crown him emperor of a new Roman Empire in St. Peter's basilica on Christmas Day in 800, uniting much of Western Europe under his rule and papal influence.

As late antiquity transitioned into the early Middle Ages without a strong imperial presence in the West, the church's role as a unifying and defining societal force continued to grow. Christian influence remained prominent in law codes, and monasteries played critical roles as places of education and learning as well as prayer and support. Thus while the history of Christianity in Europe shares the complex early Mediterranean history of Christians everywhere, the unique role of the papacy, especially following the fifth-century dissolution of the Western Roman Empire, comes to distinguish the Latin church by the end of late antiquity.

Bibliography

Barton, Carlin A., and Daniel Boyarin. *Imagine No Religion: How Modern Abstractions Hide Ancient Realities*. New York: Fordham University Press, 2016.

Buentgen, Ulf, et al. "Cooling and Societal Change during the Late Antique Little Ice Age from 536 to around 660 AD." *Nature Geoscience* 9 (Mar. 2016) 231–36.

Castelli, Elizabeth. *Martyrdom and Memory: Early Christian Culture Making*. New York: Columbia University Press, 2004.

Cohen, Samuel. "Religious Diversity." In *A Companion to Ostrogothic Italy*, edited by Jonathan J. Arnold et al., 503–32. Brill's Companions to European History 9. Leiden: Brill, 2016.

Demacopoulos, George. *The Invention of Peter: Apostolic Discourse and Papal Authority in Late Antiquity*. Divinations: Rereading Late Ancient Religion. Philadelphia: University of Pennsylvania Press, 2013.

Harper, Kyle. *The Fate of Rome: Climate, Disease, and the End of an Empire*. Princeton History of the Ancient World. Princeton: Princeton University Press, 2017.

Knust, Jennifer Wright. *Abandoned to Lust: Sexual Slander and Ancient Christianity*. Gender, Theory, and Religion. New York: Columbia University Press, 2006.

Kraemer, Ross Shepard. *The Mediterranean Diaspora in Late Antiquity: What Christianity Cost the Jews*. New York: Oxford University Press, 2020.

Lee, A. D. *Pagans and Christians in Late Antiquity: A Sourcebook*. Routledge Sourcebooks for the Ancient World. New York: Routledge, 2000.

McCormick, Michael, et al. "Climate Change during and after the Roman Empire: Reconstructing the Past from Scientific and Historical Evidence." *Journal of Interdisciplinary History* 43 (2012) 169–220.

Rebillard, Éric. *Christianities and Their Many Identities in Late Antiquity, North Africa, 200–450 CE*. Ithaca: Cornell University Press, 2012.

Rosen, William. *Justinian's Flea: Plague, Empire, and the Birth of Europe*. London: Penguin, 2007.

Severus of Minorca. *Letter on the Conversion of the Jews*. Edited and translated by Scott Bradbury. Early Oxford Christian Texts. Oxford: Clarendon, 1996.

Watts, Edward. *Hypatia: The Life and Legend of an Ancient Philosopher*. Women in Antiquity. New York: Oxford University Press, 2017.

———. *Riot in Alexandria: Tradition and Group Dynamics in Late Antique Pagan and Christian Communities*. Transformation of the Classical Heritage. Berkeley: University of California Press, 2010.

2

Christianity Negotiates the Western Middle Ages

PETER SHERLOCK

MEDIEVAL EUROPE ENDURED FOR a thousand years. Its origins were in the gradual disintegration of the Western Roman Empire and its conclusion in the intellectual, theological, and political revolutions of the Renaissance and Reformation. Despite the awkward term *medieval*—literally "Middle Ages," a title that implies an absence or deficiency—this period saw Christianity flourish and transform from a missionary movement to a powerful, almost universal institution in Western Europe that sought to dominate its members, eliminate its rivals, and keep its neighbors at bay. In this era Christian ideas became more important than ever, codifying Christian theology on the one hand and diversifying its expression in mystical and practical forms. A striking characteristic of Christianity in what might be termed the era of Christendom is its ability to reinvent itself, drawing on beliefs and practices from within and without and above and below, and allying itself with rulers and kingdoms for its own purposes. Medieval Christendom consequently proved itself adept at handing on both Christian beliefs and the exercise of power by Christians to future generations. This prevailing dynamic came at an enormous cost, however, as new, combative movements arose within Christianity that sought to exterminate dissent, eliminate enemies, and enhance worldly wealth. The same dynamic also produced works of art, architecture, and literature of astonishing beauty; spiritual practices that sought to know and experience God in myriad ways; and institutions such as universities, hospitals, and monasteries that shaped contemporary and future ideals of human society for both Christians and non-Christians alike.

Recovering Christendom

In the sixth and seventh centuries, Christianity in Western Europe was the religion of a former empire. Its structures carried with it the memory of imperial rule—the concept of Christianity as a state religion, organized around bishops and dioceses that corresponded to political centers and boundaries, with the pope as its titular head—but the Christian God was still in competition with the gods of other religions. In places such as Germany much of the former Roman ecclesiastical system had collapsed, while Islamic rulers were occupying Spain and reaching into southern France. Yet if we fast forward to the eleventh century, most of Western Europe identified as Christian, and Christianity was easily accessed, whether in the local village church, monastic house, or increasingly grand cathedral.

Critical to this change was the role of the Franks who were beginning to consolidate power and who saw in Christianity a useful ally. In the mid-eighth century their leader, Pepin III, entered into an alliance with Pope Zachary (reigned 741–752). In return for sacred recognition of their legitimacy as rulers, the Franks would provide military force to assist the church in regaining control from the Lombards over its lands in the Italian Peninsula. The deal worked: Pepin was anointed king in 751 by Frankish bishops, and in 756 Pepin invaded Italy, seizing the Lombards' lands and returning them to the papacy. This transaction was momentous, establishing a vital thread between the pope and his bishops, and kings and emperors. For many centuries, the church and rulers existed in uneasy tension. While the pope might make kings, giving sacred authority to rulers, the church was also vulnerable to the will of these same rulers and to shifts in the balance of power across kingdoms. Another consequence of this moment was a turning away of the papacy from the Byzantine Empire and Eastern Church, towards the west and north.

Pepin's son Charles the Great, or Charlemagne, inherited his kingdom in 768 with a determination to expand its borders and to grow Christianity's reach. He did so with military force, successfully conquering rival groups from northern Spain to Bavaria, including the slaughter or enforced conversion of thousands of Saxons. Charlemagne articulated his understanding of the relationship between pope and monarch within the church and world:

> It is our task, with the aid of divine goodness, to defend the holy church of Christ everywhere from the attacks of pagans outside and to strengthen it within through the knowledge of the Catholic faith. And it is your duty, O Holy Father, with your hands raised high to God, after the manner of Moses, to aid our armies so that by your intercession with God, who is our leader and

benefactor, the Christian people may always and everywhere be victorious over the enemies of His Holy Name, and the name of Our Lord Jesus Christ be proclaimed throughout the world.[1]

This understanding must have been shared at some level by Pope Leo III (reigned 795–816), who famously crowned Charlemagne in Rome as emperor of the Romans on Christmas Day in the year 800, a deed that paved the way for what would later become known as the Holy Roman Empire. The reference to Moses is significant, and indicates a prevailing theological theme of kingship and conquest in the early medieval period that tended to focus on the Hebrew Bible and the experience of the people of Israel.

Charlemagne put his theory of the role of church and kingdom into practice well beyond the domain of conquering other lands and peoples. He oversaw the systematic reorganization of both church and empire, promoting education, liturgical consistency, and missionary work. This included the edification and beautification of church buildings and church furnishings such as the construction of the lavish Palatine Chapel at his preferred residence at Aachen. He brought a British scholar, Alcuin, to Aachen to run the palace school. Alcuin's educational program was based on classical Roman ideals, now put to the purpose of Christian learning through study of the Scriptures, church fathers, sermons, canon law, and saints' lives. Outcomes included the preservation and dissemination of ancient texts that were copied into a new, highly legible script known as Carolingian miniscule, putting an end to the loss of classical literature and early Christian writing in the West. Another was the codification of canon law and the attempt to shape a legal system that brought imperial society into alignment with the commandments of God. As part of this codification, Charlemagne and his son Louis invested heavily in monasteries, including bringing all the monasteries in their empire under the Rule of Benedict. Monasteries came to play a vital theological role in medieval Europe as places of prayer and good works, through which men and women might intercede with God and the saints on behalf of their secular patrons. Monastic prayers and charitable deeds could be used to pay the debt for the sins that seemed necessary for Christian rulers who wanted to maintain or extend their power through war, bloodshed, and the display of their power. In this period Western Christianity was—relatively speaking—hospitable for Jews who were allowed by the emperor to live according to their own laws and to practice their religion, with some acting as merchants who could operate across the Mediterranean and into Eastern Europe.

---

1. Madigan, *Medieval Christianity*, 75.

Reform and Reorganization

Charlemagne's empire did not last, splintering within a few decades into three territories, while Western Europe faced external threats from Islam to the south, the Vikings to the north, and the Magyars to the east. For the church, the tenth century was characterized by a constant struggle against disorder, to overcome the subordination of the sacred to the profane, of the church's power to royal authority, and of the clergy to the laity. One vital and successful response was increasing investment in monastic houses. Communities that lived under the Rule of Benedict provided order and discipline that contrasted with the surrounding world. They could also represent the church's authority across Europe, from Britain to France, Germany, and Spain, well beyond the Italian Peninsula and the papal or old imperial centers of Rome and Ravenna.

In 910 Duke William I of Aquitaine established the monastery at Cluny by charter. Cluny had a profound influence, ranging from its spiritual and political influence to its architecture: for centuries Cluny Abbey was the largest church building in the world. Critical to this success was a novel element in Cluny's foundation. Duke William's charter gave the monks the right to elect their own abbot, free from outside intervention. The monks took up this freedom wisely and appointed a series of outstanding abbots who grew the community and its influence. The abbots in turn adopted another novel strategy, planting hundreds if not thousands of daughter houses that were not independent of Cluny but part of a kind of monastic empire, with the priors of each house answerable to the abbot. Thus Cluny became a religious order, an order reaching across Europe and united by a common practice that placed a high value on prayer and liturgy. This practice was not only for the monks or clergy. The liturgical demands of the Cluniac way led to the construction of impressive churches that commanded attention. Moreover, Cluny organized and orchestrated pilgrimage routes, that lay pilgrims could follow as they sought to approach the gates of heaven itself through self-denial and seeking out the benediction of saints and apostles. This included organization of the pilgrim route from Cluny to Compostela in the Iberian Peninsula, where lay the body of St. James, one of Christ's apostles.

The Cluniac monks sought to reform and purify the lives of the clergy, opposing simony—the purchase of church offices for money—and clerical marriage. This particular series of reforms reflected Christianity's self-understanding as a cult in this period. If in the Eucharist the bread and wine literally became Christ's body and blood, then the priests who administered this sacrament were handling God and needed to be "pure," free from worldly associations. The reform was successful: in 1139 the Second Lateran

Council declared that a priest could not legitimately enter into marriage. The emphasis on reform and renewal was a recurring theme in monastic history, as men and women living in religious communities sought to be faithful to the Christian Scriptures, to apostolic teaching, and to the ascetic demands of the monastic rule. Thus as the Cluniacs grew in numbers and wealth, their way of life was in turn challenged, most prominently by the Cistercian order established in 1098 at Citeaux with the purpose of living according to as literal as possible an interpretation of the Rule of Benedict.

In the eleventh century the theme of reform and renewal was advanced under successive popes. Leo IX (reigned 1049–54) was pope for only five years, but spent less than a year of his reign in Rome, preferring instead to conduct a series of tours through Northern Europe where he convened synods and councils. These enabled him to prosecute his opposition to simony and clerical marriage, but also increased papal authority through his presence. Pursuit of papal authority soon became a cause unto itself, prosecuted heavily by Gregory VII (reigned 1073–85) in the late eleventh century. Gregory contended that the pope was nothing less than the universal monarch, superior to all earthly rulers. He adopted a new title as "vicar of Christ" rather than "vicar of Peter": the pope was the representative of God on earth, not merely that of an apostle. Gregory's vision brought into focus the battle over who might ultimately control the church—kings and emperors, or popes and bishops—which would play out over and over again for many centuries. Gregory himself clashed repeatedly with the emperor, thrice excommunicating Henry IV. The conflict over who appointed bishops and clergy reached its apex in the assassination of the archbishop of Canterbury, Thomas à Becket, by a group of knights seeking to support the English monarch, Henry II, in the king's claim to exercise legal jurisdiction over the church. Unsurprisingly, theological commentary in this period began to focus less on Old Testament behavioral codes and ideas about kingship and more on New Testament texts. These included the texts that testified to the power granted by Christ to his apostles and specifically to Peter—the "Petrine" texts—as a basis for papal supremacy. But scriptural interpretation also focused on evidence for the apostolic way of life as found in Acts and elsewhere based on preaching, renunciation of personal wealth, and the sharing of goods that lay at the basis of monasticism.

The Contest for Glory

Gregory VII had advocated for an army of St. Peter that could protect the Western Church without the need to seek the aid of kings and emperors. It was common for eleventh-century popes to provide spiritual or financial rewards to soldiers engaged in, for example, wars against Muslim armies in the Iberian Peninsula. But in 1095 something new happened. Pope Urban II (reigned 1088–99) received a request for military aid from the Byzantine emperor. He responded by preaching a sermon at Clermont that appealed to Christians to make a pilgrimage to Jerusalem, remove the Islamic rulers, and create a Christian colony. Urban promised those who answered the call to "take the cross" the full remission of their sins and complete restoration of innocence. The response was unexpected and overwhelming, with tens of thousands participating in what became known as the First Crusade, the first in a series that took place over the next two hundred years.

The motivations for this extraordinary moment in European history remain a matter for debate, with numerous theological and political strands pointing to the potential of Christianity to change the behavior and aspirations of large numbers of people. Central to the Crusades was Augustine's theory of just war, a theory that permitted warfare and its attendant violence as a necessary but lesser evil only if there was just cause, legitimate authority, and right intention. Contemporary rhetoric argued that the cause was the liberation of the Holy City of Jerusalem, the authority was the pope, and the intention was Christian love. Going on crusade could also be seen as a form of armed pilgrimage, encompassing a visit to the holy places of Jerusalem and opportunity to see the lands that Jesus walked and to acquire relics of Jesus and the saints. This was a penitential activity undertaken at significant personal cost that might thereby provide spiritual benefits directly to the participant. Those who perished along the way would die as willing martyrs, free from the consequences of sin and assured of salvation. In 1099 the crusaders reached Jerusalem, defeated its rulers, and established a European kingdom there. This added a further justification for future Crusades: surely the apparent success of this First Crusade was a sign of God's blessing. The notion that Christians should be engaged in what they saw as holy war was enshrined in the founding of two orders, the Knights of the Temple (Templars) and the Knights of St. John (Hospitallers), which combined monastic vows with promises to fight the "infidel."

The reality rarely aligned, however, with the theory. Urban drummed up support for the First Crusade by making up stories of the horrors visited by Muslims upon Christian pilgrims to the Holy Land. As early as 1096 the crusader army committed its first atrocity before it had even left European soil when it massacred large numbers of Jewish people in the Rhineland. Over the next two centuries the Crusades saw Christians engaged in willful murder and theft, of other Christians such as the Cathars of southern France or the Orthodox Christians of Eastern Europe, as well as of Jews and Muslims, and deepened the fault lines between Eastern and Western Christianity. The Crusades left a bitter legacy for Christianity, creating a new theology of violence and legitimating a militancy for future generations far removed from the gospel of peace preached by Jesus. At the heart of the crusading era was a strange tension between self-denying, costly pilgrimage undertaken for the purposes of salvation, and unprovoked acts of violence against those identified as enemies of European Christendom.

The contest for both temporal and spiritual power exemplified in the Crusades found expression within Western Europe as rulers sought to outdo each other in the search for glory. We have already seen the examples of Charlemagne at Aachen and the monks at Cluny. Cathedrals and abbeys followed, symbols of the church's power and of the authority of Christianity, but also of the good works of royalty and nobility in creating places of worship that gave glory to God and served the needs of their people. Distinctive to Western Europe was the emerging "Gothic" architectural style that favored height and light and created canvasses in stone and glass for depictions of the events of Christian Scripture and history. Suger, the twelfth-century abbot of Saint-Denis, set out the theological vision for the form and function of church buildings in the inscription he placed on the doors of his abbey:

> Bright is the noble work; but, being nobly bright, the work
> Should brighten the minds, so that they may travel, through the true lights,
> To the True Light where Christ is the True Door.[2]

Medieval cathedrals and chapels tied heaven to earth, past to present and future, and led the Christian pilgrim through light towards the light of Christ. The link between heaven and earth was not only achieved through stained glass, statues, and paintings, but through the liturgical rituals and the display of relics. These sacred buildings and their venerated contents were not mere imitations of heaven, for they sought to bring the faithful directly into the presence of Christ and the saints. The architectural design regulated the behavior of the Christian worshipper, seeking to instill an internal spiritual order that matched the external form.

The search for spiritual glory and worldly honor in art and architecture had elements of a contest. Sometimes this was the age-old human contest to build something that was higher, longer, or larger than anything else—often with dangerous consequences, such as when part of the vaulting of Beauvais Cathedral collapsed in 1284, just twelve years after its completion. When

---

2. Gerson, *Abbot Suger*, 186.

the English king Henry III set out to refashion Westminster Abbey in the thirteenth century, he did so in competition with Louis IX of France. The French king assembled a famous collection of relics of Christ, including the crown of thorns and a fragment of the cross; in 1247 Henry acquired a relic of Christ's blood, which he installed at Westminster. In 1248 Louis IX completed building Sainte-Chapelle at his palace in Paris to house his collection of relics in a shimmering edifice of stained glass that aimed to imitate heaven itself. Not to be outdone, Henry commenced rebuilding Westminster Abbey, with a new shrine for his royal predecessor St. Edward the Confessor whose cult Henry promoted. In both cases the imagery of each building provided not only illustrated versions of biblical narratives, but also a history of the relics and their owners, creating a permanent record of their charitable deeds.

Teaching and Preaching

In the eleventh century, Europe's cathedrals were increasingly complemented by places of learning that sought to create an organized body of Christian knowledge. The concept of theology as the systematic exploration of Christian thought was itself invented in this period by Peter Abelard, a theologian in Paris, when he published his *Theologia Christiana* in the early twelfth century. Theologians became a resource of advice for rulers throughout the church. All this drew heavily from Islamic practice, and, increasingly, on knowledge transmitted through Islam to Christian schools—not least the recovery of Aristotle's work in Western Europe. In time, these schools would become what we know today as universities. They developed a new approach to education that became known as scholasticism. The scholastic method promoted debate, skepticism, and analysis, for if truth was created by God, then contradiction and argument were ways to find that truth. Scholastics asserted that the world was ordered by reason, and its true order could therefore be known by the application of reason. Reason could define, disseminate, and defend the faith in the world, and could also ensure the prosecution of dissidents, those who questioned authority itself.

The leading medieval theologian was a product of the scholastic method. Thomas Aquinas, thirteenth-century author of the *Summa theologiae* or the "sum total of theology," sought to integrate Aristotelian philosophy and Christian theology. Aquinas argued that human reason was created by God, as humans were endowed with a rational soul. Reasoned argument was a means to approach faith; everything had a cause, and the correct application of reason would lead to the ultimate cause of all things, God. Scholastic disputation was vital to the search for truth, for God. For Aquinas, this was no ivory-tower activity, as righteous Christian behavior itself was determined by the natural law revealed by reason. Thus, Aquinas pointed not only to the four cardinal virtues—prudence, temperance, justice, and fortitude—that might be taken up by any person of good will but also to the three theological virtues—faith, hope, and charity. It was the theological virtues that pointed to God.

Just as the project of scholasticism was to think about how to apprehend the truths of faith using reason, the thirteenth century also saw new methods for communicating those truths through the establishment of new orders known as friars, or brothers. The friars stood in the reformist tradition of the Cluniacs and Cistercians that sought a return to a purer, more authentic Christian practice. In the early thirteenth century the priest and monk Dominic believed that the church was failing to convert Cathar heretics to Catholic orthodoxy because its leaders were not walking the talk. He therefore started a campaign of preaching that was intellectually rigorous and matched by a life of poverty and simplicity so that nothing could detract from the Christian message. In 1217 Pope Honorius III (reigned 1216–27) elevated Dominic's followers into the Order of Preachers, who became known as the Dominicans or Blackfriars. The Dominicans lived an itinerant life rather than settling in communities, and were dependent on begging for survival, a recipe for ensuring that their preaching was effective. Their rigorous training and rhetorical ability later led them to be recruited as inquisitors, the main opponents of dissent.

The same period saw the creation of another order of friars, the Franciscans. Their founder, Francis of Assisi, was from a wealthy family, but after a dramatic conversion in 1209 in response to a sermon on Matt 10:9 he began to identify with the poor and outcast, especially the lepers who were excluded from European society. In an extraordinary career he traveled to Egypt to meet the sultan in 1219, and famously preached to the birds, seeking a return to the way of life of the garden of Eden. Within a few years of his death his followers were formally constituted as the Franciscans with the support of Pope Innocent III (reigned 1198–1216), while a parallel order for women, the Order of Poor Clares, was established by Clare of Assisi. The Franciscans sought to emulate the poverty and humility of Christ and the apostolic church, even traveling barefoot.

Together the Dominicans and Franciscans argued passionately for a new vision of how Christian society might operate, advocating for Christian truth grounded in a life of poverty and oriented towards the most destitute members of society, rather than towards the acquisition of power or wealth for its own sake. This sense of exhorting Christian people to greater holiness and a deeper engagement of their faith found expression at the highest levels of the church. In 1215 Pope Innocent III convened the Fourth Lateran Council, a council that resolved that Catholic Christians were required to receive the Eucharist at least once a year, and to make their confession to a priest prior to doing so. Christians were to scrutinize their lives, and to receive instruction from the clergy on how to live. Part of this instruction concerned the nature of the Eucharist itself. The Lateran Council formalized the doctrine of transubstantiation, drawing on Aristotelian philosophy, to teach that in the miracle of the Mass, the bread and wine were changed in substance by God's power into the body and blood of Christ. While the "accidents" of bread and wine remained—the eucharistic elements continued to appear to be bread and wine—their true substance had been changed. The high point of Christian liturgy became the elevation of the bread, or "host," by the priest immediately after the consecration, when the faithful might gaze directly on Christ's body.

Mystical Visions and Theology from Below

This miracle of transubstantiation was celebrated through the institution of the Feast of Corpus Christi, inspired by a nun, Juliana, who in 1208 experienced a vision in which Christ instructed her on the need for a dedicated celebration of the eucharistic elements. Juliana's vision was echoed over and over again in legendary miracles in which hosts shed blood, providing evidence of the veracity of the change of substance, this presence of the crucified Christ on earth, to the skeptic. The cult of Corpus Christi points to the physicality of medieval Christianity, and the intermingling of supernatural and natural realms at every turn. Thus Francis of Assisi was blessed—or afflicted, depending on your point of view—with the stigmata, or physical wounds that mirrored the wounds of Christ, the first person, though not the last, to receive this sign of divine approval. Christ was not the only source of such manifestations either, with his mother Mary making regular apparitions. Richeldis de Faverches was said to be an eleventh-century English noblewoman who received three visions of the Virgin Mary in which she was shown Mary's home in Nazareth and told to build a replica of it at Walsingham. Richeldis obediently commenced building the "holy house," which was miraculously moved and completed by angels, becoming a celebrated destination for pilgrims who wished to venerate Our Lady of Walsingham.

Accompanying such physical manifestations of God and the saints was the emergence of mystical theology and spiritual practices that engaged the mind as much as the body. These were especially pronounced among elite women in nunneries, who had access to education, though not to the universities. Hildegard of Bingen, a twelfth-century abbess, was an early example. Her mystical thought survives in a remarkable range of written, painted, and musical forms that draw on biblical metaphors to reimagine the relationship of God and creation and to meditate on the end of time itself. In her major work *Scivias*, Hildegard set out how she came to write down her visions by divine command, following a series of illnesses:

> I set my hand to the writing. While I was doing it, I sensed, as I mentioned before, the deep profundity of scriptural exposition . . . I spoke and wrote these things not by the invention of my heart or that of any other person, but as by the secret mysteries of God I heard and received them in the heavenly places. And again I heard a voice from Heaven saying to me, "Cry out, therefore, and write thus!"[3]

At the other end of the spectrum was Julian of Norwich, a fourteenth-century English anchorite who lived in permanent seclusion and produced the earliest surviving English works by a woman. Julian's writings record her visions of Christ and extrapolate their theological meaning, focusing on an optimistic view of divine love as overcoming sin.

Mystical experience could reach the world far beyond the cloister. Catherine of Siena was a fourteenth-century Italian woman who became associated with the Dominicans and operated outside conventual life, undertaking diplomatic negotiations on behalf of the pope. Catherine engaged in ascetic practices such as fasting, or eating only the eucharistic host, seeking physical union with God through deprivation of the flesh, and she is famously recorded in art as entering into a mystical union with Christ. Her writings present her mystical ideas through scholastic method, yet are fundamentally grounded in her ecstatic experiences.

Perhaps most dramatically, in the early fifteenth century the adolescent Joan of Arc claimed to see visions in which angels and saints told her of the French king's victory over the English. Dressed in men's clothes and wearing a suit of armor, she called herself "Joan the Maiden" and participated in the French army's victories, though she was ultimately tried and executed for heresy.

Mysticism thus operated within the structures of medieval Christianity, but constantly threatened to overturn them by empowering women, opening up a direct line of communication to God, and potentially threatening ecclesiastical and political authorities. The church managed potential disruption through accommodating its doctrines and liturgies to popular

---

3. Hildegard of Bingen, *Scivias*, 60–61.

demand. We have already seen how the Feast of Corpus Christi was instituted following a vision given to a nun. The most notable example of church teaching being responsive to popular theological movements is the doctrine and devotion connected with the Virgin Mary. Known in the Eastern Church as *theotokos*, or God bearer, in the West she assumed the much stronger title of Mother of God. Popular devotion included pilgrimages to shrines such as Walsingham, the dedication of churches in her honor as "Our Lady," and the belief that Mary . The most remarkable phenomenon was the rise of the idea of the immaculate conception, the belief that in order to conceive and bear Jesus as her son, Mary herself must have been born without sin. The doctrine was a popular subject in art and in devotions, such as praying the rosary. The fourteenth-century mystic Bridget of Sweden reported a vision in which Mary herself revealed that her parents had conceived her through a sinless act of sexual intercourse free from lust. The immaculate conception was heavily debated by medieval theologians, with Aquinas objecting that if Mary were free from sin at her conception, then Jesus's redemption was not necessary; the doctrine did not become official church teaching until the nineteenth century.

The most effective doctrinal development in medieval Western Europe centered on the fate of the dead, and the relationship of the living and the dead. Here, church teaching and popular piety merged to create an extraordinarily strong theological economy centered around the exchange of prayer, good works, and money in return for the reduction of the debt owed for sin not only in mortal life but in the life to come. This concept solidified in the twelfth century, elaborating an idea first proposed by the early church fathers Origen and Clement who imagined a realm in the afterlife somewhere between the extremes of heaven and hell. Purgatory was the name given to this third realm, in which the dead were not sentenced to eternal damnation for their sins but could pay off the debt of sin through penance over time. As shown in Dante's account of the afterlife, suffering in purgatory was real and to be avoided, but it was not permanent. The underlying belief was that it was possible through works to change one's fate in the afterlife. The number of years in purgatory accrued by certain types of sin could be calculated, as could the reduction of time for penance or prayers. An elaborate economy of death and salvation resulted: as penance could be done by the living as well as the dead, so too might good works be done by one person for the benefit of others. This theological and pastoral development was a unique feature of Western European Christianity.

The influence of the concept of purgatory was unexpectedly augmented in the mid fourteenth-century. The outbreak of plague in the 1340s and 1350s killed between one-third and two-thirds of the population across

Europe. Christian societies crippled by death, grief, and loss surely turned anew to the fascination with the fate of the dead in the afterlife. The commemoration of the dead was soon dominated by purgatory, with the names of the dead rehearsed in prayer, memorials to the dead calling on the living to pray for their souls, and bequests used to pay priests to sing Mass for the benefit of the souls of the departed. This system grew in complexity with the invention of the concept of the indulgence, which would later be so vehemently attacked by Luther and the early reformers in the sixteenth century. An indulgence could be purchased, the financial transaction justified as a form of donation or fundraising towards good works such as building churches, monasteries, hospitals and schools. Down payments on sin might even be made in advance, such as prior to initiating warfare or bloodshed.

Conclusion

In the fourteenth century the negotiation of power between the papacy and Western European kingdoms and empires took a new turn. The pope's claim to be a spiritual monarch above earthly kings was questioned following conflicts between Pope Boniface VIII (reigned 1294–1303) and Philip IV of France. Although Boniface reiterated the theory of papal supremacy, his successor Pope Clement V (reigned 1305–14) removed the papal court from Rome to Avignon, much closer to French influence, where it remained until 1376. The fracturing of papal power continued as rival groups of cardinals separately elected two popes, one at Avignon and the other at Rome. A new movement, conciliarism, arose, seeking to solve the papal schism through agreements reached at church councils. Yet if a council could determine who was or was not the pope, then presumably even within the spiritual realm the papacy was contingent on and subordinate to another human institution. Initially the conciliar approach made things worse, leading to approval of a third pope at the Council of Pisa. The schism was finally resolved in 1415 when the Council of Constance arranged the removal of all three rival popes and successfully installed a single, new pope in Rome.

By the fifteenth century, Christianity held sway across Western Europe both in popular culture and in the corridors of power. It attained that position through its attractiveness to kings and emperors as a means of giving sacred approval to their power, and maintained it by the genius of popes, bishops, and bureaucracies who found ways to manage the tension between regal and ecclesial authority. A major strength was the cycle of reform and renewal, especially in the monastic orders, as each generation sought to unpick the decay and corruption of time and human nature and to exemplify a new understanding of the Christian life. An extraordinary feature of the medieval Western Church was the systematic organization of Christianity, from its theology and bureaucracy to its liturgy and discipline, a feature symbolized in the design of cathedrals, abbeys, and churches and their appearance throughout the European landscape. Vitality also came from the ability of mystics and visionaries to break through cultural and political barriers, and from the power of popular practice to inform doctrinal change.

Late medieval Christendom contained many vulnerabilities. The papacy had endured decades of schism, with rival claimants to be the vicar of Christ. An emerging conciliar movement promised peace through theological consensus but threatened to overshadow papal and monarchical rule. Christian xenophobia had hardened into regular and systematic persecution of dissenters, whether Jews or "heretics" who dissented from church teaching. The strength of Islamic empires raised an existential risk for Western Christendom, a risk made material by the fall of Constantinople and the Eastern Empire in 1453. Finally, the European realization that there were other lands and other peoples beyond the Atlantic Ocean challenged medieval cosmology as the boundaries of the known world were exploded.

Bibliography

Cassidy-Welch, Megan. *Crusades and Violence*. Past Imperfect. Amsterdam: ARC Humanities, 2023.
Furlong, Monica, ed. *Visions and Longings: Medieval Women Mystics*. London: Mowbray, 1996.
Gerson, Paula Lieber, ed. *Abbot Suger and Saint Denis: A Symposium*. New York: Metropolitan Museum of Art, 1986.
Hildegard of Bingen. *Scivias*. Translated by Columba Hart and Jane Bishop. Classics of Western Spirituality. New York: Paulist, 1990.
Jordan, W. C. *A Tale of Two Monasteries: Westminster and Saint-Denis in the Thirteenth Century*. Princeton: Princeton University Press, 2009.
Le Goff, Jacques. *The Birth of Purgatory*. Translated by Arthur Goldhammer. Chicago: University of Chicago Press, 1984.
Madigan, Kevin. *Medieval Christianity: A New History*. New Haven: Yale University Press, 2015.
Monagle, Clare. *The Scholastic Project*. Past Imperfect. Kalamazoo: ARC Humanities, 2017.
Robson, Michael. *The Franciscans in the Middle Ages*. Monastic Orders 1. Woodbridge, UK: Boydell, 2006.
Rubin, Miri. *Mother of God: A History of the Virgin Mary*. New Haven: Yale University Press, 2010.
Southern, R. W. *Western Society and the Church in the Middle Ages*. Pelican History of the Church. London: Penguin, 1970.
Tyerman, Christopher. *The World of the Crusades: An Illustrated History*. New Haven: Yale University Press, 2019.

3

Christianity Transforms in the Reformation

Alec Ryrie

The city of Constantinople, on Europe's eastern edge, had once been the capital of the Christian world. By the sixteenth century it was under Muslim rule, and there was every reason to think that Christendom's long retreat west was only going to continue. And then rumors began to appear that something was going very wrong in the Christian world: people called "Lutherans" were on the rampage. This was how it looked to Abraham ibn Megas, the (Jewish) court physician to the Ottoman sultan:

> The Lutherans . . . destroy their stelae, demolish their towers and burn the graven images of their gods. So they abrogated and devastated much of the unworthy faith they possessed. . . . This congregation has cast off all faith in icons and priests, and has discarded the form of this worthless creed. . . . Their faith has reverted to a state of primeval flux. Where there are a thousand of them one cannot find ten men willing to rely upon a single doctrine or consent to a given line of reasoning. Thus they are in a state of formlessness, ready to take shape, since faith has departed.[1]

He can be forgiven for taking some pleasure from this outbreak of Christian chaos; and also for being bewildered by it. Why, after a thousand years of apparent institutional stability, had Western Christendom so dramatically blown itself to pieces? Five hundred years on, this question is still open. But while we may not be able decisively to answer it, it will teach us something about what this dramatic collapse—the event Christians themselves call "the Reformation"—actually means.

---

1. Ben-Sasson, "Reformation," 273–74.

An Inevitable Reformation

Here is one story. During the Middle Ages, the church in Europe was corrupt. Popes luxuriated in gilded splendor in Rome and lived lives of depravity. Ordinary priests everywhere exploited their social position to extract wealth from the peasantry. The church conspired to keep knowledge of the Bible and of Christian doctrine from the common people, instead befuddling and terrifying them with mummery. Priests were ignorant and knew only how to mumble the service in Latin. Dissatisfaction with and contempt for the church was growing; so was hunger for the true gospel. A series of brave reformers—Peter Valdes in the twelfth century, John Wyclif in the fourteenth, Jan Hus in the fifteenth, and many others—all championed the cause of the common Christians against this vast corrupt conspiracy; but all of them had been defeated, because the one part of the church that really operated effectively was its secret police, the Inquisition.

Finally, or so the story goes, it all came crashing down. Another brave Reformer, a German professor of theology named Martin Luther, nailed his ninety-five theses to the door of the castle church in Wittenberg on October 31, 1517. Those theses were simply a challenge to one small area of the church's authority and practices, but the blows of the hammer on that door were enough to awaken a restless Christian Europe. Luther had found a way to give voice to the shared anger of all Western Christians. Within a few short years, half of Europe had been set ablaze by Luther and his allies preaching what they called the "pure gospel" and putting their new translations of the Bible in the hands of the common people. For a brief, heady moment it looked as if they would sweep all before them, washing away all the old corruption.

But it was not to be. The old church regrouped and fought back; partly on the battlefield, giving us the terrible age of the religious wars, and partly, ironically, by heeding many of the Reformers' criticisms. During the so-called Counter-Reformation, the Catholic Church transformed and renewed its own disciplines and cracked down on corruption. The result was that it managed to retain control of rather more than half of Europe. Nevertheless, the new "Protestant" Churches that derived from Luther's original protest put down roots especially across Northern Europe. From there they would spread out to the world.

This story has some elements of truth in it. Some parts are plainly wrong: the legend of Luther nailing his theses to the castle door, for example.[2] But the central claim, that the events we now call "the Reformation"

2. Marshall, *1517*.

were a mass revolt against medieval corruption, has just enough truth in it to be seriously misleading. It is true that virtually every thinking Western Christian in around 1500 believed that the church was in desperate need of reform; but this does not prove either that the dam was waiting to burst, or that the torrent that was eventually unleashed was a consequence of the medieval church's failures.

That universal consensus on the need for reform is less significant than it appears. Of course, the church in 1500 needed reform: churches always need reform. They are staffed by human beings, some of whom will inevitably be timeservers, fools, or villains. For a thousand years, the church in Latin Europe had been facing acute crises and chronic problems, and it had survived and flourished by generating reform from within itself. In many ways, it was in better shape in the early sixteenth century than ever before. There was nothing on the scale of the existential threats of previous centuries—the crusade against the supposed heresies of the Cathars and the Waldensians, the effective capture of the papacy by the kings of France, the catastrophic schism of 1378–1417. Priests were better educated and better disciplined than ever before, for all that everyone accepted there was still much more to be done. And there were now finely-honed systems for—as the church saw it—protecting their flock from malicious ideas spread by the willful troublemakers who were classed as "heretics."

The worst that can be said about the Western Church in the late fifteenth and early sixteenth century is that it had a leadership vacuum. As a body, the church was buzzing with reforming energies of all kinds, some modest and local, some naïve and idealistic, some shrewd and far reaching. But the papacy, one of whose roles had long been to act as ringmaster to this exuberant and sometimes quarrelsome circus, was a shrunken institution that had never properly recovered from the schism a century earlier. It still claimed a mighty authority, but in fact it struggled even to maintain its own political independence. The office had for many decades been almost exclusively held by Italians, most of them drawn from a few competing families, and many of them spiritually unimpressive individuals who did nothing to counter Rome's reputation for corruption. The challenges the church faced in this period were neither new nor especially severe, but one novelty was that the papacy seemed less like part of the solution and more like part of the problem.

This did not make a sudden or spectacular collapse of the united Western Church inevitable or anything like it. But it did mean that, if a sudden crisis did erupt, the church's response to it might be brittle, misjudged, or ineffective.

Publicity, Print, and Politics

Here is another story. Throughout the medieval period, the church in Europe had experienced a cycle of reform, corruption, and renewed reform. And yet this was not merely a cycle, but a spiral, widening with each turn. The monastic redoubts to which Western Christendom retreated after the fall of Rome were at the center of the spiral, but at each turn it reached further out, taking the gospel out to royal courts, to expansive monastic reform movements like the Cluniacs and the Cistercians, to cathedral schools and the new universities, and then breathing new life into the parishes and producing movements of lay piety such as the Brethren of the Common Life in the Netherlands. The final and most dramatic sweep of this spiral came in the fifteenth century, when the humanist scholars of the Renaissance started talking about putting the Bible into every Christian's hands and expanding the spirituality of the monastery to encompass the whole of society. Laypeople, ordinary Christians, were being drawn into the life of the church and empowered within it as they had not been since late antiquity. It was inevitable that this movement of bottom-up empowerment and the church's increasingly rigid and suspicious hierarchy would eventually collide. We call the collision "the Reformation."

It is plainly true that lay Christians were being slowly, unsteadily empowered and also being more rigorously governed. A decisive element of this was technological. The race to produce a viable means of printing books using movable metal type was won in 1454 by the German craftsman Johannes Gutenberg, with competitors hot on his heels, and the new technology spread remarkably rapidly. The capacity to produce books in greater numbers, with greater accuracy and at much lower cost than ever before, led to an astonishing boom in the book business. Indeed, it produced Europe's first tech bubble: a series of printers piled into the business and overextended themselves, producing a string of bankruptcies in the 1490s.[3] In this new world, a zealous, eloquent, or publicity-hungry scholar such as the peripatetic Dutch monk and satirist Desiderius Erasmus could reach a mass audience in a way that had never been done before. His *Enchiridion* (1501), sometimes published as *Handbook of the Militant Christian* in English, was translated into a dozen languages and went through scores of editions.

Was Luther's Reformation simply the inevitable next step? This much is true: it is impossible to imagine his movement succeeding without print. Whether or not Luther nailed his theses to a door is trivial; what matters much more is that he sent them to a printer, and that the printer then

---

3. Pettegree, *Book in the Renaissance*.

decided, on his own initiative, to translate this inflammatory little text into German in the hope of generating some more sales. What made the Reformation possible was that Luther bypassed the existing structures of power and scholarly debate by appealing directly to a mass readership in German, a language in which he discovered he could write accessibly, arrestingly, unforgettably, mixing soaring ecstasies with brutal street fighting, with a knack for vivid images and analogies, and a sense of paradox that made his arguments seem almost irrefutable. Luther and his printers between them discovered a new literary form, the mass-market pamphlet. A printed copy cost roughly the same as a hen in sixteenth-century Germany, but it could be spicier and provide more lasting nourishment. The printers who caught this wave permanently changed the rules of religious debate, which was meant to be a game for informed adults, played in the decent obscurity of Latin behind university walls. Luther flung open the gates. Now anyone who could read German, or who knew someone who could read German, could join in. Over Luther's thirty-year public career he produced 544 separate books or pamphlets, slightly more than one every three weeks; in total, at least 3,183 editions.[4] Since, at a very conservative estimate, each edition would have run to over a thousand copies, that is well over three *million* books by Luther in circulation—easily enough for every literate German speaker in Europe to have one. None of Luther's supporters and cheerleaders came anywhere near these sales; nor, more to the point, did his opponents, one of whom wrote ruefully in 1520, "Every day it rains Luther books.... Nothing else sells."[5] We can forgive them for being flabbergasted: no one had ever seen anything quite like this before. Equally, we can understand why Protestants would later hail the invention of printing as a near-miraculous providence.

But this picture of an inevitable, print-fueled Reformation does not really work. Yes, Luther had a larger audience than ever before and a means of reaching them. But sixteenth-century Europe was neither a democracy nor a paradise of free speech. Printing was an industrial process dependent on expensive equipment, and its entrepreneurs had to bear all the costs up front; in other words, this was a business that was easy for censors to control, much more so than in the ages when books were hand copied. And the church's heresy-hunting machinery was generally swift to crack down on attention-grabbing dissidents. It is no surprise, then, that in the late 1510s a vivid writer with a pungent critique of the church establishment could find an audience for a few weeks or months. Other outspoken celebrities had

4. Edwards, *Printing, Propaganda*, 18.
5. Hendrix, *Martin Luther*, 101.

come and gone before. The question then is, how did this particular passing scandal metastasize into a permanent schism?

The church was quick enough to oppose and condemn him (perhaps too quick): he was excommunicated by the pope in 1520 and condemned by the Holy Roman Empire in 1521. By rights he should have been arrested and silenced—either by being persuaded to recant his errors or, if absolutely necessary and only as a last resort, by being burned as an impenitent heretic. The truly remarkable thing about Luther is not that he defied the inquisitors, but that he succeeded.

The simple explanation for this is sheer political chance. Luther had a powerful protector, Elector Frederick III of Saxony, who was not just his local prince but was also the founder of Wittenberg University, the university where Luther was a professor, and while he had no particular interest in Luther's theology, Frederick liked having a celebrity on his staff, and strongly disliked interfering outsiders who tried to tell him what to do in his own university. And he was in a position to make this stick, because he was one of Germany's most powerful princes, especially during the years 1518–19, when he was a key player in the Holy Roman Empire's long-running succession crisis, meaning that it would be a bad time for anyone to risk making an enemy of him over some loudmouth professor. Even once that particular crisis was over, the new emperor, Charles V, had no appetite for a confrontation with Frederick: he had more urgent problems to deal with, not least the apparently relentless northward march of the Ottoman Turks. Luther and his movement survived by a series of political accidents, giving them just long enough to put down ineradicable roots.

But this is not good enough as an explanation either. The reason Elector Frederick went to so much trouble to protect Luther was that he had put Wittenberg University on the map; the reason Charles V didn't move against the Lutherans in the 1520s was because he knew it would take an army, not just a few inquisitors. What underpinned these "chance" escapes was Luther's celebrity: all those books. And the reason the books had an impact was not just because of the new technology that produced them, but because in them, Luther had something to say, something that caught the attention of the age.

The Power of an Idea

As one historian has summarized the problem: "The old Church was immensely strong, and that strength could only have been overcome by the explosive power of an idea."[6] What was that idea?

To begin with, most of Luther's eager readers and hearers thought Luther was following in the footsteps of Erasmus, who, like many great medieval reformers before him, had called for the Christian life to be radically simplified. Erasmus poured scorn on religious practices that seemed to him superstitious or empty rituals; he wanted to distinguish the essential and eternal core of Christian faith and practice from the flummery and corruption with which he believed it had become encrusted. A Christian, he argued passionately, was called to live a Christlike life, not to quibble over the doctrinal niceties beloved of medieval theology. Christians could learn everything they truly needed to know from the Bible itself. Since Luther agreed with a great deal of this, it was easy to mistake him simply for a more outspoken ally of the Dutchman. This was what some of Luther's early opponents thought, famously joking that Erasmus laid the egg and Luther hatched it. But Erasmus himself vehemently denied it, and he was right. More experienced heresy hunters, with their finely honed antennae, spotted right away that Luther's subversion ran far deeper.

Luther's famous doctrine of *justification by faith alone*—the heart of his theology, and an idea that was anathema to Erasmus—arose directly from his personal experience. His "conversion" and theological "breakthrough" have been much mythologized and overinterpreted, but this much we know: as an Augustinian friar in the late 1500s and early 1510s, Luther was consumed by awareness of his own sinfulness and, from bitter experience, despaired of his ability to overcome it. It seemed to him that corruption and sin were pervasive in him; no thought was pure, no motive was unmixed, and so everything he did, said, and thought only dug him in deeper. Whether in a single thunderclap of a moment, or through a slow dawning of realization, by 1517 or 1518 he had arrived at a very radical solution to his problem. It was true that he could do nothing to break the power sin had over him; he was enslaved to it. But God could break it. God could forgive him, and did not need Martin Luther's help to achieve this. Luther could do nothing to save himself and, he now realized with a stunning simplicity, he did not need to. Christ had already done it all, dying and rising for his sins. All he needed to do was to believe that it was so, laying hold of Christ with

---

6. MacCulloch, *Reformation*, 110.

a pure faith: a faith that was not one of his own filthy deeds, but was God's freely given gift to him.

For Luther, this realization was a transforming liberation. The crushing weight of his despair was lifted from him by the realization of freely given, utterly undeserved, but utterly transformative forgiveness. It was an idea that certainly drew on deep wells of the Christian tradition, in particular on Augustine of Hippo and on Paul; but this particular formulation of it was new, and its implications were far reaching. The idea that Christians are saved through faith and by God's grace was a truism that all Christians could accept, but Luther's insistence that we are saved by faith *alone* was an unexpected turn. It made a great deal of what had once constituted the Christian life seem at best unimportant, at worst an active distraction. In Luther's favorite book of the Bible, the Letter to the Galatians, Paul argues that "if righteousness come by the law, then Christ is dead in vain" (Gal 2:21 KJV).[7] To place your trust in anything other than Christ is to imply that Christ's sacrifice was futile or unnecessary. In which case, the church and most of its ministry almost evaporates. Almost everything that Christians *do*, up to and including celebrating the sacraments, can seem pointless. In this view, the only real purpose of the church is to preach the word: a purpose at which Luther believed it was failing badly. There is no difference between priests and laypeople; in fact, Luther argued in one of his most eye-catching ideas, all Christians are priests. Pilgrimages, relics, saints, processions, fasts, all the rich, ritual life of the church: sweep them all away.

Erasmus wanted to rid the church of superstition so Christians could focus on living good lives. Luther believed—he *knew*—that living a good life was impossible, and that if you think you can, you are clutching at straws while teetering on the brink of hell. Luther's opponents, not least Erasmus, were horrified by this, and accused him of the heresy of *antinomianism*: the belief that God's free forgiveness of our sins is a licence to sin afresh. This was a slander, and Luther argued passionately that in his system, justified Christians do good deeds out of simple gratitude, not in some grubby attempt to barter their way into heaven. Yet the idea would not go away. Luther and his theological allies were not antinomians: but if you were an ordinary Christian looking for a religious system that would not police your morals too heavy-handedly, Luther's doctrine had its attractions.

And this of course is the point. Luther was hardly the first or the last Christian to find a novel solution to his own spiritual crisis. What made this case remarkable is how some aspects of his personal experience resonated with a wider public. It was outwardly familiar: this was another message

---

7. Luther, *Table Talk*, 20.

of simplification, like Erasmus's. But it was accompanied by a new sense of joyful, almost anarchic moral liberation—that you could shake off all the church's religious burdens and turn to Christ alone, that Christ had indeed made *you* a priest—all that found a ready audience. And at the same time, Luther was saying that you could abandon all the tedious and costly good works that the medieval church required; and that also had its appeal.

These doctrines also bristled with problems, the most obvious being that they contradicted the established teachings of the church, and in some cases had already been formally condemned as heresy. The way Luther responded to that challenge was even more electrifying. He had, he insisted, learned his doctrines simply from studying the Bible, which no less an authority than Erasmus had said was all a Christian needed. A series of spokesmen for the hierarchy explained forcefully to him that the church alone could interpret the Bible authoritatively, and that his reading of it was simply wrong. By 1519 Luther had been backed into a corner, and reached perhaps the only possible conclusion. If the church disagreed with his own understanding of the Bible, then, obviously, he was right and the church was wrong. When he was brought before the parliament, or diet, of the Holy Roman Empire in the German city of Worms in 1521, Luther was formally commanded to recant his heresies, and he replied:

> Unless I am convinced by the testimony of the Scriptures or by clear reason (for I do not trust either in the pope or in councils alone, since it is well known that they have often erred and contradicted themselves), I am bound by the Scriptures I have quoted and my conscience is captive to the Word of God. I cannot and will not recant anything, since it is neither safe nor right to go against conscience.[8]

This was Luther's famous doctrine of 'Scripture alone." Again, there is nothing radical about a Christian valorizing the Bible. What was shocking was Luther's rejection of every other authority. His conscience—and by implication, every Christian's conscience—was directly subject to the word and to *nothing else*. His opponents could try to persuade him he was wrong—at least in theory—but they could not compel him. The fact they were trying to do just that made Luther conclude, very quickly, that popes and councils were more than just error prone. Since they were openly opposing the gospel that he himself was preaching, which Luther passionately believed to be the true gospel of Christ, he could only conclude that the pope was antichrist, and his legions of bishops and friars and inquisitors were all slaves to the devil.

8. Luther, *Career of Reformer II*, 112.

If Luther's doctrine of justification by faith alone, his rejection of all the ritual structures of the church, caught the popular imagination, so too did this doctrine of Scripture alone, its rejection of all the church's authority. That torrent of books and pamphlets heaped scorn and mockery on the church. The wealth and self-importance of priests, the corruption of the popes, that gang of effete Italian sybarites, in contrast to the simple, manly virtues of Germans: people had grumbled about these things for decades. Now Luther offered a simple, devastating explanation. They were not the church of Christ at all; they were the church of antichrist, the synagogue of Satan. (The sideswipe at Judaism there was quite deliberate.) Who had more moral authority in this situation: corrupt Italians defending the system that kept them rich and powerful, or brave German preachers brandishing a printed Bible and defying all the powers of church and state to reveal the shocking truth, that Christ had set his people free but the church had kept them in chains?

So these two ideas—justification by faith alone, and Scripture alone—were able to catch public attention, to suddenly crystallize centuries' worth of rumbling discontent with the hierarchy, to fully exploit print's potential for reaching a mass audience for the first time, and to keep Luther alive for long enough for the flame to spread. For a short while in the early 1520s, it seemed as if this movement might sweep all before it: that all Germany, maybe all Western Christendom would embrace Luther's gospel and the whole church would be renewed. In which case, we would remember this as another, perhaps the most dramatic, in the sequence of great intrinsic reforms of the medieval church. It could easily have happened. Churchmen across Europe, including some very close to the centers of authority in Rome, felt the force of Luther's ideas, and brilliant minds were hard at work on how to absorb, direct, and accommodate his piercing insights without overthrowing the whole structure of the church. A bolder, more capable, and less compromised papacy could have taken the lead in such a thing. Or a new reforming council of the church, something for which Luther and his allies had been calling almost from the start, could have taken the whole matter in hand. It could have happened. But it did not.

From Reformation to Schism

Perhaps the impossibility of success was baked into Luther's protest from the beginning. By rejecting the idea of a single, uniting, magisterial authority and appealing instead to the free Christian's conscience governed by Scripture alone, he replaced what he saw as religious tyranny with what his enemies ever since have called religious anarchy. At the Diet of Worms, where Luther made that epochal appeal to his conscience, one of the churchmen present, Johann Eck, responded with horror that Luther was "completely mad." This was not just abuse. His point was that, if believers were allowed to defy the Church by simply appealing to conscience and Scripture, "we will have nothing in Christianity that is certain or decided."[9] The point is undeniably true. Luther was sweeping away the old structures and old authorities, but what would he put in its place? And what if someone disagreed with him?

It quickly became clear that Luther himself was not the problem. For all his radical principles, his views about what should actually change in the life of the church were quite cautious, even conservative. He even continued to dress as a monk as late as 1522, even though in his system monasticism made no sense; by the time he married in 1525, most of his allies and fellow travelers had already done so. Indeed, by this stage he was being left behind by his own revolution. Increasingly he found himself in a war on two fronts, the "Romanists" to one side and those whom he called the "fanatics" on the other. "Fanatics" turned out to be a capacious category. Some—including former friends from his own university—wanted a thoroughgoing purge of Christian worship, ridding the church of anything that sniffed of "superstition": Luther thought this new legalism was worse than the old kind. Others pressed further still, into nakedly social and political territory. Applying Luther's principle of sweeping everything away and judging everything against the Bible, these radicals noticed that Bible teaches that the early Christians had no private property but held their goods in common; that idolaters ought to be put to death; and that the ancient patriarchs had had multiple wives. The church and tradition said no: But who cares about them?

This ferment boiled over during the vast peasant uprising that swept across Central Europe in 1524–25, the so-called German Peasants' War: the biggest mass rebellion in European history before the French Revolution. The rebellious peasants mixed traditional grievances about rents, taxes, and local rights with new and dangerous ideas such as distributing church property to the poor and electing priests. Luther's idea that they should not be required to believe anything unless it could be proved to them from the Bible was particularly popular. It was terrifying for the whole of the ruling class, a group that for these purposes definitely included Martin Luther. He wrote a pamphlet titled *Against the Robbing and Murdering Hordes of Peasants* and called for them to be suppressed by whatever means were necessary. The princes of Germany did not exactly need his permission, and the rebels would no doubt have been defeated anyway, but it is Luther certainly

---

9. Luther, *Career of Reformer II*, 113.

shares in the responsibility for the roughly one hundred thousand deaths in the wake of the rebellion.

It was the defining catastrophe of the Reformation and the end of the best chance of a universal solution. The first flush of naïve enthusiasm was over, and most of Western Christendom scurried back to the safety and good order of the old church. Most, but not all. In some places, and for some princes and city councillors, Luther's critique had sunk in too deep to be abandoned. And in the wake of the frightening radicals of the war, Luther himself now looked reassuringly moderate. So, with the emperor still devoting all his energies to stopping the onslaught of the Ottoman Turks, a handful of German cities and territories began peeling away from the old church and setting up new structures along the lines Luther had suggested within their borders. This was an admission of defeat by the Reformers: they were having to abandon their hopes of reforming the whole of Christendom and accept the much less satisfactory alternative of piecemeal change. In 1529 the emperor Charles V had the imperial diet pass a resolution condemning these schismatics, but it failed to pass unanimously. Five German princes issued a formal "protestation" against it. As a result, they, and then their allies and descendants down to the present, became known as Protestants.

At least the exhilarating, frightening chaos of the early 1520s had been suppressed, but the fundamental problem of how to unite Reformers who acknowledged no universal authority other than their own consciences was not and never would be solved. The radical revolutionary tradition continued, although persecuted ferociously by both the old church and the emerging new "Protestant" establishments. For many—but not all—of the radicals, the breach with the past was vividly symbolized by their rejection of infant baptism: their conviction that baptism must be a deliberate choice made by an adult meant that they had abandoned the old idea of a universal, national or international church, a community that one was born into. In 1534, a few of these revolutionaries succeeded in seizing the western German city of Münster and turning it into an apocalyptic kingdom, whose rulers abolished private property, instituted polygamy, beheaded naysayers, and waited for Christ's imminent return: they were instead besieged and butchered by a joint Protestant-Catholic army, and Münster would remain a byword for terrifying radicalism for centuries to come. After that the radicals retreated to the margins, forming withdrawn communities, which, despite mostly being committed to pacifism, continued to suffer grievous persecution. The new Protestant establishment was determined to prove that these alarming radicals were completely different from themselves. The truth was that their principles were uncomfortably close.

Not that the new Protestant establishments themselves were united. In 1529, the year of the protestation, Luther and his most serious rival, the Swiss preacher Huldrych Zwingli, held a summit conference in Marburg in a desperate attempt to settle the differences between them: and it failed. Zwingli, who was killed in battle two years later, stood at the head of an alternative Protestant tradition that we know as "Reformed" or (from the name of a second-generation leader who became its most unifying figure) as "Calvinist." The split between the Reformed and the emergent "Lutheran" establishment was as bitter as it is hard to pin down. The neuralgic theological disagreements—over the nature of the Eucharist or the doctrine of predestination—were real enough, but were symptoms of a deeper differences in mood and ethos. The Lutheran churches were skeptical about institutional or moral reform, convinced that righteousness in this world is unattainable, and concerned above all to confront sinners with their need for grace in a fallen world. The Reformed churches taught that, as God's covenanted people, the new Israel, his church needed to embrace individual and corporate holiness. There is something in the crude stereotype that Lutherans believed that whatever is not forbidden is allowed, while Calvinists believed that whatever is not allowed is forbidden. And both were convinced that the other side was making a dreadful mistake.

Not that these differences were purely matters of theology and worship. Lutheran churches had first been established through the patronage of friendly (and sometimes overbearing) princes, and they remained committed to that Christian model, reaching back as far as the emperor Constantine, of a symphony between church and state, a symphony that secular politicians usually conducted. Calvinism, which grew up in the raucous republican city-states of Switzerland, was never so quietly obedient. Luther had very little to offer sympathizers of his reform who happened to live under rulers who remained Romanists: he compared underground networks of dissidents to rats. Jean Calvin, a French Reformer who spent most of his career in exile in Geneva, made his name by supporting and resourcing the "rats," in France, the Netherlands, and elsewhere. These formidably organized, bottom-up movements for religious revolution provoked increasingly alarmed church establishments into crackdowns and, by the 1560s, had tipped large parts of the Continent into open religious war. For nearly a century, Europe's religious parties fought one another to a standstill, a collective trauma in which no one emerged victorious, the Continent's religious dividing lines were entrenched in the way that only violence can, and all of the religious factions were transformed into battle-hardened parties, sharply defined against one another and all but unrecognizable from the naïve and idealistic visions of their first founders.

Perhaps none was transformed more than the party that, on the face of it, represented the greatest continuity: the body that, from this period onwards, we can unproblematically call the Catholic or Roman Catholic Church. After two decades of paralyzed and ineffectual response to the Luther crisis, the old church confronted an existential choice in the 1540s. The many thoughtful Catholics keen on finding a reconciliation with Luther's movement seemed to have that elusive prize in their grasp at a carefully stage-managed summit conference in 1541, when the emperor Charles V, desperate to put an end to this debilitating schism, managed to persuade chosen representatives of both sides to agree to a statement on the doctrine of justification. But by now there were too many other issues poisoning the water, and neither Luther himself nor Pope Paul III had any desire for a deal. With that avenue closed, the pope at last summoned a council of the church, designed not to pursue reconciliation with the Protestants but instead authoritatively to reject their teachings. However, Charles V insisted that this council should also act decisively to put the church's house in order: to pursue structural, financial, disciplinary, educational, and moral reform alongside its traditionalist doctrinal agenda.

It was a tall order. The Council of Trent took eighteen years, from 1545 to 1563, to complete its work; for most of that time, in fact, it was suspended, and it seemed unlikely it would ever be able to finish. When it did complete its work, in a sudden surge of activity in 1562–63, it seemed like it might have failed: although it passed some fine-sounding decrees, it also fudged some of the most difficult issues and left the enforcement and implementation of its decisions to the pope. Pope Pius IV, a scion of the Medici House, which had treated the papacy like a political trophy for decades, promised that this time it would be different. And remarkably, it was. The moral and institutional renewal of the papacy from the 1560s onwards, which after a century of intermittent absence began to take its responsibilities with a new and consistent seriousness, was the underpinning of the so-called Counter-Reformation and of a Catholic resurgence that, until the eighteenth century, seemed to have the Protestants on the defensive.

For Catholics, the tragedy was that it took a catastrophic schism for the church actually to embrace the renewal it had long been obvious it needed. For Protestants, the irony was that they had managed to spur the old church into saving itself. It is perhaps true that a Reformation of some kind was inevitable in the sixteenth century. But the Reformation that was most likely was the one that, in fact, the majority of European Christians experienced: a Reformation that took place within the embrace of the Catholic Church itself.

Bibliography

Ben-Sasson, Haim Hillel. "The Reformation in Contemporary Jewish Eyes." *Proceedings of the Israel Academy of Sciences and Humanities* 4 (1969–70) 239–326.

Edwards, Mark U., Jr. *Printing, Propaganda and Martin Luther*. Berkeley: University of California Press, 1994. Reprint, Minneapolis: Fortress, 2004.

Hendrix, Scott H. *Martin Luther: Visionary Reformer*. New Haven: Yale University Press, 2015.

Luther, Martin. *Career of the Reformer II*. Edited by George W. Forell. Vol. 32 of *Luther's Works*. Philadelphia: Fortress, 1958.

———. *Table Talk*. Edited and translated by Theodore G. Tappert. Vol. 54 of *Luther's Works*. Philadelphia: Fortress, 1967.

MacCulloch, Diarmaid. *Reformation: Europe's House Divided, 1490–1700*. London: Lane, 2003.

Marshall, Peter. *1517: Martin Luther and the Invention of the Reformation*. Oxford: Oxford University Press, 2017.

Pettegree, Andrew. *The Book in the Renaissance*. New Haven: Yale University Press, 2010.

4

Christianity Navigates the Enlightenment and the Age of Empire

AMBROGIO A. CAIANI

CHRISTIANITY AND ENLIGHTENMENT ARE no longer depicted as implacable adversaries by historians. Admittedly, the intellectual and scientific ferment that emerged in the eighteenth century did pose many challenges for clergymen and theologians across Europe. Yet, as scholars like David Sorkin have shown, new ideas and calls for reform were interpreted by Catholics, Protestants, and Orthodox Christians as opportunities that could strengthen their respective faiths. There has been a growing sense that Christianity and Enlightenment were in dialogue with each other, rather than pitilessly opposed. Some scholars have used the labels of Christian and Catholic Enlightenment to describe discrete groups of intellectuals and philosophes who tried, during the eighteenth century, to reconcile reason with their faith.[1] Yet, these attempts to revise our understanding of the Enlightenment's complex relationship with Christianity have tended to come from the Olympian vantage point of philosophy, intellectual thought, and, to an extent, theology. It is true that the Enlightenment was not intrinsically opposed to religious faith, but it did foster an attack on organized religion. A growing revulsion for established churches and confessional states precipitated one of the most severe crises that faced Christianity in its millennial history.

There is an argument to be made that the eighteenth and nineteenth centuries witnessed what could be loosely defined as a "second Reformation." Not since Luther and the Thirty Years' War would the papacy encounter such a challenge to its authority. No fewer than three popes were forced to leave Rome during the age of revolutions. Similarly, Protestantism

1. Sorkin, *Religious Enlightenment*.

and Russian Orthodoxy saw movements of spiritual renewal emerge that condemned the clerical establishment. The turmoil of revolution, and the Napoleonic Wars, damaged the political, cultural, and economic position of established churches. Having said this, these struggles concerned the politics of religion rather than religion per se. Unlike the sixteenth-century Reformers, the philosophes and revolutionaries of the eighteenth century had little to say about the economy of salvation or Christ's teachings. Their priority was to subordinate the church to the power of the reforming state. Enlightened statesmen sought not just to regenerate politics, society, and economic life, but were determined to clip the wings of privileged corporations; the church was at the top of their list.

This led to decades of religious turmoil, where Europeans were asked to decide between the state and their Christian faith. After 1815, rationalism had failed to deliver the humanitarian and liberal state heralded by the Enlightenment. In the early nineteenth century, many Europeans, guided by Novalis and François-René de Chateaubriand, turned to their Christian heritage to provide answers to life's most fundamental questions.[2] The collapse of the ancien régime had cast many adrift. People were atomized, isolated, and unable to resume their pre-1789 existence. Conservatives, reactionaries, and radicals alike turned to Christianity as the potential cement that would bind new organic communities together to withstand unprecedented social, political, and economic change. Thus, Christianity entered a period of sustained religious renewal.

This chapter will examine how Christianity in Europe interacted with the forces of Enlightenment, revolution, spiritual renewal, and imperial expansion. While this was an age of deep religious crisis, it was not one of secularism. The separation of church and state sanctioned first by the United States Constitution in 1787 and, briefly, by the French Directory between 1795–1801 was the exception, rather than the rule.[3] Secularism as a clearly defined notion emerged only in the final decades of the nineteenth century. Its ultimate incarnation was found in 1905, with the law on separation of church and state passed by the Emile Combes government in France.[4]

Reform and Christianity

Ancien régime Europe was characterized by the alliance of throne and altar. This described the equal partnership that existed between monarchies and

2. Gilley and Stanley, *World Christianities, c. 1815–1914*.
3. Wood, *Power and Liberty*.
4. Silva, *Separazione*.

the clergy within their realms. In Catholic Europe, Orthodox Russia, and, to a lesser extent, in the Protestant North, the First Estate was an independent, wealthy, and powerful corporation embedded within the fabric of the state. Intellectuals, and a nascent reading public, felt uneasy, as the eighteenth century unfolded, with the privileged position of state churches.[5] The reasons for dissatisfaction were manifold. It was not merely the laity who criticized their pastors. In many ways the Enlightenment unleashed a civil war within the clergy itself. This pitted reforming priests against powerful prelates and monks unwilling to disturb the status quo.

The excess of wealth and political power, held by the episcopacy at the expense of the lower clergy, drew the most condemnation. Similarly to the Reformation of the sixteenth century, there were stormy debates on the appropriate manner of worshipping God within all Christian denominations. In an age characterized by reason, conspicuous, mystical, and flamboyant devotion seemed out of place. There was a sense that the superstitious and miraculous should be relegated to the mists of medieval barbarism. Even the Catholic world was not immune to such tendencies towards devotional understatement. Intellectuals like Ludovico Muratori, Scipione de' Ricci, Adrien Lamourette and Joseph Valentin Eybel sought to reduce feast days and the worship of relics and to limit ornamentation within churches. Even the papacy was not immune to the allure of rationality. Pope Benedict XIV drew up strict guidelines on the canonization of saints, especially when it came to the vexed issue of miraculous intercession.[6] Rational scientific and medical explanations were to be preferred, where possible, to divine or supernatural intercessions.

Enlightened reformers argued that Christian faith was principally about the cultivation of the spirit rather than sensuality. Eighteenth-century Europe witnessed the resurgence of Jansenism, a seventeenth-century heresy that was critical of moral laxity and papal claims to supremacy.[7] There was a growing disdain for the baroque, or enthusiastic piety of the masses, on Europe's peripheries. A better trained clergy would lead the faithful away from quasi pagan devotions towards a more reasoned faith in Christ and the church's teaching.

Priests and religious who did not deliver social benefit were viewed with increasing suspicion and hostility. In Catholic and Orthodox Christianity, a barrage of criticism against monasteries and their inmates emerged.

---

5. Israel, *Revolutionary Ideas*.
6. Messbarger et al., *Benedict XIV and Enlightenment*, 151–74.
7. Doyle, *Jansenism*.

Their contemplative and sedentary life was decried as parasitical.[8] Thanks to publications like Denis Diderot's novel *The Nun*, convents came to be viewed (somewhat unfairly as it turned out) as dens of iniquity, where innocent maidens were incarcerated by degenerate families.[9] In Russian Orthodoxy, the situation was even more fraught. Here the celibate monks, known as the "black" clergy, monopolized access to the episcopacy. This meant that the secular "white" clergy, made up of married parish priests, who ministered to serf communities, were excluded from power within the Orthodox establishment.[10]

Critics created the impression that Christianity was ripe for reform. This mirrored the process whereby enlightened absolutists had sought to enhance the efficiency of their states.[11] Reformism did not just drive secular politics, but embraced the politics of religion too. Old-fashioned portrayals of godless reformers working to destroy the Christian faith simply do not reflect reality. Many enlightened bureaucrats and clergymen shared the same mindset; this inspired them to improve dioceses, seminaries, and monasteries. Several bishops (like William Warburton, Jean Soanen, Scipione de' Ricci, or Christoph Anton von Migazzi), priests, and religious were sympathetic to the absolutist state's quest to erect efficient and humanitarian polities. They believed that a poorer and more pastorally focused church would strengthen and renew Christianity rather than weaken it.

Jansenists, Methodists, Pietists, and reform Catholics were highly sympathetic to attempts by Joseph II, Charles III, Peter Leopold, Bernardo Tanucci, Pedro Rodríguez de Campomanes, and Sebastião José de Carvalho e Melo, Marquês de Pombal, to transform the state and the church into utilitarian institutions. Despite resistance on the part of the papacy, these reformers scored notable victories in cementing the supremacy of the rationalizing state over the clerical establishment. In 1773, Clement XIV, despite his personal misgivings, was forced to abolish the Jesuit order.[12] The Society of Jesus, founded by Ignatius de Loyola during the sixteenth century, had been one of the bulwarks of papal authority in early modern Europe. Its disappearance from 1773 to 1814 made manifest how Catholic reformers were determined to create national churches that were only loosely federated with a papacy whose role was to be relegated to the symbolic.

---

8. Beales, *Prosperity and Plunder*.
9. Choudhury, *Convents and Nuns*.
10. Freeze, "Russian Orthodoxy, Church, People."
11. Scott, *Enlightened Absolutism*.
12. Van Kley, *Reform Catholicism*, 218–40.

This led to a resurgence in Catholicism and Russian Orthodoxy of neo-conciliarist tendencies, reprising the ancient and medieval notion that the body of the church in council superseded the authority of the hierarchy. Such calls for the democratization of church governance led to several crises throughout the eighteenth century. One need only think of the reestablishment of a "Catholic" diocese in Utrecht, Richerism in France, Febronianism in the Holy Roman Empire, the punctation of Ems, and the synod of Pistoia.[13] Such incidents highlighted that clergymen were deeply divided over the limits of episcopal authority (especially the papacy).

An existential threat to the established churches emerged during the eighteenth century, the resurgence of religious toleration. Louis XIV's revocation of the Edict of Nantes in 1685 had led to the flight of many Huguenots towards Protestant Northern Europe. The Sun King's persecution deprived France of some of its best minds and entrepreneurs. The Bourbon monarchy's loss was Britain, Holland, and Prussia's gain. These refugees proved resourceful and high-achieving diasporas that benefitted greatly the states to which they fled.[14] Throughout the eighteenth century, the early modern confessionalization of the state was perceived as an obstacle to progress. Enlightened Christians believed that faith supported by reason had little to fear from heresy. Thus, enlightened absolutism, gradually, came to embrace religious toleration.

Frederick the Great's toleration of Catholics and Jews drew much praise from the philosophes in Paris. The barbaric judicial murders of the Protestant Jean Calas and the Chevalier de la Barre for blasphemy made France seem a bigoted theocracy in comparison. In contrast, Saint Hedwig's Cathedral in Berlin, whose construction began in 1747, stands as testament to the city's neoclassical renewal under the Frederician regime. More importantly, this building is a Catholic basilica that embodies Frederick's prioritization of religious toleration. Frederick believed strongly that a poly-confessional state could unlock the potential of all his subjects.[15] The removal of barriers would enable all to contribute fully to the life of the state, regardless of religious conscience.

He was followed by Joseph II who, in 1782, issued a patent of toleration, and eventually even by the lethargic Louis XVI, whose 1787 edict of toleration reversed the wrongs of the revocation of 1685.[16] In Russia, Catherine the Great followed the inspiration of her Catholic and Protestant

13. Blanchard, *Synod of Pistoia*.
14. Stanwood, *Global Refuge*.
15. Kloes, "Dissembling Orthodoxy."
16. Beales, *Joseph II*, 177–86.

counterparts. She offered protection to "Old Believers" and other schismatics who had suffered persecution since the seventeenth century at the hands of the Orthodox Church. After the first partition of Poland in 1773, she welcomed a very substantial Catholic and Jewish minority into her empire. After some robust negotiations, she forced Pius VI to concede her supremacy over both church and state within her empire. Russia's autocrat received the right to nominate bishops to vacant dioceses within her domains, as if she were a Catholic monarch.

Great Britain fared poorly when it came to establishing religious toleration, despite its parliamentary and representative institutions. On the British archipelago, the question of how to accommodate Irish and recusant Catholics within the state proved intractable. After all, the Glorious Revolution of 1688 had created a political settlement based on the exclusion of Catholics from public life and office. Proposals to alleviate the burden of penal laws erupted into mass violence with the Gordon riots of 1783.[17] Irish and British Catholics would have to wait patiently for progress to be made. It was only during the early nineteenth century that agitation on the part of Daniel O'Connell and Catholic associations began to achieve results. This, eventually, culminated in 1828 in the repeal of the Test and Corporation Act, followed swiftly by Catholic Emancipation in 1829.[18] Such toleration embraced Nonconformists, who continued to grow exponentially in the nineteenth century. Their refusal to accept the authority of the Church of England represented a huge challenge to the British state. Evangelical Christians would form the backbone of radical politics in Britain throughout the eighteen and nineteenth centuries. They were to have a determining role in the campaign to abolish the slave trade, which culminated in 1807.[19]

Churches in Revolution

If any event was to catalyze, and eventually derail, the process of the enlightened reform of the Christian church, it was the French Revolution. Initially at least the Estates General in Versailles and the National Assembly in Paris were not anti-religious. Their goals mirrored the eighteenth century's ambitions for a rationalization of the Gallican church. They increased toleration by granting full civil rights to Jews and Protestants, thus eroding Catholicism's monopoly on public worship.[20] The confiscation of church

17. Haywood and Seed, *Gordon Riots*.
18. Fraser, *King and the Catholics*.
19. Ryrie, *Protestants*, 183–208.
20. Goldfarb, *Emancipation*, 62–90.

land and the dissolution of the monasteries, between 1789 and 1790, was not dissimilar to what Catherine the Great, Frederick II, and Joseph II had accomplished within their own domains.

Even the controversial Civil Constitution of the Clergy of July 12, 1790, was not intrinsically anti-religious. Its goal was to reduce the number of dioceses in France and to make bishops and priests the salaried officials of the state. Ultimately, the real bone of the contention was that this legislation was presented to the papacy as a fait accompli, and the revolutionaries in Paris refused to negotiate. Even more divisive was the oath to uphold the French Constitution, which had to be taken by all bishops and priests. This transformed allegiance to the revolutionary state into a crisis of conscience. Pius VI, after a long delay, condemned this oath in 1791.

After this turning point, the revolution assumed increasingly religious undertones, which had been far from the intention of the deputies in Paris. With almost the totality of the ancien régime episcopate rejecting the Civil Constitution and only half the priesthood adhering to it, 1791 heralded a growing schism within the Gallican church. The new constitutional church, born of the revolution, was condemned by Rome, and its members viewed as quislings by loyal Catholics. The peripheries of France witnessed significant resistance to the Civil Constitution. In the south of France significant sectarian violence emerged. Protestants tended to support the revolution that had emancipated them, whereas Catholics resisted it. Events like the *bagarre* of Nîmes and the two camps at Jalès left hundreds dead. It was just the beginning. Adherence to traditional Catholicism was a vital factor in sparking the revolts of the Vendee, Brittany, Normandy, and Languedoc.

The fall of the monarchy, and the revolutionary wars, radicalized events beyond recognition. Priorities shifted as the new republic grew increasingly anti-Christian in outlook. The mass wave of dechristianization that erupted in 1793 was not official government policy. Yet, it unleashed a campaign of vandalism that did untold damage to the fabric of countless churches, monasteries, and Gothic cathedrals.[21] Mass intimidation elicited forced marriages and the abdication of thousands of priests. Indeed, Jean-Baptiste-Joseph Gobel, constitutional archbishop of Paris, relinquished his miter and crosier at the bar of the National Convention. This act of political expediency did not save him from the guillotine. Members of the Committee of Public Safety were fearful that the destruction of Christianity, and its replacement with atheism, would damage the republican virtue they wanted to instill in the population. They were determined to create a new civic religion. To do this, the Gregorian calendar was abolished due to its religious

---

21. Van Kley, "Christianity as Casualty."

connotations, and replaced with a decimal republic calendar. New religions, like the Cult of the Supreme Being and theophilanthropy, tried to supplant Christianity to replace it with deistic and pantheistic forms of worship.[22] Founding a new faith based entirely on politics proved unsuccessful.

What surprised revolutionary elites in Paris was how attached to their faith the Catholic masses of the peripheries remained. The situation exploded when, between 1795 and 1799, the armies of the French Republic entered Italy. Flash points like the Viva Maria riots in Tuscany and the Sanfedisti revolts in Calabria demonstrated that there were hundreds of Vendees simmering beyond the borders of France. Christians did not appreciate it when their faith was dismissed as backward and superstitious. The kidnapping, exile, and death of Pius VI in Valence in 1799 was a public relations disaster for the French Directory. After a century of benign neglect, and a certain intellectual disdain, the religion of the masses of the peripheries of Europe piqued the attention and, eventually, the patronage of the papal curia.

Initially, the rise of Napoleon seemed to provide Catholicism with much needed respite. His negotiation of a concordat, in 1801 with the newly elected Pope Pius VII, seemed to herald a new relationship between church and state. On the surface it appeared that the papacy accepted much of the changes wrought by the French Revolution. The loss of church property, the dissolution of the monasteries, the reduction of dioceses, and that clergy would become salaried officials of the state, all found confirmation in this agreement. Yet, article 3 represented something of a papal revolution. Napoleon wanted to depose all the ancien régime bishops who fled France during the 1790s. Under this clause the pope's right to remove bishops who had committed no crime or heresy, but merely for administrative purposes, was implicitly sanctioned. It was the first step in the slow road to spiritual absolutism that would eventually find its culmination in the first Vatican Council and its declaration of papal infallibility in 1870.

Yet, the concordat of 1801 was built on a fundamental misunderstanding. For Pius VII it was an extraordinary agreement, granted to allow the Gallican church to rebuild itself from the embers of revolution, whereas for the French government it enshrined the subordination of the church to the state. Indeed, the consular and later imperial government contracted similar treaties with Lutherans, Calvinists, and Jews within their domains. Catholicism had not resumed its monopoly on public worship as in the past. Problems multiplied, as Napoleon, after his coronation in Notre Dame (where he was anointed by the pope himself) in 1804, won an uninterrupted string of military victories, making him master of Europe. For him,

---

22. Smyth, *Robespierre and the Festival*.

the concordat was to be exported unilaterally to the rest of Europe. This infuriated the papacy, who felt that it was a usurpation of its prerogatives and retaliated by refusing to confirm Napoleon's episcopal nominees. This created a crisis over investiture that culminated in the kidnapping of Pius VII from the Quirinal palace in July 1809. Pius VII would remain a prisoner of Napoleon for the better part of five years. The entire college of cardinals, and the Vatican archives, were transported to Paris, where they would remain till 1814.[23]

The religious dimension of the Napoleonic Wars has been a field of growing interest. Those irregulars who fought Napoleon in Spain, Calabria, Parma, and the Tyrol were inspired to defend not just their homeland, but their faith as well. In central Italy, passive resistance, in the form of the refusal to collaborate or recognize the French Empire, led to the arrest, imprisonment, and deportation of thousands of Catholic priests.[24] The faithful on the peripheries of Europe clung to popular Catholicism and defended their clergy against the encroachments of the empire. Napoleon's invasion of Russia prompted a damascene conversion in Tsar Alexander I. Although brought up by Frédéric-César de LaHarpe, a radical tutor, in the ideas of the Enlightenment, the Russian monarch weaponized orthodoxy in the defence of Mother Russia in 1812. Many serfs acted as partisans to defend their faith and carried icons into battle to vanquish the godless invaders. Religious undertones pervaded the correspondence of the allied leadership of 1813–14. Metternich, Nesselrode, and Alexander's letters invoked the language of crusade in their battle against the French Empire.[25] Napoleon as antichrist became an important trope in his growing black legend.

Christianity Revived

Europe was not restored by the Congress of Vienna but changed deeply. The confidence that reason alone could consolidate Christianity had been shaken. Confessional states and Catholic theocracies (excluding the papal states) would disappear from the map. France's attempts to subordinate Christianity to the state left a mixed legacy. Governments of the restoration proved unwilling to reestablish the alliance of throne and altar. There was little appetite for the First Estate to reemerge as an independent and powerful corporation. Monastic and ecclesiastical properties remained confiscated, not

---

23. Caiani, *To Kidnap a Pope*, esp. ch. 5.
24. Esdaile, *Fighting Napoleon*.
25. Rey, *Alexander I*, 297–326.

to be returned to their original owners. Gradually, religious toleration was extended to every European polity (excluding the papal states) by 1848.[26]

The post-Napoleonic period witnessed a notable religious revival across the Continent. It embraced all three major Christian traditions. Anglicanism, despite the reverberations of Catholic emancipation, undertook major church building and diocesan revival campaign. Nonconformism continued to grow exponentially in the Celtic fringe and in cities.[27] In the British Isles the struggle between high church Anglicanism and Evangelicalism was at the heart of this revival. Several clergymen known as Anglo-Catholics were sympathetic to pre-Reformation devotional practices. The Oxford Movement defended centuries of hierarchical and liturgical practices. Its success was compromised when some leaders, like John Henry Newman and Henry Manning, converted to Catholicism, eventually becoming prominent cardinals.[28]

The Orthodox tradition, too, experienced a process of revival. Female religious in convents increased at least tenfold, and their male counterparts grew impressively. This search for an authentic orthodoxy, or a pristine Christianity, influenced Russian culture and literature profoundly during the nineteenth century. One need only read the novels of Fyodor Dostoevsky or Leo Tolstoy to gain a glimpse into this Romantic rediscovery of Slavic Christianity.[29] The character Pierre Bezukhov, in Tolstoy's masterpiece *War and Peace*, personified the Christian experience post-Napoleon. Bezukhov begins as an indifferent deist and becomes an enthusiastic Freemason, only to rediscover finally the beauty of primitive Christianity.

Proto-nationalist orthodoxy was to undermine the Ottoman dominance over the Balkans. The Greek wars of independence that so inspired British and French Romantics had a decidedly religious dimension. When the ecumenical patriarch in Constantinople, Gregory V, refused to condemn the Greek struggle for independence, he was hanged publicly in Istanbul.[30] This martyrdom backfired on the sultan, galvanizing Greek resistance and making it impossible for the Ottomans to retain control of the Aegean. The new kingdom of Greece that emerged in 1832 fostered the birth of a new Greek Orthodox Church that was autocephalous. This allowed for a Greek Christian revival that would fuse Greek identity and religion closely

---

26. Clark and Kaiser, *Culture Wars*.
27. Jones, *Revival of Evangelicalism*.
28. Duffy, *John Henry Newman*.
29. Medzhibovskaya, *Tolstoy and Religious Culture*.
30. Mazower, *Greek Revolution*, 33.

together—a process that was replicated in much of the Balkans, as the Ottoman hegemony disintegrated slowly.[31]

It was in the Catholic world that renewal was most pressing, given that it was this Christian tradition most affected by the revolutionary and Napoleonic crises. In Restoration France, missionaries traveled the countryside preaching and seeking converts. Mission crosses scattered around the hexagon are testament to this campaign to bring back the lost sheep of revolution into the fold. More sinister were the book-burning campaigns that saw Voltaire and Rousseau consigned to the flames. Louis de Bonald, Joseph de Maistre, and Félicité de Lamennais urged a fusion of civil with religious society. They saw it as the only way to restore a healthy Christian society capable of withstanding the centrifugal forces of individualism, industrialization, and revolution—in essence, a theocratic and paternalist society, whereby clergy and aristocracy would resume their natural leadership.

Yet, the Catholicism that emerged after 1815 was very different from that of the eighteenth century. The autonomous churches of Gallicanism and the Reichskirche were beyond reconstruction. There was little nostalgia for the reform Catholicism, Jansenism, and neo-conciliarism that had characterized the age of Enlightenment. Many saw such movements as guilty of collusion with the revolutionary and Napoleonic regimes. A new generation of bishops and priests no longer looked domestically for leadership, but rather to Rome. Inspired by their persecution during the Napoleonic Empire, they looked to the papacy for guidance. This pro-Roman outlook was known as "ultramontane," taken from the Latin *ultra montes*, meaning beyond the mountains (the Alps). The nineteenth century was to be the ultramontane century par excellence.

To dismiss such tendencies as mere conservatism is to misunderstand the remarkable vitality of ultramontane Catholicism, which, after the 1820s, splintered into disparate groups. After several trans-European revolutions in Europe, Catholics were keener than ever to stabilize their societies, and became convinced that Rome was key role to this objective. The 1830s saw the emergence of "social Catholicism" and "liberal Catholicism." Although technically distinct, there was significant cross-fertilization between these two movements.

Social Catholicism, as the name implied, sought to harness the moral authority of the church to defend the weak, especially industrial workers, from the rapaciousness of nascent capitalism. Lamennais, in his later career, was deeply committed to the improvement of the material conditions of the working proletariat. So too was the former Napoleonic prefect Alban

---

31. Vovchenko, *Containing Balkan Nationalism*.

de Villeneuve Bargemont, who published a three-volume treatise entitled *Christian Political Economy*, which advocated the creation of a religious welfare state. Social Catholicism, cyclically, raised its head to then enter dormancy throughout the nineteenth century. It reached its culmination in 1891 with the publication of Leo XIII's encyclical *Rerum Novarum*. This text condemned exploitative capitalism and recognized that workers had the right to form Catholic trade unions to bargain collectively for fair wages and better conditions.

Liberal Catholicism's key mouthpiece, at first, was the newspaper *L'Avenir* edited by Lamennais between 1830 and 1831. It advocated that the church could only benefit from its separation from the state. There was optimism that Rome would benefit from liberalism and the freedom of the press. Liberals theorized that Catholics, shorn of coercion and the tutelage of the corrupt state, would develop a deeper faith in Christ's teachings. These men, who wrote for *L'Avenir*, endorsed ethnolinguistic self-determination in Italy, Belgium, Poland, and Ireland. Lamennais, Jean-Baptiste Henri Lacordaire, Charles Forbes René de Montalembert, Vincenzo Gioberti, Antonio Rosmini, Daniel O'Connell, and Adam Mickiewicz, all supported a liberal church, less obsessed with hard political power and more pastorally engaged.[32] They saw proto-nationalism as an opportunity for the church.

They came into direct conflict with Rome when the papal legations of Emilia-Romagna erupted in revolution in 1830–31. Only Habsburg military might restored the pope's authority over these provinces. The liberal Catholic notion that the papacy would be strengthened by losing its temporal power struck at the heart of one of the pillars that sustained Catholicism's independence. Gregory XVI condemned *L'Avenir* and thus pushed the volatile Lamennais into the arms of Christian socialism.

Matters were catalyzed further by the Italian Risorgimento. This cultural and political reawakening called on Italians to throw off the yoke of foreign domination and federate together. Gioberti and Rosmini, known as neo-Guelfs, believed that the pope could serve as head of an Italian federation of states.[33] The election in 1846 of Giovanni Maria Mastai Ferretti as Pius IX was a turning point. Ferretti had a reputation for being progressive and sympathetic to Italian nationalism. Initial indications seemed favorable, as the pope undertook many liberal reforms, which, eventually, included a constitution, representative bodies, and lay participation in the governance of Europe's last theocracy.

32. Harrison, *Romantic Catholics*.
33. Hill, *Persecuted Prophet*, 155–61.

All changed when Europe exploded into continent-wide revolution in 1848. Calls on Pius IX to join other Italian states in an anti-Austrian war proved too much. His refusal to declare war radicalized the situation. The pope's chief minister, Pellegrino Rossi, was lynched by a mob in Rome on November 15, 1848. Humiliatingly, Pius IX was forced to flee in the night and seek refuge at Gaeta, in the nearby kingdom of the Two Sicilies. The revolutionaries in Rome proclaimed a short-lived republic. It required military intervention from France, Austria, Naples, and Spain to quell this insurrection. Once Pius IX was restored, he entered a reactionary phase of his pontificate, dismantling his earlier reforms. He embarked on the twin policies of preserving his kingdom intact and gaining spiritual absolutism over the church. The first proved a lost cause, as Italian nationalism brought an end to papal rule. In contrast, the First Vatican Council (the first ecumenical council convened since Trent in the sixteenth century) used conciliarism to consolidate papal power rather than undermine it. The declaration of papal infallibility in 1870, ironically, provided Pius IX with spiritual absolutism in the very year when Italian troops breached the walls of Rome and put an end to his temporal rule. As High Macleod has put it, Catholicism entered a sustained process of self-ghettoization in which Catholics shunned contact with the secular state to avoid contamination from modernist errors.[34]

Religious revival during the nineteenth century fostered an unprecedented phase of Christian missionary expansion across the globe. The clergy doubled, and female religious increased roughly eightfold. In Europe's rural peripheries there is evidence of something akin to a devotional revolution. Marian apparitions throughout the century and resurgences in pilgrimages highlighted the deep spiritual need of communities to live and benefit from their faith.[35]

Imperialist Expansion: The European Church outside of Europe

As Europe expanded beyond its boundaries in its second age of imperialism, missionary activity accelerated. The Anglican Church Mission Society, founded in 1799, sent evangelizers throughout the globe to spread the Bible and preach the word of God. Their global coverage was impressive, but their ability to make converts remains unclear.[36] The Catholic Church had to play significant catch-up in terms of global missionary activity. It was only under Gregory XVI that the *propaganda fide* was restructured, and a new impetus

34. McLeod, *Religion and the People*, 36–53.
35. Pazos, *Nineteenth-Century European Pilgrimages*.
36. Etherington, *Missions and Empire*.

was given for missionary activity beyond Catholicism's heartlands. Cardinal Lavigerie's foundation of the "White Fathers" in 1868 proved a remarkable success. In the closing decades of the nineteenth century, they evangelized much of sub-Saharan Africa. When it comes to missions, orthodoxy's focus was Eurasian. Russian missionaries did contact the Ethiopian Orthodox Church, but little came from these encounters. Attempts to convert the Muslim population of the Eurasian steppes proved unsuccessful, especially as the tsarist regime preferred toleration to conversion in these delicate regions.[37]

It is striking that the arrival of missionaries often laid some of the groundwork for the conversion of informal empire into direct colonial rule. Famously, Jules Ferry stated that "anticlericalism was not for export" and that Catholic missionaries, until the early twentieth century, were seen as a tool of empire in the scramble for Africa and the conquest of much of Indochina. Having said this, missionaries were not mere stooges. They could be whistleblowers for the worst excesses of imperial rule. This was certainly the case in the Congo, where Protestant missionaries denounced Leopold's brutal colonial regime long before the press intervened.[38]

The ages of Enlightenment and empire were a time of fundamental change for Christianity in Europe. Historians are moving away from older narratives that saw this as an age of religious indifference and growing secularism. Such a view is teleological and unhelpful. Admittedly, established churches saw their authority eroded by reforming monarchies and revolutions. This was especially traumatic for Catholicism, which had invested heavily in the alliance of throne and altar. Yet, even for Anglicanism and Russian Orthodoxy, their monopoly of religious power was greatly unsettled. These trends were counterbalanced by a nineteenth-century process of Christian resurgence. Clergy and faithful increased impressively throughout the Continent until the 1870s. Post-Napoleonic churches were different from those of the previous century. The umbilical cord that connected church and state had been severed in many states, and, where it survived, it proved less than nourishing. In the Orthodox and Catholic worlds, growth occurred mainly in rural peripheries. This was a rising cause of concern and did cause some alarm. Christianity may have flourished in village hamlets, but in major cities and industrial centers it was in retreat. How to bring the Christian message of the "good news" to urban societies and the industrial proletariat was to be the great challenge of the twentieth century.

37. Werth, *Tsar's Foreign Faiths*.
38. Thomas, *Mental Maps of Empire*, 136.

Bibliography

Beales, Derek. *Joseph II: Against the World, 1780–1790*. 2 vols. Cambridge: Cambridge University Press, 2009.

———. *Prosperity and Plunder: European Catholic Monasteries in the Age of Revolution, 1650–1815*. Cambridge: Cambridge University Press, 2003.

Blanchard, Shaun. *The Synod of Pistoia and Vatican II, Jansenism and the Struggle for Catholic Reform*. Oxford Studies in Historical Theology. Oxford: Oxford University Press, 2020.

Caiani, Ambrogio. *To Kidnap a Pope: Napoleon and Pius VII, 1800–1815*. London: Yale University Press, 2021.

Choudhury, Mita. *Convents and Nuns in Eighteenth-Century French Politics*. Ithaca, NY: Cornell University Press, 2004.

Clark, Christopher, and Wolfram Kaiser, eds. *Culture Wars: Secular-Catholic Conflict in Nineteenth-Century Europe*. Cambridge: Cambridge University Press, 2003.

Cottret, Monique. *Histoire du jansénisme: XVIIe–XIXe siècle*. Pour l'histoire. Paris: Perrin, 2016.

Doyle, William. *Jansenism: Catholic Resistance to Authority from the Reformation to the French Revolution*. Studies in European History. Basingstoke, UK: Palgrave, 2000.

Duffy, Eamon. *John Henry Newman: A Very Brief History*. Very Brief Histories. London: SPCK, 2019.

Esdaile, Charles J. *Fighting Napoleon: Guerrillas, Bandits and Adventurers in Spain 1808–1814*. London: Yale University Press, 2004.

Etherington, Norman, ed. *Missions and Empire*. Oxford History of the British Empire Companion. Oxford: Oxford University Press, 2005.

Fraser, Antonia. *The King and the Catholics: The Fight for Rights, 1829*. London: Weidenfeld & Nicolson, 2018.

Freeze, Gregory L. "Russian Orthodoxy, Church, People and Politics in Imperial Russia." In *The Cambridge History of Russia*, edited by Dominic Lieven, 2:284–305. Cambridge: Cambridge University Press, 2006.

Gilley, Sheridan, and Brian Stanley, eds. *World Christianities, c. 1815–1914*. Vol. 8 of *The Cambridge History of Christianity*. Cambridge: Cambridge University Press, 2006.

Goldfarb, Michael. *Emancipation: How Liberating Europe's Jews from the Ghetto Led to Revolution and Renaissance*. New York: Simon & Schuster, 2009.

Harrison, Carol E. *Romantic Catholics: France's Postrevolutionary Generation in Search of a Modern Faith*. Ithaca, NY: Cornell University Press, 2014.

Haywood, Ian, and John Seed, eds. *The Gordon Riots: Politics, Culture and Insurrection in Late Eighteenth-Century Britain*. Cambridge: Cambridge University Press, 2012.

Hill, John. *Persecuted Prophet: Antonio Rosmini*. Cippenham, UK: Gracewing, 2014.

Israel, Jonathan I. *Revolutionary Ideas: An Intellectual History of the French Revolution from The Rights of Man to Robespierre*. Princeton: Princeton University Press, 2015.

Jones, Andrew Michael. *The Revival of Evangelicalism: Mission and Piety in the Victorian Church of Scotland*. Scottish Religious Cultures, Edinburgh: Edinburgh University Press, 2022.

Kloes, Andrew. "Dissembling Orthodoxy in the Age of the Enlightenment: Frederick the Great and his Confession of Faith." *Harvard Theological Review* 109 (2016) 102–28.

Mazower, Mark. *The Greek Revolution: 1821 and the Making of Modern Europe*. London: Penguin, 2021.

McLeod, Hugh. *Religion and the People of Western Europe, 1789–1989*. Oxford: Oxford University Press, 2000.

Medzhibovskaya, Inessa. *Tolstoy and the Religious Culture of His Time: A Biography of a Long Conversion, 1845–1885*. Plymouth, UK: Lexington, 2009.

Messbarger, Rebecca, et al., eds. *Benedict XIV and the Enlightenment: Art, Science, and Spirituality*. Toronto Italian Studies. Toronto: Toronto University Press, 2016.

Pazos, Antón M., ed. *Nineteenth-Century European Pilgrimages: A New Golden Age*. London: Routledge, 2021.

Rey, Marie Pierre. *Alexander I: The Tsar Who Defeated Napoleon*. NIU Series in Slavic, East European, and Eurasian Studies. DeKalb: Northern Illinois University Press, 2012.

Ryrie, Alec. *Protestants: The Radicals Who Made the Modern World*. London: Collins, 2017.

Scott, Hamish, ed. *Enlightened Absolutism: Reform and Reformers in Later Eighteenth-Century Europe*. Problems in Focus 1. Basingstoke, UK: Palgrave, 1990.

Silva, Cesare. *La separazione dello stato dalla Chiesa in Francia del 1905*. Miscellanea Historiae Pontificae 71. Rome: Pontificia Universita Gregoriana, 2020.

Smyth, Jonathan. *Robespierre and the Festival of the Supreme Being: The Search for a Republican Morality*. Studies in Modern French and Francophone History. Manchester, UK: Manchester University Press, 2016.

Sorkin, David. *The Religious Enlightenment: Protestants, Jews, and Catholics from London to Vienna*. Jews, Christians, and Muslims from the Ancient to the Modern World. Princeton: Princeton University Press, 2011.

Stanwood, Owen. *The Global Refuge: Huguenots in an Age of Empire*. Oxford: Oxford University Press, 2020.

Thomas, Martin. *Mental Maps of Empire and Colonial Encounters*. Vol. 1 of *The French Colonial Mind*. France Overseas: Studies in Empire and Decolonization. London: University of Nebraska Press, 2011.

Van Kley, Dale K. "Christianity as Casualty and Chrysalis of Modernity: The Problem of Dechristianization in the French Revolution." *American Historical Review* 108 (2003) 1081–104.

———. *Reform Catholicism and the International Suppression of the Jesuits in Enlightenment Europe*. Religion and Global Politics. London: Yale University Press, 2018.

Vovchenko, Denis. *Containing Balkan Nationalism: Imperial Russia and Ottoman Christians, 1856–1914*. Oxford: Oxford University Press, 2016.

Werth, Paul W. *The Tsar's Foreign Faiths: Toleration and the Fate of Religious Freedom in Imperial Russia*. Oxford Studies in Modern European History. Oxford: Oxford University Press, 2016.

Wood, Gordon S. *Power and Liberty: Constitutionalism in the American Revolution*. Oxford: Oxford University Press, 2021.

Section Two

The Story of Christianity Adapts to the European Context

5

The Orthodox Story of Christianity in Europe

Andrew Louth

To TELL THE ORTHODOX story, we begin at the beginning, even though this overlaps with chapter 1, which concerns the emergence of the Christian church during late antiquity.[1]

The Beginnings

The primitive apostolic church, which consisted of first disciples of Jesus, had at its core the community in Jerusalem, and it may be presumed that these disciples spoke some form of Aramaic, the lingua franca of the Middle East. Barely a couple of decades after the death and resurrection of Christ, Christians came to realize that the gospel was for the gentiles as well as for Jews, and that gentile converts were not required to become Jews (that is, circumcision was not required, nor observance of the Torah). The church had a worldwide mission, and so the language of the church became Greek, the lingua franca of the Roman Empire: for which reason the writings that came to constitute the New Testament are in Greek, and what Christians came to call the Old Testament was the translation into Greek (by Jewish scholars) known as the Septuagint, the "Seventy" (after the number of scholars engaged, according to tradition, in the translation). Until the end of the third century, evidence for Christianity is overwhelmingly Greek; Aramaic-speaking Christianity continued, but the earliest evidence for literature in Syriac, the Edessan dialect mostly used by Christians, is only from the second century. Latin-speaking Christianity is a still later development. The Orthodox story of Christianity sees itself as the continuation of the original Greek-speaking Christianity that

1. For a concise account see Ware, *Orthodox Church*.

saw its mission as worldwide (or "ecumenical," that is, belonging to the "inhabited world," as the Romans hubristically called their empire).

Persecution and Martyrdom

Christians for some centuries faced persecution by the Roman Empire. The nature and extent of that persecution is much discussed, but what is beyond question is that martyrdom came to be branded on the memory of the church. The martyrs were regarded as present in the heavenly courts, with a special concern for the earthly communities from which they came; celebration of their memory was at the heart of the emerging cult of the saints, who were heavenly intercessors, whose martyrdoms were celebrated as their "heavenly birthdays."

Despite persecution, for the most part early Christians protested their loyalty to the empire and prayed for the health and success of the emperors. Even during the period of persecution, the governing structures of the church were modeled on the administrative structures of the empire, each city having a single Christian community under a bishop, who was himself responsible to the bishop of the provincial capital, the metropolis; even broader structures seem to have been emerging in these early centuries.[2]

Conversion of the Emperor and the Beginnings of a Christian Empire

The period of imperial persecution ended with the "Great Persecution" under Diocletian and his fellow emperors, which was followed by the rise of Constantine and Constantine's conversion.[3] What that conversion meant for Constantine himself is difficult to assess, but for the church it meant a sudden change from being persecuted to be supported by the empire, with church building supported from imperial funds, and a new Christian capital city, built by Constantine (and his sons), and named after him Constantinople—Constantine's city—although more widely known as "New Rome." This city became the site of the imperial court, and so the real capital of the Roman Empire. The "conversion" of the empire, however, was a much more gradual process, with regions remaining pagan into the sixth century at least, though the legal status of Christians became more entrenched, and with Emperor Justinian's revision of Roman law there emerged the vision of a Christian empire, with the imperial office (*imperium/basileia*) and the

---

2. On persecution and martyrdom, see Ste. Croix, *Christian Persecution, Martyrdom*.
3. See Potter, *Constantine the Emperor*.

priestly office (*sacerdotium/hierateuma*) both derived from God and mutually supportive: an arrangement known as *symphonia*, "harmony."

This *symphonia* was manifest in the emperor, though a layman, taking an increasing interest in the affairs of the church. The already existent system of synodal government, though in an inchoate form, became regulated, and was capped by synods or councils ("synod" was the Christian term, both in Greek and in Latin) with authority throughout the whole empire, called ecumenical (Greek: *oikoumenikos*, pertaining to the whole inhabited world; the rest of the world consigned to "barbarians"), called by the emperor. The concern of the emperors extended into matters of doctrine, where what mattered above all was to achieve peace and unity throughout the church, so that the prayers of the church for the emperor might be the more effective with God.[4]

Alongside the emergence, after persecution, of a church with structures reflecting the empire (qualified, it must be said, in the by-now-Latin West, where sacerdotal authority was regarded as apostolic, and thus independent of imperial authority and indeed its source), there emerged (or became more manifest) the phenomenon of monasticism. From the beginning this took a variety of forms—hermits devoted to prayer, groups of hermits, and "coenobitic" communities under the authority of an abbot, as well as, to begin with, more informal communities of extended families in country estates or in cities. Synodal legislation makes clear a certain tension between monastic communities, which sought to preserve a sense of distance from the world, and the church, increasingly a feature of Roman society, ruled by bishops.

Monasticism, in its various forms, rapidly became an important feature of the church life, often keen to be involved in church affairs, sometimes, even, a focus for opposition to the decisions of episcopally governed synods. Synods sought to clarify the church's faith—the doctrine of the Trinity and the incarnation—and set down rules (canons) for Christian living. These aims were not achieved without controversy. The councils of the fifth century—Ephesos (431) and Chalcedon (451), the Third and Fourth Ecumenical Councils—achieved doctrinal clarity at the expense of agreement, the former excluding the Church of the East, the latter those churches known as Oriental Orthodox, principally in Egypt (the Coptic Church), Ethiopia, Syria, and Armenia.[5]

By the time of Justinian (r. 527–65), the structure of the church had become settled, at least in the East, with a synodal structure, its highest organ of authority being ecumenical synods, called by the emperor, though increasingly sacerdotal/episcopal bodies. The monastic order complemented this imperial

4. The concept of *symphonia* is set out in the preamble to novel 6: see Miller and Sarris, *Novels of Justinian*, 1:97–98. For a sympathetic account of Justinianic *symphonia*, see McGuckin, *Eastern Orthodox Church*, 122–30.

5. On councils and Chalcedon, see Price and Whitby, *Chalcedon in Context*.

structure, possessing its own spiritual authority, based on the single-minded spiritual life of the monks (and nuns) and its appeal to ordinary Christians. Also, however, by the time of Justinian, the Roman Empire was not what it had been—the regions grouped round the Mediterranean, with its natural borders the Rhine-Danube Rivers to the north, the Tigris/Euphrates Basin to the east, the Atlas Mountains to the south, and to the west the Atlantic. On his accession to the imperial throne, the territories Justinian ruled were much diminished: North Africa had fallen to the Vandals, and from Spain to Italy to the Goths and Franks. The Roman Empire survived in the West as little more than a legal fiction, as the leaders of the invading tribes sought imperial titles to mark their assumed authority. During Justinian's reign, there was a remarkable recovery of the empire in the West, but nevertheless at its greatest extent it was much reduced from the empire Constantine had governed, recovering only North Africa, the coastal regions of Spain and Provence, and much of Italy, but still facing challenges from other "barbarian" tribes.

The Rise of Islam

The real political threat to the Christian Roman Empire of Justinian was to come from elsewhere, for the seventh century saw the rise of Islam and the rapid conquest by Arab tribes united by Islam of the eastern provinces of the empire from Syria, through Palestine, to Egypt, followed by a slower progress though North Africa, eventually to Spain. As well as seizing these Roman provinces, the whole of the Sassanian Empire (Persia/Iran) fell to Islam, leading to the establishment of an Islamic Empire, with its capital first in Damascus (under the Umayyads) and then in Baghdad (under the Abbasids), stretching eventually from Spain to the Hindu Kush, and permanently changing the political geography of the region.

The rise of Islam and the conquest of the eastern provinces of the Roman Empire constituted a challenge to the Christian church as great, if not greater than, the end of persecution and the embrace of the church by the Roman Empire in the fourth century.[6] This challenge was more palpable to the church in the Eastern Roman Empire than to the church in the West. It is also true, as Pirenne argued (though the detail of the arguments have been much discussed), that one effect of the Islamic conquest was to drive a wedge between Western and Eastern Christendom, and in particular between Rome and Constantinople. The Islamic conquests, entailing the loss of the Fertile Crescent, seriously depleted the resources of the Roman Empire, and eventually led to administrative changes, which put the empire

6. For a concise account of the impact of Islam, see Fowden, *Before and after Muḥammad*.

on military footing, with provinces ruled by civilian governors yielding to *themata* (themes) under the military.

Despite the fact that the ecclesiastical structures had been modeled on the imperial structures, these ecclesiastical structures remained unchanged, continuing to reflect the older imperial structures. Moreover, three patriarchates had been lost to the empire—Alexandria, Antioch, and Jerusalem; what survived there had minimal links with the imperial church. The first century after the Islamic conquest saw, paradoxically, creative developments in the Orthodox liturgy: developments beginning in Jerusalem and spreading to Constantinople at the beginning of the ninth century. A new verse composition, the canon, emerged, associated with three churchmen, all hailing from Damascus and associated with Jerusalem: John Damascene, Cosmas of Maïuma, and Andrew of Crete. The songs of the Byzantine liturgy were to play an incomparable role in preserving the Orthodox faith in the coming centuries.

The Iconoclast Controversy

A century after the Islamic conquest, there broke out in the Byzantine/Roman Empire the iconoclast controversy. The origins of the controversy are unclear, even the sequence of the events and their interpretation; the historical sources all come from the side of the winning party, the defenders of icon veneration, and none of them are contemporary with the events they relate. Iconoclasm (or "iconomachy," as it was called: struggle against icons, rather than smashing of icons) entailed the removal (and destruction) of icons, that is, depictions of Christ, his mother, and the saints, and the rejection of their veneration as idolatry. The origins and development of the making and venerating icons in Christian practice is disputed. Once, it was confidently asserted (and it still is) that the rejection of religious art was inherited by the church from Judaism, but this is belied by the existence of religious art in second-century Palestinian synagogues. Christian objections to pagan art, too, were once regarded evidence of an aniconic or anti-iconic attitude, but they may have simply been objections to paganism. One point, at least, seems clear: iconoclasm was a matter of imperial policy, rather than a spontaneous movement among Christians.[7]

Our concern is primarily with the place of iconoclasm in the Orthodox story. That depends on our general view of the controversy; nevertheless, it is the legacy of the controversy that is our primary concern. It is difficult to deny that iconoclasm was, in some respects at least, a reaction

---

7. On iconoclasm, see the revisionary Brubaker and Haldon, *Byzantium in Iconoclast Era*; Humphreys, *Companion to Byzantine Iconoclasm*.

against the military and political success of the new religion Islam, which had, at the very least, reservations about visual art in a religious context. It is, however, difficult to articulate what this really means. Iconoclasm seems to have begun with an imperial edict of Emperor Leo III (r. 717–41). He did not, however, introduce iconoclasm immediately; it was not until 726, or 730, if ever (no edict survives). Patriarch Germanos resigned in 730, in protest, it is claimed. The first comprehensive defence of icons and their veneration came not from within the empire, but from a monk of Jerusalem, John Damascene, who wrote three treatises, or rather a treatise that he revised twice, between 726 and probably about 745.

His arguments in favor of icons are wide ranging, but can be summarized thus: first, veneration of icons is not idolatry, as condemned by the second of the Ten Commandments; furthermore, there is evidence for religious art in the Old Testament itself and even veneration (*proskynēsis*) of sacred objects, which is to be distinguished from true worship (*latreia*), due to God alone; second, icons and their veneration are entailed by the incarnation, in which God took on a human form that can be circumscribed (as God in himself cannot be); third, aversion to icon veneration suggests a negative attitude to matter, which is dualistic and smacks of Manichaeism. In 741 Leo died and was eventually succeeded by his son, Constantine VI, whose attitude to icon veneration was more determined, and who called an ecumenical synod in 754, held in the imperial palace at Hiereia. This synod produced a definition (*horos*) in favor of iconoclasm, the text of which we have, as it was read out and refuted at the sixth session of the Second Ecumenical Synod of Nicaea held in 787.[8] There can be deduced from the *horos* a coherent argument against icons, which in essence asserts that the only way in which Christ asked to be remembered was in the Eucharist, which he instituted. This is the only true icon of Christ; painted (or woven or embroidered) icons are human inventions, the very making of which is contrary to Christ's command and constitutes idolatry. The first phase of iconoclasm came to an end with the accession of Constantine's infant son, Leo, whose mother, the empress Irene, soon abandoned iconoclasm and introduced the icons, which were affirmed at Nicaea II. By the end of the century, the empire was in a parlous state, and eventually in 815 the new emperor, Leo V, reintroduced iconoclasm. By the time of the death of his son, Theophilos, iconoclasm had lost its hold; icon veneration was restored, again under an empress, Theophilos's widow, Theodora, regent for her infant son, Michael III. This was set out in the *Synodikon of Orthodoxy*, a piece of performative liturgy, held on the First Sunday of

---

8. For the sixth session of Nicaea II with the *Horos* of Hiereia, see Price, *Acts of Second Council*, 2:425–546.

Lent in 843, and repeated annually thereafter (initially in Constantinople, though eventually it spread to the whole Orthodox world).

The importance of the iconoclast controversy for the Orthodox story has several aspects. First, the "triumph of Orthodoxy," expressed in the restoration of the icons, endowed icons with a central place in the practice of Orthodoxy—a place both public, in churches and public spaces, and private, in personal devotion—a central place and a *necessary* place. Icons were no longer optional, and there lay a difference with the West. The popes in Rome had no intention of obeying the imperial edict—icons were not to be destroyed—but neither did they imbue icons with a necessary place in Christian worship. Henceforth, the fashioning of icons in the Orthodox East would be governed by the devotion that was their due. This was much less so in the West; indeed, there were those in the West who rejected the Eastern attitude to icons. Furthermore, as icons became regarded as a necessary part of the Orthodox heritage of worship, so in the missionary expansion of the faith, which gained ground in the wake of iconoclasm, Orthodox Christianity would be marked by its veneration for icons. There were other collateral consequences of the triumph of Orthodoxy. Although it can hardly be maintained that the monastic order as a whole was behind icon veneration, it was certainly the case that certain monks, especially the monks of monasteries that followed the Studite reform, led by Theodore the Studite, a charismatic monastic leader, played a major role in the defense of icons during the second period of iconoclasm. (Modern scholars have sometimes argued that women were notable supporters of icons, but apart from the fact that icon veneration was reintroduced on both occasions by regent empresses there is little more than speculation in support.)

The most important collateral was political: during the eighth century Italy faced invasion by the Lombards. Tension between the pope and emperor over iconoclasm, together with the Roman Empire's military preoccupation with the Muslim Empire, meant that popes had to look elsewhere for military protection and found it in the nascent Carolingian Empire. In this way, the iconoclast controversy added to the growing rift between Latin West and Greek East.[9]

Renewed Missionary Activity in the Ninth Century

The end of iconoclasm introduced a period of renewed confidence in Christians both in the Orthodox East and the Latin West, a confidence manifest in a revival of education and learning, liturgical development, and a deeper

9. For Rome's relationship with the Byzantine Empire in the iconoclast era, see Noble, "Papacy."

interest in theology, and indeed in science and other forms of learning. One manifestation of this greater confidence can be found in an awakening awareness of lands beyond the traditional frontiers of the Roman Empire that led to renewed missionary activity. Both Latin and Greek missionaries were engaged in this missionary expansion. In the mid-ninth century, Prince Rostislav of Moravia is said to have requested missionaries from Byzantium to preach Christianity to his people who spoke a form of Slavic. Rostislav's motives remain unclear, but the Byzantine emperor responded by sending two brothers, Methodios and Constantine, natives of Thessaloniki, who had learnt some Slav from the tribes settled in the Thessalonikan hinterland. Together they devised a Slavonic alphabet in order to translate the liturgy and some scriptural texts from Greek to Slavonic. Their activities in Moravia attracted the attention of Pope Nicholas I (d. 857), who invited them to Rome. They were given a warm welcome in Rome, perhaps because they had with them relics of the early Roman bishop Clement, which they had acquired on an embassy to Cherson (present-day Crimea) by Pope Hadrian, Nicholas's successor.

There Constantine became ill and died, having taken the monastic habit under the name of Cyril. Methodios was consecrated Archbishop Sirmium and returned to Moravia. There he died, his mission apparently unsuccessful.[10] His disciples, who included Clement, Naum, and Gorazd, later made their way to Bulgaria to play a role in the establishment of Slavic Orthodoxy in that country. For though Cyril and Methodios's mission to Moravia had no immediate success, about the same time as they were in Moravia, Boris, the Khan of Bulgaria, was considering the merits of adopting Christianity, whether Western or Eastern. He was in touch with both Latin pope and Byzantine emperor, and wavered—in the end, making up his mind, concentrated as the Byzantine emperor marshaled troops along the border; Bulgaria was too close to allow it to be aligned with Latin Christianity and the burgeoning Carolingian Empire. Boris's conversion—he took the name Michael, after his godfather the emperor Michael III—provoked a backlash after his abdication and retirement to a monastery. Boris returned from seclusion and sought again to reestablish Christianity, not this time in its Greek form, but using the fruits of Cyril and Methodios's mission, Orthodox Christianity in Slavonic dress, with the help of Clement and his companions.[11]

In this way was established the principle that Orthodox Christianity, at least, could take a Slavonic form, unlike Western Christianity, which insisted on Latin. Such a principle was clearly attractive in some ways but had

---

10. On the Cyrillo-Methodian mission, see Vlasto, *Entry of the Slavs*, 29–85; and more briefly, Louth, *Greek East*, 172–76.

11. On Clement and his companions, see Obolensky, *Six Byzantine Portraits*, 8–33.

limitations: whereas Latin converts took over a developed Latin culture, Slav converts to Orthodoxy had limited access to the rather more impressive Greek culture, for the need for translation of literary texts created what one might call a "linguistic filter." Aspects of Orthodox life and culture that could bypass this filter therefore came to assume greater prominence—and that included icons and other aspects of visual culture, such as architecture, music, ceremonial, which were able to make a more immediate appeal, as well as monastic communities, making their home in newly Christian territory and consolidating the Christian presence.

The Conversion of the Rus'

A century later, Orthodox Christianity spread into the land of the northern Slavs, who were governed by the Rus', Vikings originating from Scandinavia. The symbolic date is 988, with the conversion of the people of Kyiv (Kiev) and their Grand Prince Volodymer (or Vladimir).[12] The details are complex and must be passed over, but with the conversion of the principality of Kyiv, the Orthodox Church was established among the Rus', ruled by a metropolitan (of Kyiv and all Rus') appointed by the ecumenical patriarch. Such converted territories, which included Bulgaria and Serbia, had political ties with the Byzantine Empire, without being incorporated: they formed what Professor Obolensky called the Byzantine Commonwealth.[13] The metropolitan of Kyiv, for some centuries, was almost invariably Greek, though the language of the church was Slavonic: his jurisdiction came to extend to other Rus' principalities further north.

In the thirteenth century, this whole Orthodox area began to suffer from invasion by Mongols from the east, called Tatars. Kyiv was vulnerable and was ravaged by the Tatars in 1240; soon after, it was abandoned as a center for ecclesiastical administration. Kyiv's metropolitan see began a complex odyssey in two directions: in the northeast around Vladimir and Suzdal, and in the southwest around Galicia (Galich) and Volhynia. Constantinople found it increasingly difficult to cope, and eventually the metropolitanate of Kyiv settled in Moscow, the emerging center of political resistance to the Mongols. The region around Moscow saw a revival of Orthodox life associated with the monastery founded by St. Sergii, influenced by hesychast monks from Mount Athos. From this sprang a golden age of iconography, the most prominent star of which was the monk Andrey Rublev.[14]

12. For the early history of the Russian Church, see Fennell, *History of Russian Church*.
13. Obolensky, *Byzantine Commonwealth*.
14. Meyendorff, *Byzantium and the Rise*, esp. 96–144.

The Growing Rift between East and West

Meanwhile, relations between West and East deteriorated, the first public evidence of which is to be found in Photios's reaction to the presence of Latin missionaries in Bulgaria.[15] The missionaries had added *filioque* to the Nicene Creed, so that the creed asserted that the Holy Spirit proceeded from the Father and the Son (*filioque*): this, Photios regarded as heresy. As time passed other differences were noted, especially in areas where Latins and Greeks lived side by side and came to know one another and their customs, for example, in southern Italy after the incursion of the Normans in the eleventh century. For the church in southern Italy (and Sicily) had been largely of Greek lineage. In this context it was liturgical differences that became prominent: differences in the beginning of Lent—Ash Wednesday among the Latins; Clean Monday, two days earlier, among the Greeks—but especially the kind of bread used in the Eucharist—for the East used ordinary leavened bread, while the West had come to use bread baked without yeast, unleavened bread or *azyma* (ἄζυμα).

Such differences became bones of contention between East and West. However, the real cause for the growing rift was the independent development over the centuries of Latin and Greek Christianity. The traditional date of the eventual schism is 1054, when anathemas were exchanged between a papal embassy to Constantinople, led by Cardinal Humbert and Ecumenical Patriarch Michael Keroularios, but at the time this was scarcely regarded as decisive (contemporary sources largely ignore it). In 1071, however, the Byzantine armies were defeated by the Seljuk Turks at Manzikert and the emperor seized. Political chaos ensued in Constantinople, which was halted by the accession in 1081 of Alexios I Komnenos. Alexios found himself emperor of an empire beset on all sides: Normans were making incursions through the Balkans, while the Seljuks remained a threat from the East. In 1095 Byzantine envoys appealed for help against the Seljuks from Pope Urban II, who later that year called for a Crusade to support the Eastern Christians and recover from the Turks the Holy Sepulchre. In the Holy Land, the crusaders found the natives, whether Byzantines or Arab Christians, just as foreign as the Arab Muslims from whom they were rescuing the holy sites. One effect of the Crusades was the extinction, more or less, of Arab Christianity that had coexisted with Arab Muslims for about six hundred years. The Fourth Crusade, in 1204, abandoned its ostensible mission for the easy pickings to be found by sacking the Christian capital of Constantinople,

---

15. On the estrangement of East and West, see Chadwick, *East and West*; Louth, *Greek East*, esp. 305–18.

leaving a sense of resentment against the West among Christians of the East that proved enduring.

Nevertheless, Byzantium's only hope lay in Western military support, which itself depended on papal support. Councils were held—at Lyon in 1274, and then at Ferrara in 1438, moving to Florence in 1439—at which the Byzantine delegates accepted what amounted to submission to the pope. Such submission was rejected back in Constantinople, and after Florence the Grand Prince of Moscow rejected the proposed union, he seized the opportunity to promote himself as leader of the Orthodox world. In 1453, Constantinople fell to the Ottoman Turks; finally there was extinguished an empire that traced its history back to Augustus's declaring himself emperor in 27 BC, and its existence as a Christian empire back to AD 330.

The "Babylonian" Captivity of the Orthodox Church

Under the Tourkokratia, as the Orthodox Christians called their period under the Turkish yoke, from 1453 to 1918, the ecumenical patriarch was quickly reinstated by Sultan Mehmet as head of the *Rum millet* (the "Roman people"), as the Christian subjects of the Ottoman Empire were called, thus assuming an important position, though also humiliating in many ways, and completely subject to the sultan.[16] His responsibilities to the rest of what had been the Byzantine Commonwealth became increasingly difficult to fulfill; the metropolitan of Moscow and all Rus' came in practice to be appointed by the Orthodox bishops of Rus', and in 1588, the ecumenical patriarch acquiesced in granting the Russian Church autocephaly, with the metropolitan becoming patriarch of Moscow and all Rus'. A century later, in 1686, the ecumenical patriarch ceded to the Moscow patriarchate formal jurisdiction over Muscovite Orthodoxy.

Meanwhile, Orthodox Christians to the southwest of Kyiv found themselves ill served by the newly established Moscow patriarchate, and in 1596, at a synod held in Brest, the Union of Brest, by which Christians of the Eastern Rite accepted papal authority while maintaining their liturgy and canon law, was embraced by the metropolitan of Kyiv, Galich, and all Rus', five of his bishops, and their people. They came to be known as Ukrainian Greek Catholics.[17]

The Greek Orthodox Church survived the nearly four hundred years of the Tourkokratia, during which it largely fell to the monastic order to preserve the Orthodox tradition. In the eighteenth century, moves were made

---

16. Runciman, *Great Church in Captivity*, 159–207.
17. Gudziak, *Crisis and Reform*.

to revive Hellenic consciousness, some of the proponents of which, notably Kosmas of Aetolia, suffered martyrdom.

The leadership of the Russian Church by the patriarch proved to be short lived (a little over a century), before the patriarchate was allowed to fall into desuetude, eventually to be replaced by a committee called the Holy Synod, appointed by Tsar Peter under the terms of his *Spiritual Regulation* (1721). This was part of a comprehensive attempt to westernize (and bring up to date) the Russian Empire, including the church. Tsar Peter inherited a schism (*raskol*) in the church, instigated by the penultimate patriarch Nikon. The schismatics were known as Old Believers, who refused to accept the revision of the service books and their ritual (including the way of making the sign of the cross), and who faced harsh persecution from Peter and his successors.

Beginnings of Renewal: The *Philokalia* and the Rise of National Churches

A beginning in the change of fortunes in the Orthodox Church can be symbolized by the publication in Venice in 1782 of an anthology of ascetic and mystical texts by St. Nikodimos of the Holy Mountain and St. Makarios, bishop of Corinth, called the *Philokalia*. This was part of a many-faceted revival in the church, emanating from the monastic communities on Mount Athos. A Slavonic version of similar material, called the *Dobrotolyubie* (a calque of *philokalia*, which in Greek means an anthology), was translated by St. Paisy Velichkovsky. It was the Slavonic version that was to have the most immediate success, stimulating a monastic revival throughout the Slav lands and nurturing spiritual fatherhood, *starchestvo*, and the practice of the Jesus Prayer. It was also part of an intellectual rebuttal of Peter's westernization, at the center of which were the Slavophiles, who laid stress on Russia's authentic Orthodox tradition.[18]

Matters progressed much less rapidly outside the Russian Empire, as the other Orthodox nations, all part of, or vassals of, the Ottoman Empire, sought to achieve national independence through armed uprising against the Ottomans. The ecumenical patriarch's claim to grant autocephaly to national churches, thus recognizing their political independence, following the case of Russia in 1588, was exercised on behalf of Greece in 1850, Serbia in 1879, and Romania in 1925.

18. Walicki, *Slavophile Controversy*.

The Orthodox World after World War I

The end of World War I in 1918 inaugurated a new era for the Orthodox Churches, in the process creating a diaspora of Orthodox Christians fleeing their native lands. The Ottoman Empire was disbanded as part of the peace settlement. Greece had the "great idea" (μεγάλη ἰδέα) of invading the diminished state of Turkey, the successor to the Ottoman Empire, with a view to making Constantinople once again their capital. It was an utter disaster, the Greek forces being driven back by the Turkish army. The "alien" populations in each country were exchanged: Muslims, long settled in Greece, "returning" to Turkey, and the Orthodox in Turkey returning to a Greece they had never known. This led to the emigration of many of the exiles abroad, creating a Greek diaspora in Europe, and not least in the British Isles, America, and Australia.

The Russian Church also entered a new era, as the collapse of the Russian state with the abdication of the tsar threw open the gates to the Bolshevik Revolution, as a result of which hundreds of thousands of Russians fled. Among these was a special group—intellectuals, regarded as unsympathetic to the regime, exiled by Lenin's decree of 1922. Many of these settled in Paris, eager to share the riches of Russian Orthodoxy with intellectuals in the West. Other Orthodox countries, such as Serbia and Romania, found themselves facing new challenges as a result of the peace settlements at the end of both world wars.[19]

A Tale of Two Patriarchs

Two patriarchs in particular faced a new state of affairs: the ecumenical patriarch of Constantinople (now Istanbul, no longer a capital city) and the patriarch of Moscow and all Rus', the latter having been reinstated at the Reform synod of 1917/18—the only decision to be acted on, as the synod was cut short by the Bolshevik Revolution. For the ecumenical patriarch, the challenge was to find a role in a world in which he risked becoming simply the bishop of Istanbul. Various strategies were adopted: putting his authority as the first see in Orthodoxy behind the burgeoning ecumenical movement; seeking worldwide leadership by promoting concern for the environment. A further, more questionable, way was to claim, on the basis of canon 28 of the Council of Chalcedon (AD 451), which granted to the See of Constantinople the right to ordain bishops working among 'barbarians,'

---

19. For Russian religious thought after the Revolution, both abroad and in Russia, see Emerson et al., *Russian Religious Thought*, 435–639 (pts. 5–6).

universal jurisdiction over Orthodox Christians living in the "diaspora," that is, in non-Orthodox countries (with the right to grant autocephaly), that is, North and South America, Australia, and European nations traditionally Catholic or Protestant.[20]

The newly-established Moscow patriarchate found itself head of the Orthodox Church in the Soviet Union, a state committed to the liquidation of Christianity. Forced into humiliating compromise, the (still only acting) patriarch gained some state recognition through his support of Russia during World War II (the "Great Patriotic War"). Everything changed—rather more quickly than anticipated—with the fall of Communism. The church regained favor; church and monastic buildings were restored to the church. However, the church remained fearful of the West that Russians had been taught during the Cold War to fear and hate: something sustained among Orthodox Christians, not least the hierarchy, with their fearful rejection of Western values, consumerism, and moral decadence. *Ruskiy Mir* (the Russian world) could have simply been a network for promoting Russian culture, but its agenda is much more alarming and is actively promoted by the present patriarch, Kirill, long committed to promoting and nurturing it. It has provided ideological justification for the war in Ukraine, since Kyiv as the baptismal font of Russian Orthodoxy is regarded as the religious heart of Russia.[21]

There has developed a "game of thrones" between the two patriarchs, who have become pawns in an increasingly warlike confrontation between the United States and a Russia hankering after the respect it once commanded as the Soviet Union. One of the victims of this—not the most heartrending, but maybe the most long lasting—has been world Orthodoxy itself, being torn apart by the chasm opening up between the two patriarchates, a chasm given canonical force by Patriarch Kirill's excommunication of the ecumenical patriarch and all in communion with him.

Bibliography

Brubaker, Leslie, and John Haldon. *Byzantium in the Iconoclast Era, c. 680–850.* Cambridge: Cambridge University Press, 2011.

Burgess, John P. *Holy Rus': The Rebirth of Orthodoxy in the New Russia.* New Haven: Yale University Press, 2017.

Chadwick, Henry. *East and West: The Making of a Rift in the Church.* Oxford History of the Christian Church. Oxford: Oxford University Press, 2003.

---

20. On the ecumenical patriarchate in modernity, see Kitromilides, *Religion and Politics.*
21. On post-Communist Russian Orthodoxy, see Burgess, *Holy Rus'.*

de Ste. Croix, G. E. M. *Christian Persecution, Martyrdom, & Orthodoxy*. Oxford: Oxford University Press, 2006.

Emerson, Caryl, et al., eds. *Oxford Handbook of Russian Religious Thought*. Oxford Handbooks. Oxford: Oxford University Press, 2020.

Fennell, John. *A History of the Russian Church: To 1448*. London: Longman, 1995.

Fowden, Garth. *Before and after Muḥammad: The First Millennium Refocused*. Princeton: Princeton University Press, 2014.

Gudziak, Borys A. *Crisis and Reform: The Kyivan Metropolitanate, the Patriarch of Constantinople, and the Genesis of the Union of Brest*. Harvard Series in Ukrainian Studies. Cambridge: Harvard University Press, 2001.

Humphreys, Mike, ed. *A Companion to Byzantine Iconoclasm*. Companions to the Christian Tradition 99. Leiden: Brill, 2021.

Kitromilides, Paschalis M. *Religion and Politics in the Orthodox World: The Ecumenical Patriarchate and the Challenges of Modernity*. London: Routledge, 2019.

Louth, Andrew. *Greek East and Latin West: The Church AD 681–1071*. Church in History 3. Crestwood, NY: St Vladimir's Seminary Press, 2007.

McGuckin, John Anthony. *The Eastern Orthodox Church: A New History*. New Haven: Yale University Press, 2020.

Meyendorff, John. *Byzantium and the Rise of Russia: A Study of Byzantino-Russian Relations in the Fourteenth Century*. Cambridge: Cambridge University Press, 1981.

Miller, David J. D., and Peter Sarris, eds. *The Novels of Justinian: A Complete Annotated English Translation*. 2 vols. Cambridge: Cambridge University Press, 2018.

Noble, Thomas F. X. "The Papacy in the Eighth and Ninth Centuries." In *The New Cambridge Medieval History*, edited by Rosamond McKitterick, 2:563–86. Cambridge: Cambridge University Press, 1995.

Obolensky, Dimitri. *The Byzantine Commonwealth: Eastern Europe, 500–1453*. London: Weidenfeld & Nicolson, 1971.

———. *Six Byzantine Portraits*. Oxford University Press Academic Monograph Reprints. Oxford: Clarendon, 1988.

Potter, David. *Constantine the Emperor*. Oxford: Oxford University Press, 2013.

Price, Richard, trans. *The Acts of the Second Council of Nicaea (787)*. 2 vols. Translated Texts for Historians LUP. Liverpool: Liverpool University Press, 2018.

Price, Richard, and Mary Whitby, eds. *Chalcedon in Context: Church Councils, 400–700*. Liverpool: Liverpool University Press, 2009.

Runciman, Steven. *The Great Church in Captivity: A Study of the Patriarchate of Constantinople from the Eve of the Turkish Conquest to the Greek War of Independence*. London: Cambridge University Press, 1968.

Vlasto, A. P. *The Entry of the Slavs into Christendom: An Introduction to the Medieval History of the Slavs*. Cambridge: Cambridge University Press, 1970.

Walicki, Andrzej. *The Slavophile Controversy: History of a Conservative Utopia in Nineteenth-Century Russian Thought*. Oxford: Clarendon, 1975.

Ware, Timothy. *The Orthodox Church: An Introduction to Eastern Christianity*. Rev. ed. London: Penguin, 2015.

6

The Catholic Story

SHAUN BLANCHARD

THE STORY OF CATHOLICISM in Europe in the last century and a half combines continuity and discontinuity in oxymoronic, sometimes paradoxical ways. For example, a "papalization" of Catholicism began in the wake of the age of Enlightenment and revolutions and reached a kind of zenith with the First Vatican Council's proclamation of papal infallibility in 1870. This papalized Catholicism, also called "ultramontanism" ("over the mountains" in Rome), was ultimately challenged by powerful currents of decentralization ascendant since the mid-twentieth century. And yet, especially when we consider the recent figure of John Paul II and the current pontificate of Francis, Catholicism in Europe—and globally, for that matter—is every bit as centered around the person of the pope, his utterances, and his jurisdictional authority as was the church of a hundred years ago.

A second paradox: the Catholic Church, since the nineteenth century, has functioned as one of the primary brakes against the process of "modernization," at least insofar as secular and liberal opponents of the church (and, often, their Catholic antagonists) have conceived of that process. Nevertheless, it is undeniable that the Catholic Church has itself modernized and indeed acted as a modernizing force throughout this entire period. This chapter covers over a century and a half of the complex and rich history of Europe's largest Christian Church. Such a study must be thematically circumscribed, and thus we will mainly explore these two aforementioned phenomena: first, the push and pull of papal centralization and conciliar decentralization internal to modern European Catholicism; second, the (external) relationship between the Catholic Church and so-called modernity.

The Papalization of Catholicism (1870–1914)

Whatever hopes there were that Pius IX (pope from 1846 to 1878) would lead the European church in a liberal direction were dashed by the revolutions of 1848. After that shock, Pius IX declared war on a modernity that he believed had declared war on religion, or at least on true religion. Pius IX rode the wave of an ultramontane movement that surged up "from below" as much as it was dictated "from above." A network of ultramontane journalists around Europe, most notoriously the Frenchman Louis Veuillot (1813–83), lavished praise on papal resistance to liberal modernity and castigated any Catholic intellectual or even prelate deemed insufficiently papalist. Ultramontanism, in contrast to conciliarism, had been a theo-political position for centuries. But a popular ultramontane *movement* was a new phenomenon. Aided by a pugnacious press and dovetailing with styles of architecture (neo-Gothic) and devotion (warmly Marian), the ultramontane movement captured the hearts of zealous priests, missionaries, and laypeople around Europe.[1]

Much of this ultramontane ethos, and its propensity for shotgun-blast–style invective, now seems bitter and intellectually narrow. This attitude produced Pius IX's *Syllabus of Errors* (1864), an infamous list of complaints against modernity. However, ultramontanism should be credited with fostering resolute Catholic subcultures in Europe and around the world. The spiritual energies cultivated or formulated for the first time by this "ultramontane revival" were powerful.[2] For example, Pius IX tapped into the widespread devotion to the Virgin Mary—complete with statues, apparitions, and miraculous healings—that enjoyed a zenith in the nineteenth century. In 1854, the pope dogmatically "defined" that Mary had been conceived without original sin, a long-held Catholic belief that had never been formally taught at this highest level. Marian devotion served as a boundary marker vis-à-vis Protestants and secularists. The Mother of God's images and titles often held implicit political or ideological connotations (as did the popular Sacred Heart of Jesus devotion). But probably most importantly, the 1854 definition served as a test run for the dogma of papal infallibility. Also marking the ultramontane movement was a *personal* devotion to the pope that went far beyond abstract respect for the office. For the first time, portraits of the pope graced living rooms and kitchens.[3]

---

1. O'Malley, *Vatican I*; Chadwick, *History of the Popes*; Schatz, *Vaticanum I*.
2. McGreevy, *Catholicism*, 29–108.
3. Duffy, *Saints and Sinners*, 291–93.

In December of 1869, Pius IX convened an ecumenical council: that is, a gathering of all the world's Catholic bishops to deliberate and legislate with and under the pope. It was the first in over three hundred years. This First Vatican Council rebuked rationalism and all forms of state interference in church matters. In July 1870, the council defined that the pope could, under certain circumstances, teach a doctrine infallibly (or without error), even without the consent of the other bishops. This was a crushing blow to the remnants of the once-mighty Gallican and conciliarist traditions, which emphasized the pope as the head of the episcopal college, but not as absolute. In the political realm, governments around the world were on alert. Anxious to soften the blow, nervous intellectuals like the English convert John Henry Newman (1801–90) minimized the new teaching as much as possible, emphasizing its limits and the primordial rights of conscience. This was a crucial endeavor in culture-war–riven France as well as in anti-Catholic societies like Victorian England and Kulturkampf Germany.[4]

To observe that the papacy had recovered some ground since Pope Pius VI died in a French prison in 1799 would be quite the understatement. Cardinal Henry Edward Manning (1808–92), another (very different) convert from Anglicanism, now boasted that "ultramontanism is Catholic Christianity"—an assertion that would have been laughed at in the eighteenth century.[5] Nevertheless, the infallibility proclamation had a compensatory feel in the face of the end of the temporal power. The papal states, a sovereign domain in central Italy that had existed in some form for over a millennium, fell to the forces of Risorgimento (Italian national unification). Italian armies ended Vatican I's deliberations, and the infallible Pius IX lived out his days a (self-imposed) prisoner of the Vatican.

The next pope, Leo XIII (reigned 1878–1903), was no less the old-style autocrat, but he was far more prudent and intellectually subtle. Pius IX had harshly rebuked Catholics liberals who advocated for a "free church in a free state," like Count Montalembert. Leo, on the other hand, had learned the lessons of the era of Kulturkampf and Risorgimento. He encouraged Catholics to make the best of whatever state they lived in, and even directed French Catholics—particularly prone to reactionary intransigence and monarchist nostalgia as a counter to aggressive French secularism—to "rally" to the republic. While traditionalists felt betrayed, Leo's policy of *ralliement* evinced the power of a pragmatic Catholicism that could face the new pluralistic reality, and then carefully curate its own subculture within it. This ability

---

4. Howard, *Pope and the Professor*; O'Gara, *Triumph in Defeat*.
5. Cited in Blanchard, "Settling Old Scores," 51.

was pivotal to the institutional success and growth of modern Catholicism, from Cologne and Liverpool to Beijing and Sydney.

The age of Leo XIII inaugurated a conservative and clericalist Catholic modernization. While Catholic leaders rejected socialism, not least since it threatened church property and autonomy, they also became wary of an unrestrained capitalism that was exploiting the working masses. Heeding good counsel from people who knew the harsh on-the-ground realities of life in industrial Europe, Leo published the encyclical *Rerum Novarum* (1891). It was paternalistic, and in places fanciful and unrealistic. Nevertheless, it had real moral vision, and sanctioned a distinctively Catholic social teaching, undergirded by networks of lay and clerical activists and, later, by the burgeoning new tradition of papal social encyclicals. The latter paved the way for the quite recent phenomenon of the pope speaking as a global moral voice: from Paul VI's pleas before the UN for an end to war (1964) to Pope Francis's addresses on climate change.

Author of eighty-six encyclicals, Leo XIII was not shy about asserting his authority on all manner of topics. The Catholic Church knew best on all matters, and the pope could speak for it directly. Nevertheless, Leo XIII valued good scholarship and critical minds. He made Newman a cardinal, opened the Vatican archives, and promoted Scripture scholarship and personal Bible reading. While Leo shared his predecessors' bleak evaluation of modern thought, he was proactive, and asserted an alternative in answer. The encyclical *Aeterni Patris* (1879) ushered in the hegemony of "neo-scholasticism" as the reigning theological and philosophical system for Catholics. This system, which relied upon a revamped Thomism (referring to the medieval scholar-monk Thomas Aquinas), had the strength of providing an intellectual framework for global Catholicism and a shared system for seminary education. But this neo-scholasticism had some glaring drawbacks. One was that it tended to rest on a classical worldview that struggled to integrate historically conscious scholarship.

The next pope, Pius X (reigned 1903–14) was in the mold of his most recent namesake. For Pius X, the church was under assault not just from without but also from within, by a shadowy and ill-defined force called "modernism." In response, Pius X, who had the strengths but also the limitations of a simple pastor, launched a relentless campaign against any hint of "modernism" in the Catholic Church. This crusade quickly spun out of control, degrading into a witch hunt. While there were a few figures who had strayed far from any semblance of traditional Christianity (e.g., the French biblical critic Alfred Loisy), anti-modernism cast a pall over Catholic scholarship just when it needed to reckon honestly with philosophical developments and new critical methods.[6]

And yet, as is to be expected, paranoia and repression were far from the whole story. Pius X was effective in carrying forward an "anti-modern modernization" of the Catholic Church.[7] Though he was deeply autocratic and clericalist, the pope empowered the laity through lowering the age of first communion and promoting frequent communion. The forces that grouped under the term *Catholic Action* were also beginning to take shape. These lay initiatives, though firmly under the oversight of the clergy, were a dynamic force within a Catholic subculture that was becoming more socially and politically aware and active.

The Church between War and Totalitarianism (1914–58)

Ironically, nationalists had been suspicious of Catholicism for the same reasons that early modern "reform Catholics" had persecuted the Jesuits: their international character, ultramontanism, and potential to form a subversive "state within a state." World War I, however cataclysmic for Christian Europe overall, helped reconcile Catholics with their respective nation-states.[8] French clergy, subject to conscription under the anticlerical laws of the Third Republic that Pius X had so vehemently denounced, earned the respect and love of their countrymen for fighting bravely. English Catholics, suspected of divided loyalty since the Reformation, proved they were every bit as patriotic as their fellows.[9]

The archbishop of Bologna, Giacomo della Chiesa, was unfortunate enough to be elected Pope Benedict XV in the apocalyptic year of 1914. A man of peace, he strenuously sought reconciliation between the competing powers, which earned him few political friends. He also sought peace within the church, ending the anti-modernist McCarthyism and rebuking those who added a modifier to "Catholic" to further denominate themselves (checking the growing fad of styling oneself an "integralist" Catholic, that is, comprehensively anti-liberal).

Though papal infallibility still dominates discussion, another teaching of Vatican I has had far more practical importance: the pope's essentially unlimited jurisdictional authority over the entire church. The fruit of this teaching became enshrined a half-century later in the 1917 Code of Canon

6. Wolf, *Antimodernismus und Modernismus*.
7. Arnold, "Authority and Integralism," 36.
8. McGreevy, *Catholicism*, 134.
9. Jenkins, *Great and Holy War*.

Law, which confirmed that the pope had the right to appoint all the world's bishops (another prerogative unthinkable as late as the eighteenth century).[10] While this papal centralization had obvious problems, it did allow forward-thinking popes to take decisive action for the good of the growing global church. For example, Benedict XV sincerely believed that Catholicism was universal and thus not coterminous with European ethnicities, ideas, or customs. He published the missionary encyclical *Maximum Illud* (1919), which advanced the indigenization of the clergy and aided inculturation. The next pope, Pius XI, consecrated six Chinese bishops and one Indian.[11]

Like the rest of European society, the Catholic Church reeled under the political turmoil and instability of the interwar period. Pius XI, elected in 1922, was a formidable character, willing to butt heads with the powers of the day. Judging that the far-right *Action Française* movement was co-opting the gospel, Pius XI condemned it. *Action Française* was led by the nonbelieving anti-Semite Charles Maurras (1868–1952), but Pius XI's condemnation still made many "integralist" Catholic indignant.[12] A French cardinal, Louis Billot (1846–1931), even handed in his red hat.

When Pius XI rebuked grasping state totalitarianisms in *Quas Primas*, a 1925 encyclical that established the Feast of Christ the King, he primarily had enemies from the left in mind. In the wake of the Russian revolution, the pope and many other Catholic leaders became totally absorbed with anti-Communism. The alleged appearance of the Virgin Mary in Fatima (Portugal), and her calls to pray for "the conversion of Russia," helped bring anti-Communism to the pews. A consuming fear of Communism led to a "the enemy of my enemy is my friend" mentality, paving the way for dalliances with dangerous bedfellows. Though not initially friendly with Benito Mussolini, Pius XI ultimately came to an agreement with his Fascist regime. Practical ties were strengthened by a concordat, or bilateral political agreement, in February 1929. Pius XI was, understandably, anxious to resolve the "Roman question" that had bedeviled relations between the church and the Italian state since Pius IX's intransigence in the face of Risorgimento a half-century earlier.[13] But in succumbing to a thug like Mussolini, Pius XI sacrificed moral credibility (for example, he did not condemn Italy's cruel and pointless invasion of Ethiopia).[14] Fascists were certainly reliably anti-Communist, but they would ultimately tolerate no challengers or

10. McGreevy, *Catholicism*, 322.
11. McGreevy, *Catholicism*, 159–61; Duffy, *Saints and Sinners*, 337.
12. Weber, *Action Française*.
13. Kertzer, *Pope and Mussolini*.
14. Duffy, *Saints and Sinners*, 342.

counter-narratives. Thus, Mussolini required that the pope throw the Catholic political party, Fr. Luigi Sturzo's *Partito Populare*, under the bus.

Similar dynamics played out in Germany, where a fascist dictator of far more consequence than Mussolini had arisen. While Pius XI sought to preserve Catholic Action, he was willing to sacrifice the Catholic *Zentrum* Party if it meant peace with Adolf Hitler's increasingly hegemonic Nazi Party.[15] A *Reichskonkordat* with Germany was thus signed in 1933, after skillful negotiations led by a diligent papal diplomat named Eugenio Pacelli. Though National Socialism had some Catholic elements in its origins,[16] Hitler's totalizing ideology rejected any other mediating power structure in the Reich. Ultimately, everything needed to be totally subjected to the Führer.

It should have surprised no one when Hitler began to systematically violate the concordat. Pius XI was furious. He penned a searing attack on the Nazi regime and had it smuggled into Germany and read from every pulpit on Palm Sunday, 1937. The only encyclical ever written in German, *Mit brennender Sorge* (With burning anxiety), condemned Hitler's betrayals of the church and Nazi racial doctrine, though in general terms. Anti-Semitism was not named. Pius XI geared up for more confrontation with the German dictator he had come to loathe. He solicited an encyclical on the evils of racism from some Jesuit theologians, but died before it could be published. The next pope shelved the idea.

Cardinal Pacelli, the former papal diplomat to Germany, was elected in 1939 as the Second World War broke out. He took the name Pius, though he adopted a far less confrontational stance than his fiery predecessor.[17] Accused of being "Hitler's pope" by his foes, and christened a saint by his followers, Pius XII was neither. He was a deeply cautious man caught in a harrowing situation. Though he viewed Hitler as an enemy and saved many Jews from certain death, Pius XII failed to deliver the kind of prophetic denunciation of Nazism that might very well have thundered from the Vatican had Pius XI lived a little bit longer.[18]

There was an abundance of Catholic intellectual ferment in the interwar period among artists, writers, philosophers, theologians, activists, and politicians.[19] Catholics took comfort in ancient traditions, but they were by no means deaf to the need to adapt to changing realities. For example, some French clergy launched a "Worker Priest" movement, living among the

15. Duffy, *Saints and Sinners*, 340–41.
16. Hastings, *Catholicism and the Roots*.
17. Ventresca, *Soldier of Christ*.
18. Ventresca, *Soldier of Christ*; Kertzer, *Pope at War*.
19. Baring, *Converts to the Real*; Schloesser, *Jazz Age Catholicism*.

people they hoped to serve. These priests took up working-class occupations to better understand the average French person, remove unnecessary social or cultural barriers, and consequently better share the gospel. This missionary experiment was eventually suppressed by conservatives in the hierarchy.

Pius XII's relation to reform is not easy to generalize. He continued, even advanced, a triumphalistic view of papal authority. For Pius XII, no subject was too arcane for papal deliberation and comment. He addressed not only politicians and soldiers, but midwives and even beekeepers, careful to read up on the latest scholarship before he spoke. Aided by the radio, Pius XII was more directly the "ordinary and immediate pastor" (cf. Vatican I) of all Catholics than any prior pope. But he was also scholarly, and not closed off to cautious reform. For example, Pius XII restored a more ancient way of celebrating the Easter Triduum services that is now beloved by Catholics. He softened rhetoric on non-Catholics, and rebuked an American Jesuit who claimed only Catholics could reach heaven. But this openness had firm limits, and in the 1950 encyclical *Humani Generis*, Pius XII sternly cautioned those "new" theologians who his advisors feared were covert Modernists. Those chastened were soon vindicated at the largest meeting in the history of the world.[20]

"Letting in Fresh Air": Pope John XXIII and Vatican II (1958–65)

The disarmingly charming Angelo Roncalli (1881–1963) was not the most likely candidate to instigate revolutionary change in the Catholic Church. Roncalli, the plump and elderly patriarch (archbishop) of Venice was elected Pope John XXIII in 1958. Most expected he would give the church a breather. The world—not to mention the cardinals listening to him—was accordingly shocked when Roncalli, a few months after his election, announced that he intended to convene an ecumenical council. Held from 1962 to 1965 in four autumn sessions of about three months each, the Second Vatican Council ultimately produced sixteen documents on a vast range of topics. It is not an exaggeration to consider Vatican II the most important event in the life of European Catholicism since the French Revolution, or even the Reformation.[21]

John XXIII aimed to renew the Catholic people and to initiate an "ecumenical" dialogue with the "separated brethren"—that is, with non-Catholic

---

20. O'Malley, *What Happened at Vatican II*.

21. See O'Malley, *What Happened at Vatican II*; Alberigo and Komonchak, *History of Vatican II*.

Christians like Protestants and the Eastern Orthodox. Tightly connected to this agenda were serious concerns about evangelization and the church's credibility. The pope and many others feared, not without evidence, that the Catholic Church was losing its ability to communicate the gospel to modern people. While there were many signs of growth and vitality in Europe and globally, astute Catholics sensed an oncoming crisis when they considered how irrelevant the faith had become in some former heartlands. The title of a book cowritten by two French priests, *La France, pays de mission?* (Is France missionary territory?), succinctly captures these concerns.[22] The fact that such a book could be written as early as 1943 complicates any tidy *post hoc, ergo propter hoc* narrative surrounding Vatican II and decline of European Catholic practice. The successes and failures of Vatican II are central when taking stock of contemporary Catholicism, demographically or otherwise.[23] However, in the European context, Vatican II should be seen as part of an attempted response to a secularization of society that was already advancing.

The European and global backdrop of the 1960s sheds light on the multifaceted and interconnected questions addressed at Vatican II. The council opened on October 11, 1962, a mere seventeen years after World War II. In the thick of the Cold War, Catholic anti-Communism ran as deep as ever, but the violence and persecution unleashed by fascist regimes made many Catholics wary of any totalitarianisms, even those that combated Communism and promised to protect the church through concordats. John XXIII condemned atheistic systems but refused to enlist in the culture war polemics between Soviet and Western blocs. He even made friendly overtures to Soviet Premier Nikita Khrushchev.[24] Pope John's encyclical *Mater et Magistra* (1961) raised conservative eyebrows: it read more like a commendation of a Christian democratic socialism than the virulent anti-Communism and old-style paternalistic conservatism of recent popes.

After World War II, thinkers like the dynamic couple Jacques (1882–1973) and Raïssa Maritain (1883–1960), long popular among liberal Catholics in Europe and the Americas, moved from the periphery to the center of Catholic intellectual life.[25] Jacques Maritain advocated for an "integral Christian humanism" that resisted secularism while championing liberalism and democracy. Partly out of a concern for the credibility of the church in the "developing world," European Catholic leaders increasingly

---

22. Godin and Daniel, *France, pays de mission?*
23. Bullivant, *Mass Exodus.*
24. Duffy, *Saints and Sinners*, 356.
25. Moore, *Kindred Spirits.*

supported decolonization and independence. For African Catholic leaders like the Francophone Léopold Senghor (1906–2001), the first president of Senegal, the cause of African political autonomy was "inseparable from native leadership in the church."[26]

When John XXIII used one of his favorite buzzwords, *aggiornamento*, he was talking about bringing Catholicism "up to date" in light of these pluriform realities. Combined with *ad extra* (external) concerns and impulses was another reformist current within mid-century Catholicism called *ressourcement*.[27] This tendency wanted to go backwards, not forwards—to reach behind Counter-Reformation ecclesiology and ultramontane neo-scholasticism to purportedly more pure sources of Catholic faith and life. For some thinkers, this could mean reading Aquinas in his own words and within his own context, rather than filtered through commentaries and interpretive traditions that they saw as stagnant or distortive. For all *ressourcement* thinkers, the Bible and the ancient church fathers formed the indispensable foundations for theological thinking. Closely linked were concerns that the church's liturgy needed reform and that Catholics had a duty to present their faith to other Christians along lines that were less triumphalistic and more ecumenical.

Ressourcement was a global Catholic phenomenon. But its leaders were mainly clerical and mainly European: French Jesuits and Dominicans, German priests in Munich and Tübingen, Belgians at Louvain, Europeans studying Scripture at the *École Biblique* in Jerusalem.[28] *Ressourcement* was suspected of neo-modernism under Pius XII, but so was John XXIII, as the new pope was amused to discover when he accessed his secret file in the Vatican's Holy Office. Out from under the cloud of Roman suspicion and thrust into the limelight, *ressourcement* theologians formed the reformist vanguard during Vatican II. Figures like the French Dominican Yves Congar (1904–95) and the German priest Joseph Ratzinger (1927–2022) advised key bishops and authored many speeches. *Ressourcement* theologians guided the production of Vatican II's documents.

Remarkably, given the makeup of previous ecumenical councils, fewer than half of the 2800 bishops who attended Vatican II were from Europe.[29] Still, European theologians had an oversized influence on the proceedings. So too did high-ranking European churchmen, especially Italians, many of whom staffed key positions in the Roman Curia. Vatican II can

---

26. McGreevy, *Catholicism*, 249.
27. Flynn and Murray, *Ressourcement*.
28. Mettepenningen, *Nouvelle Théologie*.
29. Duffy, *Saints and Sinners*, 359.

still, however, lay claim to being the first global ecumenical council. Middle Eastern bishops delivered pivotal addresses in French, refusing to speak Latin as a nod to the equality of their ancient Melkite (non-Roman) expression of Catholicism. A US Jesuit, John Courtney Murray (1904–67), was an architect of the landmark decree promoting religious liberty, *Dignitatis Humanae*, a stunning departure from Pius X's anti-modernism and the spirit of Pius IX's *Syllabus of Errors*. Latin American bishops were key players in both the reformist majority bloc and among the traditionalist minority. Groups of African bishops delivered requests and offered amendments. But the globalization of Catholic leadership was far from complete. For example, only 20 percent of the 311 African bishops at Vatican II were native born (as opposed to missionary clergy). By the 1970s, however, a majority of African bishops were native born.[30]

Let us briefly survey some of the most important results of the council. The bishops voted overwhelmingly for liturgical reform in the first document promulgated, *Sacrosanctum Concilium*. Before Vatican II, the Mass was for the most part in Latin, with the priest facing away from the people and toward the altar. After Vatican II, the Mass became a predominantly vernacular affair in which the people were encouraged to vocally participate. Priests faced the congregation, with the altar between them.

A second major document, *Dei Verbum*, used *ressourcement* theology to restate Catholic theology in a way that moved away from the neoscholastic status quo. With this shift came an emphasis on personal Bible reading, an embrace of ecumenism, and, probably most radically, a recognition that Catholic doctrine develops in a dynamic and not merely syllogistic manner. Put simply, the Catholic Church at Vatican II accepted that change was not only sometimes acceptable, it could even be a sign of life and vitality—principles that Cardinal Newman had embraced in nineteenth-century Oxford when he wrestled with historical consciousness.

The latter sessions of the council, in 1964 and 1965, were dominated by debates over the nature and mission of the church (ecclesiology) and the relationship between the church and those outside it. A third key document called *Lumen Gentium* tried to sketch a kind of constitution for the modern church in which the laity were coworkers with the ordained clergy, and the pope exercised his supreme authority "collegially" with the college of bishops he headed.

A fourth major document, *Gaudium et Spes*, was an unwieldy manifesto on the church in the modern world. It addressed the sorts of things that popes weighed in on in social encyclicals, from the economy to sex

---

30. McGreevy, *Catholicism*, 371.

and marriage to modern warfare. These four texts were the foundations undergirding shorter documents drafted to tackle specific problems. For example, *Nostra Aetate*, a "declaration" addressed to non-Christians, included an extended reflection on the Jewish people and a sincere rejection of all prejudice and persecution. Such a statement was hotly debated for a number of reasons, one of them being the political complications caused by the recent establishment of the state of Israel. But in the wake of the Holocaust, Catholics, especially Europeans, were forced to reckon with centuries of anti-Semitism perpetuated by Christians and Christian institutions.[31]

When the council closed on December 8, 1965, most of the Catholic world looked on the achievements of Vatican II with a sense of hope and excitement. The pace of change was exhilarating, but also could be unsettling. Unfortunately for a church that boasts stability and timelessness as calling cards, the rest of the 1960s and the 1970s would be anything but tranquil for European Catholicism.

The Postconciliar Church: European Decline, Global Growth (1965–Present)

European Catholics did not have much time to catch their breaths. The pace of liturgical change, which in some places went beyond what church authorities had authorized, fittingly symbolized the speed of broader changes sweeping through European society in the 1960s.[32] While most Vatican II reforms had long been gestating, for the average person in the pew the impact of the before-and-after was seismic.

The first four decades of postconciliar Catholicism were led by two very different popes: first Paul VI, and then Karol Wojtyla reigned as John Paul II from 1978 to 2005 (Albino Luciani, elected in 1978 as John Paul I, died after a month). Paul VI, formerly Cardinal Montini of Milan, was elected before the council's second session, when John XXIII succumbed to cancer in June 1963. Montini was a cautious proponent of *aggiornamento* and respected figures like Maritain. But he also had a very high view of papal authority and was unafraid of offending contemporary sensibilities if he believed a nonnegotiable Catholic truth was at stake. And so, in 1968, Pope Paul reaffirmed the traditional ban on "artificial" birth control, even though a papally appointed committee had recommended a change in church teaching. Paul's encyclical *Humanae Vitae* sparked widespread discontent, especially in North America and Western Europe. Large groups

31. Connelly, *From Enemy to Brother*.
32. Harris and Ryan, *Sink or Swim*.

of clergy dissented from the ruling, married couples mostly ignored it, and even some bishops made their discomfort known, not least with the unilateral nature of the judgment (the bishops at Vatican II were instructed by the pope not to debate birth control, nor were they to debate clerical celibacy).[33]

While postconciliar European Catholicism harbored bitter reactionaries and manic revolutionaries, the great majority of Catholics were neither. Most laypeople and their priests approved of the fundamental elements of the new liturgy and appreciated many Vatican II reforms. In these ways, the *aggiornamento* of the council was a success. But the main problem facing European Catholicism was far more basic: a rising secularization that was challenging all forms of traditional religion. The church struggled mightily to meet it.

Connected with the indigenization of the clergy was the globalization of Catholic theology. Europeans, however, were often directly involved in developments outside of Europe, often through the influence of educational institutions (e.g., Louvain, Tübingen) and the Roman ecclesiastical center. Additionally, some of the most prominent liberation theologians were European born and educated before spending decades in Latin America. Jon Sobrino SJ (b. 1938) hailed from Basque Spain, while José Comblin (1923–2011) was born Joseph in Brussels. Jacques Dupuis SJ (1923–2004), one of the foremost scholars of religious pluralism, was born in Belgium and died in Rome. However, Dupuis's thought was profoundly shaped by the thirty-six years he spent as a Jesuit missionary in India. Finally, probably the most famous Catholic woman of the twentieth-century, Mother Theresa (1910–97), was born Anjezë Gonxhe Bojaxhiu in Albania before ministering to the poorest of the poor in India.

John Paul II (Karol Wojtyla), the first non-Italian elected pope since 1522, promoted the legacy of Vatican II and was enthusiastic about many conciliar developments. However, the Polish pope and his close confidante Cardinal Ratzinger were deeply disturbed by what they saw as a rising tide of "relativism" that undercut the philosophical and moral claims of Christianity. Such a mindset became manifest in popular acceptance of divorce, birth control, abortion, homosexuality, and euthanasia (to different degrees). This emphasis put the Catholic hierarchy—a body that answered to and was shaped by the pope—increasingly at odds with European society, including with many Catholics in the pews and some clergy. The general accord that Catholic leaders felt with an array of centrist or Christian Democratic parties earlier in the century—Konrad Adenauer's CDU (*Christlich*

---

33. Harris, *Schism of '68*.

Demokratische Union) in Germany,[34] the *Mouvement Républicain Populaire* active in Charles DeGaulle's France, Italy's *Democrazia Cristiana*—felt like an increasingly distant and possibly irrecoverable past in the face of a new gulf between the church and European societies.

Questions of gender and sexuality increasingly came to the surface within the Catholic Church as well. Though female participation at Vatican II was extremely limited, it was not entirely absent, and the council had set in motion a conversation about women's roles that, when combined with societal change, proved considerable. Like their male counterparts, the number of women religious (nuns and sisters) in Europe was declining, in some places precipitously. However, women were increasingly seeking, and receiving, advanced theological educations. As a result, a distinctly feminist theology arose. Today, the English-speaking world in particular boasts numerous leading feminist Catholic theologians, like the long-time Oxford scholar Janet Soskice (b. 1951). Catholic women now chair theology departments and sit on pontifical commissions. The official barrier to women's ordination to the priesthood was emphatically restated by John Paul II in 1994. This papal intervention was not positively received in many European contexts, and it also stirred up more general debates regarding ecclesial power and decision-making.

John Paul II's pontificate, which lasted over a quarter of a century, evidenced the enduring vitality of modern Catholicism as well an ominous gathering of dark clouds. On the positive side of the ledger, Wojtyla's magnetic presence provided moral authority and confident leadership to rally around. "World Youth Day" bonanzas drew screaming crowds in the six and seven figures. Many devout young Catholics attributed their vocations to the inspiring figure of John Paul II. Wojtyla's spirit was probably best evidenced in his tenacious and effective support of anti-Soviet efforts, especially in Poland.

But his celebrity pontificate also masked seriously destabilizing problems. John Paul tended to trust those who advanced his ecclesio-political agenda, be they fearless evangelizers, staunch anti-Communists, or charismatic leaders of new movements. The most infamous case of mistaken trust is the awful story of Fr. Marcial Maciel Degollado, founder of the Legionaries of Christ and Regnum Christi movements. Though evidence mounted that Maciel was a sociopathic sexual abuser and cultlike manipulator, John Paul II, to his death, refused to take action against his friend. Though Maciel was finally sidelined by Ratzinger (soon after Wojtyla's death), the continued existence of the movements founded by this criminal to ease the perpetuation

---

34. Mitchell, *Origins of Christian Democracy*.

of his cruelties makes it difficult to credit Vatican claims to take seriously the full dimensions of the abuse crisis.

Over the twentieth century, European Catholicism has undergone something of a demographic reversal vis-à-vis the rest of the global church. In 1910, two-thirds of the world's 290 million Catholics lived in Europe. By the year 2000, this ratio had flipped.[35] When Cardinal Ratzinger was elected pope in 2005, his choice of the name Benedict illustrated his profound concern in the face of this decline (St. Benedict is the patron of Europe). Ratzinger was immersed in the European intellectual tradition and eagerly read and appreciated works by Jews, Protestants, and atheists. The newly elected Pope Benedict XVI called for a fresh dialogue on faith and reason; he hoped for a renewed appreciation for Europe's Christian and Catholic roots in the face of challenges from Islam and secularism. Despite the German pope's many admirable intellectual and spiritual qualities, such a program cannot be said to have succeeded. The depths of the sex abuse crisis and cover-up were only beginning to be grasped upon the death of John Paul II. Amid some signs of hope and recovery, Mass attendance and religious vocations continued to drop. Credible rumors of widespread corruption among Vatican cliques were only further confirmed. Ever the academic, Ratzinger knew that the pope technically could resign. In February 2013, Benedict XVI shocked the world when he became the first pope to resign in six hundred years (and that earlier instance was hardly voluntary).

Ratzinger's resignation made way for the election of Pope Francis, the first bishop of Rome born outside Europe since the eighth century. Jorge Mario Bergoglio (b. 1936), former archbishop of Buenos Aires, is also the first Jesuit pope. A son of Italian immigrants, Bergoglio is marked by his global religious order and by a distinctively Argentinian style of Catholicism. Though he defends unpopular Catholic teachings on sex and gender, Francis's emphasis on environmentalism, poverty, and immigration—marked by his experience in South America—has opened up points of dialogue with modern European society. Within the church in Europe, the most important facet of Francis's agenda is his promotion of "synodality"—that is, a process of ecclesial discernment and deliberation at all levels, from laypeople in the pews to national churches to Rome. How such a process can exist vis-à-vis Vatican I's view of the papacy (substantially reaffirmed on many points by Vatican II) is unclear. But what is clear is that ultramontanism can and has taken "liberal" forms,[36] even if Francis balks at the radical agenda that synodality is taking in some European nations (e.g., Germany).

---

35. McGreevy, *Catholicism*, 136.
36. Portier, "Unintended Ultramontanism."

Conclusion

Pope Francis's calls for "synodality" are, at their theological root, attempts to recover biblical and patristic models after centuries of Counter-Reformation theology and ultramontane ecclesiology. Practically, however, they are attempts to square two perplexing circles: the relationship between the laity and the clergy, and the relationship between local churches and Rome. Vatican II began this process, but by no means completed it. The myriad questions that have been raised during the synodal process Pope Francis has called for will not be answered, it is safe to say, during Francis's pontificate, which is probably in its twilight. But the first Jesuit pope has done what he said he would do: "make a mess" (¡Hagan lío!). The task of ordering that mess could very well fall to a Third Vatican Council. At a Vatican III, it is likely that European theologians, bishops, and institutions would not play a dominant role at an ecumenical council for the first time in over a millennium—with, of course, the notable exception of the Roman papacy.

Bibliography

Alberigo, Giuseppe, and Joseph Komonchak, eds. *History of Vatican II*. 5 vols. Maryknoll, NY: Orbis, 1995–2006.
Arnold, Claus. "Authority and Integralism in Pius X." *ET-Studies* 13 (2022) 23–40.
———. *Kleine Geschichte des Modernismus*. Freiburg im Breisgau: Herder, 2007.
Baring, Edward. *Converts to the Real: Catholicism and the Making of Continental Philosophy*. Cambridge: Harvard University Press, 2019.
Blanchard, Shaun. "Settling Old Scores: *Pastor Aeternus* as the Final Defeat of Early Modern Opponents of Papalism." *Newman Studies Journal* 17 (2020) 24–51.
Blanchard, Shaun, and Stephen Bullivant. *Vatican II: A Very Short Introduction*. Oxford: Oxford University Press, 2023.
Bullivant, Stephen. *Mass Exodus: Catholic Disaffiliation in Britain and America since Vatican II*. Oxford: Oxford University Press, 2019.
Chadwick, Owen. *A History of the Popes 1830–1914*. Oxford: Oxford University Press, 1973.
Connelly, John. *From Enemy to Brother: The Revolution in Catholic Teaching on the Jews, 1933–1965*. Cambridge: Harvard University Press, 2012.
Duffy, Eamon. *Saints and Sinners: A History of the Popes*. 2nd ed. New Haven: Yale University Press, 2006.
Flynn, Gabriel, and Paul D. Murray, eds. *Ressourcement: A Movement for Renewal in Twentieth-Century Catholic Theology*. Oxford: Oxford University Press, 2012.
Godin, Henri, and Yvan Daniel. *La France, pays de mission?* Lyon: Abeille, 1943.
Harris, Alana, ed. *The Schism of '68: Catholicism, Contraception, and Humanae Vitae in Europe, 1945–1975*. Genders and Sexualities in History. New York: Palgrave MacMillan, 2018.

Harris, Alana, and Isabel Ryan. *Sink or Swim: Catholicism in Sixties Britain through John Ryan's Cartoons*. Durham, UK: Sacristy, 2020.

Hastings, Derek. *Catholicism and the Roots of Nazism: Religious Identity and National Socialism*. Oxford: Oxford University Press, 2011.

Howard, Thomas Albert. *The Pope and the Professor: Pius IX, Ignaz von Döllinger, and the Quandary of the Modern Age*. Oxford: Oxford University Press, 2017.

Jenkins, Philip. *The Great and Holy War: How World War I Became a Religious Crusade*. New York: HarperCollins, 2015.

Kertzer, David I. *The Pope and Mussolini: The Secret History of Pius XI and the Rise of Fascism in Europe*. New York: Random House, 2015.

———. *The Pope at War: The Secret History of Pius XII, Mussolini, and Hitler*. Oxford: Oxford University Press, 2022.

McGreevy, John T. *Catholicism: A Global History from the French Revolution to Pope Francis*. New York: Norton, 2022.

Mettepenningen, Jürgen. *Nouvelle Théologie—New Theology: Inheritor of Modernism, Precursor of Vatican II*. London: T. & T. Clark, 2010.

Mitchell, Maria D. *The Origins of Christian Democracy: Politics and Confession in Modern Germany*. Ann Arbor: University of Michigan Press, 2012.

Moore, Brenna. *Kindred Spirits: Friendship and Resistance at the Edges of Modern Catholicism*. Class 200: New Studies in Religion. Chicago: University of Chicago Press, 2021.

O'Gara, Margaret. *Triumph in Defeat: Infallibility, Vatican I, and the French Minority Bishops*. Washington, DC: Catholic University Press, 1988.

O'Malley, John. *Vatican I: The Council and the Making of the Ultramontane Church* Cambridge: Harvard University Press, 2018.

———. *What Happened at Vatican II*. Cambridge: Belknap, 2008.

Perreau-Saussine, Emile. *Catholicism and Democracy: An Essay in the History of Political Thought*. Princeton: Princeton University Press, 2012.

Portier, William L. "Unintended Ultramontanism." *Theological Studies* 83 (2022) 54–69.

Schatz, Klaus. *Vaticanum I, 1869–1870*. 3 vols. Paderborn, Germ.: Schöningh, 1992–94.

Schloesser, Stephen. *Jazz Age Catholicism: Mystic Modernism in Postwar Paris, 1919–1933*. Toronto: University of Toronto Press, 2005.

Ventresca, Robert. *Soldier of Christ: The Life of Pope Pius XII*. Cambridge: Harvard University Press, 2013.

Weber, Eugen. *Action Française: Royalism and Reaction in Twentieth-Century France*. Stanford: Stanford University Press, 1962.

Wolf, Hubert, ed. *Antimodernismus und Modernismus in der Katholischen Kirche: Beiträge zum Theologiegeschichtlichen Vorfeld des II. Vatikanums*. Paderborn: Schöningh, 1998.

7

The Protestant Story: National and Territorial Churches

Charlotte Methuen

PROTESTANT EUROPE SINCE THE sixteenth century has been characterized by national—or in some cases territorial—churches, through which political identity and ecclesiastical identity have been closely intertwined. Names of churches such as the Church of England or the Church of Sweden (*Svenska Kyrkan*), or in Germany the Evangelical Church in Hesse and Nassau (*Evangelische Kirche in Hessen und Nassau*) and the Evangelical Church of Kurhessen-Waldeck (*Evangelische Kirche von Kurhessen-Waldeck*), assign churches the names of political jurisdictions, some of which are still in existence while others are not. Many such church names include no indication of a confessional allegiance, although some do, such as the Estonian Evangelical Lutheran Church (*Eesti Evangeelne Luterlik Kirik*), the Dutch Reformed Church (*Nederlandse Hervormde Kerk*), or the Evangelical Lutheran Church of Denmark (*den Evangelisk-Lutherske Kirke i Danmark*), generally known as the *folkekirke*, literally "the people's church." These churches were intended to be precisely that: the church of an entire nation or territory. They were often closely integrated into the political structures of the nation or territory (that is, they were established churches) to the extent that in some cases they were state churches. They generally had their roots in what is known as the magisterial or princely Reformation, introduced by a local ruler or city council.

However, the Reformation often brought into sharp focus already existing differences and tensions. This chapter begins by describing regional and national differences in the Western Church in the pre-Reformation period. It then explores how during the sixteenth century these shaped national and territorial churches in four geographical areas: the German territories, the Nordic countries, England and Scotland, and the Netherlands. Subsequent developments are then outlined, including trends towards disestablishment. European national and territorial states took different forms, as exemplified by the areas considered.

Regional Aspects of the Pre-Reformation Western Church[1]

The pre-Reformation Western Church was not a monolithic institution. There was much local variation in liturgical practice, but also in other aspects of church life, including what is now known as church-state relations (or more precisely in this period the relationship between spiritual and secular power). These relationships were specific to particular nations or territories, with important implications for the emergence of national and territorial Protestant Churches during the sixteenth century.

Across Europe in the fifteenth century, bishops and archbishops, abbots of major monasteries, and sometimes also abbesses, exercised considerable political power. In many territories, holders of ecclesiastical offices were integrated into the structures of government. The clergy formed the first of the three—or sometimes four—"estates" that shaped the political structures of most Western European countries. Typically, the three estates comprised the clergy, the nobility, and bourgeoisie. Thus the late medieval Scottish parliament included clergy (bishops), nobility, and burghers. The English parliament consisted of a House of Lords, which included bishops (lords spiritual) and nobility (lords temporal), and a House of Commons. Monarchs were generally involved in the nomination and election of key church appointments, although the terms of their involvement varied across Europe.

The English monarch nominated episcopal candidates who were subsequently confirmed by papal edict; many high-ranking English churchmen simultaneously held important and powerful political offices. Thus, from 1515 Thomas Wolsey was not only cardinal archbishop of York but also chancellor of all England. King Ferdinand and Queen Isabella achieved similar powers of appointment in the newly united Spanish kingdom, and subsequently for their overseas territories. The French king Charles V had sought to restrict the powers of the papacy in France through the Pragmatic Sanction of Bourges of 1438. This was superseded in 1516 by the Concordat of Bologna negotiated by King Francis I with Pope Leo X, which gave the monarch of France the power to appoint bishops, to tax clergy, and to

---

1. For this section, see MacCulloch, *Reformation*; Methuen, "German Catholic Dioceses"; Methuen, "Ordering the Reformation Church."

restrict appeals to Rome. The pope was himself a territorial ruler, and Julian II was known for having personally led papal troops into battle.

Bishops, abbots, or abbesses ruled around half the plethora of German territories, with the remainder ruled by temporal princes; the resulting tensions contributed to the Protestant Reformation. While in England, Scotland, France, and Spain ecclesiastical dioceses lay geographically within the monarch's jurisdiction, in the German territories the geographical extent of most dioceses was larger than the territories, resulting in a particularly complex relationship between spiritual and secular or temporal power. German diocesan bishops ruled their ecclesiastical lands (*Hochstifte*) as well as exercising spiritual jurisdiction over other secular territories that lay within their dioceses. Of the seven imperial electors responsible for electing the emperor, three were spiritual princes: the archbishops of Mainz, Cologne, and Trier, together with the count of the Palatine, the duke of Saxony, the margrave of Brandenburg, and the king of Bohemia. While the four temporal electors—like most temporal German princes—were hereditary ranks, senior ecclesiastical posts were not. German bishops generally came from the nobility, for by the fifteenth century candidates for German cathedral canonries—the pool from which bishops were elected—were required to demonstrate noble birth. Nonetheless, ecclesiastical posts offered political opportunities for younger sons or for noble but less powerful families. The appointment of Albrecht of Brandenburg, the younger brother of Joachim I, elector of Brandenburg, as archbishop of Mainz, gave the Hohenzollern brothers two of the seven votes in the imperial election of 1519, while the archbishops of Trier (Richard von Greiffenklau zu Vollrads) and of Cologne (Hermann von Wied) were both fourth sons of noble families. Ecclesiastical office offered political power.

At the same time, temporal rulers were increasingly understood to exercise spiritual responsibility. The so-called "mirrors for princes" body of literature emphasized rulers' personal responsibility for their subjects' spiritual and physical well-being. Rulers—whether individuals or city councils—responded by appointing preachers and other ecclesiastical positions, founding religious orders, and establishing schools and universities to educate young men locally. The University of Tübingen was founded in 1477, in part so that Württemberg's youth would no longer have to travel to Italy or France for their education.

Spiritual and territorial interests were often closely interlinked. In the later fifteenth century dukes of Jülich-Berg rejected the authority of the archbishop of Cologne, within whose diocese Jülich-Berg lay, as a "foreign power," appointing a territorial dean (*Landesdechant*) to oversee ecclesiastical affairs. In Cleves, from 1521 united with Jülich-Berg, the duke asserted that "the duke of Cleves is pope in his own land."[2] Such assertions of spiritual responsibility, intertwined with territorial jurisdiction, formed the foundations on which the territorial churches would be established.

The German Territories[3]

The particular relationship between the German temporal rulers and the bishops provided fertile ground for the seeds of Reformation. Elector Frederick of Saxony was in conflict with the bishop of Magdeburg before Luther's appointment in 1511, to the extent that the bishop had effectively lost his jurisdiction over Wittenberg.[4] Frederick remained in control of the church in Electoral Saxony; Luther ensured that the implementation of reforming ideas and practices did not proceed faster than the elector was prepared to accept. It was only on Elector Frederick's death in 1525 and the accession of his brother John, who was sympathetic to evangelical theology, that the Reformation could be introduced into Electoral Saxony. A system of parish visitations was introduced across the territory to ensure conformity with evangelical theology and liturgical practice.

This pattern was replicated in other German and Swiss cities and territories: the Reformation was implemented under the leadership of the local prince, or at the initiative of a city council. Despite the 1521 Edict of Worms, which sought to suppress Luther's theology, Reformation ideas spread. The 1526 Diet of Speyer took a policy of toleration towards territories and imperial cities that had shown themselves sympathetic to reform. By the time of the Diet of Speyer in 1529, when the emperor sought to suppress the evangelical movement, the Reformation had been formally introduced into fourteen imperial cities (Constance, Heilbronn, Isny, Kempten, Lindau, Memmingen, Nordlingen, Nuremberg, Reutlingen, St Gall, Strasbourg, Ulm, Weissenburg, and Windsheim) and five territories (Electoral Saxony, Hesse, Brandenburg, Lüneburg, and Anhalt). Their rulers protested at the attempt to suppress evangelical religion, giving rise to the term *Protestant*.

Decisions about religion in the German territories were made territory by territory and city by city. Territories and cities generally introduced the Reformation by means of a church order, which made provisions for liturgical practices, established a poor chest, and regulated education. Each church order was specific to the particular territory, although increasingly

    2. Flüchter, *Zölibat*, 96–97.
    3. For this section, see Blickle, *Reformation im Reich*; Henke, "Toleration and Repression"; Herl, *Worship Wars*; Schindling and Ziegler, *Territorien des Reichs*.
    4. See Krentz, *Ritualwandel und Deutungshoheit*, 63–65.

the *Confessio Augustana*, presented to (and rejected by) the 1530 Diet of Augsburg, formed the foundation for statements of faith. A period of religious conflict was ended (temporarily) in 1555 through the Peace of Augsburg, which codified the principle of *cuius regio eius religio* (the religion of the territory is the religion of the ruler). The only religions to be recognized, however, were Catholicism and subscription to the *Confessio Augustana*. The growing influence within the German territories of Reformed theology and church order, led by Geneva and to a lesser extent Zurich, would not receive legal status until the conclusion of the Thirty Years' War. In 1648 the Peace of Westphalia required imperial cities to make provision for both Lutheran and Catholic worship and stipulated that the remaining spiritual territories (i.e., the bishoprics) must remain Catholic, but otherwise allowed territorial rulers to determine whether the church in their territories would be Catholic, Lutheran, or Reformed. Although there were and remained confessionally mixed areas,[5] in some territories the principle of *ciuis regio eius religio* was profoundly unsettling. The Palatinate changed religion nine times between 1546 (when Lutheranism was initially introduced) and 1700. Lutheran and Reformed territories within the German Empire had a church office, which, along with an office for education, was part of the territorial government. This was the *landesherrliches Kirchenregiment*, the ordering of a territory's church by the territorial ruler.

In the course of the eighteenth century, territorial confessions began to be associated with geographical areas rather than with the ruler. When the elector of Hanover ascended to the British throne as George I in 1714, Hanover's church office moved with him to London: George was Anglican in England, Reformed in Scotland, and Lutheran in Hanover. Religious diversity, often arising from migration, presented growing challenges to territorial churches. Prussia's General Law Code of 1794, the *Allgemeines Landrecht für die Preußischen Staaten*, recognized Catholic, Lutheran, and Reformed as publicly approved religious societies that could call their buildings "churches" and use bells. Other religious groups were defined as tolerated religious societies.[6]

In the final decades of the eighteenth century, those German territories which were annexed by Napoleon underwent secularization and the separation of church and state. Some of these changes were retained after 1815 in the territories returned to German jurisdiction by the Treaty of Vienna. Napoleon's intervention had reduced the number of German territories from over three hundred to thirty-nine, each ruled by a secular prince, which

---

5. Johnson et al., *Archeologies of Confession*.
6. Henke, "Toleration and Repression," 341.

now came together as the German Confederation. This massively reduced the number of Protestant territorial churches. The Articles of Confederation (*Bundesakte*) guaranteed equal rights for all "Christian co-religionists," defined as Catholic, Lutheran, and Reformed (although in fact Catholics were not everywhere granted equal rights with Protestants). The *landesherrliches Kirchenregiment* continued, with some confessional quirks: Bavaria's Catholic king became head of the Lutheran Church in Bavaria, with congregations primarily in the former territories of Franconia and Swabia; he was also head of the newly created Protestant Church, which united the Lutheran and Reformed Churches in the new territory of Rhenish Bavaria (the Rhenish Palatinate or *Rheinpfalz*) formed by the Treaty of Vienna. In Prussia, 1817—celebrated as the three-hundredth anniversary of the Reformation—marked the beginning of a process that united the Lutheran and Reformed Churches with the intention of creating a unified Prussian Protestant Church, although a side effect of the union was the creation of the Old Lutheran Church by opponents. Prussian expansion extended the United Church of Prussia to other territories, including the Rhineland and Westphalia.

A deepening association of German identity with Protestantism led during the nineteenth century to the so-called Kulturkampf, or culture war, which sought to secularize education and marriage law, and particularly to restrict the powers of the Catholic Church. This conflict escalated after German unification in 1871. Citizens gained the legal right to leave any church; following the Napoleonic pattern, responsibility for registering births, marriages and deaths, previously the remit of churches, was assigned to secular *Standesämter* (register offices); all marriages also had to be conducted in a register office, although a church ceremony might follow. By 1876 these regulations had taken effect in all the territories of the united Germany. Some German Protestant Churches became more self-governing: while the *Landesherr* was both head of state and of church, the two developed separate modes of government. The *landesherrliches Kirchenregiment*—the unity of throne and altar—was nonetheless maintained in church order until the formation of the Weimar Republic in 1919. Article 137 of the new constitution declared: "There is no state church. Every religious community organizes and administers its affairs independently." This policy initiated a radical reorganization of Protestant Churches, including electoral systems to determine the head of each church. Lutheran, Reformed, and Roman Catholic and Old Catholic Churches retained the right to collect church taxes through each territory's central tax system; religious education in public schools continued to be provided by the territorial churches; and churches continued to be closely involved in providing health and social care.

An attempt by the National Socialists to unite Germany's Protestant Churches into a single German Protestant Church (*Deutsche Evangelische Kirche*) with a unified structure headed by a *Reichsbischof* (imperial bishop) met with considerable resistance. The constitution of the Federal Republic of Germany is based on principles of freedom of religion, the separation of church and state, and self-governing *Religionsgesellschaften* (religious societies). The territorial Protestant Churches continue in Germany (along with an extraterritorial Reformed Church), but many of Germany's *Landeskirchen* now reflect political borders which no longer exist. In 1948, the German Lutheran, Reformed, and United Churches came together in a federation known as the Protestant Church in Germany (*Evangelische Kirche in Deutschland*, or EKD); within the EKD the individual territorial churches preserve their own independent structures. In 1969 the new constitution of the German Democratic Republic declared pan-German bodies illegal, and the *Bund der Evangelischen Kirchen in der DDR* (BEK) was formed. The BEK reunited with the EKD in 1991. The member churches of the EKD, the Roman Catholic Church and the much smaller German Old Catholic Church, retain and use the right to levy church tax; the existence of confessional theological faculties is confirmed through state-church treaties. Many hospitals, programs of social care, and kindergartens are run under the auspices of the churches, funded largely by taxes and the health and social insurance system. Germany has no state church, and numbers of church members are decreasing, but the member churches of the EKD and the Catholic Church nonetheless remain closely integrated into the functioning of society.

The Nordic Countries[7]

The Reformation in the Nordic countries coincided with the collapse of the Scandinavian Union—of Denmark, Finland, Iceland, Norway, Sweden, and the duchy of Schleswig-Holstein—established in 1397 by Margrethe I of Denmark. Its king, Christian II, had been an early supporter of Luther; in 1520, he invited the Wittenberg professors Andreas Bodenstein von Karlstadt, Martin Reinhardt, and Matthias Gabler to advise on the introduction of the Reformation in Denmark. In 1521 the Swedes rebelled under Gustav Vasa, and the combined kingdoms of Sweden and Finland separated from Denmark-Norway. In 1523 Christian II was deposed, fleeing to Wittenberg and then to the Netherlands. As duke of Holstein, Christian II's cousin, the

---

7. For this section, see: Aarflot, "Lutheran Perspective"; Furseth, *Religious Complexity*; Grell, "Scandinavia"; Markkola, "Lutheranism in Scandinavia"; Oftestad, "Church of Norway."

future Christian III, had attended the Diet of Worms; he was attracted by Reformation ideas. When in 1533 he succeeded his father, Frederick, to the throne, he set about introducing the Lutheran Church into Denmark and Norway. The Danish Church Ordinance of 1537 introduced a Lutheran theology with liturgy and Scriptures in Danish.

The Church in Denmark and Norway, to which later that in Iceland was joined, was a state church, headed by the monarch and run from a government ministry in Copenhagen. It was effectively Danish, and despite the official acceptance of the Reformation, Catholicism remained strong in many parts of Norway throughout the sixteenth century. A church ordinance for Norway was passed in 1607, and the Norwegian Law of 1687 regulated the Norwegian Church, with minimal differences to the Danish Church. When Norway achieved effective independence in 1814, its constitution affirmed "the Evangelical State Religion" as the "public religion of the State," requiring the monarch, members of the government, and civil servants to profess it. A proposed clause on religious liberty was not included.[8] In 1851 a dissenter law provided a degree of religious liberty, and other churches and religious communities (including Jews, but not Jesuits) were permitted to hold services and to teach. The twentieth century saw the Norwegian Church acquire a growing degree of self-government. In 2012 constitutional amendments initiated the separation of church and state, and on January 1, 2017, the state church (*statskirken*) became a separate and independent legal entity, "the Church of Norway" (*den Norske Kirke*).[9] Nonetheless, the Norwegian monarch must "at all times profess the Evangelical-Lutheran religion."[10]

The Church in Iceland separated from the Danish Church in the 1870s, as part of a long process of achieving independence. The Republic of Iceland was constituted in 1944. The Lutheran Church continued as the state church, with growing self-governance, until 1998, when it became the national Church of Iceland, with structures separate from the state; this separation was confirmed and increased by a further law in 2021. In contrast, the Danish Church remains closely integrated with the state. Although religious liberty was introduced in Denmark in 1849, the national church was retained. The monarch and the monarch's family (though not their spouses) are required to be members. The church has no central legislative body and no archbishop. The Danish Church retains considerable civic responsibilities, including the issuing of birth and marriage certificates (except in North

8. Oftestad, "Church of Norway," 33.
9. See Hofverberg, "Norway."
10. Aarflot, "Lutheran Perspective," 121.

Schleswig, which from 1864 to 1920 was under Prussian rule, where municipal offices are responsible for registering births and marriages).

Under Gustav Vasa, Sweden-Finland also introduced the Reformation, although this initially took the form of the rejection of papal jurisdiction and was not theologically well defined. In 1527, the parliament of Västerås confiscated church lands and required that the gospel be preached "purely"; in 1536, the Swedish synod introduced major changes to the order and ceremonies of the Swedish Church, instructing that the Mass was henceforth to be celebrated in Swedish; a Swedish hymnbook was published. From 1539, the leadership of the church was largely transferred from the Swedish bishops to superintendents. The theology of the Swedish Church was finally confirmed as Lutheran in the church orders of 1571 and 1593, which allied the Church of Sweden and Finland with the *Confessio Augustana*. From 1593 the Swedish monarch was expected to be Lutheran; Queen Christina of Sweden abdicated in 1654 in conjunction with her conversion to Catholicism. Almost all inhabitants of Sweden were required to be members of the Swedish Church; only Jews could form their own religious communities. From 1860, some religious toleration was introduced; members of another "approved religious community" were permitted to resign membership of the Swedish Church. In 1951 freedom of religion was enshrined in Swedish law. A church assembly was established in the second half of the nineteenth century, giving the church more control of its affairs. However, the church remained closely linked to the state.

Until 1996, the children of a member of the Church of Sweden were also regarded as members from birth, whether or not they were baptized; since 1996, a child becomes a member on baptism. This alteration reflected the changing status of the Church of Sweden, which was disestablished on January 1, 2000. The Church of Sweden no longer has an exclusive power to raise church tax: all recognized churches and religious communities collect voluntary contributions through the state tax system. However, the monarch is still required under the 1810 Act of Succession to "profess the pure evangelical faith."[11]

Late medieval Finland was already home to two forms of Christianity: western Finland was predominantly Catholic, while eastern Finland was Orthodox. Early modern Finland was under the Swedish crown, and the Reformation of Finland's Catholic Church paralleled developments in Sweden. The Finnish bishops tended to support the Reformation, resulting in a nominally princely Reformation which was effectively implemented by successive bishops of Turku. When in 1809 Finland became a grand duchy

11. Aarflot, "Lutheran Perspective," 110.

under the Russian czar, the Swedish Church Law of 1686 remained in effect. In the course of the nineteenth century, the Lutheran Church in Finland achieved considerable self-governance. The 1919 Constitution declared Finland to be a "religiously neutral country," although both the Evangelical Lutheran Church and the Orthodox Church in Finland had a particular status regulated by church laws. Both have the right to levy church tax; both receive public funding to support their provision of social services, for the maintenance of cemeteries, for church record-keeping, and for church repairs.

England and Scotland[12]

Until 1603, England and Scotland were separate (and often warring) countries with their own monarchs. They were united under one crown in 1603, but did not become one country until the Act of Union in 1707. They had distinct experiences of the sixteenth-century Reformation, which led to the formation of the (episcopalian) Church of England and the (presbyterian) Church of Scotland. Differences around church polity, including the existence of bishops and the monarch's relationship to the church, brought civil war to the British Isles during the seventeenth century. The Church of England and the Church of Scotland, while both established in law, retain different polities and very different modes of establishment.

The English Reformation began under King Henry VIII, driven by the king's desire for a legitimate male heir. While Henry remained largely uncommitted to the theological principles of the Reformation, he was appreciative of its potential financial gains: through the dissolution of the monasteries and the closure of chantries, almost all monastic lands in England were sequestrated to the crown, adding their income to his tax base. The 1534 Act of Supremacy, passed by parliament, declared the king to be "supreme head of the Church of England," removing the English church from papal jurisdiction. The title page of the Great Bible, printed from 1540, vividly illustrates the role of the king in England's new ecclesiastical structures: God communicates with the king, who passes God's message to the bishops and lords, who proclaim it to the people.

Under the boy king Edward VI, the English church became protestant in its theology and practice. In 1549 and 1552, Acts of Uniformity were passed, imposing a single form of worship through the Book of Common Prayer. Religious measures were imposed through Act of Parliament, which

12. For this section, see Muirhead, *Reformation, Dissent and Diversity*; Strong, *Oxford History of Anglicanism*.

retained bishops in the House of Lords, now nominated and confirmed by the king and his advisers. A national program of visitations ensured that parishes implemented the reforms. After a brief period of re-Catholicization under Queen Mary I, England was returned to Protestantism under Queen Elizabeth I. The 1559 Act of Uniformity declared her supreme governor of the Church of England and imposed a prayer book that was very similar to the 1552 version. Elizabethan ecclesiastical politics sought a *via media*: although the church retained the threefold pattern of ministries and was organized in dioceses, it was clearly a Protestant Church, with a vernacular Bible and liturgy, distribution of communion in both kinds, married priests, and the rejection of papal authority. Rather than taking sides in theological disputes between Protestants, the queen and government focused on ensuring conformity of practice.

In Scotland, in contrast, the Reformation was introduced in 1560 by the Scottish parliament with the support of many of Scotland's lords and lairds, but against the religious allegiance of Queen Mary of Scotland, who remained a Catholic. John Knox, Scotland's leading Reformer, influenced by Calvin's theology and by the polity of the Genevan church, sought to apply the synodical system developed by Calvin in Geneva to a much larger geographical area. The 1560 Book of Order directed that a school be provided in every parish and proposed a form of church discipline intended to create a Christian nation. The Reformation church was initially organized in dioceses overseen by superintendents (the Reformed translation of the Greek term *episcopos*, traditionally rendered "bishop"), who were expected to be elected by the parish ministers; in exceptional cases, a superintendent might be appointed. James VI of Scotland, Mary's son and successor, quickly sought to influence the appointment of superintendents; in response, a substantially revised Book of Order proposed a presbyterian structure for the Scottish church, with a kirk session in every parish, ministers and parish representatives forming local presbyteries, which in turn elected a national synod, the general assembly. Conflict with the king around Scottish church polity ensued.

Tensions were exacerbated when in 1603 James VI of Scotland succeeded Queen Elizabeth I as King James I of England. As king of England, James was supreme governor of the English Church, with the right and power to appoint bishops; as king of Scotland, he was a member of the Scottish Church, with no direct power over appointments or ecclesiastical policy. James sought to bring the Churches of Scotland and England more closely together, but his attempts to reintroduce practices into Scotland such as private baptism, kneeling to receive communion, episcopal confirmation, and the observation of Christmas and Easter, all of which in England were accepted as Protestant, were vehemently rejected as "papist." When his son and successor King Charles I, with the support of Archbishop William Laud, sought to impose a revised Book of Common Prayer in Scotland, where set liturgy had been rejected in favor of extempore prayer, conflict erupted into civil war, ultimately leading to the execution of the king. The church of the ensuing Commonwealth was congregational, rejecting not only bishops but also the national structures of Scottish presbyterianism. Charles II's supporters in both Scotland and England made the restoration of their own church and polity a condition for his restoration to the throne, but in fact in 1660 an episcopal church was reintroduced in Scotland as well as England. After the forced abdication of Charles II's brother James II, largely over his espousal of Catholicism in 1688, his daughter Mary and nephew William ascended the throne, reintroducing presbyterianism into Scotland and retaining bishops in England (although Jeffrey Stephen notes that William "would have preferred uniformity between his kingdoms"[13]). The monarch continued as supreme governor of the Church of England, while an ordinary member of the Church of Scotland; confessionally, British monarchs remain Anglicans in England and Presbyterians in Scotland.

The Act of Union of 1707 included the Protestant Religion and Presbyterian Church Act, which guaranteed "Presbyterian church government and discipline" in Scotland. Despite the ongoing existence of a Scottish Episcopalian Church, initially suppressed for its Jacobite connections (but legalized by stages in 1792 and 1864 and now the Scottish member church of the Anglican Communion), and of Scottish Catholics, particularly in some areas of the Highlands and the Western Isles, presbyterianism became closely associated with Scottish identity. This did not prevent multiple splits during the eighteenth century, or the Disruption of 1843, mostly around questions of patronage. By the end of the nineteenth century, Scotland had several smaller Presbyterian churches and three major ones: the Church of Scotland, the Free Church, and the United Presbyterian Church. The last two united in 1900 to form the United Free Church. Through the 1921 Church of Scotland Act, the British parliament confirmed the Church of Scotland's independence in spiritual matters, paving the way for the reunion of the Church of Scotland and the United Free Church in 1929.

The Restoration Church of England held many exclusive rights. Catholics and members of free churches (then known as Dissenters) could not attend the two English universities, Oxford or Cambridge, become members of parliament, or hold public office. The 1689 Toleration Act provided granted freedom to worship publicly to the majority of Dissenters, subject

---

13. Stephen, *Scottish Presbyterians*, 2.

to their swearing a modified oath of allegiance to the crown. From 1828, with the repeal of the Test and Corporation Acts (of 1673 and 1661 respectively), Dissenters were able to become members of parliament and hold public office; the Catholic Emancipation Act of 1829 extended these right to Catholics. The growing numbers of non-Anglican members of parliament raised serious questions about the Church of England's established status. In 1836, the Births and Deaths Registration Act made the registration of births and deaths the responsibility of register offices; marriages in register offices were possible from 1837.

The nineteenth century saw the end of the tithe system (which was not replaced by a system of church tax). From 1919, the Church of England gained increasing powers to determine its own liturgy and canon law through a system of parish councils, deanery and diocesan synods, and a national body, initially the Church Assembly and since 1970 the General Synod. Certain changes of doctrine or church order still require the assent of parliament. Thus the decision to allow women to be consecrated as bishops was enacted through the Bishops and Priests (Consecration and Ordination of Women) Measure 2014. Diocesan bishops are nominated by the Crown Nominations Commission, which receives a submission from the Vacancy in See Committee of the relevant diocese: the chosen candidate's name is passed to the prime minister (currently an adherent of the Sikh faith) who then presents it to the monarch for confirmation. The monarch instructs the college of canons of the cathedral of the vacant see to elect a bishop and tells them whom to elect. After the election (and consecration if appropriate), the bishop pays homage to the monarch.[14]

The Restoration Church of England was also the established church in Ireland and Wales. Disestablishment in Ireland on January 1, 1871 created the Church of Ireland; in Wales, disestablishment took place on March 31, 1920, following the delayed implementation of the Welsh Church Act 1914, and the Church in Wales was formed. Today, the four nations of the British Isles have four member churches of the Anglican Communion: the Church of England, the Church of Ireland (which has dioceses in both Northern Ireland and the Republic of Ireland), the Church in Wales, and the Scottish Episcopal Church. Of these, only the Church of England is an established church. Two established churches remain in Britain: the Church of England and the Church of Scotland, with very different forms of establishment. As supreme governor of the Church of England, the English monarch is the titular head of the Church of England, and ultimate governance of the church

14. For this process, see Archbishop's Secretary for Appointments, "Briefing"; usefully summarized by Owen, "Choosing Diocesan Bishops" and "Crown Nominations Commission."

lies with parliament and the monarch. The coronation of King Charles III in 2023 offered a clear affirmation of the relationship between king and church.

The Netherlands[15]

In the fifteenth century, what is now the Netherlands was part of the Low Countries, an alliance of seventeen small territories in present-day Netherlands, Belgium, and Luxembourg, ruled by the duke of Burgundy. In 1477, along with the rest of Burgundy, the Low Countries were incorporated into the Holy Roman Empire, and during the sixteenth century, first Emperor Charles V and subsequently King Philip II of Spain sought to impose a centralized authority. They also attempted to suppress the religious tolerance for which the Low Countries had in the course of the sixteenth century become known. From the 1560s, against increasingly vicious opposition led by the duke of Alba, William of Orange led the seventeen provinces of the Low Countries in the fight for greater religious tolerance. In 1579, however, the ten southern provinces, predominantly Catholic, declared their continued allegiance to Spain, while the seven northern provinces formed the Dutch Republic through the Union of Utrecht. This was the first free republic of early modern Europe; its existence was confirmed in the 1648 Treaty of Münster.

In the midst of this controversy, the Reformed Church emerged in the Low Countries from the 1550s; a key synod was held in Emden in 1571. Its theology was influenced by Calvin and the Genevan church, by Heidelberg and Basel, and by the experiences of exile churches such those in London and Emden. Religious toleration was a fundamental principle of the new Dutch Republic: although the Reformed Church had a privileged status, it was not a state church. Only the Reformed Church was allowed to conduct public worship, with adherents of other churches required to worship in homes or in hidden churches. The government provided subsidies to pay Reformed Church ministers and for the upkeep of buildings; Dutch Reformed clergy were required to baptize any child on request. The University of Leiden, the first in the Netherlands, was founded in 1575 with the primary purpose of educating Reformed ministers. Nonetheless, in the Netherlands, "the religious landscape always remained pluriform" and "the public church was the church of a minority."[16]

---

15. For this section, see Kroenig, *Great Power Rivalry*, ch. 7, "The Dutch Republic and the Spanish Empire"; Marnef, "Netherlands"; Wood, *Going Dutch*.

16. Marnef, "Netherlands," 361.

This situation remained stable until the Napoleonic invasion in 1795 and the subsequent Batavian Revolution. A more centralized state ensued, and in 1815 the United Kingdom of the Netherlands was formed out of the Dutch Republic, the Spanish—by then Austrian—Netherlands, and the prince-bishopric of Liège. King William I sought to unite these disparate territories into a modern nation, hoping to establish a unified Dutch Church, integrating Protestants and Catholics or, failing that, a church that united the Reformed and Lutherans. He failed; coining the name Dutch Reformed Church (*Nederlandse Hervormde Kerk*), he gave the Reformed Church established status in law.[17] However, this establishment was short lived. After the majority Catholic Southern Netherlands achieved independence as Belgium in 1830, the Dutch Reformed Church became the largest church of the Netherlands, and in the course of the nineteenth century, it came to be known as the *volkskerk*. From 1848, the legal separation of church and state was imposed, one of the earliest in Europe. Clarifying where responsibility lay for education, welfare, and church property took some time. For several decades the government department of public worship continued, with pastors to be paid by state funds. In 1879, over 99 percent of the population was still listed on the rolls of the Dutch Reformed Church.

By the middle of the twentieth century, the Roman Catholic Church in the Netherlands was larger than the Dutch Reformed Church. From the 1960s, church membership declined steadily. In 2004, the Dutch Reformed Church, the Reformed Churches in the Netherlands (*Gereformeerde Kerken in Nederland*), and the Evangelical Lutheran Church in the Kingdom of the Netherlands (*Evangelisch-Lutherse Kerk in het Koninkrijk der Nederlanden*) formed the Protestant Church in the Netherlands (*Protestantse Kerk in Nederland*).

Conclusion

National and territorial churches emerged in the course of the Protestant Reformation as the result of a close integration of political and ecclesiastical identity. The principle of *cuius regio eius religio* had by the seventeenth century given way to an understanding that a territory had a faith to which the ruler would be expected to conform. As migration and the emergence of free churches produced more confessionally mixed populations, the idea that a territory would have a unified religion became more problematic. By the mid-twentieth century, religious tolerance had come to be generally accepted, reflecting the fundamental right to freedom of religion or belief that had become enshrined in European constitutions

17. Wood, *Going Dutch*, 7.

after the First World War and which in 1948 was enshrined in the Universal Declaration of Human Rights.[18] By the turn of the twenty-first century, the majority of those churches that had been closely allied to the state had become disestablished, with the notable exception of the Church of Denmark, and to some extent the Church of England.

Bibliography

Aarflot, Andreas Henriksen. "A Lutheran Perspective." In *Church Laws and Ecumenism*, edited by Norman Doe, 106–27. Law and Religion. London: Routledge, 2020.

Archbishop's Secretary for Appointments. "Briefing for Members of Vacancy in See Committees." Church of England, Jan. 2020. https://www.churchofengland.org/sites/default/files/2020-06/briefing-for-the-vacancy-in-see-committee-january-2020.pdf.

Blickle, Peter. *Die Reformation im Reich*. 4th ed. Stuttgart: Kohlhammer, 2015.

Flüchter, Antje. *Der Zölibat zwischen Devianz und Norm: Kirchenpolitik und Gemeindealltag in den Herzogtümern Jülich und Berg im 16. und 17. Jahrhundert*. Norm und Struktur: Studien zum sozialen Wandel in Mittelalter und früher Neuzeit. Cologne: Böhlau, 2006.

Furseth, Inger, ed. *Religious Complexity in the Public Sphere: Comparing Nordic Countries*. New York: Palgrave Macmillan, 2018.

Grell, Ole Peter. "Scandinavia." In *The Reformation World*, edited by Andrew Pettegree, 257–76. Routledge Worlds. London: Routledge, 2000.

Henke, Manfred. "Toleration and Repression: German States, the Law and the 'Sects' in the Long Nineteenth Century." In *The Church and the Law*, edited by Rosamond McKitterick et al., 338–61. Studies in Church History 56. Cambridge: Cambridge University Press, 2020.

Herl, Joseph. *Worship Wars in Early Lutheranism: Choir, Congregation and Three Centuries of Conflict*. Rev. ed. Oxford: Oxford University Press, 2008.

Hofverberg, Erin. "Norway: State and Church Separate after 500 Years." Library of Congress, Feb. 3, 2017. https://www.loc.gov/item/global-legal-monitor/2017-02-03/norway-state-and-church-separate-after-500-years/.

Johnson, Carina L., et al., eds. *Archeologies of Confession: Writing the German Reformation 1517–2017*. Spektrum: Publications of the German Studies Association 16. Oxford: Berghahn, 2017.

Krentz, Natalie. *Ritualwandel und Deutungshoheit: Die frühe Reformation in der Residenzstadt Wittenberg (1500–1533)*. Spätmittelalter, Humanismus, Reformation 74. Tübingen: Mohr Siebeck, 2014.

Kroenig, Matthew. "The Dutch Republic and the Spanish Empire." In *The Return of Great Power Rivalry: Democracy versus Autocracy from the Ancient World to the U.S. and China*, 99–112. New York: Oxford University Press, 2020.

Lok, Matthijs. "The United Kingdom of the Netherlands (1815–1830): A Case of Failed European Nation Building?" In *Les nations européennes entre histoire et mémoire, xixe–xxe siècles*, edited by Francis Démier and Elena Musiani, 37–43. Nanterre, Fr.: Presses universitaires de Paris Nanterre, 2017.

---

18. See https://www.un.org/en/about-us/universal-declaration-of-human-rights.

MacCulloch, Diarmaid. *Reformation: Europe's House Divided 1490–1700*. London: Lane, 2003.

Markkola, Pirjo. "The Long History of Lutheranism in Scandinavia: From State Religion to the People's Church." *Perichoresis* 13 (2015) 3–15.

Marnef, Guido. "The Netherlands." In *The Reformation World*, edited by Andrew Pettegree, 344–364. Routledge Worlds. London: Routledge, 2000.

Methuen, Charlotte. "The German Catholic Dioceses and Their Bishops on the Eve of the Reformation." In *The Oxford Encyclopedia of Martin Luther*, edited by Derek R. Nelson and Paul R. Hinlicky, 1:521–38. Oxford: Oxford University Press 2017.

———. "Ordering the Reformation Church in England and Scotland." In *"Church" at the Time of the Reformation: Invisible Community, Visible Parish, Confession, Building . . . ?*, edited by Anna Vind and Herman Selderhuis, 65–90. Refo500 Academic Studies 72. Göttingen: Vandenhoeck & Ruprecht, 2021.

Muirhead, Andrew T. N. *Reformation, Dissent and Diversity: The Story of Scotland's Churches, 1560–1960*. London: Bloomsbury T&T Clark, 2015.

Oftestad, Bernt T. "The Church of Norway: A State Church and a National Church." *Studia Theologica* 44 (1990) 31–37.

Owen, Peter. "Choosing Diocesan Bishops in the Church of England." Peter Owen, Jan. 9, 2002; last revised Jan. 23, 2023. http://peterowen.org.uk/articles/choosing.html.

———. "Crown Nominations Commission: Changes to the Rules." Thinking Anglicans, July 9, 2019. https://www.thinkinganglicans.org.uk/crown-nominations-commission-changes-to-the-rules/.

Schindling, Anton, and Walter Ziegler, eds. *Die Territorien des Reichs im Zeitalter der Reformation und Konfessionalisierung*. 7 vols. Münster: Aschendorff, 1989–97.

Stephen, Jeffrey. *Scottish Presbyterians and the Act of Union 1707*. Edinburgh: Edinburgh University Press, 2007.

Strong, Rowan, ed. *The Oxford History of Anglicanism*. 5 vols. Oxford: Oxford University Press, 2017–19.

Wood, John Halsey, Jr. *Going Dutch in the Modern Age: Abraham Kuyper's Struggle for a Free Church in the Netherlands*. Oxford Studies in Historical Theology. New York: Oxford University Press, 2013.

8

The Protestant Story: Nonconformists, Radicals, and Sects

Mark W. Lee

Over the three centuries that followed the onset of the Protestant Reformation, numerous so-called free churches emerged across Britain and Continental Europe. Distinct from the Protestant state churches, such as the Lutheran Church in northern Germany and Scandinavia, the Reformed Church in Switzerland and the Netherlands, and the Anglican Church in England and Wales, the free churches were independent of state control and governance. Most of them were born in a climate of persecution. In England, for instance, non-Anglican Protestants—Baptists, Congregationalists, Presbyterians, Quakers, and others—were subject to legal penalties until 1689. For non-Trinitarian Christians, such penalties persisted until 1813. And all Nonconformists in England were denied the right to vote or hold public office until 1828.

As John Coffey has observed in his introduction to the first of four volumes of the recently published *Oxford History of Protestant Dissenting Traditions* (2017–2020), the history of Protestant nonconformity has frequently been portrayed with the long view in focus. Denominational histories—a genre now long since in decline—thus narrated the backstories of independent, separatist types who formed their own versions of dissent groups. The rise of fascism in 1940s Europe then saw their reconstrual among liberal historians as preservers of traditional Western democratic principles, as they saw them. And Marxist histories such as Christopher Hill and E. P. Thompson rendered these independents as contemporary social activists.[1] As Coffey notes, it was the historian Patrick Collinson who first identified this historiographical mode as a "vertical" one, which has since

---

1. Coffey, "Introduction," 11, 19–20.

been displaced in academic history by "horizontal" investigations that aim to "locate [Nonconformists] not within the long story of Dissent, but within their host societies."[2]

The more recent approach has uncovered the layers of complexity in the history of Protestant Nonconformists, radicals, and sects in Europe. These were not simply persecuted separatists who foreshadowed an Enlightenment conception of religious liberty; often, they had designs on reforming state power in their own image.[3] Moreover, their relationships to their conforming counterparts were frequently congenial and collaborative. This chapter aims to capture something of this complexity. Focusing especially on the British context in the seventeenth and eighteenth centuries, it highlights four key themes: the emergence and stigmatization of Protestant "enthusiasms," the formation of denominational identities, the cultivation and spread of "heart religion," and the story of heterodox dissent.

Defining Radicalism and Nonconformity

We begin, though, with two key definitions, starting with "radicalism." Despite its current associations with fanaticism, the etymology of the word relates more specifically to primitivism: the notion of returning to the roots of a practice or belief system. The so-called radical Reformers of the sixteenth century—those who wished to push the Reformation further than magisterial Reformers such as Martin Luther and John Calvin—were intent on recovering the doctrines and practices of the early church, which they believed had been lost or corrupted over the intervening centuries of Christian history.[4] This core assumption gave rise in the sixteenth century to numerous types of "radical," which the historian George Hunston Williams has wrangled into three main categories (more recently adopted and slightly modified by Carlos Eire): "Anabaptists, Spiritualists, and Evangelical Rationalists (Anti-Trinitarians)."[5] Despite the many differences within and across these categories, there are also important commonalities between them. Most, for instance, rejected infant baptism; and most held that the true church was a *voluntary* community, "composed," in Eire's words, "of only believers."[6]

---

2. Coffey, "Introduction," 11; see also Collinson, "Towards a Broader Understanding."
3. Rose, "Dissent and the State," 313.
4. Eire, *Reformations*, 250.
5. Eire, *Reformations*, 253.
6. Eire, *Reformations*, 250.

The word "nonconformity" refers to how individual ecclesial communities relate to the state churches. It has been used to refer both to insiders who refused to conform to certain practices of the state churches to which they belonged, and to religious sects that operated outside the state churches. In England, as Michael Watts observed in his classic three-volume study of English and Welsh Dissenters, its application shifted from the first sense (nonconformism from within) to the second (separatism) when, after 1662, "the state required of its clergy their 'unfeigned assent and consent' to everything in th[e] Prayer Book [of 1559]."[7] While the word "nonconformity" captures each species of radical discussed above, its meaning is far broader and more elastic than the word "radical." In England, Presbyterians were Nonconformists, and Episcopalians comprised the state church. In Scotland, the roles were reversed.[8] In neither place were Presbyterians (or Episcopalians, for that matter) anything like the radicals encompassed in Williams's threefold taxonomy.

Enthusiasm

Protestant radicalism emerged as part of the broader crisis of authority that attended the Reformation. The doctrine of *sola scriptura* (by Scripture alone) opened a floodgate of new theological and ecclesiological possibilities. Some radicals in the "spiritualist" camp, such as the Zwickau prophets in sixteenth-century Wittenberg, even abandoned Scripture, relying instead upon the immediate guidance of the Holy Spirit. The rejection of traditional authority was frequently paired with a millenarian eschatology: a conviction that the "last days" prophesied in the biblical books of Daniel and Revelation had arrived, that Christ's return was imminent, and that the church had entered a stage in which new things could be expected. In Acts 2:17, the early Christians had been promised that "in the last days, . . . your sons and your daughters shall prophesy, and your young men shall see visions, and your old men shall dream dreams" (KJV)—an echo of Joel 2:28. The arrival of the last days thus had radical implications in two key ways: prophetic dreams and visions could now be expected—even by ordinary people—and should be deemed spiritually authoritative; and women—not just men—were among those who could prophesy and exercise spiritual authority.[9]

The word "enthusiasm" was used to encapsulate this whole dynamic. In its broadest sense, it was used as a pejorative term for a specific

---

7. M. Watts, *From the Reformation*, 1.
8. Coffey, "Introduction," 14.
9. Brown, "Introduction," 6.

epistemological mode, in which the individual looked only to their own standards on matters of religious belief and conduct.[10] In the sixteenth and seventeenth centuries, it was applied especially to radicals who set the standard of authority in religious experience: the direct apprehension of the divine will, manifested in bodily agitations (convulsions, trance states, and the like), dreams, and visions. The public disturbance caused by the Zwickau prophets and their ilk posed a threat to the vision of the magisterial Reformers; and to confront it, Luther turned to rhetoric. These were not legitimate men of God, he insisted, but sufferers of *Schwärmerei*—a form of "self-delusion" marked, in Anthony La Vopa's words, by "a mistaken conviction that one had become a receptacle of a divine inspiration or an immediate revelation."[11]

This was precisely the sense in which seventeenth-century Anglicans used the term *enthusiasm* when condemning the radicals in their own context. Its etymological associations, notably, were actually positive. The Greek roots, *en theos*, referred literally to the indwelling of God, and evoke an ancient Hellenic worldview wherein Plato, for instance, could celebrate the "godsent" forms of madness that yielded prophetic insights, relieved tormented consciences, and inspired poetic genius.[12] But in the sermons, pamphlets, and treatises of early modern Anglicans such as Méric Casaubon (1599–1671) and Henry More (1614–87), "enthusiasm" was reconstituted as a medical category—"an Effect of Nature . . . mistaken by many for either Divine Inspiration, or Diabolical Possession," as the subtitle of Casaubon's *Treatise Concerning Enthusiasme* (1655) would have it. Its victims, in the view of these authors, were the members of the various radical sects that had emerged during the period of the English Civil War: the Quakers, Ranters, Diggers, Fifth Monarchists, and Muggletonians. As "advocates," in Hillel Schwartz's words, "of extensive sovereignty for prophecy, inspiration, and mystical insight," their existence was a threat to elite power.[13] And the threat was formidable. The Puritan commander of the parliamentary army, Oliver Cromwell, claimed to have been acting upon a divine mandate when he led the rebellion against Charles I and the Royalists. Enthusiasm, in England, was implicated in no less than regicide.[14]

The radical effects of "enthusiasm" were not merely political and religious, but also social. The advent of the last days, as we have seen, generated

10. Heyd, *"Be Sober and Reasonable,"* 8–9.
11. La Vopa, "Philosopher and *Schwärmer*," 88.
12. Plato, *Phaedrus*, 27–29; La Vopa, "Philosopher and *Schwärmer*," 88.
13. Schwartz, *Knaves, Fools, Madmen*, 2.
14. Pocock, "Enthusiasm," 10–11.

expectations that women, too, would prophesy and preach. And so they did. Quaker women in the 1650s, for instance, traveled near and far to spread the news about the "inner light" that was accessible to all, irrespective of gender or status. In a particularly striking example, the Quaker missionary Mary Fisher (ca. 1623–98) traveled to present-day Turkey to evangelize the ruler of the Ottoman Empire, Sultan Mehmed IV, with whom she managed to gain a sympathetic audience at a military encampment at Adrianople.[15] Beyond what it reveals about the tremendous authority that religious experience could confer, this example epitomizes "the potential of religious radicalism," in Sylvia Brown's words, "to transcend confessional, national, ethnic, or sexual difference." Fisher, Brown adds, preached a "universal light" that is "not shared out but is the same light in all," and so, permitted "the possibility of intimate communion with the 'Other.'"[16] Radicalism indeed was not always a force of division and sectarianism; it could also build seemingly improbable bridges.

The longer-term survival of these radical sects in England depended in large part upon their ability to curb their more radical tendencies, and to adapt their "spiritualist" impulses to a politically and intellectually hostile environment. Their work was cut out for them. As J. G. A. Pocock has observed, the Anglicanism that emerged from the seventeenth century was one shaped largely in reaction to the threats of the perceived "enemies within and without—Catholic, Calvinist, and enthusiast."[17] Isabel Rivers has further expounded the latitudinarian philosophy that hence emerged: a "new [Anglican] orthodoxy"[18] grounded in "the essentially rational basis of religion," where reason was coextensive with the status quo, and unreason with the political and social radicalism encouraged by the enthusiasts' intervening deity.[19] The sects that established themselves as denominations, then, were those that mitigated the perceived excesses in their ranks—an effort that was part of the broader process of institutionalization to which we will turn next. "Independents, Baptists, and Quakers," Rachel Adcock relatedly observes, "curtail[ed] women's more authoritative roles as teachers or prophets" through the latter half of the seventeenth century.[20] Moreover, Quakers and Methodists, as Phyllis Mack has shown, internalized "religious experience from public prophecy to dreaming," a sequence that dulled

---

15. Brown, "Radical Travels," 40.
16. Brown, "Introduction," 10–11.
17. Pocock, "Enthusiasm," 12.
18. Rivers, *Whichcote to Wesley*, 1.
19. Rivers, *Whichcote to Wesley*, 35.
20. Adcock, "Women and Gender," 456.

the radical edge of the spiritualist impulse by rendering it a principle of personal transformation. And yet, despite this privatizing turn of "enthusiasm," Quakers were adamant that the character development afforded by devotional attentiveness to one's dreams should issue in social action.[21] As unlikely as it might have seemed to a seventeenth-century latitudinarian, Quakers would find themselves, by the end of the eighteenth century, at the vanguard of the development of "moral treatment" in English and American lunatic asylums, a form of therapy that emphasized sobriety and self-restraint.[22] Agents of unreason no more.

Denominational Identities

In England, Nonconformity moved from the margins of society in the early modern period to become, by the Victorian period, a major force in the nation's religious culture. An 1851 census revealed that half of the nation's churchgoers (18.62 percent of the total population) attended Dissenting chapels.[23] This transformation came about as part of the process through which separatist groups and sects became established denominations. Historians divide these denominations between two major categories: Old Dissent and New Dissent. Old Dissent comprises those groups that had survived the formal and informal forms of discrimination to which they had been subjected in the seventeenth century: Presbyterians, Baptists, Congregationalists, and Quakers. New Dissent refers specifically to the Methodist Church, which originated in the 1730s as part of the evangelical revival movement within the Church of England under the leadership of Anglican clergymen George Whitefield and John Wesley, and then, in 1794, separated from the Anglican Church.[24]

The transition of the congregations of Old Dissent from persecuted minorities to become settled denominations hinged on two key developments. The first is what Max Weber referred to as the "routinization of charisma": the process of institutionalization that involved the formation of denominational networks, synods, conferences, and associations.[25] The second is the more informal way in which denominational identities developed around the theme of persecution. As John Coffey has observed, names such as "Anabaptist" and "Quaker" were initially used as pejorative terms,

21. Mack, "Dreaming and Emotion," 178.
22. Scull, *Madness in Civilization*, 202.
23. M. Watts, *Crisis and Conscience*, xv.
24. Coffey, "Introduction," 7–8.
25. Max Weber, quoted in Coffey, "Introduction," 23.

but were eventually embraced by the groups at which they were aimed as part of their embattled identities. Lived experiences of persecution became, after the Act of Toleration in 1688/89, communal memories, propagated and reinforced through the writing of denominational histories.[26]

These denominational histories are in large part responsible for the simplistic narratives of English Nonconformity that historians in recent years have been keen to dismantle. English Puritanism was not born as a separatist movement. Rather, it emerged during the Reformation as part of a contest between rivaling factions over the shape the Church of England should take. The Puritan faction thought that the Elizabethan settlement—the political and religious policies implemented under Elizabeth I from 1559 to 1563—had not pushed the Reformation agenda far enough. After all, the settlement had left the episcopacy—the system of governance under bishops—in place. It had kept the clergy in their traditional vestments. It had done too little, they lamented, to slough off the material and spiritual entrapments of the Roman Church. Puritans had no qualms, on the other hand, with the church's marriage to the state. They simply wished to compel the church-state establishment to take a different—more distinctly Reformed—direction. By losing this internal power struggle, they became Nonconformists—a status they would temporarily shed in the 1640s and 1650s, when, under Cromwell, the episcopacy was abolished. By the same blow, of course, Episcopalians became the new "Nonconformists."[27] "'Dissent' and 'Establishment,'" as Coffey observes, "are relative categories."[28]

English Nonconformity, then, was born amid struggle for control of the established church, and resorted to separatism only when the struggle was lost.[29] The distinct doctrines and practices of the congregations that would eventually comprise Old Dissent emerged from the heterogenous, yet undifferentiated, community of the Puritans, who, before the Elizabethan period, had been committed to *reforming* Anglicanism, not departing from it. New Dissent had a similar relationship to the Church of England, beginning as a renewal movement of "Methodistical" insiders, and then subsequently breaking away to form a nonconforming church. As we shall see, New Dissent was fueled both theologically and devotionally by, among other sources, Old Dissent, which likewise inspired a renewal of personal piety among Protestant groups in Continental Europe. It is to the devotional culture—the "heart religion"—of Protestant Nonconformity that we now turn.

26. Coffey, "Introduction," 19–29.
27. Coffey, "Introduction," 5–8.
28. Coffey, "Introduction," 14.
29. Coffey, "Introduction," 16; also see Rose, "Dissent and the State."

Heart Religion

A central concern across the sects of Protestant Nonconformity was the notion that religion should be a matter of sincere, heartfelt conviction for each individual believer.[30] Referred to variously as "heart religion" and "vital religion," this concern was not unique to Nonconformists, nor to Protestants—nor even, indeed, to Christians. Ted Campbell has identified a similar turn to the heart in the seventeenth century among French and Spanish Catholics (the Jansenists and the Quietists) and Hasidic Jews in Eastern Europe.[31] For Protestants in particular, heart religion emerged as a reaction against nominal Christianity (where the religious identity of the individual goes no deeper than their outward affiliation with and conformity to the labels and tests of the state church or denomination of which they are a part) and academic theology.[32] The cultivation of piety, heart "religionists" insisted, was not the exclusive duty of clerics and theologians; it was the responsibility of ordinary people too.

In England, Nonconformity was at the epicenter of heart religion. It was among the Puritans in particular that the concern to extinguish nominalism generated, from the early seventeenth century, a spate of theological and devotional texts—works of "practical divinity"—that served as a crucial source for the emergence of heart religion among Pietists on the Continent and, a century later, among evangelical revivalists (the progenitors of New Dissent) in Britain. And such activity did not stop at writing. Puritans developed a range of new communal practices that aimed, in David Ceri Jones's words, "to stimulate a red-hot spirituality, and then to maintain its intensity": "Bible reading, a feast of sermons, meditation, small cell groups, prayer meetings, [and] fast days."[33] Heart religion, then, was not just an individual affair; it was a communal concern.

As a *communal* phenomenon, heart religion had the paradoxical effect of both sharpening denominational identities and blurring confessional boundaries. On the former tendency, Elizabeth Clarke and Robert Daniel have written about the "devotional exceptionalism" that formed among "Presbyterians, Independents, Quakers, Baptists and other religious movements," as their "congregational and domestic devotional performances crystallized their sense of religious identity and sharpened their resolve."[34]

---

30. Campbell, *Religion of the Heart*, 2.
31. Campbell, *Religion of the Heart*, 2.
32. Coffey, "Introduction: Sources and Trajectories," 9; Hempton, *Church*, 41.
33. Jones, "George Whitefield," 96–97.
34. Clarke and Daniel, "Introduction," 3.

Particularly in the period of state persecution, when Dissenting worship could incur fines and prison sentences, household piety played a key role in the formation of Nonconformist congregational identities. Anne Hughes has noted, for instance, the ways in which a Derbyshire family's distinctly Presbyterian identity was sharpened and sustained by the devotional use of sermon notes.[35] Denominational distinctions also played out in the contrasting ways in which communities engaged with pious literatures. In Scotland, where the established church was Presbyterian, the nonconforming Episcopalians embraced the devotional writings of French Quietists such as Madame Guyon (1648–1717). By contrast, a stronger aversion to all things "popish" made the Scottish Presbyterians and English Dissenters more wary about—though, as we shall see, not entirely averse to—Catholic mystical spirituality.[36]

Despite these different denominational inflections, heart religion is ultimately more striking for its transconfessional and transnational dynamics.[37] It emerged, after all, as a reaction against nominalism and the cerebral Christianity of the academy.[38] While some—Calvinist Evangelicals, in particular—were more committed than others to containing vital religion within confessional bounds,[39] others, such as the German Pietist William Boehm (1673–1722), advocated, in Daniel Brunner's words, "a movement of transconfessional Christianity that transcended labels, Anglican, Lutheran, or Pietist."[40] For later seventeenth-century Puritans, ecumenism was not merely an unintended consequence of the heart-ward turn, but the implication of a conscious effort to move past the interconfessional strife that had roiled the English population through the century's middle decades.[41] Coffey relatedly notes Richard Baxter's efforts in his devotional and theological writing to chart a course between Calvinism and Arminianism, "prefigur[ing] the broad tent approach of later evangelicals."[42]

Suitably, then, Puritan devotional writing became a core part of what Patricia Ward has called the "ecumenical devotional canon" that emerged in the eighteenth century, as readers of various Protestant stripes sought "useful examples and guidelines that would lead to a deeper inner life."[43] Puritan

---

35. Hughes, "Soul Preaching to Itself."
36. Coffey, "Introduction: Sources and Trajectories," 23.
37. Coffey, "Between Puritanism and Evangelicalism," 32.
38. Hempton, *Church*, 41.
39. Coffey, "Introduction: Sources and Trajectories," 23–24.
40. Brunner, "'Evangelical' Heart," 87.
41. Coffey, "Introduction: Sources and Trajectories," 3.
42. Coffey, "Introduction: Sources and Trajectories," 4.
43. P. Ward, "Continental Spirituality," 53.

influence was not limited in this regard to Britain. Historians have noted the mass translation of English Puritan works into German in the seventeenth and eighteenth centuries, which has been described as a key influence on the development of German Pietism.[44] The canon was not limited, moreover, to Protestant texts. Catholic spiritual works such as the medieval theologian Thomas à Kempis's *Imitation of Christ* were embraced not only by the "mystics of the northeast"—the Scottish Episcopalians mentioned above—but even by English Nonconformists of a more anti-Catholic bent such as the minister and educator Thomas Rowe (1657–1705), who could recommend the *Imitation* as "a very useful companion for all Christians" because its "naturall and unaffected pathos . . . proceeded doubtless from the heart of the Author, & touches the hearts of readers."[45]

The devotional writings of English Puritans, German Pietists, and Catholic mystics in turn became key sources for the emergence of evangelical revivalism in the 1730s, and thus, by extension, for the consolidation of New Dissent in the form of the Methodist Church in the late eighteenth century. Old Dissent was especially key in this respect. Bruce Hindmarsh has written recently about the influence of "the practical biblical emphasis of Puritan-Nonconformist divinity" on the evangelical revivalist George Whitefield's (1740–70) spiritual and theological formation. Despite his initial scruples, as an ordained Anglican, about reading too much Dissenting literature, Whitefield immersed himself in the writings of late Puritan authors such as Richard Baxter (1615–91), Joseph Alleine (1634–68), and James Janeway (1636–74), and so was guided to his Calvinistic convictions.[46] These writings were then embraced more widely by evangelical ministers—Dissenting and Anglican alike—who recommended them devotionally to their congregations and readers. The Anglican evangelical clergyman and friend of John Wesley's, David Simpson, for instance, recommended to his readers the works of seventeenth-century Puritans such as Baxter, Milton, and Bunyan in a list of books "best calculated to advance the spirit of religion in the soul."[47] Such lists reinforce the historian John Walsh's observation that "if the evangelicals themselves had been asked what their Revival was intended to revive, they would have had a ready answer. It was a restatement of the 'good old divinity' of English Puritans and Reformers."[48]

---

44. W. Ward, *Protestant Evangelical Awakening*, 10–13; Coffey, "Introduction: Sources and Trajectories," 2.

45. Quoted in Stephenson, "Isaac Watts's Education," 277–78.

46. Hindmarsh, *Spirit of Early Evangelicalism*, 15, 28.

47. Simpson, *Plea for Religion*, 343–44; quoted in Rivers, *Vanity Fair*, 91.

48. Quoted in Hindmarsh, *Spirit of Early Evangelicalism*, 78–79.

Simpson's book recommendations further attest to the ecumenical character of early Evangelicalism, and to the ongoing cooperation the movement saw between contemporary Nonconformists and Anglicans. So, alongside Kempis's *Imitation of Christ*, Simpson promoted the seventeenth-century Scottish Episcopalian Henry Scougal's *Life of God in the Soul of Man* (1677), one of the key books through which, as Hindmarsh observes, themes of Continental mystical piety such as the "Union of the Soul with God" were mediated to Protestant British readers.[49] And, finally, Simpson's list featured the works of *contemporary* Nonconformists: namely, Elizabeth Singer Rowe's (1674–1737) *Devout Exercises of the Heart* (1737), Isaac Watts's (1674–1748) *Discourses on the Love of God* (1729), and Philip Doddridge's *Rise and Progress of Religion in the Soul* (1745).[50] Watts and Doddridge—both Congregationalist ministers—were active supporters of Whitefield's and Wesley's evangelical Anglican ministries; and, as John Coffey has shown, the tradition of Dissenting hymnody to which they both contributed constituted some of the connective tissue between the Puritanism of the seventeenth century and the revivalism of the eighteenth.[51]

Heterodox Dissent

While the majority of Nonconformists in eighteenth-century Britain were Calvinists, there were a growing number in this period who questioned or flatly rejected traditional doctrines such as the Trinity and predestination, particularly within Presbyterian congregations.[52] Known as rational Dissenters, they, perhaps more than any other Dissenting group, have been associated in denominational histories with the liberal principles of reason, liberty, and tolerance.[53] And the connection is by no means baseless. In the 1770s and 1780s, as the historian John Seed has observed, the most radical Dissenting chapels embodied the values of freedom of conscience and religious tolerance advocated by rational Dissenters such as Joseph Priestley (1733–1804) and Richard Price (1723–91). Their guiding principle, Seed argues, was not a specific doctrinal position, such as the Socinian denial of the Trinity and of Christ's divinity, but "the Priestleyan ideal of a free public sphere untrammeled by central authority."[54] In a similar vein, David

49. Hindmarsh, *Spirit of Early Evangelicalism*, 80.
50. Simpson, *Plea for Religion*, 343; cited in Rivers, *Vanity Fair*, 91.
51. Coffey, "Between Puritanism and Evangelicalism," 47.
52. Wykes, "Rational Dissent, Unitarianism," 2–3.
53. Hotson, "Arianism and Millenarianism," 9.
54. Seed, "Gentlemen Dissenters," 316–24; quotation on 324.

Wykes has shown that rational dissent "sheltered a wide variety of opinions, orthodox as well as heterodox," and "was characterised [above all] by an absolute belief in an individual's right to exercise private judgement in matters of religion."[55] This conviction proved costly. With the onset of the French Revolution in 1789, rational dissent in England provoked anxious comparisons to the infidelity of revolutionaries on the Continent—concerns that culminated in the Priestley Riots in 1791, during which three Dissenting chapels in Birmingham were burned to the ground.[56]

Nevertheless, teleological approaches are no less problematic when applied to the history of rational dissent than in other contexts. Heterodoxy and rationalism, after all, are not synonymous in the history of Protestant radicalism. An illuminating example is furnished by the trial and execution in 1612 of an alehouse keeper named Edward Wightman. Among the doctrinal transgressions for which Wightman was burned at the stake was his denial of the Trinity; yet he also claimed, in the more "enthusiastic" mode of the Spiritualists, that he was the Holy Ghost.[57] Hardly a beacon of Enlightenment values. Just as problematic is the frequency with which anti-Trinitarian views were combined, among Protestant radicals, with millenarian beliefs in the coming apocalypse. As Howard Hotson has noted, historians have associated millenarian radicals not with reason and liberty, but "with messianic tyranny, mass delusion, and violent fanaticism."[58] And yet, even the so-called "father of Unitarianism," the Spanish humanist Michael Servetus (d. 1553), was a convinced millenarian whose writings pondered the imminent downfall of the antichrist.[59] The many expressions of heterodox dissent, then, have to be parsed carefully in the light of their distinct cultural contexts. The sixteenth-century heterodoxy of Servetus was of an entirely different genus from the eighteenth-century "rational religion" of Priestley.

Another long-standing interpretation of heterodox Nonconformity that has recently faced scrutiny—this one related specifically to the rational dissent of Priestley's context—is that it was a "cold and polite religion," bound up with processes of secularization or with the engines of capitalism.[60] Analyzing the participation of rational Dissenters in abolitionism and other philanthropic activities, Anthony Page has argued, contrariwise, that they cultivated an alternative form of "vital religion" to the evangelical "heart

55. Wykes, "Rational Dissent, Unitarianism," 4.
56. Seed, "Gentlemen Dissenters," 325.
57. Atherton and Como, "Burning of Edward Wightman," 1215–16.
58. Hotson, "Arianism and Millenarianism," 10.
59. Hotson, "Arianism and Millenarianism," 12.
60. Page, "Rational Dissent, Enlightenment," 747.

religion" discussed above. Theirs, Page contends, was a "rational piety," "a combination of individualism, sociability, and reformist activism," fueled in part by their own experiences and communal memories of persecution, from which they derived sympathy for "victims of legal discrimination."[61] Ruth Watts has relatedly commented on the "fervent love of liberty and civil reform" with which students of England's most radical Dissenting academies were inculcated.[62] While historians such as Roy Porter and John Brewer have cautioned against overestimating the extent of rational Dissenters' reformist activities,[63] Page and Watts rightly highlight the dimensionality of rational dissent as it was incarnated in real communities. The heart mattered, too, not just the head.

Conclusion

The stories of radicals, Nonconformists, and sects in Protestant Europe frequently defy the stereotypes and teleological narratives we encounter in denominational and Marxist histories. The explosion of new, and often ecstatic, religious experiences among radical sects in the sixteenth and seventeenth centuries—denigrated as *Schwarmerei* by Luther and "enthusiasm" by Anglican elites—had the contrasting effects of reinforcing sectarian divisions in certain contexts and bridging formidable divides in others. Nonconformist denominations (Quakers, Presbyterians, Baptists, Congregationalists, Methodists, and others) were not born as fully formed separatist groups, but emerged and consolidated their identities amid intricate negotiations for power and respectability. In the sphere of worship and devotion, Nonconformists were not detached outsiders, but were instrumental in the development of heart religion in Britain and Continental Europe, often engaging fruitfully with their conforming neighbors in both regions. And early modern heterodox Dissenters were not forerunners of Enlightenment values, nor were eighteenth-century rational Dissenters passionless devotees of Reason. Across time, the heterodox varieties of dissent were felt, not merely thought. Nonconformists and radicals were indeed a complex lot, as their lived experiences make plain.

61. Page, "Rational Dissent, Enlightenment," 746–47.
62. R. Watts, "Harriet Martineau," 638.
63. Seed, "Gentlemen Dissenters," 299.

Bibliography

Adcock, Rachel. "Women and Gender." In *The Post-Reformation Era, c. 1559–c. 1689*, edited by John Coffey, 454–71. Vol. 1 of *The Oxford History of Protestant Dissenting Traditions*. Oxford: Oxford University Press, 2020.

Atherton, Ian, and David Como. "The Burning of Edward Wightman: Puritanism, Prelacy and the Politics of Heresy in Early Modern England." *English Historical Review* 120 (2005) 1215–50.

Brown, Sylvia. "Introduction." In *Women, Gender and Radical Religion in Early Modern Europe*, edited by Sylvia Brown, 1–14. Studies in Medieval and Reformation Traditions 129. Leiden: Brill, 2007.

———. "The Radical Travels of Mary Fisher: Walking and Writing in the Universal Light." In *Women, Gender and Radical Religion in Early Modern Europe*, edited by Sylvia Brown, 39–64. Studies in Medieval and Reformation Traditions 129. Leiden: Brill, 2007.

Brunner, Daniel L. "The 'Evangelical' Heart of Pietist Anthony William Boehm." In *Heart Religion: Evangelical Piety in England & Ireland, 1690–1850*, edited by John Coffey, 72–92. Oxford: Oxford University Press, 2016.

Campbell, Ted A. *The Religion of the Heart: A Study of European Religious Life in the Seventeenth and Eighteenth Centuries*. Eugene, OR: Wipf & Stock, 2000.

Casaubon, Méric. *A Treatise Concerning Enthusiasme, as It Is an Effect of Nature: But Is Mistaken by Many for Either Divine Inspiration, or Diabolical Possession*. London: RD, 1655.

Clarke, Elizabeth, and Robert W. Daniel. "Introduction." In *People and Piety: Protestant Devotional Identities in Early Modern England*, edited by Elizabeth Clarke and Robert W. Daniel, 1–21. Seventeenth- and Eighteenth-Century Studies 11. Manchester: Manchester University Press, 2020.

Coffey, John. "Between Puritanism and Evangelicalism: 'Heart-Work' in Dissenting Communion Hymns, 1693–1709." In *Heart Religion: Evangelical Piety in England & Ireland, 1690–1850*, edited by John Coffey, 29–49. Oxford: Oxford University Press, 2016.

———. "Introduction." In *The Post-Reformation Era, c. 1559–c. 1689*, edited by John Coffey, 1–38. Vol. 1 of *The Oxford History of Protestant Dissenting Traditions*. Oxford: Oxford University Press, 2020.

———. "Introduction: Sources and Trajectories of Evangelical Piety." In *Heart Religion: Evangelical Piety in England & Ireland, 1690–1850*, edited by John Coffey, 1–28. Oxford: Oxford University Press, 2016.

Collinson, Patrick. "Towards a Broader Understanding of the Early Dissenting Tradition." In *The Dissenting Traditions: Essays for Leland H. Carlson*, edited by Robert Cole and Michael E. Moody, 3–38. Athens: Ohio University Press, 1975.

Eire, Carlos M. N. *Reformations: The Early Modern World, 1450–1650*. New Haven: Yale University Press, 2016.

Hempton, David. *The Church in the Long Eighteenth Century*. I. B. Tauris History of the Christian Church. London: Tauris, 2011.

Heyd, Michael. *"Be Sober and Reasonable": The Critique of Enthusiasm in the Seventeenth and Early Eighteenth Centuries*. Studies in Intellectual History 63. Leiden: Brill, 1995.

Hindmarsh, D. Bruce. *The Spirit of Early Evangelicalism: True Religion in a Modern World*. New York: Oxford University Press, 2018.

Hotson, Howard. "Arianism and Millenarianism: The Link between Two Heresies from Servetus to Socinus." In *Continental Millenarians: Protestants, Catholics, Heretics*, edited by John Christian Laursen and Richard H. Popkin, 9–35. Millenarianism and Messianism in Early Modern European Culture 4. Dordrecht: Springer Netherlands, 2001.

Hughes, Anne. "'A Soul Preaching to Itself': Sermon Note-Taking and Family Piety." In *People and Piety: Protestant Devotional Identities in Early Modern England*, edited by Elizabeth Clarke and Robert W. Daniel, 63–78. Seventeenth- and Eighteenth-Century Studies 11. Manchester, UK: Manchester University Press, 2020.

Jones, David Ceri. "George Whitefield and Heart Religion." In *Heart Religion: Evangelical Piety in England & Ireland, 1690–1850*, edited by John Coffey, 93–112. Oxford: Oxford University Press, 2016.

La Vopa, Anthony J. "The Philosopher and the *Schwärmer*: On the Career of a German Epithet from Luther to Kant." *Huntington Library Quarterly* 60 (1997) 85–115.

Mack, Phyllis. "Dreaming and Emotion in Early Evangelical Religion." In *Heart Religion: Evangelical Piety in England & Ireland, 1690–1850*, edited by John Coffey, 157–80. Oxford: Oxford University Press, 2016.

Page, Anthony. "Rational Dissent, Enlightenment, and Abolition of the British Slave Trade." *Historical Journal* 54 (2011) 741–72.

Plato. *Phaedrus*. Translated by Alexander Nehamas. Indianapolis: Hackett, 1995.

Pocock, J. G. A. "Enthusiasm: The Antiself of Enlightenment." *Huntington Library Quarterly* 60 (1997) 7–28.

Rivers, Isabel. *Vanity Fair and the Celestial City: Dissenting, Methodist, and Evangelical Literary Culture in England, 1720–1800*. Oxford: Oxford University Press, 2018.

———. *Whichcote to Wesley*. Vol. 1 of *Reason, Grace, and Sentiment: A Study in the Language of Religion and Ethics in England, 1660–1780*. Cambridge Studies in Eighteenth-Century English Literature and Thought 8. Cambridge: Cambridge University Press, 1991.

Rose, Jacqueline. "Dissent and the State: Persecution and Toleration." In *The Post-Reformation Era, c. 1559–c. 1689*, edited by John Coffey, 313–33. Vol. 1 of *The Oxford History of Protestant Dissenting Traditions*. Oxford: Oxford University Press, 2020.

Schwartz, Hillel. *Knaves, Fools, Madmen, and That Subtile Effluvium: A Study of the Opposition to the French Prophets in England, 1706–1710*. Gainesville: University Presses of Florida, 1978.

Scull, Andrew. *Madness in Civilization: A Cultural History of Insanity from the Bible to Freud, from the Madhouse to Modern Medicine*. London: Thames & Hudson, 2015.

Seed, John. "Gentlemen Dissenters: The Social and Political Meanings of Rational Dissent in the 1770s and 1780s." *Historical Journal* 28 (1985) 299–325.

Simpson, David. *A Plea for Religion and the Sacred Writings: Addressed to the Disciples of Thomas Paine, and Wavering Christians of Every Persuasion*. 1797. Reprint, London: Tegg, 1832.

Stephenson, William E. "Isaac Watts's Education for the Dissenting Ministry: A New Document." *Harvard Theological Review* 61 (1968) 263–81.

Ward, Patricia A. "Continental Spirituality and British Protestant Readers." In *Heart Religion: Evangelical Piety in England & Ireland, 1690–1850*, edited by John Coffey, 50–71. Oxford: Oxford University Press, 2016.

Ward, W. R. *The Protestant Evangelical Awakening*. Cambridge: Cambridge University Press, 1992.

Watts, Michael. *The Crisis and Conscience of Nonconformity*. Vol. 3 of *The Dissenters*. Oxford: Oxford University Press, 2015.

———. *From the Reformation to the French Revolution*. Vol. 1 of *The Dissenters*. Oxford: Oxford University Press, 1978.

Watts, Ruth. "Harriet Martineau and the Unitarian Tradition in Education." *Oxford Review of Education* 37 (2011) 637–51.

Wykes, David L. "Rational Dissent, Unitarianism, and the Closure of the Northampton Academy in 1798." *Journal of Religious History* 41 (2017) 3–21.

9

The Story of Christianity and Other Religions

MARK R. LINDSAY

IN A RECENT ARTICLE for the Australian theological journal *Colloquium*, missiologist John Flett noted the global diversity, polycentricity, and polyvocality of Christianity, grounding his comments in the "factual observation" that "the gravity of Christianity has shifted south." Demographically, and perhaps even culturally, Flett was quite correct. Nevertheless, he qualified these remarks by a recognition that the "expected orientation"—and thus power base of global Christianity—"remains toward Europe."[1] This more nuanced observation in Flett's article speaks to a popular and often unchallenged set of assumptions—that not only is there something particularly "European" about Christianity, but that there is, and has for two millennia always been, something particularly "Christian" about Europe.

It is undeniably the case that, for much of the last seventeen hundred years, Christendom and Europe have been almost contiguous; for centuries, the *corpus Christianum* and the *civitas Dei* overlapped precisely, with the center of both being located in Rome.[2] However, the story of European Christendom is also a story of the encounter between Christianity and a host of other religions, both imported and indigenous. Such encounters inevitably entail both challenges and opportunities for the evangelizing faith and the evangelized demography. As James Russell rightly states, "Distinguishing between that which is essential to Christianity and that which may be modified or omitted to advance the process of Christianization, has always been a major problem.... When Christian essentials are considered to include substantial elements of the proselytizing party's culture, the potential for alienating the target society is high. When Christian essentials

---

1. Flett, "Plotting an Oceanic Voice," 7–8.
2. Lindsay, *God Has Chosen*, 72.

are minimalized, and indigenous cultural and religious customs readily incorporated, the likelihood of syncretism increases."³ The story of European Christianity, and its engagement with myriad non-Christian religious traditions, has been a story characterized by precisely this tension. In this chapter, some of the most decisive, alongside some of the lesser known but nonetheless formative, of these encounters will be narrated and interpreted.

Christian Encounters with Early European Folk Traditions

In his study of Constantinian religious plurality, Mark Edwards avers that "from the reign of Hadrian to the late third century, stones and monuments bearing the name of Mithras . . . are found in every province of the empire."⁴ Its ubiquity notwithstanding, the Mithraic cultus was not the only religion vying for space and adherents. Edwards goes on to say that, throughout the first three centuries of the Common Era, European religious devotion was offered also to, among many others, Astarte, Attis, Demeter, and Dionysius.⁵ What is interesting, from the perspective of this chapter, is that this religious pluriformity was apparent throughout the empire precisely during those years when Christianity was spreading beyond the Holy Lands at an extraordinary, and possibly unparalleled, pace.

By the time of the Diocletian persecution of 304 CE, Christianity had spread not only southward from Jerusalem into Egypt and northern Africa, but also northwards and into the west. There were churches throughout Spain, modern-day France, and across into Britain. Indeed, the great Carthaginian Father Tertullian had spoken of "the haunts of the Britons" being among those evangelized lands that were "subjugated to Christ" as early as ca. 200 CE, with the death of the first British Christian martyr—St. Alban— dating from possibly no more than a decade after Tertullian's report.⁶ And, while definitive statistics are now impossible to discern, there is a broad scholarly appetite for believing that by the year 300—fully a quarter of a century before Constantine's watershed intervention at Nicaea—there may have been as many as six million Christians scattered throughout the European Empire.⁷ As Robin Lane Fox has commented, "No other cult in the

---

3. Russell, *Germanization*, 11.

4. M. Edwards, *Religions of Constantinian Empire*, 112.

5. M. Edwards, *Religions of Constantinian Empire*, 113–27.

6. Tertullian, "Answer to the Jews," §7. The exact date of St. Alban's martyrdom is contested; however, the earliest date puts it at 209 CE.

7. Hopkins, "Christian Number."

Empire grew at anything like the same speed."[8] Larry Hurtado is somewhat more cautious in his conclusions. Nonetheless, he too admits that "by all reckoning there was overall an impressive and broadly consistent growth in numbers of Christians across the first three centuries."[9]

The point of all this is, quite simply, to highlight the coincidence of Christianity's remarkable early spread through Western and parts of Central Europe, and the persistence through the same period of other, quite different religious traditions. Given the evangelistic impulses of Christianity, this newer faith had not only to encounter these other religions, but also to contend for its own survival in the face of them, and even to seek to convert their followers. As Sághy and Schoolmen note, even after the "sea-change of the fourth century that made Christianity the official religion of the State," there was a continued "coexistence of various religious cultures" throughout Christianized Europe.[10]

But what did that coexistence look like? Prior to the formal toleration of Christianity as a consequence of the Edict of Milan in 313 CE, and then the declaration of Nicene Christianity as the empire's official religion by the Edict of Thessalonica in 380 CE, Christian encounter with other religions was combative. In the late first century, for example, during the so-called Flavian Dynasty, Christians were in a "precarious position." They were confronted not only by a Jewish tradition from which Christianity was by then—and often quite acrimoniously—seeking to distance itself, but also by powerful urban elites of both Greek and Roman background, "who were consolidating their own power and not inclined to tolerate a movement composed of people who denied the existence of their own gods."[11] The example of second-century apologists, such as Justin Martyr and Athenagoras, illustrates precisely the issue at hand. Writing from Rome to Antoninus Pius, and through him to the whole senate, Justin noted somewhat provocatively that "though death is decreed against those who teach or at all confess the name of Christ, we everywhere both embrace and teach it."[12] The Athenian apologist Athenagoras was even blunter in his assessment; pagan idolatry—he has in mind particularly the cults of Neryllinus and Peregrinus Proteus—was nothing other than a device wrought by the demons, "who are eager for the blood of the sacrifices."[13]

---

8. Lane Fox, *Pagans and Christians*, 271.
9. Hurtado, *Why on Earth*, 32.
10. Sághy and Schoolmen, *Pagans and Christians*, 2–3.
11. D. Edwards, *Religion and Power*, 27.
12. Justin, *First Apology*, 45.
13. Athenagoras, *Embassy for the Christians*, 26.

But not all interreligious encounter was overtly combative, and nor was it only the Greco-Roman pantheon with which emergent Christianity had to deal. Much of what would now be called interreligious dialogue occurred between an imported Christianity on the one hand, and the more localized, folk, or indigenous cults of the lands into which Christianity was taken on the other. Gregory the Great's mission to the Angles—in Mayr-Harting's opinion, an evangelistic opportunity among "honest-to-goodness heathens," rather than Arian heretics, as had been the case with the Visigoths and the Lombards—is a case in point.[14] When Mellitus took charge of Gregory's second missionary journey to England in 601 CE, his instructions were clear—destroy the pagan temples and crush their inherent idolatry. No sooner had he arrived, however, than he received new orders from the pope. Gregory now wanted the temples to be reconsecrated for Christian worship, with cattle slaughter and feastings to be permitted within them on the church's feast days, as the English people had been used to doing prior to Christianity's arrival. Acknowledging that such toleration might encourage the continued, if subterranean, observance of a pagan cultus, Gregory was missiologically sanguine. The conversion of the English would be incremental, he advised, with it being "impossible to cut out everything at once from their stubborn minds."[15]

Such repurposing of folk and pagan religiosity for Christian ends was evident in other ways too. Richard Firth Green has noted the extraordinary use made by popular mystery plays in places like Chester and York of the early medieval belief in *faeries*. So, for example, Jesus is referred to sometimes as a "changeling"—a fairy who has been substituted for a real person—and on at least one other occasion as a "mare," a term referring to an incubus fairy.[16] Thus, while the church's official position was one of utterly intractable opposition to such superstitious belief—fairies and "elvish folk" were "mere fantasies bequeathed . . . by an evil spirit"[17]—popular medieval culture, dramatized in the mystery plays of the thirteenth to the fifteenth centuries, sought ways to adjust its traditional religion to the various ecclesiastical orthodoxies. We should not therefore be surprised, says Green, to encounter throughout medieval England "fairies who swear by the Virgin Mary [and] who are eager to attend mass."[18] The end goal of such syncretistic blending may have been to raise, sotto voce, a protest against a

14. Mayr-Harting, *Coming of Christianity*, 60.
15. Bede, *Ecclesiastical History*, 1.30.
16. Green, *Elf Queens*, 127–30.
17. Green, *Elf Queens*, 1.
18. Green, *Elf Queens*, 2.

formal and alien orthodoxy. It may on the other hand, however, been a rather clever rhetorical device designed to translate Christian—and specifically Christological—motifs into language that was more readily comprehensible among a more latently traditionalist (read: pagan) audience.

This sort of religious blending is apparent also in early medieval Germany. Gregory Dix has noted that "the barbarians followed their chiefs submissively into the fold of the church . . . but that did not in fact make them responsible Christians. Their mass movements into Christianity . . . did not betoken any sort of change of heart."[19] One reason why this might have been the case is suggested by George Jones's study of ancient Germanic religiosity, in which the disparity between Germanic values of kinship loyalty—including, but not limited to, the necessity of avenging, even to death, dishonored kin—and Christian values of forgiveness and mercy, was so glaring that "there was not much to which the [Christian] missionaries could appeal."[20] Thus, rather than positing Christianity in such starkly oppositional terms—to paraphrase Tertullian, "What has Jesus to do with Odin?"—Christian missionaries to the Germanic lands instead, at least according to Jones, "sought to redefine the Germanic virtues of strength, courage, and loyalty [so as to] reduce their incompatibility with Christianity, while at the same time 'enculturating' Christian values as far as possible to accommodate the Germanic ethos."[21] In just one example, St. Odo (d. 944 CE), second abbot of Cluny, attempted in his hagiographic *Vita sancti Geraldi* to "sublimate the Germanic warrior ethos into the service of the Church," with St. Gerald himself being "explicitly set forth as a model for the *potentiores*. . . . He was rich and powerful and a warrior."[22] As Mircea Eliade has noted, genealogical descent from mythic figures like Wodan remain ingredient to Germanic sovereigns' legitimacy, even after their Christian conversions, with Wodan himself being woven into Christianized narratives as variously Noah's son or a descendant of the Blessed Virgin's cousin.[23] "Conversion to Christianity gave rise to many reinterpretations and revalorizations of [Germanic] ancestral traditions. But it never succeeded in effacing the pagan heritage."[24]

In other words, the picture that emerges from the early through to the late medieval period, and from England across through the Germanic

19. Gregory Dix, *Shape of the Liturgy*, 595–96; cited in Russell, *Germanization*, 199.

20. George Jones, *Honor in German Literature*, 41; cited in Russell, *Germanization*, 121.

21. Russell, *Germanization*, 121.

22. Barbara H. Rosenwein, *Rhinoceros Bound*, 73–75; cited in Russell, *Germanization*, 124.

23. Eliade, *From Muhammad*, 90.

24. Eliade, *From Muhammad*, 92.

lands, is one of Christian accommodation of existing religious traditions, rather than a complete replacement of the old by the new. This accommodation may have been at times reluctant, but it was—as we have seen with Gregory's advice to Mellitus—certainly pragmatic. James Russell goes even further. In his view, the vitality of the Germanic folk traditions was so strong that in fact the result was a Germanization of Christianity that became normative throughout Western Christendom—in parts, even up to the mid-twentieth century—rather than a Christianization of German myth.[25]

Lest we suggest too close a syncretistic merging of Christianity with European folk religions, it is perhaps useful to discuss briefly one form of religiosity with which Christianity seems to have had no truck at any stage of its European life, namely, witchcraft. Rodney Stark's invaluable sociological research has thankfully repudiated the long-held assumption that medieval and early modern Europe was flooded with the blood of witchcraft and witch hunts. Far from the "absurd" death tolls claimed by Andrea Dworkin, Mary Daly, and Pennethorne Hughes—no, there were not nine million European victims of witch trials—Stark argues that the real number of people executed for witchcraft was probably closer to sixty thousand across Europe, and that the most frenzied witch-hunting season was limited to the three centuries between 1450 and 1750.[26] Similarly, he notes that, while magic and sorcery were at least frowned upon, if not denounced, by the church, it was *satanism* that came to define the essence of European witchcraft, and that crossed the line from magic (to which a blind ecclesiastical eye might be turned) to religion (which could not be so ignored).[27]

Even so, witchcraft was not intrinsically condemned. Indeed, St. Boniface (d. 754 CE) declared that belief in witches was "un-Christian," while St. Agobard (779–840 CE), accepting that witches did in fact exist, nonetheless denied that they had any actual power. Such denials of the reality of witchcraft as an effective potency became enshrined in the tenth-century *canon Episcopi*, in which the notion of witchcraft as a physical manifestation was formally repudiated. Its (re)emergence as a threat to Christianity that was (a) inextricably connected to satanism, and (b) therefore something that had to be mercilessly crushed, coincided with the threat to institutional Catholicism that was represented by the Cathars and Waldensians in the twelfth century. Despite the eventual failure of this proto-Reformation, it nevertheless inspired an ever-increasing number of Christian sectarian movements—culminating in the sixteenth-century forms of Protestantism—each

25. Russell, *Germanization*, 209–10.
26. Stark, *For Glory of God*, 202–3.
27. Stark, *For Glory of God*, 206.

of which was understood, by the very repetition of Christian liturgies outside the authorization of the church, to be self-evidently confecting a devilish parody of Christian worship. Hence the stereotypical depictions of satanic masses, and the correlation of heresy with satanism and witchcraft. As Stark insists, the Protestant reforms and the era of witch hunts are "inseparable."[28]

But the equation is not one-sided. For insofar as Protestantism was equally convinced that Roman Catholicism was satanic—the Roman Mass is an abomination of Satan, says Calvin[29]—Reformers took their own witch-hunting agendas into the Catholic territories over which they gained control. In short, during the age of the European religious wars from the twelfth through the seventeenth centuries, heresy—whether it was Roman, Protestant, or proto-Protestant—was associated with a deliberate perversion of the Christian cultus, which, for that very reason, was attributed to the devil's influence. Witchcraft had become something no longer outside the boundaries of religious life with no ecclesially acknowledged reality but rather, through the media of satanically inspired liturgical perversions, a potent entity that had brought magic into consort with heresy. This conflation of satanism, witch-hunting, and intra-Christian enmity also helps explain why, in the aftermath of the Peace of Westphalia of 1648 and the greater degree of religious toleration that that brought, not only did heresy-hunting decline dramatically, so too did the prevalence of witch trials.[30]

European Christianity's Encounter with Islam

To discuss the encounter of Christian Europe with Islam—and by extension the impact of Islamic culture, art, and learning on European Christians—requires a sober acknowledgment that much of that encounter has taken place in the form of assumption and stereotype. As Maurits Berger has said of the late Byzantine period, "from a European perspective much of the interaction with 'Islam' took place . . . without any physical Muslim counterpart. In other words, talking and writing about 'Mahomet' and the 'Turk' was done mostly by Europeans who had had no encounters with Muslims themselves."[31] Berger goes on to say that such depersonalized assumptions continued to govern most Europeans' understanding of Islam until well into the modern era. One consequence of this caricaturing was a tendency towards demonization. As John Esposito has said, "The European

---

28. Stark, *For Glory of God*, 250.
29. Calvin, *Institutes*, 4.18.1.
30. Stark, *For Glory of God*, 282.
31. Berger, *Brief History of Islam*, 22.

Christian response [to Islam] was, with few exceptions, hostile, intolerant, and belligerent. Muhammad was vilified as an imposter and identified as the antichrist. Islam was dismissed as a religion of the sword led by an infidel driven by a lust for power and women."[32] Having said that, Christian engagement with Islam as a religion, and with Muslims as people, was not limited to the theoretical realm. There were innumerable examples of "real-life" encounter, many of which were momentous in both their scope and impact, and not all of them intractably negative.

From the seventh through the tenth centuries, the religious context of Europe—most especially in its southern and western regions—was decisively altered by the arrival, and then expansion, of Islamic communities. Emperor Constans II's disastrous defeat in the naval Battle of Phoenix in 655 CE paved the way for Caliph Mu'awiya I's siege of Constantinople in 674 CE and the simultaneous blockade of Chalcedon. That the Byzantine Empire managed eventually to rout the invading forces proved only a temporary reprieve in Christian Europe's attempt to protect itself against Muslim Arab incursions. Over the next fifty years, Islamic armies of the Ummayad Caliphate captured much of the Iberian Peninsula and then advanced further into western Gaul. Far from being regarded as an alternative to the hoped-for destruction of Byzantium, it was in fact understood as its necessary means. As the tradition of Caliph Uthman put it, "Only through Spain can Constantinople be conquered."[33]

The Caliphate's eventual defeat at the Battle of Tours (Poitiers) in 732 CE proved decisive, insofar as Muslim armies never ventured further into Europe until the siege of Vienna in 1683. Nevertheless, there remained considerable, and not always amicable, encounters between Christians and Muslims throughout Europe during these centuries. Some have suggested that part of the reason why the Ummayad Caliphate was able to push so hard beyond the Pyrennees was because it received active support from "third-column" Monophysite Christians who were aggrieved at their treatment by the Chalcedonian faction that dominated Byzantine Christianity. While this poses the intriguing prospect of Christian-Muslim cooperation, there is little solid evidence to support the theory.[34]

It would be easy to point to the infamous martyrs of Cordoba—a total of fifty-eight Christians who were executed by the Muslim administration in Al-Adalus between 850 and 859 CE variously for blasphemy and apostasy—as representative of normative European Christian-Muslim encounters.

---

32. John Esposito, *Islam: The Straight Path*, 67; cited in Lindsay, *God Has Chosen*, 76.
33. Al-Ma'sumi, "Earliest Muslim Invasion," 97.
34. See Collins, *Early Medieval Europe*, 151; cf. Berger, *Brief History of Islam*, 40.

Such would be an understandable conclusion, if one also wished to prioritize the recurring Arab incursions, from the Iberian invasion to the siege of Vienna, as religiously motivated wars of conquest. That, however, would be to flatten out the history of Christian-Muslim engagement into an unrepresentative caricature. For a start, it is unlikely that the Muslim incursions into Europe were for the purpose of religious conquest. That would imply a consequential forced conversion of the conquered peoples, yet such did not take place. On the contrary, while Muslim armies did wage occasional wars of conquest into the European mainland, those same armies "did not impose on their non-Muslim subjects a compulsory conversion to Islam, nor was there any Muslim missionary activity among the non-believers."[35] Rather, the encounter between European Christians and Islamic communities was variegated, and at times highly productive. As Alexandre Roberts has said in the context of the eleventh-century commerce between Byzantium and the Middle East, the two cultures "were hardly worlds apart, nor was their contact restricted to war and diplomacy. On the contrary, scholars, texts, and ideas circulated widely across their political boundaries, in both directions."[36] To put it otherwise, European Christians engaged with Muslims "on the battlefield *and* in the academy."[37]

Arguably the best example of productive Christian-Muslim engagement in Europe, from the High Middle Ages to early modernity, is the mutual intellectual dialogue that took place during the development of medieval scholasticism from the thirteenth century. One unforeseen consequence of the Muslim incursions into Byzantine territories had been the discovery of Aristotle's corpus by Islamic scholars. Between 750 CE and 900 CE, that corpus was systematically translated into Arabic from its Greek and Syriac versions. Then, over the next two hundred years, Aristotle's philosophy was pored over in minute detail by Islamic polymaths, such as the Persian Avicenna (Ibn Sina, 980–1037 CE) and the Andalusian Averroes (Ibn Rushd, 1126–98 CE), who not only translated it, but commented upon it. When Christian forces entered Spain in the 1100s as part of the centuries-long *reconquista*, this Aristotelian corpus, now in its Arabic Muslim iterations, thus became known once again to Christian scholarship. Consequently, the scholastic development in Western Christianity not only learned its Aristotle again, but also benefited from Islamic learning in ethics, theology, and science.

35. Berger, *Brief History of Islam*, 45.
36. Roberts, *Reason and Revelation*, 2.
37. Lindsay, *God Has Chosen*, 76.

To take Ibn Sina's contribution, for example, his "synthesis of Graeco-Arabic philosophy, with concerns central to all three of the Abrahamic religions, helped facilitate and prepare Latin Europe for the reintroduction of the Aristotelian scientific tradition. As such, [his] thought played an important role in the reinvigoration of philosophy in Europe, as well as the formulation of Christian theology."[38] While Avicenna's enduring theological impact was felt particularly as he was mediated by Thomas Aquinas, he made his presence known in other disciplines too. In medicine, for example, his *Canon of Medicine* was a standard medical textbook throughout Europe into the eighteenth century, while his *Book of Healing* proved invaluable to Albertus Magnus's psychological studies in the thirteenth century.[39]

Averroes arguably had a greater, but more contested, influence on the development of Western European intellectual endeavor. Employed as "one of the main guides for understanding Aristotle's teachings until the Age of the Enlightenment," Averroes was equally influential in the formulation of early modern understandings of physics, psychology, and cosmology.[40] Certainly by the seventeenth century his reputation as a *reliable* intellectual guide was being challenged. This was, in considerable part, because—in the wake of the Reformed emphasis on the doctrine of divine providence and Pierre Gassendi's revival of Epicureanism—a figure such as Averroes, who was taken to represent those thinkers "who denied providence by dismissing the role of divine intervention in the sublunary world," was an easy target.[41] Nevertheless, as Craig Martin has noted, by the close of the seventeenth century, while Averroes "might have [become] irrelevant, yet he still remained etched in the collective imagination," such had his influence been, for so long a time.[42]

It is, of course, regrettably true that the narrative of European Christian-Muslim encounter has been seismically shifted since the terror attacks of 9/11. It is difficult now to conceive of Christian-Muslim dialogue in any part of the Western world, not least Europe, that does not immediately get refracted through that lens of conflict and enmity. Such a characterization misses the vital and vivifying impact that Islamic learning, and culture more generally, had on a millennium of European Christianity. Nevertheless, as far back as the fourteenth century, Dante—that great poet of medieval Christendom—had relegated Muhammad to the eighth circle of hell, a

---

38. McGinnis, *Avicenna*, 244.
39. McGinnis, *Avicenna*, 251.
40. Bakker, *Averroes' Natural Philosophy*, vii.
41. Martin, "Providence and Seventeenth-Century Attacks," 197.
42. Martin, "Providence and Seventeenth-Century Attacks," 195.

place reserved for apostates and schismatics.[43] (Since Peter the Venerable [1092–56 CE], Islam had routinely been understood theologically as a Christological heresy.) Such a portrayal illustrates precisely why Muslims have struggled for so much of European history to be tolerated as full members of the European body politic; insofar as they were believed to represent an apostate religion, Christian Europe *had* to exclude them from any sense of ultimate belonging.[44] With that in mind, it is perhaps legitimate, albeit tragic, to see the post-9/11 narrative of Christian-Muslim encounter as more typical of the longer European history. Averroes, Avicenna, and the great cultural contributions of Islam to European society become, on this reading, significant precisely because of their *unrepresentative* character.

European Christianity's Encounter with Judaism

The Shoah—the Holocaust of the Jews under Adolf Hitler's Nazi regime—is the unhealed wound in the soul of European Christianity. While it is always dangerous to speak of historical inevitabilities, Christian Europe's nearly two millennia of hostility towards Jews and Judaism, a hostility that was born precisely out of its *Christianity*, provided the necessary, if not sufficient, ground out of which the Holocaust was made possible. In little more than twelve years, six million Jews—fully two-thirds of Europe's Jewish population—were murdered. That traditional forms of anti-Semitism have, in the years since the Holocaust, largely been discredited is in the main, according to Alvin Rosenfeld, because much of Europe "has entered a post-Christian phase," with the churches' negative doctrines about the Jews no longer holding sway among a majority of people. Recognizing this to be a positive move—while at the same time acknowledging that contemporary forms of anti-Semitism that are driven by political ideologies rather than racial or religious prejudices are emerging in force—Rosenfeld's argument simply underscores how critically important Europe's *Christianness* was to its previous forms of enmity towards Jews.[45] Much more can and should be said of Christian-Jewish encounter throughout European history, and not all of it so negative. Nonetheless, insofar as "Nazism was defeated in Europe . . . [but] antisemitism was not,"[46] the narrative must begin with an acknowledgment of this deepest of wounds, which has infected European

---

43. Alighieri, *Divine Comedy, Inferno*, canto 38, 22–34.
44. Lindsay, *God Has Chosen*, 77.
45. Rosenfeld, *Resurgent Antisemitism*, 2–3.
46. Rosenfeld, *Resurgent Antisemitism*, 1.

Christianity from the first centuries of Christian mission in Europe through to the present day.

In late fourth-century Milan, the venerable Bishop Ambrose, who was to have such an enduring influence on his North African catechumen Augustine, compiled a collection of his homilies under the title *Expositio evangelii secundum Lucam*. Its two primary characteristics were, according to Maria Doerfer, an unashamed unoriginality, and "a virulent anti-Jewish tenor." "Scarcely a passage," says Doerfer, "is free of venom."[47] True, Ambrose's animus against Jews was largely theoretical—he seems to have had almost no contact with any actual Jewish communities. This is hardly surprising, in that until the twelfth century, 90 percent of Europe's Jews remained confined to the Iberian Peninsula. Nevertheless, Jews became for Ambrose a demonic cipher that could stand not only for Jews and Judaism *as such*, but for all whom he wished to excoriate and excise as heterodox. By correlating Jews and heretics, arguing that both groups shared the same fundamental characteristics, Ambrose was able to "persuade his audience who had long learned to reject Jewishness to [also] reject non-Nicene Christianity."[48] What is of interest here is less the rhetorical manner in which Ambrose constructed (confected?) his "Jew-heretic" opposition, and more the fact that, by as early as the 380s, Milanese, if not European, Christianity was already so steeped in anti-Jewish prejudice that "Jews" could be used as a potent symbol for the demonization of any "other" to which the symbol was rhetorically attached. Two hundred years later, Gregory the Great provided further foundation for an anti-Jewish animus that would permeate ecclesiastical teaching for centuries. According to Gregory's logic, a large part of the threat posed by the Jews lay in the fact that they were not only corrupters, but that they *knew* they were, and yet nevertheless persisted in their corruption.[49] Their stubbornness was not, it could then be claimed, something from which they might repent, but rather an essential ingredient of "Jewishness." Centuries later, this idea of a Jew's indelible "Jewishness"—something that could not be washed away even by baptism—would be used to devastating effect by Hitler's Nazis against Jewish Christians, for whom conversion could thus be no escape from genocide.

In the second half of the twentieth century, the German jurist Carl Schmitt wrote of his hatred of diasporic Jews because, as essentially stateless people, they "lacked reverence for order in general and the sovereign

---

47. Doerfer, "Ambrose's Jews," 750.
48. Doerfer, "Ambrose's Jews," 761.
49. Johnson, *History of the Jews*, 206.

authority of the state in particular."⁵⁰ That they were a people without a nation-state was both a sufficient reason for hating them and a justification for seeking their expulsion from Europe. Schmitt, though, was unoriginal. Throughout Europe's earlier history, Jews had been the "eternal strangers," personifications—both individually and collectively—of Ahasuerus's myth of the stateless and eternal wanderer. From Prudentius Clemens and Johannes Molchus, through to Matthew Paris, Percy Bysshe Shelley, and even Charles Dickens, the European popular imagination has refracted Jews through the same trope so insistently prosecuted by Schmittian political theory.

And yet, as with European Christianity's encounter with Islam, the situation has always been more complicated. Alongside being targeted for their alleged religious, and later racial, perversion, Jews have also served important, even necessary, social functions in European society. As Paul Johnson has noted, "The powers-that-be favoured Jews, other things being equal. They were the best of all colonists, had useful trading networks, possessed rare skills, accumulated wealth quickly and were easy to tax." Indeed, says Johnson, Jews in Europe "flourished under the Carolingians."[51] Thus, we see the bishop of Speyer granting the Jews in his city a charter of privileges in 1084, with Emperor Henry IV extending those privileges to the Jews of Worms in 1090, and Frederick II doing the same for all Jews throughout the empire in 1236.

Official church pronouncements, arguably up until Vatican II, reflected this ambiguity, wavering between condemnations of anti-Jewish massacres on the one hand (such as the papal bulls by Innocent IV in 1247 and Gregory X in 1272) and expulsion orders from cities and towns (such as from Vienna in 1253) on the other. But ecclesial ambiguity was not reflective simply of the church's political uncertainty about what to do with the Jews. There was, in fact, an eschatological necessity in the church's mind to this bifurcated response to them. Church teaching insisted on two things at once: that Jews were "potential Christians," possible members of the "remnant" of whom the apostle Paul had spoken (Rom 9–11) and who were thus ripe for conversion; but in the ossification of their religion and the depredation of their lives, they were also witnesses to the fact that God had cast them off, choosing Christians in their place. That is, the church's *adversos Judaeos* teaching required the Jews to be visibly punished for their infidelity, and yet also protected as both a testifying artifact and as prospective converts.[52] As Bernard of Clairvaux said in the twelfth century, "The Jews are for us the

---

50. Ratip, "Katechon over Acheron," 63.
51. Johnson, *History of the Jews*, 205.
52. Hood, *Aquinas and the Jews*, 28.

living words of Scripture, for they remind us always of what our Lord suffered. They are dispersed all over the world so that by expiating their crime they may be everywhere the living witnesses of our redemption."[53]

The general population throughout much of Europe, however, was far less vacillating in its attitude. Jews were routinely depicted in European art, literature, and popular legends as sorcerers, cannibals, profaners of the eucharistic host, and even as the corporeal manifestation of Satan himself. Dan Cohn-Sherbok paints a dismal and horrifying picture: "In the Middle Ages Jews were viewed as the personification of evil. Dabbling in the occult, they were associated with devils and demons. At times, they were depicted as the devil himself; alternatively, they were seen as intermediaries between the devil and innocent human beings. Given such diabolical attributes, it is not surprising that the Jewish people were relegated to a sub-species of humanity.... As the vermin of the earth, they were a contagion in the body of Europe."[54]

Cohn-Sherbok, in the wake of the Holocaust, has read Nazi imagery back into the medieval and early modern experience of European Jewry; their being and nature were not understood in quite so simple terms as he suggests, and certainly the Jewish "threat" was not construed in such pathological ways. Nevertheless, Jews have been subject to a particular virulent, and a particularly *Christian*, form of hatred through most of European history, which has been exacerbated by Europe's (until recently) dominant cultural Christianness. For all the methodological problems of his controversial 1996 book, Daniel Goldhagen was right to say that the depiction of Jews as "fundamentally different and maleficent" was at the time of the Shoah "an axiom ... of most of Christian culture."[55] Indeed, in the light of not only the Holocaust, but also the long tradition of pogroms, exclusions, and ghettoizations—not only in Germany, but across the breadth of the European continent—it is hard to argue against Goldhagen's thesis that "antisemitism has been a permanent feature of [European] Christian civilization."[56]

Conclusion

This chapter's narration of European Christianity's encounter with other religious traditions has been necessarily selective and piecemeal. There are

---

53. Bernard of Clairvaux, "Letter to the People of England"; cited in Chazan, *Church, State and Jew*, 103.
54. Cohn-Sherbok, *Crucified Jew*, 55.
55. Goldhagen, *Hitler's Willing Executioners*, 30.
56. Goldhagen, *Hitler's Willing Executioners*, 39.

many more instances of positive engagements with Judaism and Islam, for example, than I have had space to discuss here. Similarly, the increasingly multicultural and secularized form of Europe that has emerged in the last sixty or so years has complicated the story beyond the sketch that I have presented. First, migration patterns to Europe have introduced a plethora of non-Western religions, including those from Africa, China, and the Caribbean. Second, Europe's increasing secularity has granted this religious diversity a legitimacy and toleration that would have been unthinkable even 150 years ago. I am conscious that this part of the story, too, has remained untold in this chapter.

Nevertheless, a 2018 Pew Research Center study found that most Western Europeans still considered themselves Christian, even if most did not regularly attend church. Religious observance aside, Europe remains paradoxically staunchly Christianized, and yet at the same time one of the most secular regions of the world.[57] In this context, it is instructive—and sobering—to note that the same study found that "self-identified Christians—whether they attend church or not—are more likely than religiously unaffiliated people to express negative views of immigrants ... Muslims and Jews."[58] If this is indeed the case, then it suggests that the admittedly selective narrative I have described in this chapter, notwithstanding the many instances of positive encounter that I have left untold, is likely a reasonable summary of the historic reality. That for the last nearly seventeen hundred years, to be European was to be Christian—to be anything else was to be "other," suspect, a potential threat that could best be negated by absorption (Germanic or English folk traditions), exclusion (Islam), or elimination (Judaism). If there have been happier instances of non-Christian encounter with European Christianity—and there have been—they are notable, sadly, precisely for their exceptionalism.

Bibliography

Alighieri, Dante. *The Divine Comedy*. Translated by C. H. Sisson. London: Pan, 1981.
Al-Ma'sumi, M. Saghir Hasan. "The Earliest Muslim Invasion of Spain." *Islamic Studies* 3 (1964) 97–102.
Athenagoras. *Embassy for the Christians; The Resurrection of the Dead*. Translated by Joseph Hugh Crehan. Mahwah, NJ: Paulist, 1955.
Bakker, Paul J. J. M., ed. *Averroes' Natural Philosophy and Its Reception in the Latin West*. Ancient and Medieval Philosophy 150. Leuven: Leuven University Press, 2015.

---

57. Pew Research Center, *Being Christian*, 6–7.
58. Pew Research Center, *Being Christian*, 9.

Bede. *The Ecclesiastical History of the English People*. Edited by Judith McClure and Roger Collins. Translated by Bertram Colgrave. Oxford World's Classics. Oxford: Oxford University Press, 1994.

Berger, Maurits S. *A Brief History of Islam in Europe: Thirteen Centuries of Creed, Conflict and Coexistence*. Leiden: Leiden University Press, 2014.

Calvin, John. *Institutes of the Christian Religion*. Translated by Henry Beveridge. Grand Rapids: Eerdmans, 1995.

Chazan, Robert, ed. *Church, State and Jew in the Middle Ages*. Library of Jewish Studies. Millburn, NJ: Behrman, 1980.

Cohn-Sherbok, Dan. *The Crucified Jew: Twenty Centuries of Christian Anti-Semitism*. London: Fount, 1993.

Collins, Roger. *Early Medieval Europe: 300–1000*. 2nd ed. Palgrave History of Europe. Basingstoke, UK: Palgrave, 1999.

Doerfer, Maria. "Ambrose's Jews: The Creation of Judaism and Heterodox Christianity in Ambrose of Milan's *Expositio evangelii secundum Lucam*." *Church History* 80 (2011) 749–72.

Edwards, Douglas R. *Religion and Power: Pagans, Jews, and Christians in the Greek East*. Oxford: Oxford University Press, 1996.

Edwards, Mark. *Religions of the Constantinian Empire*. Oxford: Oxford University Press, 2015.

Eliade, Mircea. *From Muhammad to the Age of Reforms*. Vol. 3 of *History of Religious Ideas*. Chicago: University of Chicago Press, 1985.

Flett, John G. "Plotting an Oceanic View: A Longitudinal Review and Analysis of Regional Theologising." *Colloquium* 54 (2022) 5–60.

Goldhagen, Daniel Jonah. *Hitler's Willing Executioners: Ordinary Germans and the Holocaust*. New York: Little, Brown and Co., 1996.

Green, Richard Firth. *Elf Queens and Holy Friars: Fairy Beliefs and the Medieval Church*. Middle Ages Series. Philadelphia: Pennsylvania University Press, 2016.

Hood, John Y. B. *Aquinas and the Jews*. Middle Ages Series. Philadelphia: University of Pennsylvania Press, 1995.

Hopkins, Keith. "Christian Number and Its Implications." *JECS* 6 (1998) 185–226.

Hurtado, Larry. *Why on Earth Did Anyone Become a Christian in the First Three Centuries?* Milwaukee: Marquette University Press, 2016.

Johnson, Paul. *A History of the Jews*. London: Orion, 1993.

Justin, Philosopher and Martyr. *Apologies*. Edited and translated by Denis Minns and Paul Parvis. Oxford Early Christian Texts. Oxford: Oxford University Press, 2009.

Lane Fox, Robin. *Pagans and Christians*. New York: Knopf, 1986.

Lindsay, Mark R. *God Has Chosen: The Doctrine of Election through Christian History*, Downers Grove, IL: IVP Academic, 2020.

Martin, Craig. "Providence and Seventeenth-Century Attacks on Averroes." In *Averroes' Natural Philosophy and Its Reception in the Latin West*, edited by Paul J. J. M. Bakker, 193–212. Ancient and Medieval Philosophy 150. Leuven: Leuven University Press, 2015.

Mayr-Harting, Henry. *The Coming of Christianity to Anglo-Saxon England*. 3rd ed. Avon, UK: Bath, 1991.

McGinnis, Jon. *Avicenna*. Great Medieval Thinkers. Oxford: Oxford University Press, 2010.

Pew Research Center. *Being Christian in Western Europe*. Pew Research Center, May 29, 2018. https://www.pewresearch.org/religion/2018/05/29/being-christian-in-western-europe/.

Ratip, Mehmet. "Katechon over Acheron: Carl Schmitt's Ambivalence and the Sovereignty of Exception." *Çankaya University Journal of Humanities and Social Sciences* 7 (2010) 59–74.

Roberts, Alexandre M. *Reason and Revelation in Byzantine Antioch: The Christian Translation Program of Abdallah ibn al-Fadl*. Berkeley Series in Postclassical Islamic Scholarship. Berkeley: University of California Press, 2020.

Rosenfeld, Alvin Hirsch, ed. *Resurgent Antisemitism: Global Perspectives*. Studies in Antisemitism. Bloomington: Indiana University Press, 2013.

Russell, James C. *The Germanization of Early Medieval Christianity: A Sociohistorical Approach to Religious Transformation*. Oxford: Oxford University Press, 1994.

Sághy, Marianne, and Edward M. Schoolmen, eds. *Pagans and Christians in the Late Roman Empire: New Evidence, New Approaches (4th–8th Centuries)*. CEU Medievalia. Budapest: Central European University Press, 2017.

Stark, Rodney. *For the Glory of God: How Monotheism Led to Reformations, Science, Witch-Hunts, and the End of Slavery*. Princeton: Princeton University Press, 2003.

Tertullian. "An Answer to the Jews." In *The Ante-Nicene Fathers*, edited by Alexander Roberts and James Donaldson, translated by S. Thewall, 3:15–18. Repr., Grand Rapids: Eerdmans, 1978.

Section Three

The Story of Christianity Encounters Modernity and Postmodernity

10

Industry, Economic Transformation, and European Christianity

JAMES KENNEDY

THE SUFFERING, INDIGNITY, AND injustice caused by the Industrial Revolution demanded a response from the church. That was the position taken by Pope Leo XIII (1878–1903) when he issued his famous encyclical *Rerum Novarum* (meaning "of new things") in 1891. The pope praised the social and economic change sweeping the world for the benefits it brought, including wonderful breakthroughs in science. But, he argued, the change also had deeply troubling effects. Industrial capitalism had dissolved the old bonds between workers and their masters, resulting in "the utter poverty of the masses" and "moral degeneracy." In casting aside the old religion and traditional worker protections, "working men have been surrendered, isolated and helpless, to the hardheartedness of employers and the greed of unchecked competition." The tragic result of this was that "a small number of very rich men have been able to lay upon the teeming masses of the laboring poor a yoke little better than that of slavery itself."[1]

Leo now urged that workers be treated not as objects but with dignity; all people, poor and rich alike, are created in the image of God. Workers must be given a just wage and should earn enough to support their families. Moreover, people should take up only the labor appropriate to their age and their sex. Laborers should not be overworked and must be given room to develop as humans and to have time free to worship. Leo saw workers' organizations as an important way to stand up for the rights of the working class. But workers must always seek good relations with their employers and never use violence against them or their property. Workers must certainly not be misled by socialism to think that ending private property would bring

1. Leo XIII, "*Rerum Novarum*," §3.

a solution to their suffering. A harmonious society depended on property rights, also for the poor. To that end, the enormous divide between the rich and the "teeming masses" needed to be narrowed.[2]

Rerum Novarum is a good place to begin the story about the relationship between Christianity and the transformative economic and social change that included the Industrial Revolution (or, as many historians say: revolutions, because of the different phases). It is a good place to begin as a way to highlight that Leo—and the church as a whole—was late to pronounce so solemnly on so important a problem. By 1891, the Industrial Revolution's impact already had been felt, at least in some parts of Europe, for decades. Moreover, the global economic system had long before *Rerum Novarum* transformed labor into a commodity, exposing workers to exploitation. There were, to be sure, Christians across denominations who spoke or acted to improve the lives of workers long before *Rerum*. As a whole, though, the churches were slow to prioritize "the social question," that is, the question of how to structurally deal with the plight of the working class. This chapter explores why this was the case. It also shows which early steps that they did undertake.

At the same time, *Rerum Novarum*, and other Christian responses at the end of the nineteenth century, had significant impact on how European societies responded to the ruptures of modern capitalism and the Industrial Revolution. They became important agents in bringing about social reforms, in organizing some of the working class to defend its interests and perhaps surprisingly, in introducing or supporting legislation that eventually crafted European welfare states.

There is a widespread assumption, still too often held by social scientists, that religion almost self-evidently declined as the modern world advanced.[3] In this view, economic changes and the industrialization and urbanization of the nineteenth and early twentieth centuries irredeemably dissolved the old bonds of faith and community. There is, however, no clear-cut evidence that links the "dechristianization" of society to urbanization and industrialization, and the reality is more complex.[4] In some ways, Christian activity was actually enlivened by these economic and social shifts, and Christian leaders developed a wide array of new organizations and strategies that met the needs of many people living in industrialized society. It was only with the far-reaching "deindustrialization" that started in the 1960s that European Christianity faced a deeper crisis.

2. Leo XIII, "*Rerum Novarum*," §3.
3. Clark, "Secularization and Modernization."
4. Pasteur, "Role of Religion," 105.

The Great Transformation

It is important to stress that our modern world is not first and foremost defined by industrialization but by the rise of a "full-fledged labor market."[5] The rise of an increasingly intertwined global economy that began in the sixteenth century made it possible for people to conceive of a radically new kind of society: where everything could be commodified, that is, bought and sold. This "great transformation," as the theorist Karl Polanyi (1886–1964) argued, included the creation of a market where the buying and selling of human labor, through market-priced wages, became a commodity just like any other.[6]

Furthermore, one could argue that the change that created the modern world was not in the first instance an "industrial" but an "institutional" revolution. All aspects of life became more measurable and more predictable by the mid-nineteenth century. Factories could now accurately measure what they could produce and how long it would take for their goods to arrive at their customers by train or steamship. Greater measurability made institutions more reliable, accountable, and honest than they had been before.[7] And they made all transactions ruthlessly efficient.

These changes dramatically rearranged the nature of society. The old dependence, for example, on one's family network for employment or security mattered less in a measurable, efficient market where one's relevant skills and one's availability mattered most. Scholars doubt Polanyi's assertion that profit-driven markets are exclusively modern.[8] But there can be little doubt that the modern economy thoroughly changed society. Old forms of economic security like the guilds disappeared, or were forbidden by the state. Family life changed to meet the demands of employers, with the "breadwinning" husband no longer working alongside his wife and children but outside the home. The very experience of time—through which productivity could now be precisely measured—became starkly different than before: a factory worker had to learn how to be punctual, and not to dally when "on the clock." Above all, perhaps, the ancient bonds of religion—so it seemed to many—lost its capacity to define communal life as it had always done time immemorial.

---

5. Van Kersbergen and Manow, "Religion," 7–8.
6. Polanyi, *Great Transformation*, 33–76.
7. Allen, *Institutional Revolution*.
8. McCloskey, "Polanyi Was Right."

Industrial Revolutions

It was in the context of this modern labor market that the Industrial Revolution began to take shape. This revolution was not only driven by technological innovations, such as respectively learning how to build steam, electric, and combustion engines. It was—given the societal change it demanded—as much a matter of organization, such as the managing of factories and their employees. This industrialization, too, would play a major part in changing Europe and European Christianity.

It would not, however, impact it evenly, or at the same time. Great Britain was—from about 1770—the first country to witness the beginning of the so-called First Industrial Revolution, made possible by a good coal supply and characterized by iron production and textile factories. By 1810, Belgium had become an important center of coal and iron production, and by 1850, western Germany constituted another industrial center. From there, industrial production, made possible by an growing rail network, would expand southwards and eastwards across Europe, eventually to Russia by the 1880s, Italy by the 1890s. By this time, steel and chemical production, along with harnessing of electricity and the use of petroleum, would usher in what is often called the Second Industrial Revolution.

Many parts of Europe, to be sure, remained rural; Germany itself became largely urbanized only after 1900 and France after 1920,[9] and some other European countries remained mostly agrarian until after the Second World War. In predominantly rural societies the church felt little need to address urban problems; the Russian Orthodox Church before Communism continued to reject capitalism as greedy and foreign.[10] But even in many of those regions the demand of industrialized cities for food changed the market economy and transformed agrarian society as well.

The Industrial Revolution, born out of these modern market logics, impacted the lives of millions of Europeans, for good and for ill. Many people easily can conjure up images of "Satanic mills"—to cite the much-discussed phrase from 1804 of William Blake's (1757–1827) poem "Jerusalem"—dark factories, exploited workers, and environmental degradation. One perennial question is whether, compared to preindustrial life, the standard of living for industrial workers actually rose or not. This has proven hard to answer. The consensus, though, seems to be is that it did after 1820 or 1830 in Britain, and that the workers of Western Europe never quite saw

---

9. Stearns, *Industrial Revolution*, 159.
10. Owen, "Industrialization and Capitalism," 221.

the depredations of the earliest English workers.[11] In fact, by the time Leo was writing in 1891, many workers in Europe saw their living conditions improve somewhat, raising the question of whether the pope's reference to "the utter poverty of the masses" was still a wholly accurate description of the working class.[12]

Still, working shifts remained long: twelve-hour days were still common in Britain at the time of *Rerum*. For many laborers it was the ever-faster rhythm of work, and the feeling of being "under the daily control of someone else," that made work most difficult.[13] By 1891, though, it mattered a good deal where one worked. Laborers in countries like Germany clearly had it materially better than in Russia, where in the years before the Revolution of 1917 workers still labored fourteen hours a day in massive, dangerous factories, and were housed with their families in apartments with no more than an iron bedstead and a straw mattress. It was one reason why Russian workers were among the most politically radicalized in Europe.[14]

Most Europeans came to recognize that modern markets needed to be, as Polanyi observed, partially "decommodified"—that is, that there had to be times and places where the market of buying and selling everything did not apply. Workers needed periods of rest, and if they fell ill or had an accident, they should be helped. Indeed, Polanyi argued, the very creation of the modern market triggered the rise of a state crafted to protect society. He saw a "double movement" in which a wholly commodified market went hand in hand with a modern regulatory state.[15] Polanyi was writing in hindsight, in 1944. In the nineteenth century, though, it was still a difficult question of how social problems in industrializing societies should be addressed. Legislation restricting child labor, first passed in the 1840s, was an early regulative initiative, partly through the efforts of devoted Christians like Lord Shaftesbury. Still the question remained. Could churches and private charities still meet their needs as they always had, or must the state play an expansive role in curbing the market? Ought Christians to focus on individual need or address collective injustice? In any event, the extent to which an interventionist state was desirable remained hotly disputed.

That was also true in Europe's Christian communities. Some believers responded to "the social question" with vision and action. But the churches

---

11. Stearns, *Industrial Revolution*, 34–35.
12. Waterman, *"Rerum Novarum,"* 29–30.
13. Stearns, *Industrial Revolution*, 71; see also 169–71.
14. Stearns, *Industrial Revolution*, 129–30.
15. Polanyi, *Great Transformation*, 111–77; Van Kersbergen and Manow, "Religion," 8–9.

initially demonstrated a hesitancy—and sometimes a serious inability—to address the social challenges brought by the Industrial Revolution.

The Church's Urban Shortcomings

Let's start with the inability of the churches to meet the demands of the industrial age. Europeans historically encountered the church through small-scale, typically rural, parish life. There the church was part of the larger social order built on deference to local aristocracy and leading families. Since early modern times, the established churches were dominated by these political and social elites.[16] However, labor migration to cities and factories often removed people from this social structure, including the church. The church would have to be a different kind of institution in large cities. But it was often hard for it to build up an effective urban presence. That required financing, staff, and infrastructure. Even if these were present, they did not always aim at securing church membership necessary for long-term support.[17]

Simply applying old parish models from the countryside to the cities, moreover, broke down, as the Scottish minister Thomas Chalmers experienced. Poor relief in the countryside was based on knowing who the recipients were; in urban Glasgow helping unknown paupers seemed to demand intrusive investigation into their situation.[18] The middle-class culture of many churches, moreover, repelled many working-class people, who often experienced the church as a completely alien community. In some cities like Berlin, where the middle class itself largely had rejected the church, workers often broke not only with it but with Christianity altogether.[19]

In short, the churches in industrialized Europe lacked capacity to connect with newly urbanized residents. Often, too, they wanted to be selective in whom they helped, preferring the "deserving poor." Churches' financial resources also were often limited. As a result, municipal governments, at least in Western Europe, came to take the lion's share of dispensing poor relief, sometimes at the insistence of Christian leaders themselves.[20] In the Netherlands, churches by law, and at their own insistence, were to help their own poor until as late as 1965, but city governments in effect had taken over

---

16. Cox, "Master Narratives," 211.
17. Cox, "Master Narratives," 213.
18. Knight, "Social Welfare," 46.
19. McLeod, *Piety and Poverty*, 107.
20. Kossert, "Religion," 49.

most of their responsibilities decades earlier.[21] The churches' struggling role in offering charity is the most important but not the only example of how the Industrial Revolution created new difficult challenges for them.

Distrust of the State

Furthermore, it took a long time before most Christians in places like England were attuned to "the social question."[22] That partly had to do with their roots as rural, elite-run institutions that had no natural affinity with, or understanding of, the industrial city and its social problems. It also had to do with the fact that churches, especially the Roman Catholic Church, were focused on other issues instead, particularly combatting the rise of the modern state. From the late eighteenth century, the modern state began a "hostile takeover of religious actors." For the well-being of all citizens, revolutionaries and liberal reformers considered it necessary to clearly subordinate religious authority to a secular one. Church property must be expropriated, education and marriage made secular, and the church itself subjected to state control.[23] The dramatic reduction of the church's authority was deeply disturbing to many European Christians, not least to the papacy itself; two popes were forced to leave Rome (in 1798 and in 1848) by anti-clerical forces.

The church's often bitter confrontation with the modern state had far-reaching consequences. It meant in the first place that many Christians focused on clawing back from the state areas that they thought out to remain under religious control—especially schools. It also made many churches, particularly but not exclusively the Catholic Church, deeply suspicious of the modern world. In 1835 Pope Gregory XVI (1831–1846), wittily expressing himself in French, equated the newly developed railroad with the "road to hell" (*Chemin de fer—chemin l'enfer*).[24] It was from this spiritual environment that Leo XIII himself stemmed, one that distrusted modern life as one linked to liberal and socialist ideas, foremost among them a vision for an anti-Christian state.

This conflict with secular elites and socialist movements was most intense where the Catholic Church had been powerful, in countries like France, Italy, and Spain. Many conservatives Protestants, too, were distrustful of attempts by the state to address the structural problems generated by

21. Van der Valk, *Van pauperzorg tot Bestaanszekerheid*.
22. Knight, "Social Welfare," 42–43.
23. Toft et al., *God's Century*, 65.
24. Cited in Zehnder, "Pope Gregory XVI."

urbanization and industrialization. This wary stance made many Christians in Germany (as in other countries) more reluctant to recognize a "social question" that demanded a response beyond traditional charity.[25] An interventionist state would destroy the spiritual bonds of charity between giver and recipient that had always held Christian community together.

Yet there were differences in the churches' response to "the social question," and poor relief in particular, that were partly shaped by specific religious traditions. These patterns could already be seen in the nineteenth century. Lutheran countries like those in Scandinavia, where church and state were tightly intertwined under the monarch, were the earliest to see a positive role for the state in dealing with these new problems (even though debates over how to divide the role of church and state persisted in a Lutheran country like Norway).[26] The Catholic Church, in contrast, preferred to find ways in which the Catholic community itself would address these issues, regarding care for the poor as an important spiritual practice. The Reformed (or Calvinist) approach, evident in a country like Britain, tended to emphasize self-help and private philanthropy as the way forward, with state support as a last resort. These characteristics would later determine the differing contours of European welfare states.[27] But in the nineteenth century churches from all confessions had to grapple with how to give effective answer to the new challenges of the Industrial Revolution.

New Charitable and Church-Led Responses

The difficulties and preoccupations of the Christian churches may suggest that the new industrial cities of Europe were bastions of godlessness, or least places that tended toward a secular bent of mind.[28] It seems more accurate to say that urbanization and industrialization promoted not so much secularism as religious and ideological pluralism, in which the range of (un)belief varied widely. New industrial cities like Manchester in England and Łódź in (what was then) Russian Poland generated "incredible religious and ethnic diversity."[29] Many urban dwellers knew little about or cared for organized religion (and it is very much the question how different this was before the Industrial Revolution).[30] But so, too, there were many expressions of active

25. Holzem, "Social Welfare," 199.
26. Tønnessen, "Christian Social Work," 300–301.
27. Kahl, "Religious Roots."
28. Stearns, *Industrial Revolution*, 88.
29. Kossert, "Religion," 40.
30. Chadwick, *Secularisation of European Mind*, 95.

faith in the cities. Glasgow, the Scottish city where Chalmers struggled to make an impact, was hailed by another observer as "Gospel City" in the 1830s for its wealth of Christian initiatives.[31]

These diverse cities were also places of sometimes fierce competition between different churches as they made competing claims for allegiance. Migration of Catholics and Protestants to the cities often had the effect of intensifying religious identity, as the difference between them became more palpable. Ethnic divisions further amplified this effect. Industrial cities, then, were places of competing kinds of religious fervor, and of secularism. They were arenas of ideological contestation, "in which adherents of rival worldviews battled it out."[32]

If the middle class dominated the established churches, furthermore, that did not prevent workers from organizing their own religious meeting places and organizations. Friedrich Engels (1820–95), the close associate of Karl Marx (1818–83), wrote in his study on the English working class in 1844 that "the workers speak other dialects, have other thoughts and ideals, other customs and moral principles, a different religion and other politics than those of the bourgeoisie."[33] Engels underestimated the religiosity of the English working class; it seems that church attendance actually rose among the working class in British cities from about 1840 to 1900 and that the "attractiveness of heaven" grew at this time in some industrial areas of Germany.[34]

Engels was partially right, though, in observing that most workers did not usually practice their religion in middle-class churches, even if the respectability of such churches attracted some.[35] Methodism, an offshoot of the Church of England, and other "free churches" were often more attuned to the hopes of part of the English working-class people, because they were grassroots movements that sprang from this group. In western Germany, Catholic workers were often looked down upon by Protestant elites and looked to their own faith community to sustain them.[36] In some parts of continental Europe, hostility to Christianity prompted some workers to all the more consciously seek out Christian community. That did not only mean attending church. Protestant and Catholic workingmen's associations arose in the 1860s to offer mutual support in difficult times.

31. Kossert, "Religion," 36.
32. McLeod, *Secularisation*, 28.
33. Engels, *Condition of the Working-Class*, 99.
34. Pasteur, "Role of Religion," 106.
35. Kossert, "Religion."
36. Holzem, "Social Welfare," 195–8.

Across the much of Europe, though particularly in Protestant areas, the period from about 1840 to about 1880 witnessed a raft of reform movements aimed at addressing social ills, many of them associated with industrialization and urbanization.[37] That included new initiatives to help the poor, often launched by convinced Christians, such as offering decent housing at a decent price or seeking to limit the often-devastating effects of alcohol addiction on workers and their families. The most famous of these, and one of the most influential, was the Salvation Army, founded in 1865, which raised money from the well-to-do and aimed its ministry at the poor. Founder William Booth (1829–1912) was widely reported to have said that were three *s*'s that characterized their mission to the poor: soup, then soap, and finally salvation. Though founded in Britain, the Salvation Army soon made impact in other European countries and across the world as well.[38] Working-class people would take leading roles in the organization.

These reform movements usually focused on the plight of individuals and typically did not advocate structural social or political change. A particularly clear example of this stance was the foundation of the Bethel Foundation in 1867 in Bielefeld, Germany. Otherwise known as the City of Charity, Bethel eventually became one of the largest social service institutions in Europe. It came to include a Worker's Colony that offered both work and housing to immigrant workers, the first such undertaking in Germany. Its founder, Friedrich van Bodelschwingh (1831–1910), did not see Bethel, however, as a way to correct injustice. Indeed, the conservative Protestant saw it more as "a Christian alternative to the secularized industrial society" rather than as an answer to "the social question."[39] Still, a host of such initiatives constituted widespread, persistent efforts by European Christians to least mitigate the effects of industrialization and urbanization—with significant impact.

There were, however, in this period Christian voices who held that the church should take a more critical stance. The Catholic bishop of Mainz, Germany, Wilhelm Emmanuel von Ketteler (1811–77), published *The Laborer Question and Christianity* (1864), working out ideas he (and a few other Reformers) had articulated as early as 1848. Politically active, Ketteler urged that workers self-organize to defend their rightful interests, that the state pass laws needed to protect them, and that the church defend such action as the execution of its historic teachings.[40] The bishop's work would

37. Van Molle, *Charity and Social Welfare.*
38. Gariepy, *Christianity in Action.*
39. Kunter, "Diakonie," 233.
40. O'Malley, *Wilhelm Ketteler.*

form an important basis for *Rerum* almost three decades later, but it was still a relatively uncommon voice.

Christian "Architectonic Critique" of the Social Order

"The social question," however, took on a new urgency in the last quarter of the nineteenth century. Increasingly, citizens of all stripes were demanding a greater say in politics. Cheap press, train, telegraph, and telephone expanded literacy, and more freedom of assembly enabled more people, to an extent greater than ever before, to join together in a shared cause. Increasingly, too, the right to vote expanded to men of lesser means in many parts of Europe. Political battles over education, the place of religious minorities in society, women's rights, and colonization were only a few important issues that seized the passions of the day. Christians and secularists, socialists and conservatives, farmers and suburbanites, workers and entrepreneurs: all alike wanted a voice to determine the future of their nation.

This political mobilization went hand in hand with the new wave of the Second Industrial Revolution, which further urbanized Britain and Germany but now also extended much more deeply into parts of Southern and Eastern Europe. As the Industrial Revolution intensified, pressure for the state to regulate the market also grew, including calls for adequate housing, social insurance, and pensions that would benefit workers. In this way "the social question" became an important political theme. The church, as noted above, came late to the issue—why was Ketteler's call not heeded earlier? It should be added, though, that "the social question" became urgent for many liberal parties only at roughly the same time that *Rerum* appeared. From this perspective, the church took on this issue about the same time that many middle-class Europeans did.

From the perspective of Leo XIII, the new concern for the plight of workers stemmed from a worry that they might, in their misery, abandon the Catholic faith, join the socialists, and oppose the norm of a church-centered social order. Recognizing the needs of the working class, then, contained a strong element of institutional self-preservation: not only for the papacy, but for the existing political system. Rising worker unrest across the Western world in the 1880s underscored this danger, and rising fears of Marxist revolution helped keep "the social question" on the political agenda. But there were also other motives. The new political visibility of working people also prompted middle-class society and the church to take a new hard look at working conditions, and with increasing sympathy. "The social question" now seemed to demand a forceful response. Abraham Kuyper

(1837–1920), then the preeminent Protestant politician of the Netherlands, had as pastor experienced firsthand the suffering of Amsterdam's poor. In 1889 he called for an "architectonic critique" of the social order.[41] Two years later he launched a "Christian social" program intended to structurally address the plight of poor.[42] Other leading Protestants made similar calls at approximately the same time.

Rerum Novarum itself was a highly influential expression of this turn in the Christian churches toward a more "architectonic" approach toward "the social question," and it since has been hailed as the cornerstone of Catholic social teaching.[43] Charity continued to have its place, but workers' legitimate interests needed to be safeguarded through effective self-representation and appropriate legislation. A just social order required it. Not all Catholics welcomed *Rerum*, and European Christians after 1891 were as divided as ever about what constituted a just social order. But the last years of the nineteenth century clearly witnessed a sea change in Christian Europe, in which Christians committed themselves to address urbanization and industrialization in more structural ways.

Christian Political and Social Engagement

Rerum Novarum clearly precipitated the rise of Christian trade unions, as Catholic workers felt encouraged by the encyclical to actively advance their own interests. Although the earliest Christian trade unions dated back to the 1870s, they rapidly multiplied after 1900 across Western and Central Europe in particular. Most of these unions were Catholic, although there were in some countries important Protestant or ecumenical variations. Usually the competing socialist unions were larger than the Christian ones, but still the Christians unions often represented a very substantial minority of workers. These unions, though, could not always count on the support of either the Catholic middle class or the church, which could still see their existence as undermining old hierarchies. These unions did press for increased wages and better living conditions for workers and their families, though their demands were typically more modest than those of the socialist unions.[44]

In continental Europe, too, the origins of Christian Democratic parties emerged in the late nineteenth century. Although they were typically led by

41. Harinck, "Herstelling van het gebouw," 53.
42. Kuyper, *Problem of Poverty*.
43. Furlong and Curtis, *Church Faces Modern World*.
44. Fardella, "Traces of the Post Secular."

the middle class and not first and foremost organized to address "the social question," these mostly Catholic parties often had close ties to the Christian trade unions and worked in coalition with them. These parties attempted to give place to workers between market individualism and socialist collectivism, in time carving out for themselves a place just right of center in the political spectrum.[45] As one legal scholar put it, these parties advocated a "Christian teaching of 'social pluralism' or 'subsidiarity,' which stressed the dependence and participation of the individual in family, church, school, business, and other associations."[46] In this way the individual could be embedded in a community that protected them the predations of the market. The encyclical *Quadragesimo Anno* (1931), penned by Pius XI (r. 1922–39), condemned the concentration of economic power in few hands that modern capitalism had brought, and urged social solidarity and strong communal bonds as an antidote.[47] This social teaching would inspire further social legislation to protect workers and their families.

European Protestants, though more fragmented, would show increasing interest in how the church could play a more active role in modern society. Heads of the established churches in Europe (and elsewhere) gathered for the first time internationally in Stockholm in 1925 to discuss the social and moral problems of society.[48] This movement would lead to the creation of the World Council of Churches, which after the Second World War envisaged a central role for both church and state in addressing the deep problems of society.[49] Many leading Protestants now came to embrace the state as the chief vehicle for moving toward a just society. Archbishop of Canterbury William Temple (1881–1944) published *Christianity and Social Order* in 1942, offering a vision for what became the British welfare state, with its attention to "healthcare, education, decent housing, proper working conditions, and democratic representation."[50]

The role of the church and other Christian organizations in the construction of the welfare state varied considerably from country to country and, as noted above, was partly shaped by religious confession (Catholic, Lutheran, Reformed). What can be said is that a myriad of Christian institutions rose in the twentieth century to help the working class in their spiritual

45. Lamberts, *Struggle with Leviathan*.
46. Witte, *Christianity and Democracy*, 9.
47. Gregg, "*Quadragesimo Anno* (1931)."
48. Oldham, "Responsible Society."
49. World Council of Churches, *Church and the Disorder*.
50. See https://williamtemplefoundation.org.uk/about-the-foundation/archbishop-william-temple/.

and material needs. Increasingly, too, many Christian organizations would work very closely with their governments, or eventually be absorbed into them.[51] The old church-state tensions had softened in most parts of Western Europe, though this obviously was not the case in Communist-dominated Eastern Europe.

End of the Industrial Age

The church eventually managed to play a significant role in large parts of industrialized, urban Europe. It remained an important institution of spiritual and moral support for a significant minority in the working class, and it created a large network of organizations to conduct its work. That included not only the unions and political parties in some parts of Europe, but social service bureaus, Sunday schools, sport clubs, and parish work, to name but a few. While still working out of the charitable traditions of the church, Christian welfare provision increasingly professionalized.[52] Moreover, Christians often supported, and made possible, legislation curbing market excesses. Christian belief both persisted and changed. Although church attendance declined in the twentieth century, it was in places still high, as in heavily Catholic cities. The church had found new ways to engage an industrialized Europe.

This changed in the 1960s when society dramatically began to shift again. Western Europe deindustrialized, as higher productivity and further technological innovation reduced the factory workforce. The service sector became more important, and the work experience more fluid. Living standards shot up. Europeans increasingly came to view themselves not chiefly as members of a community but as individuals and as consumers. The working class, too, shriveled away as a collective identity. Most Europeans no longer looked to the church, or any organization, for guidance, as they judged themselves competent to chart their own paths. This was also true of women, who had once sustained the church.[53] Citizens now relied on a welfare state for securing their lives, a development seen by some scholars as the most important factor in diminished religiosity.[54] European Christianity had adapted over time with some success to the Great Transformation and the Industrial Revolution. Postindustrial society, though, would confront it with an even greater challenge.

51. Van Molle, "Comparing Religious Perspectives," 26.
52. Van Molle, "Comparing Religious Perspectives," 21, 32.
53. Brown, *Death of Christian Britain*.
54. Norris and Inglehart, *Sacred and Secular*.

Bibliography

Allen, Douglas W. *The Institutional Revolution: Measurement and the Economic Emergence of the Modern World*. Markets and Governments in Economic History. Chicago: Chicago University Press, 2011.

Bell, G. K., ed. *The Stockholm Conference 1925. The Official Report of the Universal Christian Conference on Life and Work held in Stockholm, 19-30 August 1925*. London: Oxford University Press, 1926.

Brown, Callum G. *The Death of Christian Britain: Understanding Secularisation 1800-2000*. Christianity and Society in the Modern World. London: Routledge, 2001.

Chadwick, Owen. *The Secularisation of the European Mind in the Nineteenth Century*. Cambridge: Cambridge University Press, 1975.

Clark, J. C. D. "Secularization and Modernization: The Failure of a 'Grand Narrative.'" *Historical Journal* 55 (2012) 161-94.

Cox, Jeffrey. "Master Narratives of Religious Change." In *The Decline of Christendom in Western Europe, 1750-2000*, edited by Hugh McLeod and Werner Ustorf, 201-17. Cambridge: Cambridge University Press, 2009.

Engels, Frederick. *Condition of the Working-Class in England in 1844*. London: Allen & Unwin, 1943. https://www.marxists.org/archive/marx/works/download/pdf/condition-working-class-england.pdf.

Fardella, Joseph A. "Traces of the Post Secular: Early Catholic Social Thought, the Association of Catholic Trade Unionists and the Pursuit of the Common Good." *Political Theology* 21 (2020) 687-704.

Furlong, Paul, and David Curtis, eds. *The Church Faces the Modern World: Rerum Novarum and Its Impact*. Winteringham, UK: Earlsgate, 1994.

Gariepy, Henry. *Christianity in Action: The International History of the Salvation Army*. Grand Rapids: Eerdmans, 2009.

Gregg, Samuel. "*Quadragesimo Anno* (1931)." In *Catholic Social Teaching: A Volume of Scholarly Essays*, edited by Gerard V. Bradley and E. Christian Brugger, 90-107. Law and Christianity. Cambridge: Cambridge University Press, 2019.

Harinck, George. "Herstelling van het Gebouw onzer Maatschappij: Abraham Kuyper en de Sociale Kwestie." In *Paus Leo XIII en Abraham Kuyper: De Encycliek Rerum Novarum en de Rede over de Sociale Kwestie*, edited by Rien Fraanje, 53-60. Amsterdam: Boom, 2016.

Holzem, Andreas. "Social Welfare in Catholic Germany, 1850-1920." In *Charity and Social Welfare*, edited by Leen van Molle, 193-220. Vol. 4 of *The Dynamics of Religious Reform in Church, State and Society in Northern Europe, 1780-1920*. Leuven: Leuven University Press, 2017.

Kahl, Sigrun. "The Religious Roots of Modern Poverty Policy: Catholic, Lutheran, and Reformed Protestant Traditions Compared." *European Journal of Sociology* 46 (2005) 91-126.

Knight, Frances. "Social Welfare and the Churches in England, Scotland and Wales." In *Charity and Social Welfare*, edited by Leen van Molle, 41-70. Vol. 4 of *The Dynamics of Religious Reform in Church, State and Society in Northern Europe, 1780-1920*. Leuven: Leuven University Press, 2017.

Kossert, Andreas. "Religion in Urban Everyday Life: Shaping Modernity in Łódź and Manchester, 1820-1914." In *Christianity and Modernity in Eastern Europe*, edited by Bruce R. Berglund and Brian Porter-Szücs, 35–59. Budapest: Central European University Press, 2010.

Kunter, Katharina. "'Diakonie' (Welfare and Social Work) and Protestantism in Germany ca. 1780–1920." In *Charity and Social Welfare*, edited by Leen van Molle, 221–38. Vol. 4 of *The Dynamics of Religious Reform in Church, State and Society in Northern Europe, 1780–1920*. Leuven: Leuven University Press, 2017.

Kuyper, Abraham. *The Problem of Poverty*. Translated by James Skillen. Sioux Center, IA: Dordt College Press, 2011.

Lamberts, Emiel. *The Struggle with Leviathan: Social Responses to the Omnipotence of the State, 1815–1965*. Leuven: Leuven University Press, 2016.

Leo XIII, Pope. "*Rerum Novarum*: On Capital and Labor." Vatican, May 15, 1891. https://www.vatican.va/content/leo-xiii/en/encyclicals/documents/hf_l-xiii_enc_15051891_rerum-novarum.html.

McCloskey, Deirdre N. "Polanyi Was Right, and Wrong." *Eastern Economic Journal* 23 (1997) 483–87.

McLeod, Hugh. *Piety and Poverty: Working-Class Religion in Berlin, London and New York, 1870–1914*. New York: Holmes & Meier, 1996.

———. *Secularisation in Western Europe, 1848–1914*. London: Macmillan, 2000.

Norris, Pippa, and Ronald Inglehart. *Sacred and Secular: Religion and Politics Worldwide*. Cambridge Studies in Social Theory, Religion and Politics. Cambridge: Cambridge University Press, 2004.

Oldham, J. H. "A Responsible Society." In *Man's Disorder and God's Design*, edited by Amsterdam Assembly of the World Council of Churches, 3:120–54. London: SCM, 1948.

O'Malley, Martin. *Wilhelm Ketteler and the Birth of Modern Catholic Social Thought: A Catholic Manifesto in Revolutionary 1848*. Ta Ethika 7. Munich: Utz, 2009. https://www.utzverlag.de/assets/pdf/40846dbl.pdf.

Owen, T. C. "Industrialization and Capitalism." In *A Companion to Russian History*, edited by Abbott Gleason, 210–24. Blackwell Companions to World History. Oxford: Blackwell, 2009.

Pasteur, Patrick. "The Role of Religion in Social and Labour History." In *Class and Other Identities: Gender, Religion and Ethnicity in the Writing of European Labour History*, edited by Lex Heerma van Voss and Marcel van der Linden, 101–32. International Studies in Social History 2. New York: Berghahn, 2002.

Polanyi, Karl. *The Great Transformation: The Political and Economic Origins of Our Time*. New York: Farrar & Rinehart, 1944.

Stearns, Peter N. *The Industrial Revolution in World History*. 4th ed. New York: Routledge, 2018.

Toft, Monica Duffy, et al. *God's Century: Resurgent Religion and Global Politics*. New York: Norton, 2011.

Tønnessen, Aud V. "Christian Social Work in an Age of Crisis and Reform: The Case of Norway." In *Charity and Social Welfare*, edited by Leen van Molle, 281–301. Vol. 4 of *The Dynamics of Religious Reform in Church, State and Society in Northern Europe, 1780–1920*. Leuven: Leuven University Press, 2017.

Van der Valk, L. *Van Pauperzorg tot Bestaanszekerheid: Armenzorg in Nederland 1912–1965*. Amsterdam: International Institute of Social History, 1986.

Van Kersbergen, Kees, and Philip Manow. "Religion and the Western Welfare State: The Theoretical Context." In *Religion, Class Coalitions, and Welfare States*, edited by Kees van Kersbergen and Philip Manow, 1–38. Cambridge Studies in Social Theory, Religion and Politics. New York: Cambridge University Press, 2009.

Van Molle, Leen, ed. *Charity and Social Welfare*. Vol. 4 of *The Dynamics of Religious Reform in Church, State and Society in Northern Europe, 1780–1920*. Leuven: Leuven University Press, 2017.

———. "Comparing Religious Perspectives on Social Reform." In *Charity and Social Welfare*, edited by Leen van Molle, 7–37. Vol. 4 of *The Dynamics of Religious Reform in Church, State and Society in Northern Europe, 1780–1920*. Leuven: Leuven University Press, 2017.

Waterman, A. M. C. "*Rerum Novarum* and Economic Thought." *Faith & Economics* 67 (2016) 29–56.

Witte, John. *Christianity and Democracy in Global Context*. Boulder, CO: Westview, 1993.

World Council of Churches. *The Church and the Disorder of Society: An Ecumenical Study*. London: SCM, 1948.

Zehnder, Christopher. "Pope Gregory XVI: A 19th Century Environmentalist." Notes from the Wasteland, July 4, 2015. https://monsalvaesche.wordpress.com/category/social-justice/.

11

Empire and European Christianity

DARIN D. LENZ

IN HIS 1902 BOOK *Imperialism: A Study*, J. A. Hobson wrote, "The Chinese have watched with much concern the sequence of events—first the missionary, then the Consul, and at last the invading army."[1] Hobson's summary of how Christianity and empire were intertwined articulated what many peoples around the world seemed to have experienced since European countries began their quest to build empires in the late fifteen century. Hobson, however, was focused on the recent history of the British Empire and held that "the muscular Christianity of the last generation" had given way "to the imperial Christianity" of his day, which linked the power of the clergy and the authority of doctrine in the church "with militarism and political autocracy."[2] Hobson's critique of the relationship between Christianity and empire raised many questions about cultural conquest, capitalist expansion, and the political dominance of European powers. He recognized that Christians who supported missions hoped "to do good work about the world in the cause of humanity," but believed they were stymied in such a project because they wrongly assumed "that religion and other arts of civilisation are portable commodities which it is our duty to convey to backward nations."[3]

Hobson's critique of imperialism was focused primarily on the economics of empire, and this theme would later be rearticulated by anthropologists John and Jean Comaroff who observed in the African context that missionaries failed to create an indigenous church but did transform the worldview of Africans and incorporated them in the "industrial capitalists

1. Hobson, *Imperialism*, 215.
2. Hobson, *Imperialism*, 228.
3. Hobson, *Imperialism*, 208.

world."[4] Many of the studies that reflect on empire and European Christianity tend to focus on the ideas forwarded by Hobson and the Comaroffs or have addressed gender and race from the vantage point of postcolonialism. Some studies have also tried to explain the reciprocal effect of empire and missions as a buttress for the notion European superiority.[5] As Hobson's statement highlights, some scholars have emphasized a close relationship between empire and Christianity in the modern era, especially regarding Christian missionary activity; while others, like the Comaroffs, have shown that the relationship resulted in outcomes that were not intended but still furthered the cause of empire. Historians such as Andrew Porter, Brian Stanley, and Robert Eric Frykenberg have raised serious questions about the relationship between empire and Christianity and show that the relationship was fraught with complexity. As Porter pointedly argues about the realities of the nineteenth-century British Empire, "Religion and Empire frequently mingled, but were as likely to undermine each other as they were to provide mutual support."[6]

Just as the Roman Empire provides the political, cultural, and religious context of early Christianity, the interactions between empires and European Christianity over the subsequent centuries have been complicated, nuanced, and never easy to define. This is primarily because the relationship between empire and European Christianity was always tension filled due to competing goals. Christianity is a religion concerned with the destiny of human souls after death, while empires were focused on present economic, cultural, and political concerns. Keeping these differences in mind is essential for avoiding an oversimplified history that ignores the complexity of the past and recognizes that what was intended is often different from what happened and how the legacy of what happened is remembered.

The Great Commission and Early Encounters with Empire

Empire and Christianity have a long and complex history that spans the last two thousand years since the time of Christ. Jesus Christ directed his followers in Matt 28:19–20 to "go and make disciples of all nations, baptizing them in the name of the Father and of the Son and of the Holy Spirit, and teaching them to obey everything I have commanded you" (NIV). Known as the Great Commission, this final teaching of Christ instituted evangelism as a key Christian practice. Consequently, Christianity rapidly

4. Comaroff and Comaroff, "Christianity and Colonialism," 2.
5. Wilson, *Island Race*, 81.
6. Porter, "Religion, Missionary Enthusiasm," 245.

spread across Africa, the Middle East, and the continent of Asia to India, Mongolia, and China.[7]

A momentous change took place when the Roman emperor Constantine granted legal toleration to Christians when he issued the Edict of Milan in AD 313. The once-persecuted religious minority rose to prominence in the Roman Empire, gained respectability, and ultimately linked the spiritual authority of the church to the political power of empire. Western Christianity was heir to Greek and Latin intellectual tradition and, in the centuries that followed, a living artifact of the social, cultural, political, and religious order represented in the Roman Empire. Pious-minded rulers, starting with the Frankish ruler Charlemagne, attempted to unify and expand Christianity in Europe by establishing the kingdom of God on earth in the form of a reborn empire in the early ninth century called the Holy Roman Empire. For about the next one thousand years, the Holy Roman Empire, a conglomeration of different states, cities, peoples, and languages, would join Christianity with empire in Europe under the concept of Christendom.[8] Medieval Christians believed in the unity of church and state and embraced a unified Christian social and political order that had the emperor and the pope as earthly leaders under the headship of Christ. They referred to this unified vision of church and state as the *corpus Christianum*, and baptism determined if one was a member or not. In the intervening centuries, medieval princes, popes, and priests inspired one of the most dynamic periods of religious expression in art, architecture, theology, popular devotion, and Christianity and empire were viewed as inseparable.

Sixteenth-Century Reformations and Empire

When the Augustinian monk and priest Martin Luther posted ninety-five theses on October 31, 1517, critiquing the practices of the Roman Catholic Church, his concerns were primarily pastoral and intended to correct well-known abuses; Luther had no idea that his actions would divide Christians for the next five centuries. However, his small act of protest forwarded two major themes that affected the development of Christianity for the next five hundred. Luther emphasized the authority of biblical text and wanted to make the Bible accessible in the vernacular language of the people, but he faced enormous opposition and was excommunicated by the Roman Catholic Church and declared an outlaw of the Holy Roman Empire. Luther's reform efforts survived because he embraced the protection of his prince,

---

7. Jenkins, *Lost History of Christianity*, 3.
8. Eire, *Reformations*, 159.

Frederick the Wise, and other German princes who challenged the authority of Holy Roman Emperor Charles V. The German princes recognized that Luther offered them the ability to unify their political power in Central and Northern Europe and challenge the profane politics of Southern Europe for their own benefit. The continuation of the age-old marriage between church and state protected the Lutheran cause in Central and Northern Europe.

In the Swiss cantons, Ulrich Zwingli in Zurich and later John Calvin in Geneva presented another way to conduct reform of the church that involved the city government led by lay Christians. Due to the publication of the *Institutes of the Christian Religion*, Calvin's ideas were far more influential than Zwingli and to this day remain important for the thinking of millions of Christians around the world. Calvin put forward the idea society was based on a series of covenants between God and people, the state and people, and individuals in community. Calvin's Reformation was a legal Reformation. Where Luther married Christianity to the princely rule, Calvin tied Christianity to the republic form of politics of the city-state of Geneva and provided a model for a genuine Christian community.[9] These covenants were linked directly to social order and the power of political leaders to define the shape of righteousness in the body politic. The joining of the Protestant Churches to the state does not mean that the desire for genuine spiritual reform was not real, but that the processes long present since Charlemagne's innovation of a "supranational Western unity" remained at the forefront of religious thought.[10] Politics for the people at this time in history were inseparable from religion. Consequently, the Protestant reform movement was inclined to start and stall according to the religious preferences of rulers. Such a tenuous situation led to several wars of religion throughout Europe, which marked the epoch that followed as one of tragic violence between Protestants and Roman Catholics. In England, for example, in the sixteenth century, King Henry VIII implemented his reform agenda by claiming that England was an empire, which gave him unique powers as a monarchy over the establishment of a state church. This decision led to a back-and-forth struggle among his heirs over whether England was a Protestant or Roman Catholic nation, which included a bloody civil war and the Glorious Revolution of 1688/89 that decided once and for all that England was a Protestant nation.

Throughout Europe, the Reformers' successes were contingent on maintaining, gaining, or preserving political power. The only group from the Reformations of the sixteenth century who rejected the close alignment

---

9. Manschreck, *Christianity in the World*, 216.
10. Balling, *Story of Christianity*, 131.

of church and state were the Anabaptists. The Anabaptists began as Dissenters from Zwingli's reforms in Zurich. They rejected infant baptism and the linking of church and state in any way, and were pacificists. For their adherence to a radical reading of the Bible, the Anabaptists were brutally persecuted by Protestants and Roman Catholics alike throughout Europe for sedition against church and state. Religion was a political identity at this time and remained so through the coming centuries.

Roman Catholicism and Empire

Christopher Columbus's arrival in the West Indies in 1492 inspired a dynamic new era in the history of the Roman Catholic Church. The indigenous civilizations of the Caribbean and Central and South America, combined with the broad expanse of North America, contained unknown numbers of souls who knew nothing about the gospel. Columbus, like the Spanish conquistadors who followed him, was always thinking about the wealth that could be extracted from the soil and the indigenous peoples along how to expand the Spanish Empire. Empire came first for the Spaniards, Portuguese, and other Roman Catholic Europeans who would follow in the Americas. As the decades and centuries passed, Roman Catholicism soaked into the fabric of Latin American life and transformed indigenous religious rites, holy sites, and material objects with new Christian meanings. The opening of the Americas was one step toward the global shift of empires and European Christianity to the Southern Hemisphere.[11]

In 1498 Vasco da Gama finally joined Europe with Indian by sea. Soon after, Portuguese, Italian, Spanish, and other European traders and missionaries soon arrived in sufficient numbers to introduce Christianity to East Asia. Christianity entered the royal courts of China as an intellectual competitor to Confucian thought. Matteo Ricci and Michele Ruggeri, Jesuits devoted to making Christianity culturally acceptable to Chinese social mores, made inroads among the Chinese political and intellectual elite. India saw a steady stream of missionary friars, like Roberto de Nobili who accommodated Christianity to the caste system to make the religion accessible to the peoples of the subcontinent.[12] In Japan, Roman Catholics achieved some of their greatest successes among the peasants and political elite inhabiting the southern island of Kyushu. Christian missionaries were welcomed and tolerated by the local rulers until internal politics and fear of European conquest placed the religion at odds with the Tokugawa

---

11. Hastings, "Latin America," 334.
12. Bugge, "Christianity and Caste," 89–90.

government who rejected Christianity, declared the religion illegal in 1614, and persecuted Christians until the faith nearly vanished from Japan.

Roman Catholicism thrived in Europe and Latin America, while it gained footholds in Asia that persisted, despite vicious persecution, until rediscovery by a second wave of missionary activity that took place primarily among Protestants in the nineteenth century. Key to Roman Catholic missionary success in this period was cultural accommodation to existing religious practices, aligning religious identity with the power of European empires, and adapting personal piety to the context of different cultures. Roman Catholic missionaries, especially those affiliated with the Dominicans, Franciscans, Jesuits, and Augustinians, were generally perceptive to how their ideas and even their European culture would be received by the majority culture in which they were introducing the gospel. In the late seventeenth century and beyond, Protestant missionaries from Europe would also face these same issues.

European Protestants and Empire

The desire for global trade and acquiring natural resources resulted in Protestant European kingdoms establishing colonies. The English, Dutch, Danes, Germans, and other Europeans who were Protestants took Christianity to the outposts of their slowly growing empires. Despite their notoriety for serious piety, which placed them in opposition to the Church of England and the English monarchy, when Puritans began to migrate across the North Atlantic to Massachusetts Bay Colony in the early seventeenth century, they failed to win many Native American converts. Protestant missions in eighteenth-century New England could not match the success of the French Jesuits living among the native tribes in the region and to the north in New France. The intellectual religious orientation of the Puritans did not connect to the indigenous peoples who preferred the rites and the rituals of Roman Catholic missionaries who practiced of a form of Christianity that could be recognized as spiritual due to liturgical practices and the use of material items like crucifixes, rosaries, and images.

Back on the continent of Europe, the devastating consequences of the Thirty Years' War (1618–48) left Central Europeans in a moral abyss in the second half of the seventeenth century. Philipp Jakob Spener, a Lutheran minister, wanted to revitalize the everyday spiritual lives of lay Christians and reinvigorate the churches. Spener gave life to the Pietist movement, which took hold in German speaking lands. At the newly founded University of Halle, August Hermann Francke, Spener's most successful disciple, gave Pietism a transatlantic and global reach through his philanthropic ventures, support of missions, publications, communication networks, and the activities of his former students. Bartholomaüs Ziegenbalg and Heinrich Plütschau, students of Francke, were recruited to serve as missionaries to Tranquebar, South India, for King Frederick IV of Denmark. Arriving on the subcontinent in 1706 they quickly addressed languages issues. Ziegenbalg's linguistic abilities allowed him to translate the entirety of the New Testament and most of the Old Testament into Tamil.[13] Ziegenbalg and Plütschau also followed Francke's model from Halle, setting up "free" or charity schools to educate Christians and non-Christians alike, which encouraged literacy and the ability to read the Bible.[14]

Another of Francke's students, Count Nikolaus Ludwig von Zinzendorf, would become the leader of the Moravians. In fact, Protestant Christian expansion in the eighteenth century can be looked at as the Moravian century for missionary work. Although others, such as the Lutheran missionary Christian Fredrick Schwartz, served as mouthpieces of the gospel outside of Europe, Moravian influence spread across the broadest geographical distance, reaching from Greenland and North America to South America to South Africa, and contributed to developing a fervent Protestant missionary ideology, impressing even non-Moravians who admired their zeal.[15] The Moravians proved to be much more adaptable and fruitful in their work for Christian expansion, especially among indigenous peoples and enslaved peoples in the Dutch and British West Indies and South Africa. They often found their beliefs and aims to be in tension with the prevailing social and political norms of the colonial administrators of the Europeans' empires in which they were missionaries.[16] Promoting spiritual liberty and spiritual equality meant that they, too, would suffer the destruction of missions by empires who viewed their activities as subversive.[17] Although the eighteenth century would have some success stories, it would not be until the nineteenth century that Protestants, as a whole, could legitimately make any claim that they could promote the expansion of Christianity that rivaled Roman Catholics'. According to historian Philip Jenkins, "Up to the end of the eighteenth century, large-scale missionary efforts were strictly the preserve of Catholic powers, a point of superiority proudly stressed by

---

13. Rajan, "Johann Philipp Fabricius," 1300–1301.
14. Liebau, "Faith and Knowledge," 1184–86.
15. Clebsch, *Christianity in European History*, 222.
16. Gibbs, "Christian Ignatius Latrobe," 71–73.
17. Gibbs, "Christian Ignatius Latrobe," 78.

Catholic controversialists."[18] Consequently, Protestant Churches remained isolated from the larger context of European imperial expansion until the eighteenth century.

The major impetus for Protestant missionaries did not come from the expansion of empires as it did for Roman Catholicism. Rather, the roots of modern missionary movement can be traced directly to the Great Awakening of the 1740s. Andrew Walls explains that the "modern missionary movement was a child of the Evangelical Revival, but it was a late child."[19] Consequently, missions were not a product of the link between empire and religion but rather a spiritual rebuttal to the society, culture, and the politics of the era. At the time of the birth of the modern missionary movement, Christians were considering anew their moment in history and when the kingdom of God might be established as recounted in the biblical book of Revelation. As Brian Stanley has noted, Christians were certain "that the church stood on the brink of the last days of history," and, consequently, men and women believed that through the conversion of non-Christian people around the world through missionary labor they would initiate Christ's empire on earth.[20]

The unlikely model for modern missions began with William Carey, a self-educated English cobbler, who launched on a shoestring budget one of the most influential missionary ventures in history. Carey, a Baptist, appealed in writing for Protestants to use the "means" for the proclamation of the gospel and then went about forming a missionary society in 1792 to further the cause.[21] Following his own advice, Carey moved to India to preach the gospel. However, Carey's main achievement was not with making converts—he had few. Instead, Carey's missionary labor in India must be seen in terms of how it ignited the imagination of thousands of men and women over the following century who set aside personal wealth, health, and comfort for the rigors of a life lived adapting to a foreign land, language, and culture. Carey's example did not simply triumph in Great Britain alone. Carey ignited a transatlantic missionary movement that tied European and American Christians together to establish the kingdom of God on earth, a rival empire to European empires. Carey showed how someone who was merely a cobbler, but "independent, hard-working," and a self-learner could effectively preach the gospel in a foreign land.[22] The missionary movement

18. Jenkins, *Next Christendom*, 33.
19. Walls, *Missionary Movement*, 160.
20. Stanley, *Bible and the Flag*, 74.
21. Porter, *Religion versus Empire*, 45.
22. Walls, *Missionary Movement*, 161.

soon owed the fruits of its success to the labor of men and women who generally came from modest backgrounds and worked with a passion to teach people around the world about Christ.

Although Protestant ministers played a role in the organization of missionary societies and even served on the mission field, as a whole the Protestant missionary efforts of the nineteenth century were primarily led, directed, and made triumphant by people who had never been to seminary nor earned their living from standing in the pulpit on Sunday morning. Unlike Roman Catholics who relied on a select group of highly trained priests and religious orders to establish and maintain overseas missions, Protestants used the resources of the laity who brought their professionals skills from skilled trades, farming, medicine, education, and business with them to their missionary work. Over the next two centuries hundreds of missionary societies would be established by the Dutch, Germans, English, Scots, Swiss, French, Danes, Swedish, Irish, and other European nations and in colonies and former colonies around the world. Magazines, books, and tracts would tell the story of missions and help bolster the cause of the empire of Christ in a global network that connected Japan, New Zealand, and Australia with India, the United States, Europe, and the African continent.

Those who followed Carey's example were heirs of a social conscience informed by evangelical activism. Evangelicals were bedfellows of reform movements in Europe and North America that sought to end slavery and promote temperance. For example, the famed nineteenth-century Scottish explorer and missionary to Africa David Livingston made "ending the Portuguese and Arab slave trade," as Dana Robert recalls, "the divine purpose of his life."[23] Social activism was not always welcome in European colonies where economic profitably was never assumed, nor were political and military dominance certain. Missionaries became the social conscience of empire. Often they acted to moderate abuses that European businessmen, settlers, and government officials benefited financially from ignoring.[24] For example, in the late nineteenth century missionaries exposed the Belgian king's, Leopold II, ruthless oppression of Africans in the Congo Free State and help stop the violence through making his policies and practices known to the world.

---

23. Robert, *Christian Mission*, 83.
24. Woodberry, "Missionary Roots," 254.

Christian Unity, Women, Bible Translation, and University Students

In 1860 at a conference of missions held in Liverpool, England, Rev. Thomas Green called those present to set aside denominational differences and not see each other as Baptists, Methodists, Presbyterians, Dissenters, or members of the Church of England, but rather recognize that "they were all fighting under one banner, the banner of the cross of Christ."[25] Green's assertion about Christian unity was one of the innovative elements in European Christianity in the nineteenth and early twentieth century. The idea that they were fighting together was not meant to be taken as using weapons in actual combat, but rather as being engaged in a spiritual war to win the world for the empire of Christ. Missionaries from across Europe and the United States saw themselves as part of a shared work for God's glory. The fight for the empire of Christ could use earthly elements to forward the gospel message but sought the transformation of human souls as the primary goal. Missionary activity flourished with the establishment of missionary boards, voluntary societies, and the activism of laypersons to encourage, fund, and go out as missionaries. Consequently, Protestant missionary work in the nineteenth century evoked a new form of Protestant piety centered on the ordinary Christian who made the ultimate act of devotion by going abroad to proclaim the gospel. This focus on the lay missionary piety in the nineteenth century had three transformational effects on Protestant Christianity that are important for the expansion of world Christianity and the development of the ecumenical movement that would seek unity among Christians from diverse church traditions and theological perspectives.

First, as the needs of the missions outpaced the men who were willing to go to a foreign land, women began to fill the void. Single women came to have a role and influence overseas that would not have been tolerated in the nineteenth century. Unencumbered by the traditional domestic duties that weighed heavily on married women missionaries, single women eventually assumed a leading role in the missionary movement. Women founded charitable organizations, they preached and discipled converts, and they challenged the cultural norms that non-Western women encountered in China, India, Korea, Africa, and elsewhere. Women also encouraged indigenous Christian women, such as Pandita Ramabai in India, to lead and speak with authority regarding the things of God. Married missionary women also became models for how Christian churches and a Christian society should function. Family prayer times, prayer circles, and women's guilds all served

---

25. Secretaries to the Conference, *Conference on Missions*, 14.

to link Christianity with broader notions of community and were copied by non-Western Christians as they formed their own churches.[26]

The next aspect of Protestant missionary work that has proven to be extremely important for the development of identity in the postcolonial twentieth century was the development of written vernacular languages. Following Luther's original impulse to make the Bible accessible to ordinary people in their own tongue, Protestant missionaries from Ziegenbalg forward began to make strides in capturing on paper languages that previously existed only in oral form. Translation of Scripture from one language to another is nothing new in the history of Christianity and was a major element in the work of the church even in antiquity. During the nineteenth and through the twentieth century, Western missionaries gave new emphasis to the mastering of the languages, literature, and culture of the people they encountered. This work, of course, required collaboration with indigenous peoples who were essential to the success of missionaries gaining any knowledge of the languages or cultures that they wanted to understand. The energy Protestant missionaries and their indigenous helpers invested in Bible translation made an enormous impact on world cultures and resulted in more languages being put into written form than at any other point in history. As Walls points out, "The specifically Christian 'sacred' use of the vernacular has given some primal cultures a resilience against the solvent of rapid change leading to loss of identity, and enabled a preservation of part of the local focus in the very act of producing a broader identity."[27] Simply stated, by creating a biblical text based on the vernacular languages of indigenous peoples, missionaries were able to lay the foundation for the rise of a global Christianity that made every culture, place, and people redeemable through the words of the gospel.

The third and final contribution to the rise of the empire of Christ around the world came from an unlikely place. College and university students were encouraged to take up the cause of missions from the early 1820s onward. At the University of Halle, Friedrich August Tholuck encouraged his students to become missionaries to the Jews, while the renowned Scottish churchman Thomas Chalmers at the University of St. Andrews also encouraged his students to take up the cause of missions.[28] The excitement for missions among university students reached a fever pitch in the aftermath of the preaching of the American evangelist D. L. Moody who inspired the famed "Cambridge Seven" in 1885 to give up their lives of privilege and

---

26. Garrett, *Footsteps in the Sea*, 37.
27. Walls, *Missionary Movement*, 70.
28. Piggin and Roxborogh, *St. Andrews Seven*, 111.

head to China as missionaries with Hudson Taylor's China Inland Mission. In their wake, North American and European college and university students took up the cause of missions through the end of century and into the next century as part of the World Student Christian Federation that sought to win the world for Christ in their generation.[29]

Early Twentieth-Century Changes

When the World Missionary Conference met in Edinburgh, Scotland, in 1910 there was a heightened sense of eschatological expectation that the world was on the precipice of seeing "the Kingdom of God come with power."[30] This ecumenical gathering about the current state of Christian missions sensed that an opportunity to finally make the empire of Christ a reality was near. Things were changing, but not in the way that they imagined. In 1906, the Pentecostal Movement was born in Los Angeles, California, at the Azusa Street Revival and quickly spread to Europe and around the world. This revival was the result of a deep desire to overcome the challenge of acquiring foreign languages that missionaries faced. Pentecostals initially believed that the baptism of the Holy Spirit would provide "authentic languages (*xenolalia*) given for the proclamation of the gospel in the end times."[31] Pentecostals were essentially a missions-motivated group of radical Evangelicals who wanted to receive a shortcut for acquiring foreign languages so that ordinary people could go out and witness to the gospel overseas.[32] This change, however, did not happen.

Despite misconstruing what spirit baptism would provide, Pentecostalism became the leading form of global Christian practice during the twentieth century. Pentecostalism, in fact, may have "accelerated the development of indigenous churches in China," as Daniel Bays acknowledges, because Pentecostals mirrored "traditional folk religiosity with its lively sense of the supernatural."[33] In addition to connecting at a cultural level, Pentecostalism provides everyone spiritual gifts for prophecy, healing, and speaking in tongues through spirit baptism. Bays argues that the spiritual gifts acquired through Spirit baptism allowed Chinese Christians to "claim equality with, or superiority to any foreign missionary."[34] The cultural, polit-

29. Tatlow, *Story of the SCM*, 67–69.
30. Stanley, *World Missionary Conference*, 1.
31. Anderson, *Introduction to Pentecostalism*, 34–35.
32. McGee, *Miracles, Missions*, 90–107.
33. Bays, "Protestant Missionary Establishment," 63.
34. Bays, "Protestant Missionary Establishment," 63.

ical, and military advantages of empire were being undone by a movement that sought to empower anyone who accepted Christ as Savior. Over the course of the twentieth century, Pentecostals transformed the spiritual landscape of the world by offering indigenous peoples a counterweight to empire through spiritual empowerment.

The First World War that raged from 1914 to 1918 altered European Christianity and people's relationship to empire. A deep sense of cynicism became part of Western culture as the war exposed the fallacy of moral and civilizational superiority. German missions faltered in the wake of the war when Germany lost its colonial possessions. Christians and the state churches who had supported their national interests during the war were questioning whether their loyalty to the nation was appropriate. Even though Christianity remained an essential part of people's lives throughout Europe, missionary societies witnessed a significant decline in the number of young people willing to devout their lives to missionary service overseas. During the postwar years there was an ongoing movement to creating an ecumenical, universal Christian identity, which had been carried on from the interdenominational focus of missions in the late nineteenth century. The ecumenical movement tried to build bridges among Christians to further camaraderie and harmony. Sadly, as the Second World War soon revealed, the age of world unity and cooperation had not arrived.

The End of Empire and the Expansion of Christianity

Not until the period after World War II did a new form of independent but distinctly Protestant Christianity emerge from the period of decolonization that swept across Africa, Southern and Eastern Asia, and the Pacific Islands. European nations, some more slowly than others, gave up their colonies in the decades after the Second World War. When Western nations abandoned their colonies in Africa and Asia, Protestant Christianity did not disappear as a relic connected to European empires, but rather began to thrive as it was freed from dependency on Westerners. In Africa, foreign missions continued to flourish through much of the twentieth century, but African independent churches grew dramatically due to the influence of Evangelicals and Pentecostals.[35] Thanks to the spread of Pentecostalism, Protestant Christianity was better able to connect with the aspirations of people around the world. Pentecostal piety challenged Catholicism in Latin America and soon began to expand dramatically.[36] Catholicism remained an important

35. Isichei, *Christianity in Africa*, 335.
36. Schreiter, *New Catholicity*, 71.

force in global Christianity, although it lacked the dynamics necessary to expand as it once had and saw a significant decline in the number of priests and members. Likewise, Protestant Churches in Europe during the twentieth century fell under the spell of secularization and, subsequently, saw serious declines in church membership and failed to continue supporting world missions as they once had. However, Protestantism saw the seeds planted by missionaries during the nineteenth century continue to bloom during the twentieth century when tens of millions of people around the world embraced Christianity as empires vanished from the global, political landscape in the post-World War II period.

Conclusion

Tsou Mingteh observes, when explaining the activities of Christian missionaries in the late Qing period, that "some got involved in political activities, but on the whole, Protestant missionaries worked among the people at the bottom of society and preached the gospel to save their souls without becoming politically involved. Most showed little direct concern for China's secular development."[37] Mingteh's observation is important for reflecting on the relationship between empire and European Christianity. Although there were always some missionaries who were paternalistic and advocated for commercial, imperial, and civilizational goals as the way forward for non-Western peoples, as Mingteh notes, this was not uniform, and many missionaries stayed focused on establishing the kingdom of God on earth.

Christian missions were a complex undertaking that involved a high level of risk combined with minimal funding, health risks, and major cultural, linguistic, and political challenges for any willing participant. Protestants followed the flags of empires wherever they went in order to establish the empire of Christ. Empires left many unintentional consequences for the places that were once colonies. In like manner, missionaries, quite unintentionally, engaged in a massive cultural preservation program through translation efforts to make the Bible available in indigenous languages. They established the foundation for indigenous churches to thrive in Africa, Latin America, Asia, Australia, New Zealand, and the Pacific Islands after their European empires had given up their colonies. In the postcolonial period, Protestant Christianity has taken on new life revitalized by separation from European empires and the influence of Western churches. In Africa, Asia, and Latin America, the form of Christianity that has taken hold is morally and ethically conservative and attuned to the authority of the biblical text,

37. Mingteh, "Christian Missionary," 87.

embraces a spirit-filled piety, and exuberantly evangelizes non-Christians, often in Europe, North America, and other parts of the world. Today, the expansion of the empire of Christ remains a foremost concern of those Majority World Christians whose nations were once colonies of European empires.

Bibliography

Anderson, Allan. *An Introduction to Pentecostalism: Global Charismatic Christianity.* Introduction to Religion. Cambridge: Cambridge University Press, 2004.

Balling, Jakob. *The Story of Christianity from Birth to Global Presence.* Translated by the author. Grand Rapids: Eerdmans, 2003.

Bays, Daniel. "The Protestant Missionary Establishment and the Pentecostal Movement." In *Pentecostal Currents in American Protestantism*, edited by Edith L. Blumhofer et al., 50–67. Urbana: University of Illinois Press, 1999.

Bugge, Henriette. "Christianity and Caste in XIXth Century South India: The Different Social Policies of British and Non-British Christian Missions." *Archives de Sciences Sociales des Religions* 43 (July–Sept. 1998) 87–97.

Ching, Wen. *The Chinese Crisis from Within.* Edited by G. M. Reith. London: Richards, 1901.

Comaroff, Jean, and John Comaroff. "Christianity and Colonialism in South Africa." *American Ethnologist* 13 (1986) 1–22.

Eire, Carlos M. N. *Reformations: The Early Modern World, 1450–1650.* New Haven: Yale University Press, 2016.

Garrett, John. *Footsteps in the Sea: Christianity and Oceania to World War II.* Suva, Fiji: University of the South Pacific Press, 1992.

Gibbs, Jenna M. "Christian Ignatius Latrobe, 'Liberty of Conscience,' and Slavery in the West Indies and the Western Cape, 1780s–1830s." In *Global Protestant Missions: Politics, Reform, and Communication, 1730s–1930s*, edited by Jenna M. Gibbs, 69–89. New York: Routledge, 2020.

Hastings, Adrian. "Latin America." In *A World History of Christianity*, edited by Adrian Hastings, 328–68. Grand Rapids: Eerdmans, 1999.

Hobson, J. A. *Imperialism: A Study of the History, Politics and Economics of the Colonial Powers in Europe and America.* Morrison, NC: Lulu, 2018.

Isichei, Elizabeth. *A History of Christianity in Africa: From Antiquity to the Present.* London: SPCK, 1995.

Jenkins, Philip. *The Lost History of Christianity: The Thousand-Year Golden Age of the Church in the Middle East, Africa, and Asia—and How It Died.* New York: HarperOne, 2008.

———. *The Next Christendom: The Coming of Global Christianity.* New York: Oxford University Press, 2002.

Liebau, Heike. "Faith and Knowledge: The Educational System of the Danish-Halle and English-Halle Mission." In *Communication between India and Europe*, edited by Andreas Gross et al., 1181–214. Vol. 3 of *Halle and the Beginning of Protestant Christianity in India*. Halle: Franckeshen Stiftungen, 2006.

Manschreck, Clyde L. *A History of Christianity in the World: From Persecution to Uncertainty.* Englewood Cliffs, NJ: Prentice-Hall, 1974.
McGee, Gary B. *Miracles, Missions, and American Pentecostalism.* American Society of Missiology Series 45. Maryknoll, NY: Orbis, 2010.
Mingteh, Tsou. "Christian Missionary as Confucian Intellectual: Gilbert Reid (1857–1927) and the Reform Movement in the Late Qing." In *Christianity in China: From the Eighteenth Century to the Present*, edited by Daniel H. Bays, 73–90. Stanford: Stanford University Press, 1996.
Piggin, Stuart, and John Roxborogh. *The St. Andrews Seven: The Finest Flowering of Missionary Zeal in Scottish History.* Edinburgh: Banner of Truth Trust, 1985.
Porter, Andrew. "Religion, Missionary Enthusiasm, and Empire." In *The Nineteenth Century*, edited by Andrew Porter, 222–45. Vol. 3 of *The Oxford History of the British Empire.* Oxford: Oxford University Press, 1999.
———. *Religion versus Empire? British Protestant Missionaries and Overseas Expansion, 1700–1914.* Manchester: Manchester University Press, 2004.
Rajan, Rekha Famath. "Johann Philipp Fabricius and the History of the Tamil Bible." In *Communication between India and Europe*, edited by Andreas Gross et al., 1299–317. Vol. 3 of *Halle and the Beginning of Protestant Christianity in India.* Halle: Franckeshen Stiftungen, 2006.
Robert, Dana L. *Christian Mission: How Christianity Became a World Religion.* Malden, MA: Wiley-Blackwell, 2009.
Schreiter, Robert J. *The New Catholicity: Theology between the Global and Local.* Faith and Cultures Series. Maryknoll, NY: Orbis, 1997.
Secretaries to the Conference, The, eds. *Conference on Missions Held in 1860 at Liverpool: Including the Papers Read, the Deliberations, and the Conclusions Reached; with a Comprehensive Index Shewing the Various Matters Brought under Review.* London: Nisbet, 1860.
Stanley, Brian. *The Bible and the Flag: Protestant Missions and British Imperialism in the Nineteenth and Twentieth Centuries.* Leicester, UK: Apollos, 1990.
———. *The World Missionary Conference, Edinburgh 1910.* Studies in the History of Christian Missions. Grand Rapids: Eerdmans, 2009.
Tatlow, Tissington. *The Story of the Student Christian Movement of Great Britain and Ireland.* London: SCM, 1933.
Walls, Andrew F. *The Missionary Movement in Christian History: Studies in the Transmission of Faith.* Maryknoll, NY: Orbis, 1996.
Wilson, Kathleen. *The Island Race: Englishness, Empire and Gender in the Eighteenth Century.* London: Routledge, 2003.
Woodberry, Robert D. "The Missionary Roots of Liberal Democracy." *American Political Science Review* 106 (2012) 244–74.

12

War and European Christianity

MICHAEL SNAPE

DUE TO THE FUNCTIONAL pacifism that came to prevail in mainstream European Christianity under the nuclear shadow of the Cold War, the significance of religious factors in European conflicts in the nineteenth and twentieth centuries, and the enduring significance of war in the development of European Christianity, has been greatly underestimated by historians. From the 1970s until the early years of the twenty-first century, for example, perspectives on the role of the British churches in the First and Second World Wars were usually formulated in reproachful, quasi-pacifist terms. The Cold War morality lesson was clear: contrary to the perceived pacifism of the New Testament, these churches had fallen prey to militarism and hyper-patriotism—with predictable, catastrophic results. Their surfeit of patriotic zeal and marked deviation from the apparently clear admonitions of Jesus (e.g., "Blessed are the peacemakers" [Matt 5:9 KJV]; "Resist not evil" [Matt 5:39 KJV]; "My kingdom is not of this world" [John 18:36 KJV]) had sapped the moral authority of the churches and accelerated the process of secularization that had been in evidence since the European Enlightenment and Industrial Revolution.

According to this viewpoint, the emptying churches of the interwar period were natural counterparts to Britain's many—often vast—military cemeteries. Furthermore, and against the mournful and menacing backdrop of the later twentieth century, only such dissidents as the (few) conscientious objectors of the First World War, or the critical voice of Bishop George Bell of Chichester, who famously condemned the Allies' area bombing of Germany during the second, warranted serious scrutiny (and, implicitly, emulation). But, as more recent scholarship has shown, the religious landscape and dynamics of British society during and after the two world wars was much more complex than this. As Leon Trotsky famously observed, "War is the locomotive of history," and the religious changes wrought by the two global wars of the twentieth century, in Great Britain and elsewhere, were many, varied, and seldom unilinear. This chapter will explore these and many other conflicts, their changes, and their consequences, drawing attention to developments across Europe from the French Revolution to the present.

Religion and War in an Era of Secularization

It is a hoary, if untenable, assumption that wars of religion ceased in Western Europe with the 1648 Treaty of Westphalia, which ended the Thirty Years' War (1618-48). Underpinned by William Lecky's monumental *History of the Rise and Influence of the Spirit of Rationalism in Europe* (1865), the idea that such conflicts had exhausted themselves by the mid-seventeenth century was a function of Lecky's argument that Cardinal Richelieu's alignment of France with Protestant powers such as Sweden in the Thirty Years' War "prepared the way for the general secularisation of politics,"[1] a view that could be justified (for example) by Oliver Cromwell's (anti-Spanish) alliance with Catholic France in the late 1650s. According to this understanding of the ineluctable, secular trajectory of European statecraft, in the subsequent, more tolerant Age of Enlightenment, to say nothing of subsequent eras, religion had no place as a driving force in interstate conflicts. But this is to gravely misread the nature of the conflicts that plagued the Continent after Westphalia. Throughout the supposedly secular wars of the age of Enlightenment, for example, religious rivalries continued to play themselves out, often as facets of much wider conflicts: in Ireland, Catholic Jacobites versus Protestant Williamites during the Nine Years War (1688-97); and, in France and Hungary, Protestant revolts against Catholic Bourbon and Habsburg rule, respectively, during the War of the Spanish Succession (1701-15). Moreover, two generations later, in the Seven Years War (1756-63), Frederick the Great of Prussia (despite his own religious skepticism) could still be hailed in Britain as a Protestant hero due to his victories over the newly allied forces of Catholic France and Austria (Britain's recent alliance with Austria during the preceding War of the Austrian Succession [1740-48] was conveniently forgotten, as was Frederick's dalliance with France).

However, it was the French Revolution, and the quarter-century of war that followed, that showed the endurance of religion as a propellant of European conflict. The seismic shock of the overthrow of the ancien régime in

1. Lecky, *History*, 2:70.

France, and the existential threat posed to throne and altar by an infidel and avowedly aggressive French Republic from 1792, galvanized conservative religious forces and forged some striking new alignments. In 1794, and while refugee Catholic clergy from France were being sheltered by King George III, and Catholic rebels in the Vendée and elsewhere menaced the French Republic from within, British troops were deployed to the papal states to protect Pope Pius VI from the depredations of the invading French. And, if Islam fueled resistance to the French invasion of Egypt in 1798, Christian faith stoked resistance to the armies of the French Revolution as far afield as Great Britain (where numerous volunteer regiments were formed, and their colors consecrated by Anglican clergy in the face of a feared invasion) and the kingdom of Naples, where Sanfedisti guerrillas (led by a cardinal) posed a potent challenge to the occupying French. Significantly, and in the person of Horatio Nelson, a clergyman's son from Norfolk and a devout (if morally wayward) Anglican, Great Britain found its greatest hero of the Revolutionary and Napoleonic Wars. And, despite Napoleon's 1801 concordat with Pope Pius VII, these profound cleavages endured throughout the Napoleonic era, a situation not helped by Napoleon's imprisonment of the same pontiff in 1809. While Napoleon was widely billed as the antichrist in popular Protestant prophecy in Great Britain, a crusading, anti-French Catholicism stirred and sustained Spanish and Portuguese resistance to Napoleonic occupation throughout the Peninsula War of 1808–14. Again, in the Tyrol (1809) and in Russia (1812), too, guerrillas and regular armies alike were galvanized by a militant piety, a spirit that also animated many Protestant Germans throughout the War of Liberation of 1813—a struggle that gave rise to Prussia's (later Germany's) famous Iron Cross medal. This consistent trope of the Napoleonic Wars culminated in Prussian soldiers singing the hymn *Nun danket alle Gott* as Napoleon's final defeat unfolded at the Battle of Waterloo (1815).

During many of the interstate and civil wars of the nineteenth century (with many of the latter carrying the political DNA of the French Revolution), a marked religious element was also present. While it persisted, inevitably, in Orthodox Russia's recurrent wars with the Ottoman Empire (1828–29, 1853–56, and 1877–78), it was also self-evident in Western Europe. In Spain, for example, recurrent conservative rebellions (1833–40, 1846–49, and 1872–76) saw ultra-Catholic Carlists clash with their liberal, constitutionalist compatriots. In Italy, too, during the middle decades of the nineteenth century the forces of conservative religion and political reaction were closely arrayed in opposing the more liberal (and secular) forces of Italian unification. In the Crimean War (1853–56), the mobilization of Protestant Britain, Catholic France, and Orthodox Russia all involved the invocation (or resurrection) of a sense of religious grievance, whether Catholic/Protestant tensions over the custodianship of the Holy Sepulcher or the freedom of Protestant missionaries to evangelize in the vast Russian Empire. Again, in the wars of German unification, and though the conflict with Lutheran Denmark (1864) was harder to spin, Protestant German nationalists were galvanized by brief and victorious wars against Catholic Austria (1866) and the France of Napoleon III (1870–71). Even in proverbially neutral Switzerland, the potency of religious divisions was readily apparent, as in its Civil War of 1847, in which federal (largely Protestant and liberal) forces prevailed against the breakaway, Catholic, and conservative cantons of the *Sonderbund*.

Because these enmities had never completely faded, as the recent Balkan Wars (1912–1913) had just shown, it was predictable that historic religious animosities and alignments should resurface in the First World War (1914–1918). In the Balkans, and on the Eastern Front, Europe's only major Catholic power, Austria-Hungary, engaged in a costly and often brutal war with the Orthodox powers of Russia and Serbia. Similarly, German atrocities in Belgium and northern France (the massacre of civilians, the burning of the library of the Catholic University of Louvain, and the shelling of Reims Cathedral) lent themselves to a lurid narrative (widely rehearsed among Catholics in Allied countries), which cast the imperial German army (which was partly Bavarian and at least one-third Catholic) as a marauding Lutheran horde. In Great Britain (now allied with Orthodox Russia and the avowedly secular French Third Republic) an even older crusading trope was revived by its struggle against the Ottoman Empire in the Dardanelles and Palestine, a self-image confirmed by the capture of Jerusalem (a feat that had eluded Richard the Lionheart) in December 1917. If the First World War—and the inevitable divisions of Catholic Europe—had seen the Vatican take an avowedly neutral stance under Pope Benedict XV, the (mis)fortunes of war created a fresh ideological menace over which neutrality was impossible. With the defeat and collapse of tsarist Russia, and the emergence of a new, atheistic Soviet Union after the Civil War that followed the Bolshevik Revolution of October 1917, new battle lines were inevitably drawn. As the Bolsheviks were initially bent on exporting Communist revolution, Protestant and Catholic Christianity served as a vital rallying point for conservatives across Europe—whether in the Finnish Civil War (1918), the Russo-Polish War (1918–1921), the Communist risings in Berlin and Munich (1918–1919), or the crushing of the Hungarian Soviet Republic (1919). However, in European terms, these enmities reached their apogee in the Spanish Civil War (1936–1939), in which a militant, neo-crusading Catholicism served as the chief binding agent in the cement that held together General Franco's motley coalition of monarchists (of various stripes), Fascists, and center-right republicans. Furthermore, religious divisions were still capable of fueling, even defining, conflicts devoid of this type of left/right polarization. For example, the Anglo-Irish War (1919–1921) demonstrated once again the deep confessional fault lines that separated Irish Nationalists (who were largely Catholic) from Unionists (who were largely Protestant).

Despite the strident atheism of the Soviet Union, and the secularism of Nazism and Italian Fascism, the Second World War (1939–1945) continued to manifest the religious dimensions of conflicts waged in what was a deceptively secular age. Christian anti-Bolshevism was a mainstay of Finnish resistance to Soviet invasion in the so-called Winter War (1939–1940) and was also harnessed in Hitler's "crusade against Bolshevism," which was launched under the crusading moniker of Operation Barbarossa in June 1941. If this appeal helped spur the efforts of Hitler's partners (Lutheran Finland, Orthodox Romania, and Catholic Hungary) it also helped to generate a significant number of volunteers from occupied Europe and even neutral nations such as Franco's Spain. However, amidst the bloody and near-apocalyptic struggle on the Eastern Front, it was a further irony that Stalin likewise called on the deep reservoirs of Russian faith and Orthodox identity. Despite having presided over the fiercest persecution of the church in Europe since the days of Diocletian, Hitler's invasion sponsored a response in kind: churches (even monasteries) were reopened, the Moscow patriarchate restored, church collections (totaling 150 million rubles) funded the purchase of weaponry, and in 1945 Red Army tanks rolled into Berlin even emblazoned with the Orthodox cross. Such, indeed, was the extent of Orthodoxy's rapprochement with Stalin's regime that, in turn, it later fell victim to renewed persecution under Khrushchev's policy of de-Stalinization. And the renascent faith of Mother Russia also played well in relation to Stalin's principal European ally, namely Great Britain. Confronted after the fall of France in June 1940 with the fact of being the last redoubt of "Christian civilization" in a Europe dominated by secular totalitarianism, there was a conspicuously Christian edge to Great Britain's war effort. Reflected in the masterly rhetoric of Winston Churchill (himself little more than a deist), in the image of St Paul's Cathedral standing untouched amidst the blitz, and in the self-image of Britain's armed forces (the crusader's cross was a favored trope in army insignia, while RAF Bomber Command wrought vengeance on Germany in operations such as Gomorrah, the firebombing of Hamburg in the summer of 1943) Britain's war effort was at least as sacralized as any previous conflict. While General De Gaulle's Free French forces rallied under the ancient symbol of the cross of Lorraine, atavistic fury was unleashed on a murderous scale in the Balkans, where the Axis defeat and occupation of Yugoslavia exposed the enduring and mutual enmities of Orthodox Serb, Catholic Croat, and Muslim Bosniak. Moreover, the darker identities of some European Christians were also revealed in the most terrible dimension of the Second World War, namely Hitler's war against the Jews. Inflamed by the widespread (if relatively recent) identification of European Jewry with Bolshevik subversion, Christian Europe's most ancient hatred was instanced by numerous Christian perpetrators (and bystanders) from the Baltic to the Black Sea, and from the English Channel to the Caucasus. Indeed, complicit Fascist organizations such as Slovakia's Hlinka Guard, Hungary's Arrow Cross, and Romania's Iron Guard (formerly the Legion of the Archangel Michael) flaunted their association with the Christian heritage of their native countries.

The defeat of Hitler's Germany did not, however, exhaust the religious dynamic of notionally secular conflicts. The drawing of the Iron Curtain, the postwar triumph of Communism in Eastern Europe, and the formation of NATO and the Warsaw Pact occurred in the context of a global Cold War (1947–1991) in which the forces of the believing "free world" were pitted against the atheistic forces of the Soviet Union and the People's Republic of China. While belief and nonbelief helped define the protagonists in this worldwide struggle, in Christian Europe the ramparts were strengthened by the transnational growth of Christian democracy as a political force, in the weaponizing of religious persecution in its propaganda, and even in the use of American military bases (a new phenomenon) as resources and focal points for the evangelistic efforts of Billy Graham. And, yet again, largely detached from this wider confrontation, religious (or religiously inflected) conflicts continued: between Protestants and Catholics in Northern Ireland, for example, and between Orthodox and Muslim Cypriots. With the end of the Cold War, and the implosion of Communist Yugoslavia in the early 1990s, the religious and ethnic divisions of its peoples were once again resurgent, and more than forty years of Communist and atheistic rule were exposed as having done nothing to dull the edge of much older religious identities and hatreds. Still more recently, the capacity for religious tensions to drive and inflect conflict in post-Communist states has been seen in the Russo-Ukrainian War, the largest war to have erupted in Europe since 1945. In addition to old and bitter enmities between Orthodox Russian and Ukrainian Catholic, a new factor has obtruded with the formal recognition of an independent Orthodox Church of Ukraine, a supreme symbol of Ukrainian nationhood, by the ecumenical patriarch of Constantinople in 2019.

War and Religious Change

Given Europe's persistent history of conflict, war has profoundly impacted the development of European Christianity. In the realm of high politics, military (rather than moral) victory or defeat has helped determine the fate of communities, churches, and whole confessions. Although examples are legion, the expansion of Protestant Prussia was marked by the forced acquisition of largely Catholic territories—Silesia in the War of Austrian Succession, much of the Rhineland after the Napoleonic Wars (to say nothing of much of Poland in the Partitions of the late eighteenth century). Ultimately, Prussian victory in the German wars of unification forged a united Germany that was two-thirds Protestant. Conversely, the defeat of Nazi Germany in 1945 led to a fifty-year partition of Germany, East and West, and the creation of a German Federal Republic in West Germany that was principally Catholic. Similarly, the collapse of the predominantly Catholic Austro-Hungarian Empire in the First World War led (among other things) to the creation of a tri-faith Yugoslavia, whose disintegration resulted in civil wars that left in their wake a patchwork of states with marked Orthodox, Catholic, or Muslim majorities. However and if war has helped to redraw the religious map of modern Europe and reconfigure the religious profiles of its component states, it has also driven internal political change. For example, the lot of British and Irish Catholics around the turn of the nineteenth century was significantly improved by the succession of wars waged by Protestant Britain between 1775 (and the beginning of the American Revolutionary War) and 1815 (and the Battle of Waterloo). Within the space of forty years, Catholic Ireland became the British Army's main recruiting ground, a process marked by incremental political concessions culminating in Catholic Emancipation in 1829. Similarly, external threats served to forge a greater degree of religious accommodation on both sides during the First World War. In France, the vaunted *Union Sacrée* (the quasi-religious terminology was telling in itself) bound Catholics, Protestants, Jews, and secularists together in an alliance that, however imperfect, was at least an improvement on the poisonous religious politics of the prewar Third Republic. Likewise, in Germany, the remarkable show of solidarity in the Reichstag (one in which Protestant nationalists and liberals, Catholics, and secular socialists united to vote war credits) was hailed, in a surfeit of optimism, as a new Pentecost.

Whether or not the Holy Spirit descended on the Reichstag in August 1914, the exigencies of war offered fruitful opportunities for the churches and for church agencies. Given a general and growing impression—which transcended national, confessional, and denominational boundaries—that the nineteenth century had seen not only the alienation of much of the industrial working class but an undue feminization of church life, the First World War seemed to offer an opportunity for the churches to recoup their influence among young, working-class males. In most of the belligerent armies (including that of France's avowedly secular Third Republic, which conscripted its clergy in any case), the huge expansion of military chaplaincy offered the scope to mix with constituencies rarely encountered in civilian life. However, besides the influence and example of formal chaplaincy and, in many armies, of "soldier priests" and their equivalents, the war also called upon the vast charitable resources of the European churches. Whether expressed in medical or in welfare work, organizations ranging from the pan-Protestant Young Men's Christian Association to female Catholic nursing orders applied themselves to the manifold challenges of war—often subverting, in the process, well-established prewar norms and assumptions. To a large extent, this pattern was repeated in the Second World War where, even in the ideologically hostile environment of Germany's *Wehrmacht*, army chaplains and soldier clergy continued to minister, though chaplains were excluded from the more thoroughly nazified *Luftwaffe* and *Waffen SS*. If the French clergy continued to serve as combatants in the French Army (both before the disaster of May-June 1940 and afterwards in the Free French forces) in Poland the Catholic clergy were a mainstay of the Polish resistance and some even served as chaplains in the Communist-led Polish People's Army.

Inevitably, the experience of war, especially in the twentieth century, stirred the intellectual and creative energies of European Christians. Among the most influential theologians of the late twentieth centuries were the First World War chaplains G. A. Studdert Kennedy (whose vision of the suffering God was later popularized by Jürgen Moltmann) and Paul Tillich, who (like Studdert Kennedy) was decorated for his ministry in the trenches of the Western Front. Among Christian philosophers, their experience of war in the front line marked the Jesuit priest Pierre Teilhard de Chardin (a stretcher bearer in the French Army) and Ludwig Wittgenstein (an officer in the Austro-Hungarian army). Among a similar crop of Christian intellectuals who served in uniform during the Second World War were Donald MacKinnon (a British Army chaplain and later professor of divinity at Cambridge), Jürgen Moltmann, and the future Pope Benedict XVI (both of whom were conscripted, teenaged antiaircraft gunners captured by the Allies at the end of the war). The example of Benedict XVI illustrates a further point, for, given the impact of the World Wars, much of the churches' leadership throughout the twentieth century were inescapably marked by the scars of war. For instance, in 1940 no fewer than fifty-one French bishops were veterans of the First World War, and many of them had been decorated (perhaps an unfortunate pedigree in view of their relationship with Marshal Pétain, another hero of the First World War, and his collaborationist Vichy regime). In 1958, in electing Pope John XXIII, the College of Cardinals chose a pontiff who had been a stretcher bearer and chaplain in the Italian Army in the First World War. Similarly, in 1980, the three senior bishops of the Church of England (namely the archbishops of Canterbury and York, and the bishop of London) were all veterans of the Second. In fact, in the newly appointed archbishop of Canterbury, Robert Runcie, and for the first and only time in its history, the worldwide Anglican Communion had a leader—a former tank commander—who had undoubtedly killed people. In cultural and artistic terms, their deep experiences of war likewise impressed themselves on Christian authors and artists of all kinds. In Great Britain, the First World War produced perhaps the greatest Christian fantasies of the twentieth century in the form of C. S. Lewis's *Chronicles of Narnia* and J. R. R. Tolkien's *Lord of the Rings*. Although they appeared after the Second World War, both Lewis (an Anglican) and Tolkien (a Catholic) were inspired by their experience as infantry officers in the First World War, and stressed common themes of conflict, comradeship, and redemptive suffering.

However, it was not only countless individuals, famous and obscure, who were indelibly marked by the trauma of war, but the built infrastructure of Christian Europe—including its schools, hospitals, and other institutions, as well as its churches and cathedrals. While the cathedrals, churches, monasteries, and convents of Spain were laid waste in the Peninsular War, and despoiled once again in the Spanish Civil War, the two world wars (and the second in particular) generated an almost endless European litany of devastated cathedrals, churches, and shrines. Despite the notional protection of article 56 of the Hague Convention of 1899, large and prominent ecclesiastical structures were often natural targets, or (at best) located where collateral damage was unavoidable, especially from aerial bombing. While St Martin's Cathedral in the Belgian city of Ypres became symbolic of the city's suffering during the First World War, the second saw the bombing of Rome and the deliberate destruction of ancient cathedrals as far afield as Coventry (1940) and Warsaw (1941). To add to this catalog of ruin, the ancient Abbey of Monte Cassino, the historic cradle of Western monasticism, was first pulverized by Allied bombing before becoming the focus of the hardest battle of the Italian campaign (it eventually fell to the Free Polish soldiers of the "Anders Army" on Ascension Day 1944).

Such grim legacies, to say nothing of the use of nuclear weapons against Japan in August 1945, help illustrate why the world wars spurred renewed engagement with the just war tradition in European Christianity, even among those Protestant Churches (like the Anglican) in which its study had been marginalized since the Reformation. However, and whatever the challenges posed by the principles, corollaries, and application of *jus ad bellum* (going to war—just cause, right intention, etc.) and *jus in bello* (the conduct of war—proportionality, discrimination, etc.), there was always the choice of eschewing St. Augustine, St. Thomas Aquinas, and their elaboraters in favor of outright pacifism, an approach that (unsurprisingly) exerted a growing appeal among Catholics and mainstream Protestants as the twentieth century wore on. Hitherto limited to the historic "peace Churches" such as the Mennonites and Society of Friends (or Quakers), or (for more sectarian reasons) to newer denominations such as the Jehovah's Witnesses and Christadelphians, pacifism after 1918 also appealed to the humanitarian instincts and theological optimism of liberals in the Anglophone Protestant Churches in particular, winning vocal adherents among Methodists, Presbyterians, and Anglicans alike. If briefly curtailed by the nature of Nazism and the resultant character of the Second World War, it revived with the onset of the nuclear age. In the postwar German Democratic Republic, Communist tutelage and the catastrophe of the war itself served to defang the traditional militarism of German Protestantism, but a spirit of pacifism also seeped into the Catholic Church, encouraged by the apparent impossibility of reconciling nuclear war with the principles of just war theory and by the functionally pacifist position of Pope John Paul II (who, as a military cadet before the Second World War, had refused to wield a rifle). If, by the turn of the twenty-first century, many Western European Christians preferred to emphasize "peace building" and a "just peace" discourse, and to eschew the classic just war tradition in favor of a newly identified "presumption against war," their assumptions were strengthened by the growth of the twentieth-century ecumenical movement. Although primarily associated with the needs of the overseas missionary enterprise, another driving concern of early ecumenists (and of liberal Protestants more broadly) from before the First World War was the promotion of international amity through the transnational cooperation of the churches. In this sense, the gestation and work of the World Council of Churches, which was finally inaugurated in Amsterdam in 1948, should be seen as a Christian counterpart of the League of Nations and its successor, the United Nations.

What, then, was the effect of war on Christian belief? This deceptively simple question invites crude, even stereotypical answers, perhaps the most clichéd being that the horrors of war ineluctably act as a solvent to personal faith. However, this truism ignores the scale and complexity of the issue, for there is no more a typical experience of war than there is a typical experience of peace. For example, despite the misery and destructiveness of the Revolutionary and Napoleonic Wars, the First World War, and even the second, many corners of Europe (and even of its belligerent states) were left untouched by fighting that raged elsewhere. As in all conflicts, losses were unequally shared within nations and among communities—a situation marked in Great Britain after the First World War by the phenomenon of several dozen "thankful" or "blessed" villages, which lost none of their menfolk in the nation's bloodiest conflict (some of these, in fact, went on to survive the Second World War unscathed). As this situation implied, even for those in uniform, the fortunes of war dictated that years could be spent without seeing or hearing a shot fired in anger, whereas (quite apart from vulnerable civilians) others might be exposed to the horrors of the battlefield for months, if not years, on end. Additionally, the many variables of religious, cultural, family, and even occupational background make generalizations hard to sustain, as does the fact that, as Richard Schweitzer helpfully points out, the spectrum of personal belief is both broad and fluid and, it might be added, inherently idiosyncratic.[2] Finally, the science (or art) of the religious pollster, denied to previous generations, was still in its infancy even in the Second World War, and gauging the prevalent religious mood was often the self-appointed task of highly subjective (and often contradictory) religious pundits. Ultimately, therefore, one can find plenty of anecdotal evidence to illustrate the loss or gain of faith at an individual level, so it is perhaps best to frame an answer in terms of broader societal currents and developments in the life of the churches.

One of the beguiling aspects of our period is that it coincides with the classic chronology of a slow, inexorable process of secularization unfolding across Europe. Naturally, Europe's recurrent conflicts can be billed as fueling this process, a perception that has been widely attached to the First World War, famously labeled the "seminal catastrophe" of the twentieth century by the American diplomat and historian George F. Kennan. However, secularization has many and often conflicting metrics, and in practice, high levels of church affiliation in any society can be entirely consistent with low levels of church attendance (and, indeed, a certain measure of anticlericalism). Significantly, such a situation characterized much of Catholic and Protestant Europe for most of the nineteenth and twentieth centuries. Furthermore, correlation is very far from causation, and the generally downward trajectory of churchgoing in Great Britain after 1918, for example, was largely a function of the steady growth of secular leisure pursuits, notably the rise of the "Continental Sunday," whose malign effects had been identified by Sabbatarian commentators long before 1914. Furthermore, in appraising the declining social significance of Christianity in European societies, it is

2. Schweitzer, *Cross and the Trenches*, 17–62.

notable that a new chronology of secularization is gaining ground, which identifies its decisive phase as the years 1958–74, or the "long 1960s," years of comparative peace and prosperity in Western Europe after two decades of conflict, postwar austerity, and Christian renewal and reconstruction. If the process of secularization was therefore much more abrupt than has long been supposed (Hugh McLeod has described the "long 1960s" as possibly "marking a rupture as profound as that brought about by the Reformation"[3]), it is vital not to fall into the trap of projecting the dynamics and trajectory of religious change in Northern European countries (Great Britain, Germany, France, Scandinavia, and the Benelux countries) onto the countries of Southern or Eastern Europe, whose cultural and political circumstances were often radically different. Besides the countries of the former Yugoslavia, in post-Communist societies such as Hungary, Poland, Ukraine, and Russia, the post-Cold War era was one of the restoration and reassertion of Christian identity and church influence.

The broad and varied impact of war can be seen in the ebb and flow of Christian life in Great Britain since the French Revolution, an instructive longitudinal survey in that Britain participated in most of the major European wars of our era. Of course, the history of every country is different, and Britain was exceptional in that it never experienced a major invasion, let alone defeat and occupation, throughout this two-hundred-year period. Nevertheless, Britain was a prime protagonist in the French Revolutionary and Napoleonic Wars (the only major power, in fact, to be consistently anti-French); it fought against Russia, and alongside France, Sardinia, and the Ottoman Empire, in the Crimean War; it came to lead the Allied war effort against Germany in the First World War; it fought Hitler's Germany throughout the second (suffering the devastation of many of its towns and cities at the hand of the Luftwaffe and Hitler's V-1 and V-2 rockets); and was a stalwart member of NATO throughout the Cold War. However, and despite this litany of major conflicts, and the losses, deprivation, and destruction they entailed, at no point did the threat or impact of war trigger a lasting and discernible downturn in the churches' fortunes. On the contrary, the febrile climate and upheavals of the French Revolutionary and Napoleonic Wars fueled the growth of evangelical Protestantism in all its guises, seeing the appointment (and assassination in 1812) of Britain's only evangelical prime minister (namely, Spencer Perceval) and witnessing the phenomenal growth of Methodism in all its guises, especially at the lower levels of British society. Similarly, and while scarcely of the same scope or duration, the Crimean War stimulated new forms of Christian philanthropy, threw up

3. McLeod, *Religious Crisis of 1960s*, 1.

new Christian martial heroes, and stoked the connected, mid-Victorian cults of "muscular Christianity" and "Christian militarism."

Sixty years later (and notwithstanding earlier, gloomy verdicts on the effects of the First World War on British religious life) the bloodiest of all Britain's conflicts saw a marked increase in public religious practice in its immediate aftermath and generated a religious (rather than secular) cult of remembrance that remains a calendrical mainstay of church life to this day. Similarly, the course and nature of the Second World War saw a cultural revival of British Christianity, one instanced by the widely credited "miracle" of Dunkirk; by the range and extent of religious broadcasting by the BBC; by the unprecedented popularity of Archbishop William Temple, the leading prophet of the postwar "welfare state"; and by the embedding of Christian religious education and daily worship in all publicly funded schools in England and Wales. Finally, even the Cold War era threw up markers of religious vitality. For example, over a thirty-five-year period (1954–89) Britain hosted no fewer than eighteen of Billy Graham's evangelistic "crusades," which reportedly racked up attendances of more than nine million.[4] In a similar vein, in 1982 (and against the backdrop of nuclear escalation and an unexpected war with Argentina over the Falkland Islands) Britain experienced its first-ever papal visit, in this case from that equally formidable Cold War warrior Pope John Paul II. Indeed, and despite the secularizing impact of the "long 1960s," it could prove significant that, as late as 2001, the proportion of British adults self-identifying as Christians hovered around 70 per cent. In successive decades, and as those who lived through the existential dangers of the Second World War and Cold War gave way to younger generations who had not, this proportion slumped to under 60 per cent in 2011, and to less than half in 2021.

Conclusion

To historians of nineteenth-, twentieth-, and even twenty-first-century European Christianity, the abiding importance of religion as a motor of inter- and intra-state conflict should be far more obvious. Despite their identification as an age of protracted and ineluctable secularization, European conflicts throughout these centuries continued to evince religious dimensions and, in some cases, were propelled by markedly religious (or at least ethno-religious) factors. In this era, a notionally secularizing Europe saw conflicts between the forces of faith and infidelity (in numerous guises); between Christian confessions; between politico-religious conservatives and

---

4. Peck, "Billy Graham," para. 5.

liberals; and between Christians and Muslims. At the same time, war continued to act as a catalyst for change within Christian Europe. While their outcome could determine the religious character and trajectory of entire states and societies, the experience of recurrent conflicts, culminating with the fear of nuclear Armageddon, left an indelible mark on Christian theology, ethics, practice, and literary and cultural expression. Indeed, and as this (necessarily brief) survey has indicated, and contrary to a received Cold War wisdom concerning Christianity and conflict, it was an era of relative peace, rather than one of war, that proved most corrosive to the fortunes of Christianity in Western Europe towards the turn of the twenty-first century. If so, in coming decades the turmoil of this conflicted continent might yet produce change of comparable significance for the future of Christianity in Europe.

Bibliography

Anderson, Olive. "The Growth of Christian Militarism in Mid-Victorian Britain." *English Historical Review* 86 (1971) 46–72.
Bank, Jan, with Lieve Gevers. *Churches and Religion in the Second World War*. Translated by Brian Doyle. London: Bloomsbury, 2016.
Burleigh, Michael. *Earthly Powers: Religion and Politics in Europe from the Enlightenment to the Great War*. London: HarperCollins, 2005.
———. *Sacred Causes: Religion and Politics from the European Dictators to Al Qaeda*. London: HarperCollins, 2007.
Gregory, Adrian. "Beliefs and Religion." In *Civil Society*, edited by Jay Winter, 418–44. Vol. 3 of *The Cambridge History of the First World War*. Cambridge: Cambridge University Press, 2014.
Jenkins, Philip, *The Great and Holy War*. Oxford: Lion, 2014.
Lecky, William. *History of the Rise and Influence of the Spirit of Rationalism in Europe*. 2 vols. London: Longman, Roberts & Green, 1865.
Loconte, Joseph. *A Hobbit, a Wardrobe, and a Great War*. New York: Thomas Nelson, 2015.
McLeod, Hugh. *The Religious Crisis of the 1960s*. Oxford: Oxford University Press, 2007.
Miner, Steven, *Stalin's Holy War: Religion, Nationalism, and Alliance Politics, 1941–1945*. Chapel Hill: University of North Carolina Press, 2003.
Peck, Andy, "Billy Graham: His Impact on Britain." *Premier Christianity*, Jan. 25, 2014. https://www.premierchristianity.com/home/billy-graham-his-impact-on-britain/4.article.
Schweitzer, Richard, *The Cross and the Trenches: Religious Faith and Doubt among British and American Great War Soldiers*. Westport, CT: Praeger, 2003.
Snape, Michael. *A Church Militant: Anglicans and the Armed Forces from Queen Victoria to the Vietnam War*. Oxford: Oxford University Press, 2022.
———. "The Great War." In *World Christianities c. 1914–c. 2000*, edited by Hugh McLeod, 131–50. Vol. 9 of *The Cambridge History of Christianity*. Cambridge: Cambridge University Press, 2006.

13

Communism and European Christianity

Katharina Kunter

Is a society without social differences or classes between people thinkable? Is this just a utopia that inspires people only as a vision, or could this idea be realized on earth? And how does Christianity relate to this thought?

This is the basic question when we are looking back at the entangled history of Communism and Christianity in Europe.[1] At the same time, this is not only a history of the modern era, starting with the philosopher Karl Marx and the theory of Marxism in the nineteenth century. It is even directly connected to the emergence of the first Christian communities over two thousand years ago. Because since the very beginning, there have always been Christian individuals, movements, or groups who wanted to live in a communitarian way. They referred to the Bible. In the second chapter of the Acts of the Apostles, for example, it is written that all those who had become believers now formed a community and owned everything together. Therefore, they sold their possessions and gave to everyone as much as they needed (Acts 2:44–45).

The German-Czech philosopher and Marxist Karl Kautsky, who lived in the nineteenth century, invented the term *Christian communism* for this.[2] He distinguished "Christian communism" from "monastic communism,"[3] because the monks and nuns in the medieval monasteries of Europe also formed a community in which they shared everything with one another, and in which the individual member of the order had no possessions or privileges. One of the most famous and radical examples was the monk

---

1. Beliakova et al., *Es gibt keinen Gott!*
2. In the German original, Kautsky uses the term *urchristlich*.
3. Kautsky, *Vorläufer des neueren Sozialismus*; Boer, "Karl Kautsky's *Forerunners*." The central first part of Kautsky's volume has not yet been translated into English.

Francis of Assisi, who lived in Italy in the thirteenth century. He even made communal poverty the basis of his order, the Franciscans. As new economic structures emerged in the Early Modern period, like early forms of "capitalism," the question of what a just society should look like continued to keep theologians, philosophers, and politicians busy even more. One of these people was the English, Catholic politician and scholar Thomas More. He wrote a book in 1516 that became known as *Utopia*.

In it he discusses what a good and ideal society might look like and what are its basics. Questions like: Would there be no more wars if people could not get richer as a result of such a conflict? Do men need private property, and how does a human society develop if there are no social differences between their citizens? And, maybe most important, what role does money play? More's work and his questions continued to inspire many, even long after his death. However, there was an opposing side to utopian and philosophical designs and ideas such as those of More: this was the church of the old, feudal, and absolutist-structured Europe.

Over the centuries, it had gained a position of power in state and in society: its popes, bishops, and church officials had privileges, its church estates were often rich, and the simple and poor, faithful people had to pay for them. This church of the ancien régime, with its prosperity and power, contributed to the fact that the old social order did not change, and more and more people lived in abject poverty. There were Christians who wanted to change this. Especially when industrialization, urbanization, and the impoverishment of the people in the large European cities took hold, there were some Christians who now advocated Christian socialism. However, they did not prevail on a broad scale.

Revolutions for Human Equality

Many experienced the institution of the church in old Europe as an oppressive authority that wanted to hold on to its privileges, without justification, and thus prevented the modernization of society as well as the happiness of individual people. This was especially true for the church institutions that had historically grown to a dominant position in the various countries and parts of Europe: the different Orthodox, Catholic, and Protestant Churches. At the end of the eighteenth century, the first major attack on this power structure took place in France.[4] At the focus of the revolt were the First Estate and Second Estate of the society: the nobility and the clergy (the consecrated members of the Catholic Church). Liberty, equality, and fraternity

4. Shusterman, *French Revolution*.

was the new slogan, which had received impulses from the philosophical movement of the Enlightenment. It claimed something new: all people should have the same rights by nature.

This was a revolutionary idea, because it meant that everyone could rise above their God-given status and have the same opportunities for realization as nobles or clerics. However, from the point of view of the church, this was an attack on God's created order. For this vision and for these rights, many people in France went to the barricades and fought. With the French Revolution also came the Universal Declaration of Human and Civil Rights in 1789. This was connected by a new religious policy: state and church were separated, and society was cleansed of all Christian traditions and elements, including renaming previously church holidays, abolishing church marriage, and allowing divorce. In addition, religious freedom was introduced. It attacked the position of power of the Catholic Church in France, because now French Protestants, for example, could invoke the same rights as the Catholic Church. This significantly weakened the power position of the Catholic Church.

The plan of the French Revolutionaries was radical. The terror in France that followed the first phase caused fear among the churches and governments in Europe; they wanted to avoid French conditions in their countries at all costs. But in 1848-49, almost sixty years after the French Revolution, the ideas of democracy, human and civil rights reached broader circles outside France.[5] Christians were also actively involved in these democratization processes. But for the institution of the European churches, it remained clear: they did not want French conditions in their backyards. For them, everything connected with the French Revolution inevitably would result into chaos and ruin. In the United States, though, there was a completely different way of thinking, best illustrated by the fact that human rights and religious freedom were enshrined in the Bill of Rights in 1776. But the ideas of the French Revolution and the 1848/49 revolutions could not be stopped in Europe. Revolution as a method to enforce human equality became a new model, which was an integral part of the ideas of the labor movement as well as of Communist thinkers in the nineteenth century.

Marxism and the Role of Religion

In 1848, many of the egalitarian ideas came together in a programmatic text published in London, a publication that would become one of the most influential texts in modern history: *The Manifesto of the Communist Party*,

---

5. Sperber, *European Revolutions, 1848-1851*.

also abbreviated as *The Communist Manifesto*. Written by two Germans, Karl Marx and Friedrich Engels, it was quickly translated into almost every language in the world. Marx and Engels had similar background profiles as intellectuals, journalists, and philosophers. *The Communist Manifesto* was the program of the Communist League and explained for the first time the basic positions of Communism and what society should look like according to these Communist ideas. *The Communist Manifesto* was thus the theory of Communism. Numerous Communist and socialist workers' parties in Europe—and later worldwide—were shaped by it. It became the basis of what was later called Marxism.

Although other aspects would also be interesting to discuss, we will focus here on the role of religion in the Communist thoughts of Marx and Engels. In their work, Marx and Engels described and analyzed the development of the so-called working classes since the start of the Industrial Revolution. The situation of those poor people, mostly living in strongly growing industrial cities, was becoming more and more miserable. Family structures but also other traditional values and ways of life were breaking down because of this. Marx and Engels were looking for a theoretical and practical solution to this "worker question." For them it was clear: the grievances were so overwhelming that a radical change in society is needed. In the end, this was only possible through a revolution. To be successful, this revolution must start from the lowest strata and classes of society, from the so-called proletariat, from the workers who own nothing and have only their labor to offer. Marx and Engels thought of history as a history of class struggles; there would be no social progress and no equal and classless society unless the working class rebels against those who own everything. This, according to the Communist conception, this is the so-called bourgeois class. If there were no workers' revolutions, there would be mass impoverishment of the people, and at the same time those with property would become richer and richer.

To prevent this, the workers of all countries would have to unite to fight for this classless society. After their revolution, a new phase would begin, that of the classless society. This is socialism, which is finally followed by Communism as the ultimate vision and as a total realization. In this final state of historical development, property no longer plays a role and all people can develop freely. Religion appears in this thinking as a negative element: following the German philosopher Anselm Feuerbach, Marx and Engels consider religion as a "drug" that people need to deal with their human poverty and misery. Hence, a religion is not much more than a construction of beliefs, a projection. But what made it problematic, according to them, was that the religious beliefs and especially the institution of the church were among the important factors that were oppressing the working class. According to Marx and Engels, the clerics were against the worker's revolution, as they did not want to change the existing order. Moreover, the church and its clerics had long been alienated from the reality of workers' lives.

From the Communist point of view, religion only embodied and strengthened the positions of the bourgeois. Furthermore: if the workers would no longer have to provide slave labor for others and would be free, they would no longer need religion nor the church anymore. As a result, religion would be unnecessary and disappear. Of course, the church was afraid of this. Marx was convinced that religion would automatically disappear under socialism, as people would no longer need God and could live fulfilled lives as atheists.[6] Therefore, he did not need to fight against churches and religion. The politician and revolutionary Vladimir Ilyich Lenin, who later founded the Russian Communist Party, as well as Stalin, clearly saw this differently.

As we shall see, they considered religion and the institution of the church, especially the Russian Orthodox Church, as real enemies of the working class, and hence they had to be fought with force.

Papal Rejection of Communism

As explained, churches were against revolution, Communism, and socialism, because these movements challenged the God-given social order. Pope Pius IX was the first pope to respond to the new movement of Communism. In his November 9, 1846, encyclical *Qui Pluribus* on faith and religion, he explained why: Communism, with its idea of an equal society and its condemnation of property, seduces the young; Communism is outrageous and seeks to overthrow society from the bottom up.[7] Communism and socialism were an error that had to be rejected, he specified later.[8] His successor, Pope Leo XIII, also initially declared war on socialism in his 1878 writing *Quod Apostolici Muneris*. Socialism was a "death-bringing plague" that was disintegrating and destroying society.[9] As a result, the conditions for the workers would not change, and misery and poverty would continue to exist.

The workers' movement, the socialists, and the Communists were trying to change things, and there were many workers who were now joining them. In 1891, Leo XIII addressed the social situation of the workers for

6. Raines, *Marx on Religion*.
7. Pius X, "*Qui Pluribus*," para. 4.
8. Pius X, "*Qui Pluribus*," para. 16.
9. Leo XIII, "*Quod Apostolici Muneris*," para. 3.

the first time in his encyclical *Rerum Novarum* and discussed how their situation could be improved and capitalism limited. Workers would have to receive fair wages and be protected from exploitation by the state and other organizations. But Leo's reflections did not mean the acceptance of socialism and Communism. The denial of Communism remained part of Catholic thinking well into the twentieth century.[10]

Russian Revolution and Orthodox Church

The revolutionary events in Russia that erupted in 1905 and 1917/18 also supported profound social and political changes. As these are very much interrelated and as it is difficult to view them separately from one another, the term *Russian Revolution* has meanwhile gained acceptance among researchers as the definition of an overall event.[11] This refers to the transformation process that turned the Russian tsarist empire's agrarian class system into a "modern" one-party dictatorship of the Communist Party based on mass industrialization, as well as the political transformation from Russia into the Soviet Union.

The revolutionary upheavals in the Russian Empire began in 1905 in St. Petersburg in front of the Winter Palace, the residence of Russian tsar Nicholas II. Tens of thousands of workers protested peacefully under the leadership of Orthodox priest Georgi Gapon for better working conditions, for the abolition of censorship, for religious freedom, and for a representation of the people. After soldiers of the tsar shot numerous workers, revolutionary and violent uprisings against the ruling class began throughout the country. This brought two results: first, a parliament was established called the "Duma"; and second, the tsar issued an edict of tolerance on April 17, 1905.[12] With this edict, the absolute power of the Orthodox Church in Russia was broken. Now even non-Orthodox parishes were allowed to build churches and celebrate services, something that previously had been forbidden. But the tsar and the Orthodox Church still formed an "antisocial power unit" in the eyes of the workers.

The First World War, which lasted from 1914 to 1918, finally destabilized the old power structures in Russia. In February 1917, Tsar Nicholas II was forced to abdicate, and the monarchy in Russia was abolished. Russia was now a republic led by a "provisional government." In which political direction Russia would go was open. The Orthodox Church lost many

10. Paul VI, "*Octagesima Adveniens*."
11. McMeekin, *Russian Revolution*; Hildermeier, *Russische Revolution*.
12. For more information, see Werth, *Tsar's Foreign Faiths*.

privileges, the synod as the governing body of the church was abolished, and debates about ecclesiastical reforms were on the agenda. But then, surprisingly for many in the church, a new revolution emerged in October 1917. It started from the Communist Bolsheviks under the leadership of Vladimir Ilyich Lenin. The Bolsheviks (or Bolshevists) were the majority group and the radical wing of the Russian Social Democratic Labor Party. They wanted sole power and to use force and professional revolutionaries to establish a Communist state, the dictatorship of the proletariat.

In their religious policy, the Bolsheviks, like the revolutionaries of the French Revolution, first introduced the right of religious freedom. This was initially intended to break the power of the Orthodox Church, which the Bolsheviks saw as an element of the old tsarist system, with its large financial resources and strong religious hold on the people. On November 15, 1917, the "Declaration of the Rights of the Peoples of Russia" was issued, which was supplemented by the "Decree on Freedom of Conscience, Ecclesiastical and Religious Communities" of January 20, 1918.[13] These two laws declared war on the church and religion and radically curtailed their traditional effectiveness. At first sight, the decree seemed progressive: it guaranteed religious freedom, including full freedom of conscience and equality of all religions. But at the same time, it marked the end of the church's role as a social and public institution. Lenin had successfully enforced the separation of church and state in the decree. Churches were privatized, so to speak, and became increasingly viewed more as an association. Furthermore, church property, monasteries, and church buildings were nationalized. This hit the Orthodox Church as the national Church of Russia the hardest since the other non-Orthodox parishes and communities had very little property. Of high symbolic significance was the order by Stalin in 1931 to blow up the Church of Christ the Savior in Moscow. A construction of the Palace of Soviets began in its place; however, it was never finished.

Communist Struggle against the Christian Churches

After the Soviet Union was founded in 1922 and Joseph Stalin took power, oppression and terror reigned. Whereas in the initial phase of the Soviet Union persecution had been directed primarily at the Orthodox Church, now Catholics and Protestants were also affected by the Stalinist anti-religious attacks and persecutions, even if they were much smaller in number.

13. Ulianov and Dzhugashvili, "Declaration of the Rights"; and Council of People's Commissars, "Freedom of Religious Conscience." See also the accompanying decree by Ulianov et al., "Decree on Separation."

By the end of the 1920s, churches were closed en masse, as well as other church-related buildings and higher theological training and study centers. Numerous Christians were forced to leave the Soviet Union, among them the well-known Orthodox religious philosopher Nikolai Berdyaev. He went into exile in Paris where he later became an important theological voice of ecumenism.

The first monasteries were closed around 1929.[14] Another step in the fight against the churches was the "Law on Religious Associations," enacted in 1929.[15] It banned all economic, social, missionary, and educational activities of all religious communities and associations. This meant that the traditional fields of work of the churches, education, youth work, school, and religious education, as well as the extensive and varied diaconal and charitable work, were forbidden. Churches in the Soviet Union had now been reduced by the Communists to purely religious groups that were no longer allowed to carry out public work. But this was not enough for Stalin and his ruling apparatus, as they wanted to systematically destroy and eradicate religion and churches. To achieve this, they carried out numerous cruel anti-Christian and anti-church measures, most notably initiated by the Marxist ideologue Leon Trotsky and organized by the politburo.

Beginning in March 1922, church valuables such as icons were confiscated, shrines were broken into, and relics were stolen and desecrated—Bibles, Christian literature, and bell ringing were widely banned. The church was defamed and ridiculed with broad anti-religious propaganda.[16] In the 1930s, and especially then in the years of the Great Terror beginning in 1937, persecution and repression of Christians increased radically: clergy and parishioners were persecuted, imprisoned, or sentenced to death in show trials; priests, monks, pastors, and ordinary Christians were deported to penal camps in the GULAG. One of those who perished in such a penal camp was the well-known Orthodox priest and philosopher Pavel Florensky, who died in 1937 in the camp of the former monastery on Solovetsky Island.

We still do not have enough details about the cruel extent of Stalinist persecutions, deportations, and murders. The historical reappraisal of Stalinist crimes, which has been carried out by human rights organizations such as the Russian NGO Memorial in recent decades, is now no longer possible in Putin's authoritarian Russia.[17]

---

14. For more information, see Wynot, *Keeping the Faith*.
15. Matthews, "Law on Religious Organizations."
16. Impressive examples are given online at the Merrill C. Berman Collection: https://mcbcollection.com/early-soviet-anti-religious-propaganda.
17. BBC, "Memorial."

The Second World War changed Stalin's attitude toward the churches. This had tactical-strategic reasons, not substantive ones: the Soviet Union needed the support of the anti-Hitler coalition and could not afford a bad image because of its policy of extermination against the churches and Christians. The result was a new course in religious policy: Christian and religious life in the Soviet Union and its newly conquered territories was now permitted to a limited extent and no longer persecuted.[18] Externally, Stalin orchestrated this new course by meeting publicly with three metropolitans of the Russian Orthodox Church on September 4, 1943. After that, the situation for the churches in the Soviet Union improved somewhat: the Orthodox Church was again allowed to hold a church council and elect a patriarch of Moscow and of all of Russia; all Christian churches were allowed to hold services and open their churches, monasteries, and ecclesiastical institutions. They were allowed to pray together and baptize.

However, these church practices had long since ceased to resemble prerevolutionary religious life. The fear of terror and persecution brought forth conformist and statist church leaders. The Communist state established an authority to control all activities of the churches and their believers. This government authority later existed in all other socialist states; it was called the Council for Religious Affairs and was located in the Council of Ministers of the Soviet Union (like the respective socialist countries). Thus, even after 1943, the Soviet state ensured that church and religion continued to decline in importance. State permission had to be obtained for all church activities, and church writings continued to be censored. Churches were allowed to operate only in the narrow religious space, and even this was strictly controlled.

The Communist Regimes in Central and Eastern Europe and the Churches after 1945

After the end of World War II, the Soviet Union had considerably enlarged its own territory; now Western Ukraine, Western Belarus, northern Bukovina, Bessarabia, the Carpathian region, and Latvia, Lithuania, and Estonia were part of the Soviet Union. In addition, Poland, Czechoslovakia, the eastern part of Germany (the later German Democratic Republic, GDR), Hungary, Romania, Bulgaria, Albania, and Yugoslavia—even if the situation was somewhat freer here—now belonged to the Soviet Union's sphere of power and established their own Stalinist-style regimes. In all these countries, socialist religious policy followed the Soviet model: first, religious

18. Chumachenko, *Church and State*.

freedom was granted in the constitutions immediately after the Communist takeover. As in the Soviet Union, this was intended to break the power of the respective majority church in the country by strengthening the minority churches as confessional competitors.

In Czechoslovakia and Hungary, for example, this was historically the Catholic Church, which the Communists regarded as a leftover of the Habsburg Empire. Moreover, the Catholic Church was part of the universal church and connected with the Vatican; the Communists also wanted to break this affiliation. In the shadow of this early Communist fight against the Catholic Church, there were margins and new freedoms for Protestants. Therefore, there were Protestants who were initially in favor of the new socialist regimes. The Czech theologian Josef L. Hromádka was one of them. He was convinced that the emergence of nationalism, National Socialism, and fascism were related to bourgeois society and its failure. Consequently, he said, Christianity, after the end of World War II, must now make a new start and adopt a socialist position. Only this would bring a renewed and peaceful society.

However, the reality was different: in the late 1940s and 1950s, there was severe persecution of churches in all socialist countries. Depending on the denomination, this affected Catholics, Protestants, and Orthodox Christians. Christians who resisted the Communists' seizure of power or advocated democracy were persecuted, arrested, tried in show trials, and murdered. A major battlefield from the Communists' point of view was church youth work. It attracted thousands of young people. However, because the Communist party wanted to take and ideologize the youth, they tried to criminalize the churches' youth work. To this end, they even introduced a new socialist ritual, a youth ceremony (*Jugendweihe*). The *Jugendweihe* was a Communist ceremony in which fourteen-year-olds were given adult social status. It was a Communist substitute for the Protestant confirmation—and it was so successful in the long run, that even after the fall of the GDR, it is still celebrated in eastern Germany. One example of how the Communist Party attacked church youth work was the *Junge Gemeinde* (young congregation) in the GDR, which was the churches' youth work in GDR.[19] Pupils and students who attended the *Junge Gemeinde* had to justify that at school and were even brought before a school tribunal. There they were pressured to leave the *Junge Gemeinde*. The pupils who did not do so and remained steadfast in their faith were arrested and banned from school. They were then unable to graduate from high school, for example, or to study. It was

---

19. Ueberschär, *Junge Gemeinde im Konflikt*.

not until the summer of 1953 that the Communist Party of the GDR, on Moscow's instructions, withdrew its repression of the students.

After Stalin's death in 1953 and the process of de-Stalinization, the way in which the Communists attacked Christianity changed: now the anti-religious and anti-church methods came across as somewhat "softer," but no less effective. The propaganda relied on a supposedly scientifically based atheism; from there they attacked churches and Christianity as irrational, anti-modern, and inhumane. In the long run, this strategy was successful. Today, for example, Estonia, Czechoslovakia, and the areas of the former East Germany are among the most secularized areas of Europe.

Beginning in the late 1960s and 1970s, the Communist Party and state developed new methods to continue to diminish and control the churches. These included defaming, polarizing, and isolating independent and system-critical Christians, recruiting agents and "unofficial collaborators" (*inoffizielle Mitarbeiter*) for the state security and using them to infiltrate church leadership, synods, church administrations, and the various church milieu.[20]

Christian Life and Theology under Communism

The Communist attacks on and repressions of the churches changed Christianity not only socially and ecclesiastically, but also religiously.[21] After the end of the Second World War, popular piety established in the interwar period with full church services and the deep-rooted traditions of baptism, confirmation, marriage, and funerals survived for a while. But after the churches were pushed back by the Communist state from their public activities, Christian professions and employees disappeared from schools, education, the media, and diaconia. Even national folkloric religious festivals, such as St. John's Day on June 23/24, which in Estonia, for example, was the most popular church festival next to Christmas, were banned or at least deliberately deprived of their religious elements.[22]

Because theological faculties and church training centers were closed and controlled by the state, there were few young church members, and they were under particular pressure to justify themselves. A career in the church was no longer attractive.

Nevertheless, people could also find a space of freedom in the church from a repressive state system that was geared toward state conformity. Those who decided to be a member of the church showed courage. Being a

20. Conway, "'Stasi' and the Churches."
21. Kunter, "Evangelische Volksfrömmigkeit."
22. Salo, "Anti-Religious Rites in Estonia."

confessing Christian in Communism meant to stand by one's decision and justify one's faith in an atheistic and anti-religious environment. There could be professional disadvantages for oneself or for one's children and families. In the GDR, children from Protestant pastor families were often not admitted to high school and were not allowed to study. So being a Christian did cost something. But one also gained something for it: faith, hope, a community that strengthened in everyday life, and a more robust identity.

Since the late 1970s, the effects of the Communist "land reform" and expropriations have been evident in the churches. Traditional ties and social hierarchies in the countryside were dissolved. Because the Communists proclaimed the workers' and peasants' state and socially favored workers and peasants, there was a broad "de-bourgeoisification."[23] This had an effect especially on Protestantism, because Protestantism was historically more rooted in the bourgeoisie. More people who came from the middle class and worked in technical professions now entered the congregations.

If one investigates the period of the Communist regimes after World War II until their collapse in 1989/90, it becomes apparent that the radical suppression of Christian expressions of life affected women more than men. Women, even under Communism, continued to be the religious-tradition transmitters in the family and were responsible for the Christian socialization of their children. Mothers and grandmothers decided in many cases whether Christian songs were sung or Bible stories told at home, whether children were baptized or went to communion or confirmation. However, because the Communists emphasized equal rights for women and enshrined them in their constitutions, women's employment was the norm in socialist society.

Just as the so-called feminization thesis provides some justification and arguments for the secularization of Western Europe,[24] the formal equality and professional activity of women under Communism is also a reason why Christian traditions broke off in many families. Unlike in Western Europe, Christian-socialized women were also exposed to enormous state and societal pressures in their everyday working lives. On the other hand, religious-political pressure and the marginalization of Christianity led women to take on more and more tasks and activities in the congregations and churches. Since there were no longer enough men to maintain pastoral care, the provision of services, and catechetical activities in the congregations, women were now in demand. In the Soviet Union, Orthodox women

---

23. Großbölting, *SED-Diktatur und Gesellschaft*.
24. See ch. 12 in this volume.

formed new monastic and Christian communities,[25] and in the Protestant Churches women were ordained as pastors from the 1950s onward.

Theologically, the question of what it means to live as a Christian under socialism had been discussed since the mid-1950s. After the Soviet suppression of the uprisings in 1953 in the GDR, 1956 in Hungary, and 1968 in Czechoslovakia, it was clear that the Soviet Union was prepared to secure its hegemony even by force. But it was also obvious that a longer duration of the Communist regimes had to be expected. Many Christians, congregations, and churches decided to "hibernate" or to go into "inner emigration." By this they meant to belong to a Christian congregation, to celebrate church festivals at home and in the congregation, but to live outwardly a conformist life. But there were other options. For example, this was the path the Greek Catholic Church in Ukraine had chosen. It was in 1946 forcibly united by the Soviet authorities with the Russian Orthodox Church and was now attached to the Moscow patriarchate. Individual, martyr-like protest against the Communist oppression of the church was another possibility: for example, the self-immolation of the Protestant pastor Oskar Brüsewitz in 1976 has become well known.[26]

In some Protestant circles, adaptation to socialism was discussed theologically. These theologians saw that the end of the Constantinian age had come, that is, the end of the ties between church, state, and bourgeoisie. Here, in contact with a secular world, new opportunities for Christianity could also arise, they thought. In the context of the cultural movements of 1968, which awakened a new interest in Marxist-inspired liberation movements in the West, a small group of Christian theologians began to engage more seriously with Marxism in terms of content. The humanist and anticolonial dimensions of Marxism in Christianity had to be taken seriously, in their opinion. On the Catholic side, the congresses of the International Pauline Society at the end of the 1960s played an important role, with the well-known West German theologians Johann Baptist Metz and Karl Rahner among the participants. In Czechoslovakia, the Christian-Marxist dialogue initiated by the philosopher Milan Machovec and the Czech theologian Josef Hromádka met with broader interest. In addition, there were the bishops in church leadership who quickly, opportunistically placed themselves in socialist service and developed a theology that apologetically defended socialism. The Hungarian Lutheran bishop Zoltán Káldy, with his diaconal theology, was one of them, as was, for example, the Catholic Slovenian bishop Vekoslav Grmič.

25. Beliakova and Mironova, "Female Religious Leadership."
26. Blažek et al., "Oskar Brüsewitz."

Christians and the End of the Communist Regime 1989/90

With the election of the Polish pope John Paul I in 1978, the dynamic between the worldwide Catholic Church and the Communist state changed. John Paul I took a strictly anti-Communist course and supported the independent Polish trade union *Solidarność* (Solidarity), which was also supported by the Polish Catholic Church.[27] This was because in Poland, unlike in the other Communist countries, the Catholic Church was still broadly rooted among the people. Now *Solidarność* represented the interests of workers, advocated democracy, and went on strike in various cities of Poland—which, according to Marxist doctrine, should not be. It became a broad, visibly Catholic opposition movement.

After the Communist government imposed martial law out of fear from 1980 to 1983, the slow road to democracy began. *Solidarność* representatives participated in the "roundtables." These were rounds of talks between representatives of the socialist government and the opposition. In June 1989, Poland held its first free parliamentary elections, from which *Solidarność* arose as the big winner. Tadeusz Mazowiecki, a *Solidarność* member and active Catholic, became Poland's first non-Communist prime minister since World War II. Poland's peaceful path to democracy and Lech Wałęsa, the charismatic leader of *Solidarność* since the war, radiated hope for change beyond Poland.

Also in other socialist states, peace, environmental, and human rights groups critical of the state had emerged since the signing of the Helsinki Final Act in 1975. One of the first and best-known civil rights movements was Charter 77, which was also signed by numerous Catholics and Protestants.[28] In addition to Charter 77, other human and civil rights groups inspired by the Helsinki Final Act came up, including the Moscow Helsinki Group in 1976, as well as the Christian Committee for the Defense of the Rights of Believers in the USSR, a Ukrainian and a Lithuanian Helsinki Group, or, somewhat later, the Initiative Peace and Human Rights in 1986 in the GDR. All these groups were inspired by the Helsinki Final Act and its human rights provisions. Many individual Protestants, Catholics, and Orthodox were active here, often without support from their own church. This was because church leaders were cautious and often too close to the state.

In the GDR, many young Christians had been active in the independent peace movement since the late 1970s, working for a better environment and human rights. The Protestant Church offered these groups the

---

27. Felak, *Pope in Poland*.
28. For more information, see Kunter, "Human Rights."

opportunity to meet in church halls and thus supported them. Since 1988, three large ecumenical gatherings took place in which Christians demanded more justice in the GDR. From these platforms and activities, democratic opposition movements appeared in 1989, in which a disproportionate number of Christians were involved. The pictures of the peace prayers and the Monday demonstrations, in which the demonstrators, candles in hand, peacefully demonstrated for freedom of travel and democracy, went around the world via television and became a symbolic image for the Peaceful Revolution in the GDR. But also, when the transition from socialist dictatorship to democracy was subsequently negotiated with roundtables and talks between the Communist state and the opposition, numerous pastors and Christians were again active in the newly founded parties and then in the first freely elected government in 1990. They possessed trust and were good at public speaking and moderation.

Outlook

Not everywhere was the impact of Christianity to the end of the Communist regimes as clear as in Poland or in the GDR. But everywhere, starting in the fall of 1989, Christians took over responsibility in several ways, were courageous in a historically open situation, and did not think only of themselves.

Quite a few had the hope and vision that life would be easier for the church after the end of Communism. But it quickly became clear that the fierce struggle of Communism against the church had left deep scars. The Communists had successfully destroyed a rich Christian culture in Central and Eastern Europe. But the Communist legacy was one thing. The other was the rapid arrival in a pluralistic, democratic, and market-oriented European society. Now the churches were often only one offer in the religious market; their membership numbers fell year by year. In other countries, such as Hungary, Serbia, or Russia, church leaders entered new, nationalistic alliances with state and politics. Against this background, the question of a just and equal society remains a central issue for the churches, even after Communism.

Bibliography

BBC. "Memorial: Russia's Civil Rights Group Uncovering an Uncomfortable Past." *BBC*, Oct. 7, 2022. https://www.bbc.com/news/world-europe-59853010.

Beliakova, Nadezdha, and Ekaterian Mironova. "Female Religious Leadership during Khrushchev's Anti-Religious Campaign." *Quaestio Rossica* 8 (2020) 792–806.

Beliakova, Nadezdha, et al. *"Es gibt keinen Gott!" Kirche und Kommunismus; Eine Konfliktgeschichte.* Freiburg: Herder, 2016.
Blažek, Petr, et al. "Oskar Brüsewitz." Jan Palach, n.d. https://www.janpalach.cz/en/default/zive-pochodne/brusewitz.
Boer, Roland,. "Karl Kautsky's *Forerunners of Modern Socialism*." In *Red Theology: On the Christian Communist Tradition*, 10–27. Studies in Critical Research on Religion 10. Leiden: Brill, 2014.
Chumachenko, Tatiana A. *Church and State in Soviet Russia Russian Orthodoxy from World War II to the Khrushchev Years.* Edited and translated by Edward E. Roslof. Abingdon, UK: Taylor & Francis, 2015.
Conway, John S. "The 'Stasi' and the Churches: Between Coercion and Compromise in East German Protestantism, 1949–89." *Journal of Church and State* 36 (1994) 725–45.
Council of People's Commissars. "Freedom of Religious Conscience." Seventeen Moments in Soviet History, Feb. 2, 1918. From *Decrees of the Soviet Government* (Moscow: Institute of Marxism-Leninism, 1957), 1:373–74; orig. from *Sobranie uzakonenii i rasporiazhenii raboche-krestian'skogo pravitel'stva* 18 (1918) 272–73. https://soviethistory.msu.edu/1917-2/conflict-with-the-church/conflict-with-the-church-texts/decree-on-the-freedom-of-conscience-and-on-clerical-and-religious-societies/.
Felak, James Ramon. *Pope in Poland: The Pilgrimages of John Paul II, 1979–1991.* Pittsburgh: University of Pittsburgh Press, 2020.
Großbölting, Thomas. *SED-Diktatur und Gesellschaft: Bürgertum, Bürgerlichkeit und Entbürgerlichung in Magdeburg und Halle.* Halle: Mitteldeutsch, 2001.
Hildermeier, Manfred. *Die Russische Revolution: 1905–1921.* Frankfurt: Fischer, 2004
Kautsky, Karl. *Die Vorläufer des neueren Sozialismus* [Forerunners of modern socialism]. Stuttgart: Dietz, 1895.
Kunter, Katharina. "Evangelische Volksfrömmigkeit im kommunistischen Mittel- und Osteuropa—ein doppelter Widerspruch?" In *Reform—Aufklärung—Erneuerung: Transformationsprozesse im neuzeitlichen und modernen Christentum*, edited by Thomas K. Kuhn and Katharina Kunter, 297–310. Leipzig: Evangelische, 2014.
———. "Human Rights as a Theological and Political Controversy among East German and Czech Protestants." In *Christianity and Modernity in Eastern Europe*, edited by Bruce R. Berglund and Brian Porter-Szűcs, 217–44. Budapest: Central European University Press, 2010.
Leo XIII, Pope. "*Quod Apostolici Muneris*: On Socialism." Papal Encyclicals Online, Dec. 28, 1878. https://www.papalencyclicals.net/leo13/l13apost.htm.
———. "*Rerum Novarum*: On Capital and Labor." Papal Encyclicals Online, May 15, 1891. https://www.papalencyclicals.net/leo13/l13rerum.htm.
Marx, Karl, and Friedrich Engels. *The Communist Manifesto: A Modern Edition.* London: Verso, 1998.
Matthews, Mervyn, ed. "Law on Religious Organizations." Seventeen Moments in Soviet History, Apr. 8, 1929. From *Soviet Government: A Selection of Official Documents on Internal Policies* (New York: Taplinger, 1974), 63–70. https://soviethistory.msu.edu/1929-2/churches-closed/churches-closed-texts/law-on-religious-organizations/.
McMeekin, Sam. *The Russian Revolution: A New History.* New York: Basic, 2017.
More, Thomas. *Utopia.* Edited by George M. Logan et al. Cambridge Texts in the History of Political Thought. Cambridge: Cambridge University Press, 1995.

Paul VI, Pope. "*Octagesima Adveniens*—the Eightieth Anniversary of *Rerum Novarum*: A Call to Action." Papal Encyclicals Online, May 14, 1971. https://www.papalencyclicals.net/paulo6/p6oct.htm.

Pius X, Pope. "*Qui Pluribus*: On Faith and Religion." Papal Encyclicals Online, Nov. 9, 1846. https://www.papalencyclicals.net/pius09/p9quiplu.htm.

Raines, John, ed. *Marx on Religion*. Philadelphia: Temple University Press, 2002.

Salo, Vello. "Anti-Religious Rites in Estonia." *Religion in Communist Lands* 1 (1973) 28–33. http://biblicalstudies.gospelstudies.org.uk/pdf/rcl/01-4_5_28.pdf.

Shusterman, Noah. *The French Revolution: Faith, Desire, and Politics*. Milton Park, UK: Routledge, 2014.

Sperber, Jonathan. *The European Revolutions, 1848–1851*. Cambridge: Cambridge University Press, 1994.

Ueberschär, Ellen. *Junge Gemeinde im Konflikt: Evangelische Jugendarbeit in SBZ und DDR, 1945–1961*. Stuttgart: Kohlhammer, 2003.

Ulianov (Lenin), et al. "Decree on Separation of Church and State." Marxists, Feb. 5, 1918. From *The Bolshevik Revolution, 1917–1918: Documents and Materials*, edited by James Bunyan and H. H. Fisher, translated by Emanuel Aronsberg (London: Milford 1934) 590–91; orig. from *Sobranie Uzakonenii i Rasporiazhenii Rabochego i Krestianskogo Pravitelstva* 18 (1918) 272–73. https://www.marxists.org/history/ussr/events/revolution/documents/1918/02/5.htm.

Ulianov, V. (Lenin), and Josef Dzhugashvili (Stalin). "Declaration of the Rights of the People of Russia." Marxists, Nov. 2 (15), 1917. From *A Documentary History of Communism*, compiled by Robert V. Daniels (London: Tairis & Co, 1985). https://www.marxists.org/history/ussr/government/1917/11/02.htm.

Werth, Paul W. *The Tsar's Foreign Faiths: Toleration and the Fate of Religious Freedom in Imperial Russia*. Oxford Studies in Modern European History. Oxford: Oxford University Press, 2016.

Wynot, Jennifer Jean. *Keeping the Faith: Russian Orthodox Monasticism in the Soviet Union, 1917–1939*. Eugenia & Hugh M. Stewart '26 Series. College Station: Texas A&M University Press, 2004.

14

Social Transformation, Gender, and European Christianity

LAURA RAMSAY

CHRISTIANITY ONCE OCCUPIED AN awkward place in historical studies of women and gender.

Guided by theories of secularization and its assumptions about the limited role of religion in modernizing societies, early scholarship tended either to relegate Christian influences to the sidelines, or to represent the churches as primarily anti-modern, repressive, and reactionary forces.[1] It can certainly be argued that Christianity has patriarchal traits, that traditionally men have maintained dominant roles in church leadership, and that Christians bear responsibility for constructing and maintaining patriarchal systems of gender relations in past societies.[2] Yet, in recent decades, revisionist scholarship has forced issues of gender and religion back on to the agenda of historical inquiry, revealing a much more complex interplay between Christianity and the social and cultural transformations of the nineteenth and twentieth centuries.

Despite the diversity of their political, economic, social, and cultural structures throughout this era, European states were confronted by the challenges of various processes of modernization, including shifts in gender ideologies and the development of movements for women's emancipation. As historical actors sought to respond according to their own perceptions of the issues posed by these changes, so too did Christian institutions and individuals. They played important roles in developing solutions to these challenges that were inspired by their Christian faith, and which had lasting

---

1. For an overview of arguments about secularization in Europe, see McLeod, "Introduction," 13–19.
2. Werner, "Studying Christian Masculinity," 7.

consequences, both for contemporary understandings of masculinity and femininity and for the religiosity of European societies. This chapter provides an overview of recent scholarship in this field, including the historical development of gendered ideas about religiosity; the role of Christianity in shaping the advance of new ideas about citizenship, feminism, and women's suffrage; and women's expanding (and contested) roles within the churches.

The "Feminization Thesis"

Theories about the "feminization of Christianity"—based on a concept first introduced by Barbara Welter in the 1970s—have had a powerful and enduring influence in historical studies of Western Europe.[3] The feminization thesis encompasses a range of interrelated developments from the nineteenth century onwards, including a cultural shift towards associating Christian belief and observance with womanliness, emotion, sentimentality, and anti-intellectualism. This, in turn, had social consequences, with increasing numbers of women (as compared to men) participating in church membership and religious rites, as well as the growth of female religious orders and the rise of women's involvement in religiously motivated charitable associations.[4] The feminization of Christianity was also strongly connected to the rise of the middle-class ideology of "separate spheres," which increasingly advocated an idealized division between a "masculinized" public sphere of politics, business, and wage-earning, and a "femininized" private sphere of domestic life and moral nurturing. According to this ideology, religion became a privatized matter to be associated with femaleness and domesticity, while religious indifference and the potential to succumb to earthly temptations came to be seen as a normalized, but troubling, aspect of modern masculinity. As piety was feminized, conversely, femininity became pietized.[5] Increasingly women were assumed to be purer, more moral, and more religious than men. The wife or mother became the "angel in the house" or the "priestess of the home" whose role it was to nurture and oversee her husband's and her children's moral and spiritual health. The feminization thesis has found support from scholars studying British Protestantism as well as Catholic spirituality in Germany and France.[6]

Some historians have used the feminization thesis as a means of exploring and explaining processes of secularization. Whereas class was once

3. Welter, "Feminization of American Religion."
4. Pasture, "Beyond the Feminization Thesis," 8–10.
5. Brown, *Death of Christian Britain*, 58–87.
6. Werner, "Studying Christian Masculinity," 8–9.

seen as the main determinant of religious decline, according to the idea that the lower social classes became increasingly alienated from the churches, now gender is also regarded as exerting a significant influence on the timing and nature of long-term changes to European Christianity. Increasing hostility towards ordained ministers is interpreted as part of wider suspicion towards clerical masculinities, which were viewed as deficient in idealized masculine qualities, just as much as it was triggered by working-class antipathy towards men of a higher social class who were seen as snobbish, disapproving, and disconnected from the lives of their congregations.[7] Callum Brown is perhaps the most vociferous advocate of the importance of gender to narratives of religious change. His work on British Christianity suggests that the feminization of piety led to the churches' relative strength and stability during the nineteenth and first half of the twentieth centuries, but that a later shift in women's relationships with the churches and religion after the so-called "sexual revolution" of the 1960s prompted the rapid demise of Christianity in the late twentieth century.[8]

The feminization thesis thus provides a compelling explanatory framework; however, several scholars have warned against overgeneralizing a simple dichotomy between feminine piety and masculine impiety. Although the feminization of Christianity was a powerful contemporary ideology, women had multiple and conflicting relationships with religious institutions, beliefs, and practices, just as large numbers of men remained committed to the churches and to Christianity. We should therefore seek to recognize the variations, complexities, and ambiguities of femininities and masculinities in Christian societies, acknowledging that these cultural ideals coexisted, competed, and interacted with each other across the period, as well as differing between regions and denominations.[9]

Such suggestions have led to increased scholarly interest in the history of men, masculinity, and religious change in modern Europe. This work suggests that the feminization of Christianity prompted the churches, as well as various Christian movements involving men (such as the missionary, scouting, and Christian Socialist movements), to develop counterstrategies of "remasculinization" that sought to create a new synthesis of masculinity and Christian belief and practice.[10] During the nineteenth and early twentieth centuries, the idea of "muscular Christianity" promoted sports and

7. Delap and Morgan, "Introduction," 18.

8. Brown, "Sex, Religion"; Brown, *Death of Christian Britain*.

9. Pasture, "Beyond the Feminization Thesis"; Werner, "Studying Christian Masculinity," 7–11; Morgan and De Vries, "Introduction," 7–9.

10. See Pasture et al., *Beyond the Feminization Thesis*; Werner, *Christian Masculinity*; Delap and Morgan, *Men, Masculinities*.

physical exercise as morally, religiously, and socially valuable activities that were both Christian and manly.[11] Catholic social movements like Catholic Action and the Leagues of the Sacred Heart also represented their activities as expressions of manly Christian values, such as obedience, sacrifice, and restraint.[12] These examples further expose the limits of the feminization thesis by confirming that masculine identities could be simultaneously modern and pious.

Domesticity and Feminine Piety

Although the feminization thesis suggests that religion and morality were increasingly associated with the privatized sphere of domesticity, this had paradoxical effects. As women became defined as naturally more caring, nurturing, and pious than men, this enabled the foundation and expansion of numerous women's organizations that undertook charitable and welfare activities on behalf of the churches and Christian causes. Rather than confining them to the domestic sphere, this philanthropic work allowed women to renegotiate some of the restrictions of their assumed gender roles by encroaching on the presumedly male, public sphere and addressing a variety of political and socioeconomic issues in their capacity as women. In the context of religious revivalism and evangelism, many middle-class women were empowered to participate in missionary movements, both at home and overseas, and to work with the poor, the sick, the vulnerable, and the outcasts of society. Despite the problematic nature of their intentions, which tended towards imposing middle-class cultural norms on other social groups, their mostly working-class, female clients often stood to gain from their efforts too.[13] Christian activists included not only wives and mothers, but also unmarried women, whose involvement was justified according to the notion of "social motherhood"—the idea that even lifelong spinsters should engage in "feminine" work connected to their presumed maternal qualities and skills in domestic management. Furthermore, it was common across many European countries for women to progress from their involvement in religious and charitable causes to participation in feminist associations.[14] To this extent, female piety was connected to a restrictive gender ideology, but it could also inspire forms of feminist activism that sought to improve the economic, educational, and legal rights of women. As Jacqueline

11. McLeod, "'Sportsman' and 'Muscular Christian.'"
12. Pasture, "Beyond the Feminization Thesis," 25.
13. J. De Vries, "More Than Paradoxes," 195.
14. Evans, *Feminists*, 33.

de Vries observes, women could experience Christian faith and practice as both oppressive and empowering—perhaps even simultaneously—and each person's experience of religion was unique.[15]

The growth of female religious orders further expanded women's involvement in charitable service. In France, joining a religious order was attractive to large numbers of Catholic women from the middle and working classes, which increased the number of nuns from 12,300 in 1808 to 135,000 in 1878.[16] Across Protestant denominations, the revival of the religious order of deaconesses also enabled many women to lead semimonastic lives dedicated to social service. The first hospital and training center for deaconesses—the *Kaiserswerther Diakonie*—was founded in Germany in 1836 by Theodor and Friederike Fliedner, a Lutheran minister and his wife. Many women from across Europe trained at Kaiserwerth, and similar deaconess institutions were established in Russia, France, Switzerland, Britain, and Scandinavia during the second half of the nineteenth century.[17]

In the Lutheran countries of Sweden and Finland, deaconesses worked in areas of poor relief and health care, providing for the material and spiritual needs of local communities. By 1930, around six hundred Finnish sisters and five hundred Swedish sisters worked outside of their deaconess institutions. While this gave women opportunities for action in the public sphere, this was carefully restricted. Their work was legitimized as a natural extension of presumedly "feminine" activities and was viewed as a necessity due to the demographic surplus of unmarried women among the urban middle classes. Although deaconesses remained celibate, there was ongoing controversy about whether they could become wives or mothers. Moreover, deaconesses remained subordinate to the male clergy and doctors who supervised their work, and as their labor was defined as voluntary Christian service, their wages were either inadequate or nonexistent.[18] Feminine piety thus had contradictory consequences for women, leading some scholars to conclude that, while increased female participation in religious activities of various kinds allowed some women to achieve status and fulfill an occupation, this did not explicitly challenge the widely accepted belief in women's subordination, whether in the leadership of Christian institutions, in mixed society, or in the domestic sphere.[19]

---

15. J. De Vries, "More Than Paradoxes."

16. Ralph Gibson and Claude Langlois, cited in Kselman, "Varieties of Religious Experience," 171.

17. Jones, *Sexual Politics*, 51–2; Markkola, "Promoting Faith and Welfare," 109–11.

18. Markkola, "Promoting Faith and Welfare."

19. Anderson, "Women Preachers," 468, 483–84.

Christian Feminism and Women's Emancipation

In early feminist historiography, feminism was often defined in secular terms, and it was frequently assumed that Christian beliefs, practices, and institutions represented the antithesis of modern impulses towards women's emancipation that emerged in the late nineteenth and twentieth centuries. Revisionist scholarship has since emphasized the need to employ a more expansive definition of feminism and to acknowledge the significance of religiously motivated activism. This work has developed a more complex understanding of the ways in which individuals who campaigned for women's social advancement drew upon, benefited from, refashioned, and rejected the religious cultures they were a part of.[20]

Christian feminists united across nineteenth-century Europe in their campaigns to establish equal standards of sexual morality for both sexes and to abolish the state regulation of prostitution. This movement was led by figures like Josephine Butler (1828–1906), a British, evangelical Anglican and advocate of women's rights, through her support for women's suffrage and access to higher education and employment opportunities.[21] Guided by feminist and Christian principles, campaigners like Butler criticized systems of state regulation of prostitution in a way that combined a belief in equality with a desire to elevate the moral standards of European societies. Reformers noted that systems of licensing and regulating sex work and brothels targeted and penalized women, while ignoring their male clients, thus upholding a vastly unequal "double standard" of morality that demanded female purity, but condoned male sexual transgressions. In Britain, Butler was the honorary secretary of the Ladies National Association, an organization that successfully campaigned against the Contagious Diseases Acts (which were suspended in 1883 and repealed in 1886). She also established the British, Continental and General Federation for the Abolition of State Regulation of Prostitution in 1875 which brought together campaigners from France, Belgium, Germany, the Netherlands, Switzerland, Italy, and elsewhere (and later changed its name to the International Abolitionist Federation). Butler's Christian feminism was directly inspired by her acceptance of ideas about feminine piety. She believed that women and men were equal, but that they possessed distinct physical and mental attributes; therefore, women like her should express their inherently moral and nurturing qualities by seeking to help others, via "preventive" work aimed at elevating manhood through expectations of Christian chivalry, and "rescue" work

---

20. J. De Vries, "More Than Paradoxes," 188–90.
21. Walkowitz, "Butler [née Grey] Josephine Elizabeth."

to support women and children considered to be in material or spiritual need. By defining Christian womanhood in this way, Butler and others like her legitimized their political interventions on issues of sexuality, venereal disease, and prostitution, which might otherwise have been seen as taboo subjects, unfit for middle-class women to address.[22] To this extent, Christian campaigners like Butler inspired feminist activism across Europe and encouraged reformers to oppose women's subordination on a moral and religious platform, as well as in the spheres of political and legal reform.[23]

Christian feminist ideas were also expressed at high-profile interwar ecumenical gatherings, such as the Universal Christian Conference on Life and Work, held in Stockholm in August 1925. This international congress was attended by over five hundred delegates, representing the Protestant and Orthodox Churches (but not the Roman Catholic Church, which declined involvement) in thirty-seven nations across Europe, the United States, and the British Empire. The Stockholm conference set out to formulate a new Christian approach towards gender relations, providing further guidance on how "to think and act in modern times." Delegates rejected the "patriarchal ideal of the family," and instead called upon Christians to value women as "the fellow-disciple of Christ with equal status and value as the man." This viewpoint led the conference to condemn prostitution and the "double code of morality" which, it suggested, were driven by "disregard or contempt for woman."[24] This vision of gender equality based on Christian principles was firmly rooted in traditions of "relational feminism," which supported advances in women's rights based on the idea that each sex was equally valuable but possessed separate and distinctive qualities—rather than alternative traditions of "individualist feminism," which campaigned for women's emancipation on the basis of individual human rights, regardless of sex or gender.[25] The Stockholm conference emphasized the complementarity of the sexes in its notion that "man and woman are dependent on each other and were created for each other." Delegates therefore advocated an idealized division of labor whereby the sexes would "work together harmoniously for the benefit of humanity," with men expressing their presumed superior qualities of "strength, energy, enterprise, initiative, bold and reasonable deliberation," and women their presumed superior qualities of "deep-rooted and strong moral feeling, a passionate and intuitive sense of justice, a quick

22. P. De Vries, "Josephine Butler."
23. Summers, "Which Women? What Europe?"
24. Bell, *Stockholm Conference*, 218–23, 255–58.
25. Offen, "Defining Feminism."

and ready sympathy."[26] Christian feminism thus incorporated contradictory intentions, motivations, and strategies that were neither wholly conservative nor wholly progressive. While such viewpoints undoubtedly sit uncomfortably with our present-day sensibilities, it is important to acknowledge the persuasiveness of such arguments within their historical context. Relational feminism was certainly contradictory in demanding greater equality for women while simultaneously confirming women's (and men's) inferiority in some areas of life, but this had the significant advantage of closing the gap between progressive and conservative viewpoints, thus making arguments for changing the position of women more palatable to wider audiences, including those who might otherwise have been reluctant supporters of women's emancipation.[27]

Such contradictory impulses also characterized forms of Catholic feminism that emerged across Italy, Spain, and France in the late nineteenth and early twentieth centuries. In these countries, where faith formed such an important part of feminine identities, Catholic women were encouraged to participate in missions and charitable associations that advocated feminist causes and campaigned for equal moral, legal, and economic laws for both sexes. These Catholic feminist associations had to negotiate the challenges of their church's teaching on women's subordination, however. They thus emphasized ideas about the separate, but equal, status of women and men, and deliberately distanced their campaigns from any suggestion of sex antagonism. This resulted in activism that focused efforts on wider issues facing women and avoided explicitly political goals, which were regarded as the more contentious aims of the feminist movement that might otherwise alienate Catholic supporters.[28]

Women's Suffrage

This gap between Christian feminism and suffrage feminism caused tensions and difficulties within some European movements for women's emancipation. In France, the founder of Catholic suffragism, Marie Maugeret (1844–1928), struggled to attract Catholic support for the issue of women's voting rights.[29] In Germany, the *Deutsch-Evangelischer Frauenbund*—a Protestant women's organization that advocated women's rights from an

26. Bell, *Stockholm Conference*, 256.
27. Ramsay, "Relation of the Sexes," 563.
28. Blasco Herranz, "Conservative Feminism"; Dawes, "Catholic Church"; Hause and Kenney, "Development."
29. Hause and Kenney, "Development," 13–25.

evangelical Christian perspective—did not support women's suffrage, and the *Katholischer Frauenbund Deutschlands*—a Catholic association that positioned itself as part of the wider women's movement and campaigned for women's voting rights within the church—remained politically neutral on the issue.[30] Hence, connections between Christian faith, feminism, and suffragism were variable. For some women and men, Christian beliefs might reinforce anti-suffrage viewpoints; for others, their Christian feminist campaigning was directly linked to the issue of women's voting rights. Christian suffragists resolved that the vote was needed precisely because it would allow women to make more progress in their related campaigns on issues like access to education, better working conditions, the abolition of prostitution, and the establishment of a single standard of sexual morality. Many churchwomen were thus active participants in militant suffrage campaigning, as well as more constitutional methods of protest, sometimes as members of nonreligious suffrage societies and sometimes as members of specifically Christian associations.

International Catholic feminist campaigns developed out of the Catholic Women's Suffrage Society (CWSS), formed in London in 1911 as the world's first Catholic women's suffrage association.[31] Initially, the CWSS faced criticism and resistance for forming a separate organization and claiming to represent Catholicism on such a contentious issue, especially in the years before 1919 when the Vatican remained hostile towards women's suffrage. Although the CWSS intended to campaign using only constitutional and educational methods, it did not denounce the militant tactics used by other suffrage societies and, unlike other organizations, did not suspend its campaigns during the First World War.[32] Elsewhere in early twentieth-century Europe, similar Catholic suffrage societies emerged and expanded, such as in France where *Action Sociale de la Femme* and *Union Nationale pour le vote des Femmes* campaigned on women's issues, including their voting rights.[33] Spurred on by such developments and the strengthening of its own international connections, in 1923 the CWSS renamed itself the St. Joan's Social and Political Alliance—a move that secured its independence by abandoning the idea of any formal affiliation with the Catholic Church. This organization thus continued campaigns for women's equality into the twentieth and twenty-first centuries as part of the St. Joan's International Alliance.

30. Gerhard, "Women's Movement in Germany," 119–20.
31. Mason, "Newer Eve," 638.
32. Clark, "Catholics and the Campaign."
33. Hause and Kenney, "Development," 27–29.

The historical significance of Christianity within movements for women's emancipation is further underlined by the ways in which the churches became key battlegrounds for suffrage campaigning. In early twentieth-century Britain, militant activists purposefully targeted the established church—the Church of England—by walking out in protest during sermons, boycotting the churches of anti-suffrage clergy, and carrying out arson attacks on church buildings.[34] In addition, suffrage campaigners mobilized Christian imagery and language to create religious and moral arguments in favor of women's enfranchisement. This was a deliberate and powerful strategy at a time when Christianity remained a dominant referent of British culture.[35] Similarly, their opponents—the anti-suffragists—appealed to the forcefulness of religion by accusing suffragists of promoting ideas and methods that were unchristian, immoral, and illegal. This situation undoubtedly presented challenges for religious suffrage leagues, which had to engage in a complicated process of associating and disassociating themselves with the Christian communities and wider suffrage movement they were a part of.[36] Christian suffragists like Maude Royden (1876–1956), chair of the Anglican Church League for Women's Suffrage (CLWS), carefully managed this potential conflict by campaigning nationally and internationally on behalf of the National Union of Women's Suffrage Societies—the largest of the Edwardian suffrage organizations in Britain—but also distancing herself and the CLWS from militant activism that targeted the churches.[37] This is not to suggest, however, that Christian feminists and suffragists did not also demand changes from their own churches. To the contrary, for many campaigners the goals of women's political enfranchisement and their representation on councils of church government, as well as in the professional ministry, were viewed as interconnected issues.

Women's Ordination

Although the feminization of piety expanded women's moral authority and their opportunities to participate in some areas of church work, women remained mostly excluded from the Christian ministry and positions of church leadership. Consequently, throughout the twentieth century, as women's access to other professions expanded, the issue of women's ordination became a crucial battleground for the churches, and debates came to be

---

34. Morgan, "Feminist Conspiracy," 781.
35. Saunders, "Great and Holy War."
36. J. De Vries, "More Than Paradoxes," 199–202.
37. Morgan, "Feminist Conspiracy," 781.

framed as a way of measuring whether Christianity was a modern, outward-facing faith, or not. Some Protestant Churches across Europe began to open the ministry to women, particularly in the postwar period, but the Catholic and Orthodox Churches continue to oppose women's ordination to the priesthood and episcopacy.

The Catholic Church's position is based on theological arguments with a long history. First, the church maintains that Jesus Christ deliberately restricted the ordained ministry to men, based on his selection of male disciples. This practice was subsequently continued by the apostles, who underlined the instruction for women to "keep silence in the churches" (1 Cor 14:34–35; 1 Tim 2:12 KJV). Second, the church teaches that God created women and men in his image, to be of equal value, but to occupy separate and harmonious functions according to their different qualities of femininity and masculinity. This idea of complementarity between the sexes is held to be confirmed by the biblical symbolism of the relationship between Christ—the masculine bridegroom—and the church—the feminine bride. A third, related argument is that, since Jesus was incarnated male, only a male priest can act as an icon of Christ in the sacraments of the Eucharist and confession. Finally, the church appeals to the authority of an unbroken tradition, confirmed by successive teaching from the Vatican, which is believed to be of a supernatural order, conferred by God, and which cannot be altered in response to contemporary goals for social advancement.[38] Despite the Catholic Church's opposition to women's ordination, there are several organizations that continue to campaign for change, including We Are Church, an international movement established in Rome in 1996, and Women's Ordination Worldwide, an ecumenical organization founded in Austria in 1996.

In the Russian Orthodox Churches, even though women often outnumber men, they are excluded from the priesthood. This is partly due to historical circumstances, since Russia was largely shielded from debates about women's ordination due to the Soviet Union's policy of state atheism and persecution of religious believers. Although this situation has changed since the dissolution of the USSR, many Orthodox Christians continue to view Soviet and Western ideas about equality as antagonistic to their faith and potentially damaging to Russia.[39] Elsewhere, in Eastern Europe, Communist rule had an unusual effect on women's access to the ministry. In Czechoslovakia, some women served the faithful of the underground

---

38. Sacred Congregation for the Doctrine of the Faith, *Inter Insigniores* (1976); John Paul II: *Mulieris Dignitatem* (1988); *Christifideles Laici* (1988); *Ordinatio Sacerdotalis* (1994).

39. Kizenko, "Feminized Patriarchy?"

churches, such as Ludmila Javorová (1932–) who was ordained as a Catholic priest in 1970. Following the end of Communist rule, however, the Vatican ruled that Javorová's womanhood made her ordination invalid.

Protestant free churches—those operating independently of the state—generally experienced fewer difficulties over women's ordination, partly due to their origins, often as "breakaway" groups seeking to minimize the formalized separation of clergy and laity. In Britain, Baptists, Quakers, and early Methodists allowed for women preachers, although this was restricted as the Methodist movement developed. The Salvation Army, a non-sacramental Christian movement founded by William Booth in London in the 1860s, was the first denomination to afford women officers equal religious status to men. This was enabled by the practice of "commissioning" officers of both sexes, rather than "ordaining" them.[40] In 1917, Constance Coltman (1889–1969) was the first British woman ordained in a mainstream Christian denomination, the Congregational Union of England and Wales. Other free churches soon followed, including the Baptist Union of Great Britain (1918), the English Presbyterian Church (1921), and the Congregational Union in Scotland (1929). The Methodist Church experienced greater conflict, partly on account of its aspiration for reunion with the Church of England, but once this looked unlikely, the first Methodist women were ordained as presbyters in 1974. Thus, where churches were less concerned by the prospect of reunion or schism, the path towards women's ordination was more straightforward.

Across Europe, experiences of wartime disruption, especially during the Second World War, provided impetus for change. As men enlisted to serve in the armed forces, women gained opportunities to preach in the churches. However, most women carried out this work unordained, and their opportunities to act as priests ceased once the war ended. The experience of Elisabeth Schmidt (1908–86), who was ordained as a pastor of the Reformed Church of France in 1949 after serving in the parish of Sète during and after the war, was unique.[41] The Reformed Church did not reach a decision to ordain women in general until 1966. The established, state-supported Evangelical Lutheran Church of Denmark was also unusual in ordaining its first female pastors in 1948.

Wider social developments in the second half of the twentieth century did the most to instigate lasting changes. This included the rise of political claims for gender equality in the women's movements of the 1960s and 1970s, as well as the development of feminist theologies that promoted

---

40. Mumm, "Women, Priesthood," 190–93.
41. Grenholm, "Women's Ordination."

women's empowerment and the end of oppression, injustice, and exploitation, through the principle that Christianity transcends issues of sex and gender and recognizes the full humanity of women. In the Lutheran, national or state-supported churches of the Nordic countries, female pastors were ordained in the Church of Sweden (1960), the Church of Norway (1961), the Church in Iceland (1974), and the Church in Finland (1988). This was followed by the ordination of female bishops in Norway (1993), Denmark (1995), Sweden (1996), Finland (2010), and Iceland (2012).

Campaigns for women's ordination have nevertheless had a long and difficult relationship with the feminist movement. Some Christian activists, like the Anglican Maude Royden, connected their struggles to gain access to the priesthood with feminist and suffragist goals. Royden established her reputation as an "international preaching celebrity" in her post as an assistant preacher at the Congregational City Temple in Holborn between 1917 and 1920. She later established the Guildhouse Fellowship in London, an ecumenical place of worship where she preached until 1936.[42] Yet other advocates of women's ordination adopted ambivalent, or even resistant, stances towards feminism. Particularly in the late twentieth century, many women struggled to navigate the implications of seeking ordination and representing their viewpoints, without being represented by their opponents as embittered feminist troublemakers willing to risk schism for the sake of their personal or social goals.[43] This led to tensions within campaigning organizations, as many women tried to distance themselves, their aims, and their strategies from negative characterizations of feminism, and others felt compelled to accept their leaders' calls to wait patiently for access to the priesthood, rather than to demand immediate change.

Conclusion

Historically considered, issues of gender and accompanying signs of social and cultural transformation—whether in debates about the roles of women and men in society, voting rights, or questions of ordination—have undoubtedly presented challenges for the European churches. But it would be a mistake to underestimate the extent to which Christian individuals and viewpoints contributed to making those historical developments possible. Today, the churches have something of an image problem on issues of gender, but as this chapter has shown, Christianity has a more complex history of its relationship with the social transformations of the nineteenth and

42. Morgan, "Feminist Conspiracy," 787–88.
43. Kroll, "Eventful Journey," 1004–13.

twentieth centuries. On the one hand, the European churches contributed to important changes by shaping dominant cultural ideals of womanhood that placed piety and morality at their core and by inspiring feminist activism from a Christian perspective. But, on the other hand, issues of women's equality, and especially ordination, have been damaging to the reputation of the churches and Christian authority. If ordination debates became a way of measuring whether Christianity was a modernizing faith, then some would argue that the churches largely failed to meet this challenge. Successive opinion surveys in Britain since the 1990s have indicated that the teaching of the established Church of England and the Catholic Church was increasingly viewed by the British public as sexist and out of touch with society and many Christians.[44] Although this negative opinion was certainly heightened in the context of debates leading up to the Church of England's approval of women bishops in 2015, it seems the association of the churches with antiquated views on gender and sex is now fixed in the popular imagination.

Nevertheless, for most of the nineteenth and twentieth centuries, Christianity maintained a powerful influence in shaping European gender ideologies. Christian feminism emerged as a way for activists to campaign for women's social advancement, usually underpinned by theological arguments about the complementarity of the sexes—the equal value, but distinctive qualities, of women and men. But the rise of women's liberation movements in the late twentieth century increasingly encouraged European societies to abandon these kinds of relational feminist arguments. In this sense, continued controversies over issues of women's ordination at the turn of the twenty-first century reveal something of the growing pains experienced by some churches, as they struggled to abandon long-established ideas that had served them well in previous centuries. While some Christians developed new theological arguments about women's equality based on their humanity regardless of gender, others have paid the price of remaining wedded to earlier ideas of relational feminism that became increasingly marginalized in the postwar decades.

Bibliography

Anderson, Olive. "Women Preachers in Mid-Victorian Britain: Some Reflexions on Feminism, Popular Religion and Social Change." *Historical Journal* 12 (1969) 467–84.

Bell, G. K., ed. *The Stockholm Conference 1925: The Official Report of the Universal Christian Conference on Life and Work Held in Stockholm*. London: Oxford University Press, 1926.

---

44. Field, "Another Window."

Blasco Herranz, Inmaculada. "Conservative Feminism in Catholic Spain." In *Faith and Feminism in Nineteenth-Century Religious Communities*, edited by Ruth Albrecht and Michaela Sohn-Kronthaler, 183–202. Atlanta: SBL, 2019.

Brown, Callum G. *The Death of Christian Britain: Understanding Secularisation 1800–2000*. Christianity and Society in the Modern World. London: Routledge, 2001.

———. "Sex, Religion, and the Single Woman c. 1950–75: The Importance of a 'Short' Sexual Revolution to the English Religious Crisis of the Sixties." *Twentieth Century British History* 22 (2011) 189–215.

Clark, Elaine. "Catholics and the Campaign for Women's Suffrage in England." *Church History* 73 (2004) 635–65.

Dawes, Helena. "The Catholic Church and the Woman Question: Catholic Feminism in Italy in the Early 1900s." *Catholic Historical Review* 97 (2011) 484–526.

Delap, Lucy, and Sue Morgan. "Introduction: Men, Masculinities and Religious Change in Post-Christian Britain." In *Men, Masculinities and Religious Change in Twentieth-Century Britain*, edited by Lucy Delap and Sue Morgan, 1–29. Basingstoke, UK: Palgrave Macmillan, 2013.

Delap, Lucy, and Sue Morgan, eds. *Men, Masculinities and Religious Change in Twentieth-Century Britain*. Basingstoke, UK: Palgrave Macmillan, 2013.

De Vries, Jacqueline. "More Than Paradoxes to Offer: Feminism, History and Religious Cultures." In *Women, Gender and Religious Cultures in Britain, 1800–1940*, edited by Sue Morgan and Jacqueline de Vries, 188–210. Abingdon, UK: Routledge, 2010.

De Vries, Petra. "Josephine Butler and the Making of Feminism: International Abolitionism in the Netherlands." *Women's History Review* 17 (2008) 257–77.

Evans, Richard J. *The Feminists: Women's Emancipation Movements in Europe, America and Australasia 1840–1920*. Routledge Library Editions: Women's History Abingdon, UK: Routledge, 2013.

Field, Clive D. "Another Window on British Secularization: Public Attitudes to Church and Clergy Since the 1960s." *Contemporary British History* 28 (2014) 190–218.

Gerhard, Ute. "The Women's Movement in Germany in an International Context." In *Women's Emancipation Movements in the Nineteenth Century: A European Perspective*, edited by Sylvia Paletschek and Bianka Pietrow-Ennker, 102–22. Stanford, CA: Stanford University Press, 2004.

Grenholm, Cristina. "Women's Ordination in Western Europe." In *The Cambridge Dictionary of Christianity*, edited by Daniel Patte, 1324–25. Cambridge: Cambridge University Press, 2010.

Hause, Steven C., and Anne R. Kenney. "The Development of the Catholic Women's Suffrage Movement in France, 1896–1922." *Catholic Historical Review* 67 (1981) 11–30.

John Paul II, Pope. "*Christifideles Laici*: On the Vocation and the Mission of the Lay Faithful in the Church and in the World." Vatican, Dec. 30, 1988. https://www.vatican.va/content/john-paul-ii/en/apost_exhortations/documents/hf_jp-ii_exh_30121988_christifideles-laici.html.

———. "*Mulieris Dignitatem*: On the Dignity and Vocation of Women on the Occasion of the Marian Year." Vatican, Aug. 15, 1988. https://www.vatican.va/content/john-paul-ii/en/apost_letters/1988/documents/hf_jp-ii_apl_19880815_mulieris-dignitatem.html.

———. "*Ordinatio Sacerdotalis*: On Reserving Priestly Ordination to Men Alone." Vatican, May 22, 1994. https://www.vatican.va/content/john-paul-ii/en/apost_letters/1994/documents/hf_jp-ii_apl_19940522_ordinatio-sacerdotalis.html.

Jones, Timothy Willem. *Sexual Politics in the Church of England, 1857–1957*. Oxford: Oxford University Press, 2013.

Kizenko, Nadieszda. "Feminized Patriarchy? Orthodoxy and Gender in Post-Soviet Russia." *Signs* 38 (2013) 595–621.

Kroll, Una. "An Eventful Journey from Christian Feminism to Christian Humanism." *Women's History Review* 24 (2015) 996–1013.

Kselman, Thomas. "The Varieties of Religious Experience in Urban France." In *European Religion in the Age of Great Cities: 1830–1930*, edited by Hugh McLeod, 163–88. Christianity and Society in the Modern World. London: Routledge, 1995.

Markkola, Pirjo. "Promoting Faith and Welfare: The Deaconess Movement in Finland and Sweden, 1850–1930." *Scandinavian Journal of History* 25 (2000) 101–18.

Mason, Francis M. "The Newer Eve: The Catholic Women's Suffrage Society in England, 1911–1923." *Catholic Historical Review* 72 (1986) 620–38.

McLeod, Hugh. "Introduction." In *The Decline of Christendom in Western Europe, 1750–2000*, edited by Hugh McLeod and Werner Ustorf, 1–26. Cambridge: Cambridge University Press, 2003.

———. "The 'Sportsman' and the 'Muscular Christian': Rival Ideals in Nineteenth-Century England." In *Christian Masculinity: Men and Religion in Northern Europe in the 19th and 20th Centuries*, edited by Yvonne Maria Werner, 85–105. Leuven: Leuven University Press, 2011.

Morgan, Sue. "A 'Feminist Conspiracy': Maude Royden, Women's Ministry and the British Press, 1916–1921." *Women's History Review* 22 (2013) 777–800.

Morgan, Sue, and Jacqueline de Vries. "Introduction." In *Women, Gender and Religious Cultures in Britain, 1800–1940*, edited by Sue Morgan and Jacqueline de Vries, 1–10. Abingdon, UK: Routledge, 2010.

Mumm, Susan. "Women, Priesthood, and the Ordained Ministry in the Christian Tradition." In *Religion in History: Conflict, Conversion and Coexistence*, edited by John Wolffe, 190–216. Manchester: Open University Press, 2004.

Offen, Karen. "Defining Feminism: A Comparative Historical Approach." *Signs* 14 (1988) 119–57.

Pasture, Patrick. "Beyond the Feminization Thesis: Gendering the History of Christianity in the Nineteenth and Twentieth Centuries." In *Beyond the Feminization Thesis: Gender and Christianity in Modern Europe*, edited by Patrick Pasture et al., 7–33. KADOC Studies on Religion, Culture and Society. Leuven: Leuven University Press, 2012.

Pasture, Patrick, et al., eds. *Beyond the Feminization Thesis: Gender and Christianity in Modern Europe*. KADOC Studies on Religion, Culture and Society. Leuven: Leuven University Press, 2012

Ramsay, Laura Monica. "'The Relation of the Sexes': Towards a Christian View of Sex and Citizenship in Interwar Britain." *Contemporary British History* 34 (2020) 555–79.

Sacred Congregation for the Doctrine of the Faith. "*Inter Insigniores*: On the Question of Admission of Women to the Ministerial Priesthood." Vatican, Oct. 15, 1976. https://www.vatican.va/roman_curia/congregations/cfaith/documents/rc_con_cfaith_doc_19761015_inter-insigniores_en.html.

Saunders, Robert. "'A Great and Holy War': Religious Routes to Women's Suffrage, 1909-1914." *English Historical Review* 134 (2019) 1471-502.

Summers, Anne. "Which Women? What Europe? Josephine Butler and the International Abolitionist Federation." *History Workshop Journal* 62 (2006) 214-31.

Walkowitz, Judith R. "Butler [*née* Grey], Josephine Elizabeth (1828-1906)." *Oxford Dictionary of National Biography*, Sept. 23, 2004; last updated May 25, 2006. https://doi.org/10.1093/ref:odnb/32214.

Welter, Barbara. "The Feminization of American Religion, 1800-1860." In *Clio's Consciousness Raised: New Perspectives on the History of Women*, edited by Mary S. Hartman and Lois W. Banner, 137-57. New York: Harper & Row, 1974.

Werner, Yvonne Maria. *Christian Masculinity: Men and Religion in Northern Europe in the 19th and 20th Centuries*. KADOC Studies on Religion, Culture and Society. Leuven: Leuven University Press, 2011

———. "Studying Christian Masculinity: An Introduction." In *Christian Masculinity: Men and Religion in Northern Europe in the 19th and 20th Centuries*, edited by Yvonne Maria Werner, 7-17. KADOC Studies on Religion, Culture and Society. Leuven: Leuven University Press, 2011.

15

Diaspora and the Redefinition of European Christianity in the Twenty-First Century

DARRELL JACKSON

ON CHRISTMAS DAY, 800 CE, Pope Leo III crowned Charlemagne as emperor, orienting the See of Rome towards Carolingian Frankia and away from the Byzantine Empire. While relatively short lived (800–924), the Carolingian Empire unified territories in what are now France, Germany, northern Italy, the Low Countries, and beyond.

Although the alliance of papal and imperial powers during the Carolingian period was clearly of consequence for both temporal and spiritual rulers, the coronation of Otto as emperor, by Pope John XII in 962, was of greater significance in harnessing imperial churches and their ruling bishops to political as well as ecclesiastical service. The empire established with Otto's coronation, usually known as the Holy Roman Empire, continued in one form or another through until the early nineteenth century. Thus established, the shared influence of emperor and pope imposed a significant level of uniformity upon expressions of Christianity in the Europe of the period through until the European Reformation (frequently dated to Martin Luther's proclamation of his ninety-five theses at Wittenberg in 1517).

This admittedly brief review of twelve hundred years of European history is nonetheless instructive because it serves to highlight the medieval ecclesiastical and imperial goals of European unity and uniformity that sit in stark contrast to that which we now know as Christianity in Europe. Of course, historical evidence reminds us that the Christian emperors, monarchs, nobles, bishops, and popes have fought between themselves for the control of European territories and its peoples for the entire period of Christian presence in Europe. The goals of imperial and ecclesiastical unity and uniformity remained, in some measure, aspirational and unrealized.

Nevertheless, what might Emperors Charlemagne or Otto have made of the denominational, social, liturgical, and cultural diversity on display across a sample of typical Sunday morning Christian gatherings in Europe? What anti-imperial impulses might they have cursed as being responsible for such social diversity and religious heresy in twenty-first-century Christianity in Europe?

This chapter will argue that the long history of people on the move in Europe is constitutive of the diversity that now characterizes Christianity in Europe. Human mobility might not be the only factor to have driven religious diversity in Europe. Nevertheless, this chapter will argue that human mobility has been, and remains, one of the more significant factors.

Liturgically, ethnically, and linguistically diverse Sunday worship is only one consequence of such mobility. Migrant scholars from the Global South, especially those from former European colonies, are now more commonplace in the lecture halls of European universities. Here they have developed sophisticated postcolonial critiques of the benefits secured by Christians in Europe through their association with empire, colonialism, and European hegemony. The unmerited dominance and normativity of European theologies are but one consequence of empire, and diaspora voices now add to the diverse expressions of Christianity in Europe.

Demography and Migrant Religion in Europe

Estimating the number of Christians in Europe is challenging. The *World Christian Database* (*WCD*) is widely used and cited by scholars of religion and provides sufficiently reliable estimates of religious populations by country and region. Estimates and projections of the percentage of Europeans who identify as Christian are constantly under revision by the compilers of the *WCD*, but a trend is apparent from their work published in 2010 and 2020 respectively. In 2010, the percentage of Europe's population that identified as Christian was estimated at 80.2 percent.[1] In 2020, the *WCD*'s compilers estimated that in 2015, 77.0 percent of Europeans identified as Christian, and that by 2050, this figure would fall to 70.1 percent, a total of 501.7 million Christians in 2050.[2] Correlating migrant status with religious affiliation is a significant challenge for religious demographers, including those responsible for the *WCD*. A 2012 Pew report, *Faith on the Move*, outlined estimates for migrant religious affiliation suggested 57 percent

---

1. Johnson and Ross, *Atlas of Global Christianity*, 154.
2. Johnson and Zurlo, *World Christian Encyclopedia*, 12.

of immigrants to Europe in 2012 were Christian.[3] The lack of consistency in collecting religious affiliation across Europe continues to frustrate the efforts of scholars of religion in Europe to draw meaningful conclusions. Moreover, the diversity of languages means that, for example, francophone, russophone, and anglophone migration studies rarely intersect. The lack of relatively reliable data means one must continue to treat statistical reports *cum grano salis*.

In 2020, this author was able to use data from the 2017 *European Values Survey* (*EVS*) to calculate religious affiliation data, extrapolated from a modest sample of *EVS* respondents who indicated they were overseas born and for whom religious affiliation data was available. While the calculations did not appear in the author's copublished third edition of *Mapping Migration*, he reported them in a British research publication, concluding that "Evangelicals, Pentecostals and Muslims are more likely to be present among migrants, in percentage terms, than they are among the indigenous populations of Europe. A migrant is three times more likely to be an evangelical Christian than is a non-migrant."[4]

The relative lack of statistical data is supplemented in the best studies by qualitative data. The author's three editions of *Mapping Migration* (2008, 2016, 2020) all make use of responses from migrant Christians collated for the MIRACLE research project.[5] Together with *Mapping Migration*'s own survey research in 2016 and 2020, these survey results suggest a wide variety of ways in which migrant Christians participate in public worship and undertake clerical duties. The *Mapping Migration* 2020 survey responses from over seventy Christian denominations in Europe concludes with this observation: "The European ecclesial landscape keeps changing. Migration has increased the presence of minority churches, both in terms of numbers and the variety of church typologies. Indeed, data demonstrates the complexity of the landscape when it comes to church constituency and membership. It is evident that the percentage of churches with a migrant background—whose members [*have become*] citizens of the country where the church is situated—is significantly high."[6]

---

3. Connor, *Faith on the Move*, 26; see also 53–55.
4. Jackson, "Mapping Migration."
5. Bertelli and Peschke, *MIRACLE Project*, 9–20.
6. Jackson and Passarelli, *Mapping Migration*, 32.

Migrant Christianity in Europe and Contested Identities

In arguing that migrants exercise agency in determinedly reformulating religious practice and identities in their new countries of residence, Jackson and Passarelli describe a changing ecclesial landscape as a result of migrant forms of Christianity.[7] Furthermore, these ecclesial innovations reflect the extent to which migration is similarly a driver of wider social, cultural, linguistic, economic, and political change. Düvell notes, for example, that "migration affects both the migrants' and their hosts' national, cultural, and individual identities."[8] In the encounter between migrant and "host," individual identity may be politicized and radicalized in a way that the resultant identity politics draws heavily upon religious heritage, history, and sensibilities.

The editors of *Vista* have closely monitored European nationalisms since the first edition in 2010. It was no accident that migration and nationalism featured jointly in the first edition of the *Vista* research bulletin.[9] These two phenomena are certainly not unique to Europe, and their concurrence is mirrored in other regions where a formerly dominant religious population receives migrants from differently religious countries of origin. It is ironic that the welcome and welfare extended to migrants by Christian communities of various traditions finds its riposte in various expressions of Christian nationalism that actively resist migrants being granted residency or legitimacy.

Drawing on Pew research data, Van de Poll reviews levels of religious identity and affiliation for countries across Europe. Van de Poll identifies countries where Christianity is central to the national identity and makes the observation that increased hostility to non-Christian migrants (with little attempt to differentiate non-European *Christian* migrants) is more prevalent in those countries where Christianity defines the national identity.[10] In such circumstances, migrant Christians are faced with the dilemma of whether they should challenge the ideological assumptions, concede to the demands of the powerful, or try to engage in theological negotiation with the proponents of Christian nationalisms. For Christian communities committed to the welcome of migrants and refugees, the dilemma may be of less existential consequence, but the questions are just as real.

---

7. Jackson and Passarelli, *Mapping Migration*, 32.
8. Düvell, "Migration, Minorities and Marginality," 328.
9. Jackson, "Migration and Nationalism."
10. Van de Poll, *Christian Faith and Making*, 332–46.

Through articulations of the unique social and political history of Europe's individual nation-states, each of those states continues to invest their respective citizenries with a particular set of sensibilities and loyalties towards the nation and, to a greater or lesser degree, to its traditional forms of Christianity.

Historically, Europe's monasteries were places of hospitality, healing, service, and refuge. To a large extent, these ministries continue in the migrant and refugee departments and agencies of the Roman Catholic Church and the various Protestant and Orthodox Churches. Refugees are frequently socially marginalized and consequently among the likely recipients of the welfare and diaconal provision of churches in Europe—more likely to receive it from these than from other voluntary, not-for-profit, or community associations. This fact alone is commonly overlooked or misunderstood when nonreligious individuals ask why the churches have such an interest in migrants.[11]

The presence of migrants in Europe, and the anti-migrant rhetoric that they face, has catalyzed new forms of ecclesial practice and identity. Moreover, it has stimulated theological reflection by European theologians who have recognized their need to better understand this human phenomenon and its consequences for the churches of Europe. The results are seen in public and political theologies that engage both the phenomenon of migration and the phenomenon of nationalism. The wider social and political context also influences the way that the churchgoing population responds to migrants. There is some, albeit limited, evidence that suggests that responses to migrants are generally *less* hostile within that part of the churchgoing population that is *more* religiously active. Higher levels of church attendance and increased frequency of personal prayer can be correlated with more tolerant views of migrants and others.[12]

In many European countries, ethnic minority churches are now among the numerically largest congregations, and they exercise agency in a wide variety of ways: ecclesially, socially, and politically. Live birth rates are higher for migrant and religious populations than they are for the nonmigrant and nonreligious populations of Europe. Demographic data suggests that migrant populations will continue to grow; it also shows that migrant populations are younger, on average, than their host populations. The characteristic creative vitality and energy of migrants are notable in gaining new

---

11. The question betrays an assumption that the church is by default committed to power and ceremony. This assumption overlooks the monastic and diaconal ministries of the churches of Europe, and an emphasis upon being a servant church from the Second Vatican Council right through to Pope Francis.

12. Jackson, "More Religious," 12.

qualifications, securing employment, setting up businesses, establishing homes, raising families, and founding new Christian denominations. Contemporary accounts of Christianity in Europe are simply inadequate if they ignore migration.[13]

However, when discussing migration, it is important to distinguish between different categories of migrant. The media frequently conflate these categories, especially where the intent is to vilify nonnationals, but the more significant consequence for this chapter is that each category of migrant impacts a community and its churches in different ways. This is especially tricky to understand as it is not always or immediately obvious to which category a particular migrant belongs. It's also possible that an individual might self-identify in more than one category or in a category different than one in which the host community might have assigned them.

This point is important because the status of any particular migrant is of consequence for how we imagine their presence and capacity to contribute to the theological and social activities of Europe's churches.[14] It also highlights the need to imagine and develop a broad range of responses from within the churches of Europe.

For example, *asylum seekers*, awaiting decisions about their application for protection as *refugees* due to a "well-founded fear of being persecuted for reasons of race, religion, nationality, membership of a particular social group or political opinion" are most likely to make demands on welfare and diaconal ministries.[15] Beyond the initial response, however, the presence of refugees in the community is likely to prompt those same Christian communities to reflect more carefully upon what it means to be a servant church.

Attention to other categories of migrants serves to further extend our appreciation of their impact. *Seasonal migrant workers*, for example, working in the agricultural industry for several months of the harvest period, are clearly of more significance for rural Christianity. Migrant Christian workers are not merely an urban phenomenon, but regional and rural churches have also had to learn how to provide for the spiritual and other needs of migrant Christians.

Economic migrants and *transnational migrants* are especially fascinating categories of migrant, to the extent that they are frequently able to exercise greater personal agency due to greater socioeconomic or educational status. They might "live and/or work in networks that transcend political

---

13. Van de Poll, *Christian Faith and Making*, 325–26; see also Connor, *Faith on the Move*.

14. For a fuller set of definitions, see Jackson and Passarelli, *Mapping Migration*, 11–12.

15. See https://www.unrefugees.org/refugee-facts/what-is-a-refugee/.

borders... be bilingual, trans-cultural, have homes in more than one country, and pursue economic, political and cultural interests in more than one place."[16] One or two African-initiated denominations operate in this manner, operating from headquarters in Europe, overseeing extensive networks in the African countries from which those denominations originate.

Somewhat closely related to these latter two categories, *diaspora* Christian communities typically maintain close social, family, religious, cultural, symbolic, or other emotional ties to their family's country of origin. On those occasions where they are still to forge the same ties with the host country, they may consider themselves to exist in exile. The use of this term often implies that the migrant population is of such a size that it can sustain its own worshipping communities, often linguistically and liturgically distinct.

This brief introduction to just some of the ways we can categorize migrants suggests that theologians in Europe do well to avoid using simplistic binaries that juxtapose "forced" and "voluntary," "sending" and "receiving," and, instead, give greater attention to human agency in the case of both emigration and immigration. A final caution is in order; migrants in Europe are not uniformly "non-European" or "non-Christian." Across the larger part of the continent of Europe, the European Union (EU) is established upon the premise of the free movement of its various peoples, irrespective of from which EU member state they originate. Statistically, a migrant churchgoer is more likely in the European context to be, for example, a Polish Catholic attending Mass in Ireland, France, or the Netherlands. These observations, plus the exodus of Ukrainians in the wake of Russia's invasion of Ukraine in February 2022, are a reminder that it has never been a simple task to classify European migration. The presence of migrants in Europe continues to catalyze the reimagining of ministry, liturgy, welfare services, and theology. In 2008, the Churches Commission for Migrants in Europe published results from its MIRACLE research project and, in doing so, shone a light on the extent to which Europe's churches were places of welcome, healthy integration, and participation.

Welcome, integration, and participation were not, and are not, uniformly practiced, however. Commonly, these factors might result in contested Christian and ecclesial identities, liturgical practices, and theologies or doctrines. Andrew Walls characterizes this as an "Ephesian moment," suggesting that the early Christians in Ephesus had to decide whether the

---

16. Koser, *International Migration*, 27.

"church in all its diversity [would] demonstrate its unity by the interactive participation of all its culture-specific segments."[17]

Newly arrived migrant faith is characteristically conservative, challenging the theology and practice of mainline denominations, which are perceived as liberal or backslidden. This impacts on migrant assessments of European Christianity and shapes the way that migrant and host Christian communities might, or might not, interact and collaborate. Nonetheless, these observations serve to underscore the assessment that the diversity of Christian expression is a consequence of migrants possessing and exercising agency. These underscore the argument of this chapter that migration is fundamentally constitutive of social realities and, we might add, of ecclesial realities.

Metaphors of Christian Arrival and Presence in Europe

If our discussion so far has outlined the extent to which the diversity of Christian identity and practice in Europe is a consequence of migration, it seems appropriate at this point to take a closer look at the metaphors of Christian "arrival" and "presence" in Europe, noting especially the extent to which these obscure the mutual interchange of spiritual, liturgical, and theological imagination between migrant and host Christian communities. At the outset, it's important to note that any singular metaphor cannot hope to bear the weight of the complexity of the endeavor we call "Christianity in Europe." Yet, choices must be made if a story is to be told. The braver scholars have ventured various options, and they each have their inadequacies. Of course, in adopting such metaphors, these authors were certainly aware of those realities that could not entirely be explained by the metaphors they used. One might even acknowledge that in suggesting a metaphor, they were offering it up for scholarly reflection and critique. Nevertheless, their decisions give some insight into how our language concerning the history of Christianity has changed over the last century.

For the purposes of this chapter, the most disturbing aspect of the choice of metaphors is that few of them are able to imagine the transformation of the forms of Christianity that were allegedly doing the propagating, expanding, transmitting, crusading, or diffusing. It seems, in most instances, that the only consequence of such transmission or expansion was its imposition on, or reception by, the target population being Christianized.

Selecting the best metaphors to characterize the historical, numerical, and geographical growth of Christianity is inevitably a fraught exercise.

17. Walls, *Cross-Cultural Process*, 81.

Nevertheless, numerical increase and geographical spread call for explanatory categories. Taking a lead from Kollman, I will argue that the increasing numerical adherence and geographical spread of Christianity in Europe has "reinforced various historical factors that helped establish the normative European subject."[18] Similarly, our use of metaphors for arrival and presence in Europe lays bare several implicit self-understandings informed by the apparent normativity of approximately seventeen hundred years of Christian settlement and adherence on the continent of Europe. A critical account of both is overdue. An honest account of close to seventeen hundred years of settlement and adherence can be neither continuous, hermetically sealed, nor homogeneous. At every juncture, the movement of people has been the motion and kinesis that not only disrupts and deconstructs prior normativities, but which, in like manner, exposes the implicit assumptions upon which our metaphors rest.

One such normativity, often unexamined in the telling of European Christian history, is that our histories frequently focus on the church as institution and fail to adequately address the history of Christians as community. Walls underscores this point, noting that "church" histories require ecclesiological choice, while "Christian" history can offer accounts that integrate communal, societal, and ecclesial factors.[19] By focusing on these factors, we might hope to arrive at a more satisfactory account of the arrival and presence of Christianity in Europe and the diversity that is inextricably bound up in the interchange of migrant and resident forms of Christianity.

Latourette's compendious *History of the Expansion of Christianity* was published in seven volumes between 1937 and 1945. Latourette's reliance upon the metaphor of *expansion* is reasonably uncontroversial, for his writing catalogs the unquestionable global spread and presence of the Christian faith across two millennia.

Understood carelessly, the metaphor suggests an increase in size of something that remains unchanged in nature; after the expansion, there is simply more of the same. Of course, in the expanding of one substance, another is displaced. The expansion of Christianity must therefore presumably require the dispersion, contraction, even deletion, of alternative or preexisting ideological and/or religious practices and beliefs. The use of "expansion" by some historians suggests it is possible to use it in this manner. For example, Bartlett uses "expansion" with reference to Latin Christendom and

---

18. Kollman, "At Origins of Mission," 429.
19. Walls, *Cross-Cultural Process*, 5.

its consolidation of Roman Catholic ecclesiastical and political dominance over the realms and rulers of Europe.[20]

Perhaps unsurprisingly, those who use this metaphor enthusiastically are silent about those historical moments and human experiences we now describe with words such as "confrontation," "dispossession," "conquest," "genocide," "exile," "migration," or "crusade," for example.

Andrew Walls more typically refers to the *transmission* of faith.[21] Although closely associated with the metaphor of expansion, "transmission" suggests that something is passed on, albeit in a rather omnidirectional way. It might be said to soften the earlier metaphor, allowing for something to be handed over, for a gift to be received, avoiding the sense of there being an ultimatum, coercion, deletion, or dispossession. Transmission may be subject to interference, and it will likely require translation for the recipient must be attuned to the messenger. However, the metaphor of transmission implies an omnidirectional communication, with a transmitter and a receptor. No allowance is made, within the constraints implied by the metaphor, for the agency of the recipient in receiving the message.

Jenkins's metaphor of *the next Christendom* expresses the sense of continuity and discontinuity between the present European context and its earlier history of Holy Roman Empire.[22] His metaphor perhaps comes closest to the "dueling empires" theme at the center of this current volume. Its use cannot be anything other than intentional by Jenkins, who describes a Europe staring down a social crisis,[23] haunted by specters, and riven by ideological and religious rivalry.[24]

Jenkins is keenly attentive to the narratives that accompany a non-Western, migrant re-presencing of aspects of Christendom that are long forgotten and disavowed: new ecclesiastical expressions that strive to extend the influence and power of this or that form of Christianity over multiple spheres of human experience and organization. If Jenkins is correct, the migration of Christians to Europe heralds a renaissance of the sociopolitical vision of Christendom. This possibility provokes diverse responses. For some, this type of migrant agency is a welcome refining of moribund, domesticated forms of Christianity.[25] Christendom was a unifying enterprise that held social imagination vicariously and simultaneously defended it

20. Bartlett, *Making of Europe*, 292.
21. Walls, *Missionary Movement*.
22. Jenkins, *Next Christendom*.
23. Jenkins, *God's Continent*, 10.
24. Jenkins, *God's Continent*, 25.
25. Oliveira, *Global Reverse Mission*, 1.

ferociously. For others, Christendom represents a failed social *imaginarium*, incapable of sustaining an ethical vision committed to common good or to the nurture of a socially diverse Europe.

Though Jenkins may be guilty of using the figure of the "migrant" as a proxy for his critique of the inadequacies of the European sociopolitical vision, he nevertheless constructs his case around an accurate account of the impact of the same migrants upon Europe's religious institutes and denominations, including its churches. If he is correct, ecclesial diversity and change will result from contestation rather than transmission or expansion.

Brian Stanley's use of *global diffusion* to describe the spread of evangelical faith is worth mentioning here,[26] given the prevalence of evangelical Christian migrants and the extent to which the Christian welfare and missionary agencies that engage with migrants in Europe are frequently evangelical in character, seeing them as a "mission field."[27] Stanley's metaphor suggests that something has entered a preexisting world of ideological and/or theological convictions and commitments. Diffusion is not possible unless both worlds are susceptible to admixture or the mutual reception of respective distinctives. Nigerian Evangelicals in Europe who identify as Anglican Episcopal may be every bit as evangelical as Ukrainian Baptists. When these diaspora groups encounter one another in, for example, the Evangelical Alliance of the UK, their shared commitment to collaborate is even more remarkable, given the diversity of liturgical, ecclesial, and theological commitments involve. In diaspora, conservative evangelical Christians are as susceptible as other parts of the Christian church to an embrace of difference and diversity.

The Connecting-Disrupting Presence of Multiple Christianities in Europe

The metaphors of expansion, transmission, next Christendom, and global diffusion capture important social and ecclesial realities involved in the arrival and enduring presence of Christianity in Europe. Treated individually, however, two trends are immediately obvious. In the first instance, the metaphors of expansion and transmission have limited capacity to describe the accelerating influx of migrant Majority World Christians into Europe from the late twentieth century onwards, defined by Andrew Walls as a "great reverse migration"[28] following a shift in the center of gravity of world

26. Stanley, *Global Diffusion of Evangelicalism*.
27. Pocock and Wan, *Diaspora Missiology*, xvii.
28. Walls, *Crossing Cultural Frontiers*, 49–51.

Christianity.[29] On the other hand, those metaphors that manage to capture this moment, including that of a next Christendom, offer unsatisfactory accounts of the treatment of people on the move throughout the history of European Christendom.

Christendom has a complicated history concerning the movement of people within Europe. The social and political settlements achieved throughout Europe's history have followed the movement of people in some form or other, whether as exiles, pilgrims, mercenaries, missionaries, vagabonds, scholars, conquerors, or traders. Imagine an alternative European history that makes no reference to the Protestant Reformers in exile in Geneva, the relocation of the imperial Roman capital to Constantinople, the Waldensian presence in northern Italy, the pilgrim ways that connected a network of monasteries as centers of learning and faith, or the Moorish and Ottoman Islamic incursions. It ought to be obvious that religious diversity and the movement of people are an inextricably connected constant of European history. Unfortunately, this connection is often overlooked. Histories of Christianity frequently cast such movements as marginal, transitory, subversive, schismatic, composed of rebels, revolutionaries, and stepchildren, a threat to social stability and harmony. One might come to understand that such movements have constantly threatened the security of the "place-bound social membership" towards which Europe appears committed.

The critical philosopher Thomas Nail critiques the primacy we afford to "place-bound social membership" and argues for an account of history that reevaluates the exile, vagabond, or migrant "people in motion" as historically and socially normative and constitutive of the very social orders (including Christendom) that eventually move to circumscribe and eject such individuals.[30] Nail argues that the historical prevalence of people in motion suggests that we should treat accounts of people in motion as socially normative, even prior to any eventual ejection. Gerard Delanty reinforces this point with the candid observation that "internal migration is itself an integral part of European history. Europeans are neither racially nor ethnically homogenous, despite what they like to think of themselves."[31]

So, if kinesis or motion constitutes European social realities and norms, and we adopt Nail's terminology, we can describe this state of affairs as a "kino-politics." Nail's account challenges the dominant assumptions, internal and external to diaspora, that migrants are disruptive and deviant marginals, and creates space to reflect on continuities that more

29. Walls, *Missionary Movement*, 9.
30. Nail, *Figure of the Migrant*.
31. Delanty, *Inventing Europe*, 150.

prominently feature people in motion throughout the whole history of European Christianity. Disruption *and* continuity are equally integral to the story of diasporic Christianity in Europe.

Historical amnesia is common among contemporary European Christians. Honest historians note the historical coercion, domination, and control of Christendom in the face of uneven orthodoxy, syncretistic incorporation of paganism, and the socially disruptive "heresies" that emerged within early Christianity, even prior to Constantine, and which were incorporated into, and continue to typify, diverse forms of Christianity in Europe. Christian peoples have frequently found themselves on the move throughout the last two millennia, often compelled to do so at the behest of church authorities and hierarchs. Kreider's edited volume points to the urgency of a vital dialogue between missiologists and historians in this respect.[32]

Along with other marginal and deviant groups, migrant Christians in diaspora are frequently described in ways that obscure any sense of agency. Where this tendency is resisted, it is possible to identify diaspora theologies, imagining diaspora as a permanent "condition" out of which contextual theologies emerge. Diaspora as a context or site for the doing of theology is wholly congruent with the theological imagination of what scholars commonly describe as "world Christianity." Diaspora Christianity in Europe represents a "centering of the margins" that challenges the universalizing claims of European theologies from within the belly of the beast. From these centers, diasporan theologians such as Israel Olofinjana and non-diasporan theologians such Dorottya Nagy, for example, are equally committed to scholarly investigation that describes diverse forms of Christian theology and practice in the context of migration and diaspora Christianity in Europe.[33] Scholars from the "margins," working at the educational "centers" of Western Europe, have contributed much to developing and popularizing liberationist, postcolonialist, indigenous, intercultural, and global or world theologies, among others. This is not to say that centered places "own" these theologies, merely to observe that the "centered" diaspora site as a location for scholarly activity appears to have been crucial in the popularization and dissemination of these theologies.

As their work, and that of others, identifies diversities and transformations, it offers a mirror in which historians see a clear reflection of processes underway for centuries, and prompts a dawning realization that the so-called "age of migration" is not necessarily as novel as one might suspect.[34]

---

32. Kreider, *Origins of Christendom*, 363.
33. Olofinjana, *Partnership in Mission*; Nagy, *Migration and Theology*.
34. Castles and Miller, *Age of Migration*.

Early twenty-first-century advances in global communications, travel, and technology are certainly accelerants for the movement of people around the globe. But the phenomenon of people in motion is a fact of European history. For almost forty years the Council of Europe has been identifying cultural routes that reinforce a "sense of fraternity amongst travelers and a strong bonding with the land."[35] In 1987 the Camino de Santiago was the first of many routes to be listed, one of the earliest pilgrim routes to forge fraternity among people on the move. The camino continues to facilitate the habitual movement of the religious faithful across Europe, catalyzing the exchange and interchange of religious imagination between pilgrims from across the Continent, much as it has for centuries.

Stasis and Kinesis and an Understanding of European Christianity

It's not uncommon to read accounts lamenting the decline in attendance at European churches that simultaneously consider the accompanying growth in attendance at ethnic minority congregations to be of little consequence for the "survival of European Christianity." The assumption seems to be that European Christianity reached stasis at an unstated point in recent history and that, since this point, there has been a steady and irreversible decline. The accounts fail to allow for the entry and presence of migrant Christians in European churches throughout their history. Equally, they demonstrate an attempt to erect a false binary of "ethnic" versus European. Such accounts ignore the fact that every European Christian has an ethnic identity. Moreover, it is difficult to imagine what is meant by "European." As a continent, Europe is generally held to include approximately fifty sovereign states, highly diverse in regard to their religious heritage, sociopolitical history, and language and culture. There has never been something we might define as "the essence of European Christianity" characterized by agreement and consensus about what and who were to be described as authentically "European Christians," and certainly not one that excludes migrants.

If they provoke anything, the more recent incidences of diasporic Christianity increase awareness of diversity in Christian thought and practice. They also highlight the failure of any contemporary attempt to suggest that diasporas are disruptive of pristine forms of Christianity happily accommodated to sovereign states and their peoples, an accommodation existing since the religious settlement of 1648 following the Peace of Westphalia. The Italians may still be predominantly Roman Catholics, Romanians predominantly Orthodox, or the Norwegians predominantly Lutheran, but these old

---

35. Council of Europe, *Cultural Routes*, 4.

certainties are breaking down. Diaspora Christians are contributing their own culturally and denominationally determined theologies and practices to an inherited mix of Christian traditions that have forged evangelical and ecumenical networks, councils, and alliances, in the effort to collaborate across the ecclesial divides. This ecumenical and interdenominational endeavor is a hallmark of twentieth-century European Christianity, even as decline accelerates into the twenty-first century. Contrary to criticisms of Europe's open-door policy regarding migrants, the impact of migration upon the churches of Europe does not represent the dechristianization of Europe so much as it heralds the de-Europeanization of Christianity. In fact, it seems more reasonable to insist that recently arriving migratory and diasporic Christians may "re-presence" or "instantiate" vibrant and active expressions of Christianity. These serve only to expand the range of Christian traditions and communities that have coexisted across Europe for as long as there have been Christians dwelling there.

Re-Presencing Christianity in Europe

This chapter has invited a search for better metaphors that describe the presence and emergence of Christianity in Europe. The increasing visibility and confidence of diaspora Christians will only accelerate the search for better metaphors. Whether the chapter has succeeded in persuading its readers that this is the case remains to be seen. Nevertheless, better metaphors are necessary, for they provide the conceptual glue that hold together the narrative threads of emergence and presence, lending them their narrative coherence.

Within the scope of this volume and series, the argument has been necessarily brief and summary, perhaps too brief. Again, nevertheless, the argument calls for sustained critique, defense, and scholarly attention. Offered here, throughout this chapter, are a variety of assertions grounded in research and observation conducted by this author over the past twenty years. Thirteen of those were spent by him in coediting a quarterly, research-led publication that monitored, measured, and analyzed trends and patterns related, directly and indirectly, to the themes of European migration and diaspora that are discussed in this chapter.

Delanty deconstructs the idea of "Europe" and argues it is an identity project: "Europe can mean whatever one intends it to mean."[36] If the same is true of European Christianity, it's entirely appropriate to ask whether Christianity can ever exist in an ideal or pristine state. The genius, and burden, of the Christian vision is that Christian discipleship is a profoundly embodied

---

36. Delanty, *Inventing Europe*, 145.

and communal activity. *European* Christianity is no exception. Understood this way is why diaspora Christianity in Europe can be understood to be a re-presencing or an instantiation of what would otherwise remain a bold or lofty ideal. The Christian churches in Europe have no social reality beyond the interconnected lives and affairs of people of faith, both lay and ordained. As the lives and witness of Christian migrants become more deeply interconnected with nonmigrants, the germ of new ecclesial and theological ideas is nourished and aspiration becomes reality. The reality may only be partially realized, messy or chaotic, but together, the aspiration and its embodiment portend a new vision for the future of the Christian churches of Europe.

The re-presencing of any particular expressions of the Christian vision will not be to everyone's liking. Such activity is frequently tensive, sorely contested, often misunderstood. It might prove disruptive in some places. The act of migrants re-presencing Christian faith can be deeply disruptive, for instance, when their actions and existence expose ecclesiologies and doctrines that are little more than regional normativities wrapped in ecclesiastical pronouncements.

In 1995, Delanty warned against a "European identity tied to an adversarial framework" in which "a white bourgeois populism [is] defined in opposition to . . . the Third World."[37] Delanty's warning is as much needed thirty years later as it was when first written, but the re-presencing activity of migrants also holds out the promise of multiple instantiations of the Christian vision towards a genuine "koinonia" of difference, a fellowship of "otherness." If migrant and diaspora Christians in Europe are genuinely contributing to the redefinition of Christianity in Europe, it is to be hoped that they can successfully engage with nonmigrants in *co-defining* the reality of a lived witness to a "koinonia of difference." This, then, would embody a truly generative exercise, willingly sought by both migrant and nonmigrant, embracing the simultaneous connecting and disrupting nature of their collaborative exploration of life together in the one body of Christ that has found its home in Europe.

Bibliography

Bartlett, Robert. *The Making of Europe: Conquest, Colonization and Cultural Change, 950–1350*. Princeton: Princeton University Press, 1994.

Bertelli, Olivia, and Doris Peschke. *The MIRACLE Project—Models of Integration through Religion, Activation, Cultural Learning and Exchange*. Brussels: Churches' Commission for Migrants in Europe, 2010.

---

37. Delanty, *Inventing Europe*, 155.

Castles, Stephen, and Mark J. Miller. *The Age of Migration: International Population Movements in the Modern World.* New York: Guilford, 1993.

Connor, Phillip. *Faith on the Move: The Religious Affiliation of International Migrants.* Washington, DC: Pew Research Center, 2012.

Council of Europe. *Cultural Routes of the Council of Europe, 2019.* Council of Europe, 2019. https://rm.coe.int/en-brochure-cultural-routes-2019/168092594a.

Delanty, Gerard. *Inventing Europe: Idea, Identity, Reality.* Basingstoke, UK: Palgrave Macmillan, 1995.

Düvell, Franck. "Migration, Minorities and Marginality: New Directions in European Migration Research." In *The SAGE Handbook of European Studies*, edited by Chris Rumford, 328–46. London: SAGE, 2009.

Jackson, Darrell. "Mapping Migration and Its Impact on the Churches of Europe: 'Being Church Together.'" *Future First* 80 (2022) 6.

———. "Migration and Nationalism: New Challenges for Europe's Christians." *VISTA: Quarterly Bulletin of Research-Based Information on Mission in Europe* 1 (2010) 1–2. https://www.europeanmission.redcliffe.ac.uk/latest-articles/migration-and-nationalism-new-challenges-for-europes-christains.

———. "More Religious or More Secular?" *VISTA: Quarterly Bulletin of Research-Based Information on Mission in Europe* 38 (2021) 12–15.

Jackson, Darrell, and Alessia Passarelli. *Mapping Migration, Mapping Churches' Responses in Europe: "Being Church Together."* 3rd ed. Brussels: Churches' Commission for Migrants in Europe, 2020. https://ccme.eu/wp-content/uploads/2021/05/2021-05-20_Mapping-Migration3-2020-PDF-FINAL.pdf.

Jenkins, Philip. *God's Continent: Christianity, Islam, and Europe's Religious Crisis.* Oxford: Oxford University Press, 2007.

———. *The Next Christendom: The Coming of Global Christianity.* Oxford: Oxford University Press, 2002.

Johnson, Todd M., and Kenneth R. Ross, eds. *Atlas of Global Christianity 1910–2010.* Edinburgh: Edinburgh University Press, 2010.

Johnson, Todd M., and Gina Zurlo. *World Christian Encyclopedia.* 3rd ed. Edinburgh: Edinburgh University Press, 2020.

Kollman, Paul. "At the Origins of Mission and Missiology: A Study in the Dynamics of Religious Language." *JAAR* 79 (2011) 425–58.

Koser, Khalid. *International Migration: A Very Short Introduction.* Oxford: Oxford University Press, 2007.

Kreider, Alan, ed. *The Origins of Christendom in the West.* Edinburgh: T&T Clark, 2001.

Latourette, Kenneth Scott. *A History of the Expansion of Christianity.* 7 vols. London: Harper, 1937–45.

Nagy, Dorottya. *Migration and Theology: The Case of Chinese Christian Communities in Hungary and Romania in the Globalisation-Context.* Zoetermeer, Neth.: Boekencentrum, 2009.

Nail, Thomas. *The Figure of the Migrant.* Stanford, CA: Stanford University Press, 2015.

Oliveira, Sandro G. de. "Global Reverse Mission in Europe: An Examination of the Limiting Factors and Prospects." *Global Missiology* 18 (2021). http://ojs.globalmissiology.org/index.php/english/article/view/2506/5946.

Olofinjana, Israel. *Partnership in Mission: A Black Majority Church Perspective on Mission and Church Unity.* Rickmansworth, UK: Instant Apostle, 2015.

Pocock, Michael, and Enoch Wan. *Diaspora Missiology: Reflections on Reaching the Scattered Peoples of the World*. Pasadena, CA: William Carey Library, 2015.

Stanley, Brian. *The Global Diffusion of Evangelicalism: The Age of Billy Graham and John Stott*. History of Evangelicalism 5. Nottingham, UK: IVP Academic, 2013.

Van de Poll, Evert. *Christian Faith and the Making of Europe: Yesterday and Today*. Nuremberg: VTR, 2020.

Walls, Andrew. *The Cross-Cultural Process in Christian History*. Edinburgh: T. & T. Clark, 2002.

———. *Crossing Cultural Frontiers: Studies in the History of World Christianity*. Edited by Mark R. Gornik. Maryknoll, NY: Orbis, 2017.

———. *The Missionary Movement in Christian History: Studies in the Transmission of Faith*. Maryknoll, NY: Orbis, 1996.

Time Line: Europe

Brett Knowles

AMERICAN CHURCH HISTORIAN MARTIN Marty has aptly commented that (in religion as elsewhere), "both hurricanes and glacial forces leave altered landscapes."[1] The "hurricane" represents sudden, drastic change, the product of clearly identifiable catalytic events such as, for example, the Second Vatican Council from 1962 to 1965. By contrast, the "glacier" represents a process of gradual, subtle change, which may not be attributable to any specific causative event or series of events. These "glacial" forces therefore symbolize slow, cumulative progressions of attitudes and orientations, which cannot always be placed within a time line of dates in the same way as catalytic "hurricane" events. Nevertheless, events are significant markers of historical process, and the entries in this time line cover the history of Christianity in the continent of Europe from the first century CE up to the present day.

Europe is deemed to be that part of the Eurasian continent west of the Urals and north of the Caucasus. However, Greenland, although included in the North American continent in the United Nations, Department of Economic and Social Affairs, Statistics Division (UNSD) website, was historically seen as being part of Europe (i.e., a Norwegian or Danish colony) and is so treated here. Country locations are placed in bold type at the end of each entry and are derived from the UNSD website;[2] those territories not listed in that website are enclosed in parentheses, e.g. (**Scilly Islands**), etc.; continental entries, with no specific country location, are cited as [**Europe**]. Where the entry refers to an event in the Greco-Roman world (which comprised parts of Asia, Africa, and Europe, up to the end of Justinian's reign in 565), this is indicated by the annotation [**Greco-Roman World:** . . .] preceding the country entry.

1. Marty, "Introduction," 1.
2. See http://unstats.un.org/unsd/methodology/m49/.

Year and Event

ca. 46 The apostle Paul begins his first missionary journey to Cyprus and Asia Minor; later journeys would take him further west into Greece, Illyricum (Albania), and, eventually, to Rome and (possibly) Spain. **[Greco-Roman World: Albania, Greece, Italy, Spain]**

ca. 49 Riots break out in Rome between Christians and Jews in the reign of Claudius, resulting in the expulsion of all noncitizen Jews. **[Greco-Roman World: Italy]**

50 The apostle Paul begins writing his letters to the churches in Asia Minor, Greece, and Rome. **[Greco-Roman World: Greece, Italy]**

64 The emperor Nero persecutes the Christians as scapegoats for the Great Fire of Rome. **[Greco-Roman World: Italy]**

ca. 65 The writing of the canonical Gospels begins, with Mark being the first to be composed, possibly in Rome. **[Greco-Roman World: Italy]**

96 Clement of Rome writes as the secretary of the church in Rome on behalf of its college of presbyters to the church of Corinth, rebuking them for the disorderly deposition of their presbyters. **[Greco-Roman World: Greece, Italy]**

ca. 107 Ignatius of Antioch writes seven letters to the Christians in Asia and Rome while on his way to martyrdom. **[Greco-Roman World: Italy]**

ca. 130–140 Aristeides of Athens and Quadratus of Asia Minor write the first Christian apologies, addressed to the Emperor Hadrian, in which they defend the Christians against the popular accusations made against them. **[Greco-Roman World: Greece]**

144 Marcion of Sinope teaches that the Jewish Yahweh is an evil demiurge (a subordinate creator deity) and thus different from the Father of Jesus Christ; he rejects the entire Old Testament and most of the New (except for Luke's Gospel and ten of Paul's letters), on the basis that only Paul had really understood the gospel. **[Greco-Roman World: Italy]**

ca. 151 Justin Martyr addresses his *First Apology* to the emperor Antoninus Pius, responding to pagan criticisms of Christianity and arguing that Christian theology is, in fact, the true philosophy. **[Greco-Roman World: Italy]**

177 A vicious, but short-term, persecution breaks out in Vienne and Lyons, resulting in several Christians being tortured and executed. [**Greco-Roman World: France**]

ca. 190 Irenaeus formulates the "Rule of Faith" as a summary of the church's teaching, taught throughout the whole world (i.e., *kata-holos*—"according to the whole," from which the word "catholic" is derived). [**Greco-Roman World: France**]

ca. 215 *The Apostolic Tradition*, attributed to Hippolytus of Rome, sets out an array of liturgical standards for the discipling of catechumens (persons receiving instruction in the Christian faith) and the conduct of public liturgy. [**Greco-Roman World: Italy**]

250–251 The emperor Decius launches the first official, empire-wide persecution of the Christians (previous persecutions had been sporadic outbreaks of local mob violence, rather than the product of imperial policy); records of this persecution come from Rome, Jerusalem, Antioch, and Carthage. [**Greco-Roman World**]

251 The Novatianist schism breaks out in Rome over the readmission to communion of lapsed Christians who had apostatized or denied the faith during persecution. [**Greco-Roman World: Italy**]

312 The conversion of the emperor Constantine, through Constantine's vision of a cross of light at the Battle of the Milvian Bridge, leads to his issuing (together with his co-emperor Licinius) the Edict of Milan the following year granting full toleration to all religions (including the Christians) in the Roman Empire. [**Greco-Roman World: Italy**]

330 The emperor Constantine transfers the capital of the Roman Empire from Rome to Constantinople. [**Greco-Roman World: Italy**]

341 Ulfilas begins missionary work among the barbarian Goths, converting them to Arian Christianity. [**Germany**]

357 A small gathering of bishops, the Council of Sirmium, issues a doctrinal statement that came to be known as "The Blasphemy of Sirmium" for its defective definition of the Trinity. [**Greco-Roman World: Serbia**]

366–384 Bishop Damasus of Rome consolidates the authority of the Roman Church, emphasizing its apostolic founding by Peter, and promoting the primacy of its bishop, leading to the development of the papacy. [**Greco-Roman World: Italy**]

386 Augustine of Hippo converts to Catholic Christianity through the influence of Bishop Ambrose of Milan; as he records it in his *Confessions*, the key catalyst is a child playing in the next-door garden, calling, "Tolle, lege!" ("Take, read!," i.e., the Bible). [**Greco-Roman World: Italy**]

390 Bishop Ambrose of Milan refuses to celebrate the Eucharist in the presence of the emperor Theodosius (effectively an act of excommunication) because of Theodosius's responsibility for the massacre of seven thousand people at Thessalonica, forcing Theodosius to do public penance before being restored to communion. [**Greco-Roman World: Greece, Italy**]

410 The city of Rome falls to the Goths and other barbarian invaders, marking the symbolic end of the Roman Empire in the West. [**Greco-Roman World: Italy**]

432 Patrick arrives in Ireland about this date and converts King Lóegaire mac Néill (Laoghaire), the high king of Ireland, at Tara. [**Ireland**]

440 Pope Leo I assumes several civic as well as religious responsibilities due to the collapse of the Roman government in the Western Empire after the fall of Rome. [**Greco-Roman World: Italy**]

452 Pope Leo I makes an embassy to Attila the Hun, the leader of a devastating barbarian invasion into Europe, seeking to alleviate the effects of this offensive and to dissuade the barbarians from sacking Rome. [**Greco-Roman World: Italy**]

496 Chlodovocar (Clovis), the king of the Franks, adopts Catholic Christianity (the first barbarian king to do so) and is baptized. [**Belgium, France, Netherlands**]

527–565 The emperor Justinian seeks to restore the Roman Empire in the West, abolish the last remnants of paganism, and strengthen the Orthodox Church; he achieves these aims by building splendid churches such as the Hagia Sophia (Holy Wisdom), by codifying its liturgy, and by consolidating Roman law on a Christian basis (the Code of Justinian). [**Greco-Roman World: Bosnia and Herzegovina, Croatia, Italy, Slovenia, Spain**]

529 Benedict of Nursia founds the Abbey of Monte Cassino, the archetype for Benedictine monasteries for more than fourteen hundred years until it is destroyed in 1943 during the Second World War; the abbey's influence is reinforced by Benedict's Rule (written about the same time), which sets out the patterns of monastic community life, becoming the dominant exemplar of monasticism in Europe throughout the Middle Ages. [**Italy**]

563 Columba and his followers cross the Irish Sea to Scotland, then comprising part of the Ulster Gaelic kingdom of Dalriada, on *peregrinatio* (i.e., wandering: the characteristic Celtic monastic practice of following Christ by means of pilgrimage or voluntary exile) and found a monastery on the island of Hii (Iona) off the west coast of Scotland. [**United Kingdom of Great Britain and Northern Ireland (Scotland)**]

590 Pope Gregory I (the Great) begins his reign and dispatches papal missions to Gaul, Sardinia, and (especially) England, with Augustine of Canterbury arriving in Kent in 596. [**France, Italy, United Kingdom of Great Britain and Northern Ireland (England)**]

ca. 590 The Celtic monk Columbanus leaves Ireland to begin missionary work in Burgundy; he later bases his evangelistic work near Lake Constance in Switzerland and at Bobbio in Italy. [**France, Germany, Ireland, Italy**]

597 The papal mission to England achieves dramatic early success, with King Ethelbert of Kent and thousands of his subjects being baptized in the Thames on Christmas Day 597; Canterbury (Kent City) becomes the headquarters of the new English Church and Augustine of Canterbury its first archbishop. [**United Kingdom of Great Britain and Northern Ireland (England)**]

664 King Oswy chooses Roman Christianity over Celtic Christianity at the Synod of Whitby in Northumbria; the merger of these two churches has significant implications for missions to continental Europe, which thereafter combine the Celts' charismatic passion with the Roman talent for organization and consolidation. [**United Kingdom of Great Britain and Northern Ireland (England)**]

687 Pepin of Heristal unites the Franks into a cohesive kingdom, thus laying the foundation for the later partnership between the Frankish kings and the Catholic Church. [**Austria, Belgium, France, Germany, Liechtenstein, Luxembourg, Netherlands, Switzerland**]

690 Willibrord evangelizes the Franks in Belgium and Holland, becoming their bishop in 695. [**Belgium, Netherlands**]

711–716 The Arab armies enter Spain, defeating the Christian Visigoths and establishing al-Andalus, a province of the Umayyad Caliphate, at Cordoba in southern Spain. [**Spain**]

716 Boniface (Wynfrith) makes his first missionary journey to Frisia; six years later, he is consecrated in Rome as bishop-without-see for the German frontier regions, giving him plenipotentiary authority over the church there. [**Germany, Italy, Netherlands**]

731 The Venerable Bede completes his *Ecclesiastical History of the English People*; his text provides much of the data for later understandings of early English Christianity. [**United Kingdom of Great Britain and Northern Ireland (England)**]

732 Charles Martel and the Franks halt the Arab advance into Europe at the Battle of Poitiers. [**France**]

751 Pepin, the son of Charles Martel and grandson of Pepin of Heristal, deposes the Merovingian king Childeric and begins the Carolingian dynasty as Pepin III, inaugurating a codependent partnership between the Frankish kings and the papacy; his son Charlemagne becomes its most powerful king in 771. [**Austria, Belgium, France, Germany, Liechtenstein, Luxembourg, Netherlands, Switzerland**]

754 A band of pagan Frisians ambush and martyr the English Roman missionary Boniface, along with fifty-two companions, as he is reading the Scriptures to his neophyte Christian converts in preparation for their confirmation on Pentecost Sunday. [**Netherlands**]

779 Benedict of Aniane founds a monastery that becomes a center of Benedictine reform for all French monastic houses; his Rule of Benedict (not to be confused with the earlier Rule of Benedict of Nursia) is approved as a monastic standard at the Council of Aachen in 817. [**France**]

781 The scholar Alcuin of York becomes an advisor to Charlemagne, joining an influential group of scholars at the royal court and thereby helping to launch the "Carolingian Renaissance." [**Germany**]

800 The coronation of Charlemagne as Holy Roman Emperor during a Christmas Day Mass at St. Peter's Basilica in Rome installs him as the heir to the Caesars and thus the legitimate ruler of Europe, thereby distancing the Roman Church from Byzantine rule. [**Italy**]

814 Louis the Pious succeeds his father Charlemagne as Holy Roman Emperor; on his death in 840, the Carolingian Empire disintegrates into three fragmentary kingdoms, collapsing in the late ninth century following further barbarian invasions by the Hungarians, the Vikings, and the Moslems. [**Austria, Belgium, Czechia (Czech Republic), France, Germany, Italy, Liechtenstein, Luxembourg, Netherlands, Poland, Slovakia, Slovenia, Spain, Switzerland**]

829 After an unsuccessful attempt to evangelize Denmark (826–28) under the patronage of its king Harald Klak, Anskar goes to Sweden in response to a request from the Swedish king Björg for a missionary and organizes a small congregation at Birka, on Lake Mälaren. [**Denmark, Sweden**]

851 The Norwegian Viking chieftain Olaf the White sets up a pagan kingdom in Dublin; this would last for the next three centuries. [**Ireland**]

857 Anskar becomes archbishop of Hamburg and as such, the metropolitan of all the northern (i.e., Germanic) churches. [**Germany**]

863 Two brothers, Cyril and Methodius, begin Orthodox missions among the Slavs in Moravia at the request of Ratislav, the Slavic ruler and prince of Moravia. [**Czechia (Czech Republic)**]

864 A delegation from Constantinople baptizes Boris I, king of Bulgaria; six years later Boris persuades the emperor and the ecumenical patriarch of Constantinople to approve an independent Bulgarian church organization, subject to the ecumenical patriarch and conducting its liturgy in the Slavonic language. [**Bulgaria**]

867 Pope Adrian II approves the Old Church Slavic liturgy of Cyril and Methodius (i.e., the celebration of the Western [Roman] liturgy in the Slavic language). [**Italy**]

870 Parties of Viking Norsemen arrive in Iceland and find communities of Irish Catholics already established there. [**Iceland**]

871–899 Alfred the Great defeats the Danish invaders of Wessex, forcing their conversion to Christianity; he later promotes the recovery of Christian learning by the appointment of pious, educated, and trustworthy bishops and abbots, and by the establishment of a court school. [**United Kingdom of Great Britain and Northern Ireland (England)**]

910 The establishment of the Abbey of Cluny in Burgundy brings about a series of changes in medieval monasticism and fosters a renewal of monastic spirituality within the Western Church, based on its model of monastic independence from the local aristocracy and episcopacy. [**France**]

911 A treaty signed at St. Clair-sur-Epte between King Charles the Simple of France and the Viking chieftain Rollo grants the Vikings territory in northwestern France (the duchy of Normandy); these Viking settlers became known as "Normans" (Norsemen or North-men). [**France**]

948 Adam of Bremen records the appointment of the first Danish bishops (under the authority of the archbishop of Hamburg) in the province of Jutland during the reign of Harald Bluetooth (Harald I). [**Denmark**]

955 The Germanic emperor Otto I defeats the Magyars near Augsburg, bringing about the end of the eastern Barbarian invasions until the time of Mongols in the thirteenth century; the Magyars settle in Hungary, which thus becomes a "buffer state" between the Germanic kingdoms and the Asian barbarians. [**Germany, Hungary**]

957 The Kievan grand princess Olga visits Constantinople, where she is baptized into the Orthodox Church. [**Belarus, Russian Federation, Ukraine**]

962 The coronation of Otto as Charlemagne's successor, one and a half centuries after the end of the Carolingian era, marks the restoration of the Holy Roman Empire; this multiethnic association of territories in Western and Central Europe would continue until its dissolution in 1806. [**Germany**]

966 The baptism of Polish prince Mieszko I on his marriage to a Catholic Czech princess leads to the conversion of Poland. [**Poland**]

975 Although there is some mission influence in Hungary after the end of the Magyar invasion in 955, little progress is made until the baptism of Géza (Geisa), prince of Hungary, after his marriage to the Christian princess Adelheid of Poland; as a Christian king, he seeks (whether by persuasion or by force) to turn Hungary into a Christian country, and the number of converts multiplies rapidly. [**Hungary**]

988 The baptism of the grand prince Vladimir of Kiev by Byzantine missionaries leads to the conversion of Kievan Rus' to Orthodox Christianity. [**Belarus, Russian Federation, Ukraine**]

ca. 990 Odinkar Hvite the Elder becomes the first bishop of Skara, the oldest bishopric in Sweden. [**Sweden**]

ca. 990 Olaf Tryggvessön encounters (and is deeply impressed by) a Christian hermit in the Scilly Islands, and receives baptism from him; after becoming king of Norway in 995, he attempts to impose Christianity on his realm, dispatching missionaries to the Shetland, Faroe, and Orkney Islands, as well as to the Norse colonies of Iceland and Greenland. [**United Kingdom of Great Britain and Northern Ireland (Scilly Islands, Scotland), Faroe Islands, Greenland, Iceland, Norway**]

1004 The Icelandic Althing (parliamentary gathering) debates Christianity and the Icelanders go over to Christianity; the Icelandic Church takes institutional form in 1016 with the establishment of the first two bishoprics (Skálholt and Hólar). **[Iceland]**

1016 Olaf Haraldssön becomes king of Norway and, building on the previous gains of Olaf Tryggvessön, seeks to make Christianity permanent in his realm. **[Norway]**

1022 The Danish king Knut sends his Danish bishops to the archbishop of Canterbury for consecration, rather than to Hamburg (the metropolitan see for all of the northern nations), reflecting the increase of English missions in Scandinavia and the decline of Germanic influence. **[Denmark]**

1026 King Knut undertakes a pilgrimage to Rome, thus symbolically linking the Germanic and Roman worlds. **[Denmark]**

1046 Holy Roman Emperor Henry III deposes three rival popes and inaugurates a papal reform movement. **[Germany]**

1049 Leo IX becomes pope and begins church reform by seeking to abolish "simony" (i.e., the appointment of church officials by local lords and princes). **[Italy]**

1054 The Great Schism between the Eastern and Western Churches worsens, with the papal legate Humbert of Silva Candida and the Orthodox patriarch Michael Cerularius anathematizing each other in Constantinople; this strengthens the papal reform movement in Europe. **[Italy]**

1059 Pope Nicholas II issues the papal bull *In nomine Domini*, placing papal elections in the hands of cardinal bishops, rather than in those of the emperor and the lay aristocracy; this decree marks the implementation of a new standardized method of papal selection. **[Italy]**

1066 The Normans invade England under William the Conqueror, the last successful invasion in British history. **[United Kingdom of Great Britain and Northern Ireland (England)]**

1075 Pope Gregory VII forbids the practice of lay investiture (i.e., the bestowal of a ring and staff by a lay ruler upon a bishop or abbot, symbolizing the clergy's dependence on the local princes). [**Italy**]

1076–77 Pope Gregory VII excommunicates Holy Roman Emperor Henry IV, following a bitter dispute over the issue of papal versus imperial authority; Henry is compelled to dress in penitential garb and to wait barefoot in the midwinter snow at the Castle of Canossa for three days, before being allowed to enter and beg absolution. [**Italy**]

1084 Bruno of Cologne founds a Catholic religious order of enclosed monks, the Carthusians, at Chartreuse in the lower French Alps. [**France**]

1085 The Conquest of Toledo by King Alfonso VI of Léon marks the first step in the Reconquista (the Christian reconquest of the Iberian Peninsula). [**Spain**]

1088 The recognition of the University of Bologna by Pope Urban II makes it the first university to be established in Europe. [**Italy**]

1091 The Normans, under King Roger I of Sicily, capture Malta and are welcomed by the island's Catholic population, who had retained their faith (dating back to the apostle Paul) under tolerant Muslim occupation since 870. [**Malta**]

1095 Pope Urban II preaches the First Crusade at the Council of Clermont; this Crusade is initially in the form of a popular pilgrimage to the Holy Land, but later becomes a military expedition to free Asia Minor, Jerusalem, and the Holy Land from Muslim control. [**France**]

1098 Anselm of Canterbury writes his *Cur Deus homo* (Why God became man), marking the beginnings of scholastic theology and of Western interpretations of the atonement. [**Italy, United Kingdom of Great Britain and Northern Ireland (England)**]

1122 Holy Roman Emperor Henry V and Pope Callixtus II sign the Concordat of Worms, ending the long-standing controversy over simony and lay investiture. [**Germany**]

1123 Asser Thorkilsen, the archbishop of Lund (in the province of Skåne, southern Sweden, but then part of Denmark) ordains Arnaldur as the first bishop of Garðar, on the southern tip of Greenland; Arnaldur arrives at his see in 1126. [**Denmark, Greenland**]

1130–55 The involvement of Cistercian monks from Southern Europe contributes to the final establishment of Christianity in Sweden during the reign of Sverker. [**Sweden**]

1146 Pope Eugenius III and King Louis VII of France induce the Cistercian monk Bernard of Clairvaux to preach a Second Crusade to free the Holy Land from Muslim control; Bernard's powerful oratory and passionate sermons motivate his hearers to enlist en masse, with castles and cities often being left empty of able-bodied men as a result. [**France**]

1147 Pope Eugenius III extends the previously granted indulgences for the Second Crusade to a northern Wendish Crusade, launched to achieve the conversion of the Polabian Slavs (or Wends), one of the last pockets of European paganism; although this is largely unsuccessful, the imposition of Christianity is finally enforced there by the Teutonic Knights in the thirteenth century. [**Germany, Poland**]

1152 Cardinal Nicholas Breakspear (later to become Pope Adrian IV, the only Briton to occupy the papal throne) establishes the archbishopric of Nidaros, thus giving the Norwegian Church its own archbishopric, rather than it being subject to the Danish archbishopric of Lund. [**Norway**]

1155 King Erik IX of Sweden carries out a crusade against the Finns, demanding that they be baptized. [**Finland**]

ca. 1157 Peter Lombard completes his theological treatise *Libri quattuor sententiarum* (The four books of sentences) in Paris; these *Sentences* provide a framework for the theological and philosophical discussions of other thinkers. [**France**]

1170 Acting on the words attributed to King Henry II ("Will no one rid me of this turbulent priest?"), four knights assassinate Archbishop Thomas à Becket in Canterbury Cathedral; this event forms the basis of T. S. Eliot's verse drama *Murder in the Cathedral*, first performed in 1935. [**United Kingdom of Great Britain and Northern Ireland (England)**]

1179 The Waldenses (a "back to the Bible" movement) emerge in southern France; however, the Catholic Church strongly opposes the movement for its failure to submit to episcopal authority and excommunicates its adherents the following year. [**France**]

1195 Pope Celestine III proclaims a northern crusade against the resistant heathens around the southern and eastern shores of the Baltic; as part of this crusade, Bishop Berthold of Hanover arrives in Livonia (part of modern-day Latvia) in 1198, seeking to compel the conversion of its inhabitants to Christianity. [**Latvia**]

1198–1216 The reign of Pope Innocent III marks the high point of papal power in Europe; as the "vicar of Christ" he claims the right to intervene in secular affairs on a large scale, enforcing his will by the use of excommunication (the removal of an individual's access to the Eucharist, and hence to grace and salvation) and the interdict (an "ecclesiastical lockout," which bans all public worship or performance of the sacraments in any kingdom whose monarch will not obey the papal commands). [**Italy**]

1210 St. Francis of Assisi founds the Franciscan order, also known as the *Ordo Fratrum Minorum* (i.e., the Little Brothers), with an emphasis on apostolic poverty and mission. [**Italy**]

1215 The Fourth Lateran Council convenes as the largest ecumenical council to date (with an attendance of 71 patriarchs and metropolitan bishops, 412 bishops, more than 800 abbots and priors, and at least 8 royal ambassadors); the council defines the seven sacraments and passes other decrees for the reform of the church, the instruction of the clergy and the laity, the suppression of heresy, and a call for a new Crusade. [**Italy**]

1216 Dominic de Guzman founds the Dominican order, a mendicant religious order dedicated to preaching the gospel and to opposing heresy (hence its official title of *Ordo Praedicatorum*, i.e., the order of preachers). [**Italy**]

1219 The consecration of St. Sava, the greatest of the Serbian national saints, as the autocephalous archbishop of Serbia, strengthens that church's ecclesiastical allegiance to Constantinople, which lasts until the fall of Constantinople to the Turks in 1453 and the de facto abolition of the patriarchate ten years after that. [**Bosnia and Herzegovina, Croatia, Montenegro, Serbia**]

1227 After entering Ukraine (then a buffer zone between Catholic and Orthodox spheres of influence) six years earlier, Dominican missionaries convert and baptize its ruler, Prince Bort; a Hungarian Dominican is then appointed as the first Ukrainian bishop the following year. [**Ukraine**]

1232 Pope Gregory IX establishes the papal Inquisition to prevent allegations of heresy becoming the catalyst for mob violence and to bring a systematic uniformity and legality to the ways in which these accusations are handled. [**Italy**]

1241 Mongol armies reach the gates of Vienna, their greatest westward extent, but Europe is saved when Great Khan Ogetai dies, and they return to Mongolia to elect a new ruler. [**Austria**]

1242 Alexander Nevsky defeats the Teutonic Knights' invasion of Russia at Lake Peipus, when the heavily armored invaders fall through the ice on the northern part of the lake; this enables Russia to remain Orthodox. [**Estonia, Russian Federation**]

ca. 1251 The baptism of King Mindowe of Lithuania leads to the provision of a bishop for Lithuania, but Christianity vanishes from the country after Mindowe's death in 1268. [**Lithuania**]

1274 Thomas Aquinas, the greatest of the medieval Scholastic theologians, dies, leaving his sixty-one-volume *Summa theologiae* unfinished. [**Italy**]

1287 The Mongol monk Ṣaumā arrives in Europe on an ambassadorial mission to the pope and to the Christian courts of Europe; as part of this mission, Ṣaumā visits Rome, Paris, and Gascony (where he celebrates Mass for the English king, Edward I). [**France, Italy**]

1291 The appointment of Magnus, the first indigenous bishop of Åbo, marks the completion of the official Christianization of Finland. [**Finland**]

1302 Pope Boniface VIII issues his bull *Unam sanctam*; this is one of the most extreme claims to papal authority ever made, stating the superiority of the spiritual power over the secular order, and claiming universal papal jurisdiction: "We declare, we proclaim, we define that it is absolutely necessary for salvation that every human creature be subject to the Roman Pontiff [i.e., the pope]."[3] **[Italy]**

1305-77 The "Avignon captivity" of the papacy begins with the election of the French pope Clement V, who declines to travel to Rome and relocates the papal court to Avignon in 1309, where it remains for the next sixty-seven years. **[France]**

ca. 1340 The famous Russian ascetic, spiritual leader, and monastic reformer Sergii of Radonezh founds the Trinity Lavra of St. Sergius, the most significant Russian monastery and the spiritual center of the Russian Orthodox Church; Sergii is today seen as Russia's patron saint. **[Russian Federation]**

1346-1349 The Black Death, carried by means of rat-borne infected fleas along the overland and maritime trade routes from China, devastates Europe, with a death toll of a third to a half of the population in some areas. **[Europe]**

1378 Catherine of Siena attempts to persuade Pope Gregory XI to return the papal court from Avignon to Rome. **[Italy]**

1378 The papal Great Schism develops, with two rival claimants to the papacy (Urban VI and Clement VII); the schism intensifies with the appointment of a third pope (Alexander V) by the Council of Pisa in 1409. **[France, Italy, Germany]**

---

3. Boniface VIII, *Unam sanctam*, para. 4.

1384 The English Reformer John Wycliffe, known as "the Morning Star of the Reformation," dies; forty-four years after his death, his bones are exhumed and burned as those of a heretic by his enemies, but as seventeenth-century churchman Thomas Fuller later wrote: "They . . . burnt them to ashes, and cast them into Swift, a neighbouring brook running hard by. Thus this brook hath conveyed his ashes into Avon, Avon into Severn, Severn into the narrow seas, they into the main ocean. And thus the ashes of Wickliffe are the emblem of his doctrine, which now is dispersed all the world over."[4] [**United Kingdom of Great Britain and Northern Ireland (England)**]

1386 Lithuania formally becomes Christian because of a marriage between the royal families of Lithuania and Poland. [**Lithuania**]

1414 Despite having already been excommunicated for heresy, the Bohemian reformer Jan Hus attends the Council of Constance under a guarantee of safe conduct, but this is rescinded on the grounds that "the Church does not keep faith with heretics," and he is arrested and burned at the stake the following year. [**Czechia (Czech Republic), Germany**]

1414–1418 The Council of Constance deposes the three rival claimants to the papal throne and elects Oddone Colonna as Pope Martin V; in so doing it demonstrates that general councils have greater authority than the popes. [**Germany**]

1418 Thomas à Kempis, a German-Dutch canon regular and a member of the *devotio moderna* (modern devotion) spiritual movement, publishes his devotional book *De Imitatio Christi* (Concerning the imitation of Christ); this became a widely used handbook for the spiritual life, with the current number of editions up to the present day now standing at more than two thousand. [**Netherlands**]

1431–1449 The Seventeenth Ecumenical Council of the Roman Catholic Church, held in several stages at Basel, Ferrara, and Florence, seeks to heal the rift between the Roman and Byzantine Churches. [**Italy, Switzerland**]

---

4. Fuller, *Church History of Britain*, 1:493.

1448 A council of Russian bishops installs Jonas, the bishop of Ryazan and Murom, as metropolitan of Moscow and of all Russia; Jonas's installation (without reference to the ecumenical patriarch of Constantinople, who normally made this appointment) marks the beginnings of a de facto Russian independence from Constantinople. [**Russian Federation**]

1450s Johannes Gutenberg invents the printing press, with the first mass-produced book printed with movable type in Europe being the Latin Vulgate Bible in 1455. [**Germany**]

1479 The Catholic monarchs Ferdinand II of Aragón and Isabella I of Castile establish the Spanish Inquisition, to examine the orthodoxy of those who had converted from Judaism and Islam to Catholicism in their territories. [**Spain**]

1492 The Muslim kingdom of Grenada, the last outpost of Moorish rule, falls to the kingdom of Castile, and the last Muslims are expelled from Spain, completing the *reconquista* (the reconquest of the Iberian Peninsula). [**Spain**]

1498 The Dominican friar Girolamo Savanarola preaches renewal in Florence, where his extreme puritanism is exemplified by his "bonfires of the vanities" (the burning of objects such as art, cosmetics, and books, deemed by authorities to be occasions of sin); paradoxically, Savanarola himself is later burned at the stake. [**Italy**]

1506 Pope Julius II lays the foundation stone of St. Peter's in Rome; the fundraising required for this massive rebuilding project and for the papal sponsorship of Renaissance art reinforces resentment (particularly in Germany) at the extravagance of the papacy, contributing to the emergence of the Reformation. [**Italy**]

1510 Moscow declares itself to be the "third Rome" (i.e., the successor as head of the church after the fall of Rome in 410 and of Constantinople in 1453). [**Russian Federation**]

1514–1517 Cardinal Jiménez de Cisneros Francisco of Castile initiates the translation of the Complutensian Polyglot Bible as part of an ongoing program of reform within the Spanish monastic orders, clergy, and church; this Bible contains the Vulgate Latin translation of the Old Testament, the Greek Old Testament (Septuagint) with interlinear Latin, the Hebrew Old Testament, and an Aramaic paraphrase together with a Latin translation. [**Spain**]

1517 Martin Luther draws up the ninety-five theses, kindling the beginnings of the Lutheran Reformation; there is now scholarly debate over whether he nailed these theses on the church door at Wittenberg or whether he simply sent them to the church authorities. [**Germany**]

1521 Martin Luther appears before Emperor Charles V at the Diet of Worms, where he is condemned for his views but remains steadfast, famously reported as saying, "I cannot and I will not recant anything. . . . [Here I stand; I cannot do otherwise.] God help me. Amen."[5] [**Germany**]

1522 Zwingli's support for the proponents in the "affair of the sausages" (during which several of his colleagues had consumed a meal of sausages during Lent, thus breaking the fast before Easter) brings the Swiss Reformation into the open. [**Switzerland**]

1524–1525 More than a century of agrarian unrest in Germany culminates in the outbreak of the Peasants' War; the radical Reformation preaching of Thomas Müntzer adds a religious dimension to this social revolt. [**Germany**]

1525 William Tyndale publishes his translation of the New Testament, the first to be printed in English, at Cologne and Worms, in defiance of the 1408 Constitutions of Oxford, which strictly forbade translations of the Bible into the native tongue. [**Germany, United Kingdom of Great Britain and Northern Ireland (England)**]

1526–1529 After the conquest of Hungary, the Muslim armies under Suleiman the Magnificent advance toward Vienna in a great invasion of Islam into Christendom; their military successes are seen by Christians as an apocalyptic sign of the end of the world. [**Austria, Hungary**]

---

5. Martin Luther, as quoted in Bainton, *Here I Stand*, 185. The words in brackets do not appear in some versions of Luther's statement.

1527 The Synod of Schleitheim formulates the Schleitheim Articles, a doctrinal agreement summarizing the key features of the *Brüderliche Vereinigung* (Swiss Brethren) movement; these include (among others) the baptism of adult believers by full immersion (hence the name "Anabaptists" or "re-baptizers"), separation from the world, and the prohibition of the bearing of arms or the swearing of oaths. **[Switzerland]**

1529 The Second Diet of Speyer, convened to formulate action against the Turks (then besieging Vienna) and to halt the progress of the Lutheran Reformation, orders that Catholicism be followed in all states of the Holy Roman Empire; the Lutheran princes at the diet issue a legal appeal or "protest" against this ruling, their action creating the label of "Protestant." **[Germany]**

1534 King Henry VIII asserts the supremacy of the English sovereign (rather than the pope) over the Church of England, thus initiating the English Reformation. **[United Kingdom of Great Britain and Northern Ireland (England)]**

1534–1535 A militant radical Anabaptist group seizes power at Munster and sets up a millennial community of the elect under John of Leyden ("the king of new Zion") but are besieged by forces loyal to the exiled Catholic bishop and ruthlessly killed. **[Germany]**

1536 John Calvin publishes the original Latin edition of his seminal *Institutes of the Christian Religion* in Basel; the definitive extended edition would be published in Geneva in 1559. **[Switzerland]**

1540 Pope Paul III authorizes Ignatius Loyola's Society of Jesus (Jesuits) as a missionary order professing vows of poverty, chastity, and special obedience to the pope in matters of mission direction and assignment. **[Italy]**

1541 John Calvin begins his program of civic and religious reform in Geneva through the city council's enactment of his ecclesiastical ordinances; these measures establish the "four ministries" (pastors, doctors [i.e., teachers of Scripture], elders, and deacons), and set up the consistory as an ecclesiastical court to systematically supervise the morals of the people of Geneva, with the intention of making the town a disciplined community, living in conformity with the gospel. **[Switzerland]**

1541 The Diet of Regensburg brings together Catholics (led by Cardinal Gasparo Contarini) and Protestants (represented by Martin Bucer, Philip Melancthon, and others) in theological debate, marking the culmination of attempts to restore religious unity in the Holy Roman Empire. **[Germany]**

1545–1563 The important Council of Trent begins, with the intentions of countering the Protestants, bringing reform to the church's discipline and administration, and providing new "Roman" definitions of Catholic doctrine and practice. **[Italy]**

1546 The posthumous publication of Polish mathematician-astronomer Nicolaus Copernicus's book *On the Revolutions of the Celestial Spheres* (in which he sets out his heliocentric theory of the movements of the planets, in opposition to the church-sanctioned Ptolemaic earth-centered model) stimulates a paradigm shift in the way in which the universe is viewed, thus making an important contribution to the beginnings of the Scientific Revolution. **[Poland]**

1549 Archbishop Thomas Cranmer publishes the first Book of Common Prayer, his 1552 revision removing residual Catholic practices from its liturgy; this is revised again in 1662 after the restoration of the Stuart monarchy and becomes the standard version throughout the British imperial period. **[United Kingdom of Great Britain and Northern Ireland (England)]**

1553–1558 Following the death of King Edward VI and the attempted placing of Lady Jane Grey on the throne to safeguard Protestant gains, a Catholic reaction takes place in England under Mary Tudor (Bloody Mary) and Bishops Latimer and Ridley and Archbishop Cranmer are burned at the stake in 1555 and 1556. **[United Kingdom of Great Britain and Northern Ireland (England)]**

1555 The signing of the Peace of Augsburg provides the first permanent legal basis for the coexistence of Lutheranism and Catholicism in Germany; this politico-religious settlement, based on the formula *cuius regio, eius religio* (whose region, his religion; i.e., the inhabitants of each prince's realm are to follow that prince's religion) ends religious conflict in Germany for more than sixty years. **[Germany]**

1557 The Muslim Ottoman emperor Suleiman the Magnificent restores the Serbian patriarchate, vacant since 1463; this assists the unification of the Serbs in the Ottoman Empire, although the Turks again abolish the patriarchate in 1766. [**Bosnia and Herzegovina, Croatia, Montenegro, North Macedonia, Serbia**]

1559 Queen Elizabeth I, although favoring the Protestants, seeks to maintain a balance in England between the papal Catholics and the radical ("Puritan") Reformers by instituting an inclusive religious settlement for the Church of England in which all parties could claim that their views are maintained; this Elizabethan settlement becomes known as the *via media*, i.e., the "middle way." [**United Kingdom of Great Britain and Northern Ireland (England)**]

1559 The first national synod of the rapidly growing French Reformed (Huguenot) Churches, held in secret near Paris, approves a confession of faith and a church discipline, both following the Calvinist model. [**France**]

1560 The Scottish Parliament passes acts disestablishing the Roman Church and reforming the Church in Scotland; John Knox influences this activity by preaching a series of sermons from the book of Haggai on the rebuilding of the temple, at public services held outside the High Kirk of Edinburgh (St. Giles's Kirk), adjacent to the parliament's meeting place in the Old Tolbooth. [**United Kingdom of Great Britain and Northern Ireland (Scotland)**]

1563 Matthew Parker, archbishop of Canterbury, prepares the Thirty-Nine Articles (a revision of the earlier Forty-Two Articles of King Edward VI's reign, complemented by Johannes Brenz's Lutheran Confession of Württemberg) as a doctrinal foundation for the Church of England; these Thirty-Nine Articles would be published in their final, official form in 1571. [**United Kingdom of Great Britain and Northern Ireland (England)**]

1566 Following a temporary suspension of heresy laws in the face of the Dutch nobility's protests against Spanish Catholic rule, thousands of Protestant refugees flock back to the Netherlands, sparking a call for religious freedom and the outbreak of a Calvinist "iconoclast" Reformation in the Netherlands. [**Netherlands**]

1569 The signing of the Union of Lublin creates a single Polish-Lithuanian Commonwealth; at the same time, Ukraine becomes part of Poland and adopts a completely Catholic official religious identity, leading to the persecution of the Ukrainian Orthodox Church (which had resisted the pressures of Polonization). **[Ukraine]**

1572 Believed to have been initiated by Catherine de' Medici, mother of King Charles IX, the St. Bartholomew's Day Massacre of the French Calvinist Protestants (Huguenots) takes place, with more than twenty thousand killed. **[France]**

1572 Visionary Carmelite nun Teresa of Ávila reaches mystical heights of contemplative prayer, experiencing a "spiritual marriage" to Christ as the bridegroom of the soul. **[Spain]**

1589 The ecumenical patriarch Jeremias II of Constantinople visits Moscow, leading to its recognition as the fifth patriarchate of the Orthodox Church. **[Russian Federation]**

1596 Andrew Melville's forthright remark to King James VI (whom he calls "God's sillie [i.e., humble, lowly] vassal") sums up the attitudes of the Scottish Reformation: "There are two kings and two kingdoms in Scotland. There is Christ Jesus the King and His kingdom the Kirk [Church], whose subject King James the Sixth is, and of whose kingdom not a king, nor a lord, nor a head, but a member."[6] **[United Kingdom of Great Britain and Northern Ireland (Scotland)]**

1596 The Union of Brest-Litovsk creates the Ukrainian Greek Catholic Church, reuniting both the Roman Catholic (Polish) and the Orthodox (Ukrainian) factions into an Orthodox Ukrainian Church in union with Rome (i.e., "the Uniates"). **[Ukraine]**

1598 King Henry IV of France issues the Edict of Nantes, granting freedom of worship to the French Calvinist Protestants (Huguenots); however, this edict would be revoked by King Louis XIV in 1685. **[France]**

---

6. Andrew Melville, as quoted in Burleigh, *Church History of Scotland*, 204–5.

1604 King James I convenes the Hampton Court Conference with representatives of the Church of England (including the Puritans); this leads to the translation and publication of the Authorized Version of the Bible (also known as the King James Bible) in 1611, which exerts a formative influence on English language and religion. [**United Kingdom of Great Britain and Northern Ireland (England)**]

1610 Italian astronomer Galileo Galilei discovers the moons of Jupiter, thereby confirming Copernicus's theory of planetary movements around the sun. [**Italy**]

1618 The Protestant citizens of Prague throw the Holy Roman Emperor's regents from the windows of the council room in Hradčany Castle; although they are not injured, this act of rebellion, known as the "defenestration of Prague," leads to the outbreak of the Thirty Years' War (1618–48), the last war of religion in Europe. [**Czechia (Czech Republic)**]

1618 The Synod of Dort articulates the Calvinist Reformed faith in the Canons of Dort to resolve the Arminian controversy of that day in the light of John Calvin's teaching; these canons have since become a key confessional standard of many Reformed Churches worldwide. [**Netherlands**]

1620 French philosopher Rene Descartes postulates the idea of skeptical rationality in his dictum "Cogito, ergo sum" (I doubt, therefore I exist). [**Germany**]

1622 Pope Gregory XV creates the *Congregatio de Propaganda Fide* (Congregation for the propagation of the faith), a new, centralized body in Rome to oversee the theory and practice of Catholic missions throughout the world. [**Italy**]

1641–1646 The English Civil War breaks out between high church royalists (the Cavaliers) and Puritan parliamentarians (the Roundheads); the latter party's victory ends the Church of England's religious monopoly. [**United Kingdom of Great Britain and Northern Ireland (England)**]

1643–1649 The Westminster Assembly meets to consolidate English Reformed orthodoxy, enshrining this in the Westminster Confession of Faith, a systematic exposition of Calvinist orthodoxy and Puritan theology. [**United Kingdom of Great Britain and Northern Ireland (England)**]

1647 George Fox experiences the first of his "openings" (or illuminations of inner light) and begins to preach; this results in the formation of the Quakers, later called the Society of Friends. [**United Kingdom of Great Britain and Northern Ireland (England)**]

1648 The signing of the series of peace treaties known as the Peace of Westphalia ends the Thirty Years' War, resulting in a radically changed balance of power and the emergence of modern Europe as a community of sovereign states. [**Germany**]

1649 Following the end of the second phase of the English Civil War, and the trial and execution of King Charles I, England becomes a republican commonwealth ruled by the Rump Parliament and a council of state; this parliament is dissolved four years later, and Oliver Cromwell becomes Lord Protector of the English Commonwealth until the restoration of the monarchy under King Charles II in 1660. [**United Kingdom of Great Britain and Northern Ireland (England)**]

1652 Tsar Alexis I appoints Nikon as patriarch of the Russian Church; as patriarch, Nikon controversially attempts to restore the church to a Greek Orthodox model, leading to schism between the traditionalist "Old Believers" and the main body of the Russian Church. [**Russian Federation**]

1660 The failure of the Puritan republic after Oliver Cromwell's death in 1658 leads to the restoration of the monarchy and the crowning of King Charles II as monarch of England, Scotland, and Ireland; although Charles favors a policy of religious tolerance, the reinstatement of the Anglican Church as the established Church of England follows his accession to the throne. [**United Kingdom of Great Britain and Northern Ireland (England)**]

1673 The English Parliament passes the Test Act, limiting access to public office and education to practicing Anglicans in communion with the Church of England, and excluding Catholics and other nonconformists; this act remains in force until 1829. [**United Kingdom of Great Britain and Northern Ireland (England)**]

1675 Philipp Jakob Spener publishes his book *Pia Desideria* (Pious desires), in which he seeks to reform the lifestyle of the Lutheran Church by cultivating a personal, warmhearted relationship with Christ; this lays the foundations of the influential Pietist movement. [**Germany**]

1682 The French Catholic (Gallican) Church issues the Four Articles, a declaration of their position vis-à-vis papal authority; these are condemned by Pope Alexander VIII in 1690. [**France**]

1685 King Louis XIV issues the Edict of Fontainebleu, revoking the 1598 Edict of Nantes, thus making Protestantism illegal in France and providing the catalyst for an exodus of French Calvinist Protestants (Huguenots) to the Netherlands and England. [**France**]

1688 The Dutch Protestant Prince William of Orange invades England with influential English political and religious support, deposes the Catholic King James II, and accedes to the English throne. [**United Kingdom of Great Britain and Northern Ireland (England)**]

1694 August Hermann Francke takes up the chair of Greek and Oriental languages in the newly reorganized University of Halle and extends the influence of Philipp Jakob Spener's Pietism, emphasizing the inner life of the individual (the "religion of the warm heart"). [**Germany**]

1695 English philosopher John Locke publishes his book *The Reasonableness of Christianity*, in which he insists that the beliefs of Christianity are rational and that every individual has the ability and responsibility to achieve salvation by means of the Scriptures; his emphasis on individual responsibility provides a basis for religious toleration and freedom of conscience, helping to lay the foundations of deism and liberalism. [**United Kingdom of Great Britain and Northern Ireland (England)**]

1696 Irish rationalist philosopher John Toland argues in his *Christianity Not Mysterious* that "there is nothing MYSTERIOUS, or ABOVE Reason in the GOSPEL"[7] and that there is therefore no need for revelation in religion; in his view, Christianity is essentially a reiteration of the religion of nature. [**Ireland**]

1698 Anglican priest Thomas Bray, together with some influential friends, founds the Society for Promoting Christian Knowledge (SPCK) to promote Christian education and the distribution of Christian literature; they also set up a related Church of England missionary organization, the Society for the Propagation of the Gospel in Foreign Parts, three years later. [**United Kingdom of Great Britain and Northern Ireland (England)**]

---

7. Toland, *Christianity Not Mysterious*, 66.

1703 French Catholic trainee priest Claude-François Poullart des Places founds a Catholic educational and mission group, the Holy Ghost Fathers (or Spiritans) in Paris; after being reconstituted in 1848, this group would have major influence on nineteenth-century Catholic mission, especially in Africa. [**France**]

1721 As part of his program of the reform and westernization of all aspects of Russian life, Tsar Peter the Great abolishes the Moscow patriarchate and puts the Russian Orthodox Church under the jurisdiction of a government-controlled "most holy governing synod." [**Russian Federation**]

1722 Count Nicholas von Zinzendorf sets up a Pietist Moravian community on his estate of Herrnhut in Saxony; this community experiences an outpouring of the Spirit in 1727, leading to the emergence of the Moravians as a major missionary movement. [**Germany**]

1738 Moravian influence leads Anglican clergyman John Wesley to his "heartwarming" conversion at Aldersgate Street in London; Wesley begins field preaching (i.e., preaching in the open air) to the poor the following year, thus launching the Methodist movement. [**United Kingdom of Great Britain and Northern Ireland (England)**]

1740 Italian cardinal Prospero Lorenzo Lambertini of the Basilica of the Holy Cross in Jerusalem becomes Benedict XIV, the great pope of the eighteenth century. [**Italy**]

1773 After the suppression of the Jesuits in many European countries and overseas dominions because of their economic power and reputation for political maneuvering, Pope Clement XIV issues the bull *Dominus ac Redemptor* dissolving the order; this leads to a decline in Catholic missions worldwide. [**Italy**]

1781 English Anglican Robert Raikes, editor of the *Gloucester Journal*, publicizes the formation of Sunday schools in Gloucestershire and elsewhere, and starts a similar school for the education of the children of factory workers and farm laborers using the Bible as a textbook; this marks the beginning of the Sunday school movement. [**United Kingdom of Great Britain and Northern Ireland (England)**]

1789 The French Revolution begins with the storming of the Bastille (a medieval fortress, armory, and political prison in Paris, which symbolized royal authority and hence the abuses of the monarchy). [**France**]

1792 William Carey publishes his landmark book *An Enquiry into the Obligation of Christians to Use Means for the Conversion of the Heathens, in Which the Religious State of the Different Nations of the World, the Success of Former Undertakings, and the Practicability of Further Undertakings Are Considered* and, with several others, forms the English Baptist Missionary Society, effectively beginning the modern foreign mission movement in the English-speaking Protestant world. [**United Kingdom of Great Britain and Northern Ireland (England)**]

1793 The ascetic monastic and miracle worker Seraphim of Sarov, the most famous of the Russian *startsy* (elders), retires to a log cabin in the forests outside Sarov, where he remains for the next twenty-five years as a solitary hermit. [**Russian Federation**]

1795–1804 The formation of several voluntarist evangelical and missionary societies enlarges the constituency of the Protestant missionary movement; these significant new groups include the Congregationalist London Missionary Society in 1795; the *Nederlandsch Zendeling Genootschap* (Netherlands Missionary Society) in 1797; the Evangelical Anglican Church Missionary Society (CMS) in 1799; and the British and Foreign Bible Society in 1804. [**Netherlands, United Kingdom of Great Britain and Northern Ireland (England)**]

1799 German theologian Friedrich Schleiermacher publishes his influential *Über die Religion: Reden an die Gebildeten unter ihren Verächtern* (On religion: speeches to its cultured despisers) appealing to the role of feeling in Christian faith and focusing on the nature of religious experience. [**Germany**]

1807 As a result of more than twenty years of tireless effort by evangelical English parliamentarian William Wilberforce and other abolitionists, parliament passes the Slave Trade Act, making the slave trade illegal in Britain, although slavery itself is not finally abolished until 1833. [**United Kingdom of Great Britain and Northern Ireland (England)**]

1829 The British parliament passes the Roman Catholic Relief Act 1829, which repeals the 1673 Test Act and thereby establishes Catholic emancipation in Britain. [**United Kingdom of Great Britain and Northern Ireland (England)**]

1833 The Oxford Movement begins in England with the publication of a series of ninety Anglo-Catholic theological publications (the *Tracts for the Times*) by leaders of the movement from 1833 to 1841; this series leads to the informal title of Tractarians for adherents of the movement. [**United Kingdom of Great Britain and Northern Ireland (England)**]

1841–1842 French Spiritan priest François-Marie-Paul Libermann founds the Congregation of the Sacred Heart of Mary as a mission to newly freed slaves in the French colonies. [**France**]

1843 The Danish philosopher Søren Kierkegaard publishes his first work *Enten-Eller* (Either-or), an existential view of Christianity stressing the ethical imperatives of the maturing human conscience. [**Denmark**]

1843 The Great Disruption splits the Church of Scotland over the rights of its congregations to choose their ministers, rather than having the ministers presented to them by the local lairds. [**United Kingdom of Great Britain and Northern Ireland (Scotland)**]

1845 The Evangelical Oxford University scholar and Anglican priest John Henry Newman converts to the Roman Catholic Church, becoming one of its foremost leaders and theologians in the late nineteenth century. [**United Kingdom of Great Britain and Northern Ireland (England)**]

1848 German philosophers and political theorists Karl Marx and Friedrich Engels jointly publish *The Communist Manifesto*, a comprehensive view of history as a series of class struggles leading to the revolutionary overthrow of the bourgeoisie (the ruling class) by the proletariat (the working classes), the abolition of capitalism, and the rise of socialism (and ultimately of Communism). [**Germany**]

1852 The establishment of the Holy Synod in Greece (modeled after that set up in the Russian Orthodox Church in 1721) brings about the independence of the Greek Orthodox Church from the ecumenical patriarch of Constantinople, a process known as "autocephaly." [**Greece**]

1854 Pope Pius IX issues the papal bull *Ineffabilis Deus*, establishing the dogma of the immaculate conception of the Virgin Mary as an article of Catholic faith; this is one of only two ex cathedra papal pronouncements (which the Catholic Church in 1869–70 would declare to be infallible, since they articulated the teaching authority of the church), the other being Pope Pius XII's definition in 1950 of the dogma of the assumption of the Virgin Mary. [**Italy**]

1855 CMS Honorary Secretary Henry Venn formulates his three-self principle (in which CMS-founded churches should become self-supporting, self-governing, and self-propagating), the aim being that missions should ideally be temporary and that the national churches should become indigenous and not encumbered with paternalistic European "cultural baggage." [**United Kingdom of Great Britain and Northern Ireland (England)**]

1859 The English naturalist Charles Darwin publishes his seminal book *On the Origin of Species*, a work of scientific literature considered to be the foundation of evolutionary biology. [**United Kingdom of Great Britain and Northern Ireland (England)**]

1865 Maverick English evangelist and former Methodist minister William Booth launches the Christian Mission (later renamed the Salvation Army) in the East End of London, offering practical help to the poor and destitute, in addition to preaching the gospel. [**United Kingdom of Great Britain and Northern Ireland (England)**]

1867 The archbishop of Canterbury, Charles Thomas Longley, presides over the first decennial Conference of Anglican Bishops at Lambeth Palace; 76 of the 144 bishops in the Anglican Communion are present. [**United Kingdom of Great Britain and Northern Ireland (England)**]

1868 Pope Pius IX summons the First Vatican Council, which meets from December 1869 to October 1870; among the council's decrees is the dogma of papal infallibility (i.e., that when the pope speaks ex cathedra in definition of the church's doctrine, faith, or morals, he articulates the mind of the church, and is therefore preserved from the possibility of error). [**Italy**]

1873 The American evangelist Dwight L. Moody, accompanied by his musician/hymnwriter partner Ira D. Sankey, begins an enormously successful two-year preaching tour of Britain, with crowds of thousands attending his meetings. [**United Kingdom of Great Britain and Northern Ireland (England, Northern Ireland, Scotland)**]

1879 The Serbian Orthodox Church regains its independence from Greek Phanariot control (i.e., the control of the church by prominent Greek families in Phanar, the location of the ecumenical patriarchate), and again becomes autocephalous or completely independent in administrative matters. [**Bosnia and Herzegovina, Croatia, Montenegro, North Macedonia, Serbia**]

1885 The Wallachian, Moldavian, and Transylvanian dioceses of the Constantinople patriarchate unite to become the Romanian Orthodox Church; this follows on from the political union of Moldavia and Wallachia to form the modern state of Romania twenty-six years earlier. [**Republic of Moldova, Romania, Ukraine**]

1891 Pope Leo XIII issues his encyclical *Rerum Novarum* on the social relationships, rights, and duties of capital and labor; this declaration lays a foundation for twentieth-century Catholic social teaching. [**Italy**]

1895 Student leaders from ten European and North American countries meet at Vadstena Castle, Sweden, to form the World Student Christian Federation, a federation of autonomous national student Christian movements. [**Sweden**]

1904 The Welsh Revival breaks out at the Moriah Calvinistic Methodist Church in Loughnor under the leadership of young trainee minister Evan Roberts and expands across Wales, gaining more than one hundred thousand converts over the next twelve months. [**United Kingdom of Great Britain and Northern Ireland (Wales)**]

1905 The French Chambre des Députés passes *Le loi du 9 décembre 1905 concernant la séparation des églises et de l'état* (The law of December 9, 1905, on the separation of the churches and the state), establishing state secularism; as a result, the French state takes over church property. [**France**]

1910 The World Missionary Conference begins in Edinburgh, attended by 1,215 invited delegates from European and American missionary societies, but only 18 from the non-Western world; the conference addresses the promotion of global mission under the slogan of "The Evangelization of the World in This Generation" and, despite its colonial paternalism, is significant as a direct ancestor of the ecumenical movement. [**United Kingdom of Great Britain and Northern Ireland (Scotland)**]

1914 The assassination of the Austrian archduke Franz Ferdinand and his wife Sophie in Sarajevo, Bosnia, and Herzegovina, by nineteen-year-old Serbian nationalist Gavrilan Princip, ignites simmering tensions in the Balkans, triggers the competing alliances of the European Great Powers (Germany, Austria-Hungary, Russia, France, and Great Britain), and unleashes the First World War in Europe. [**Bosnia and Herzegovina**]

1917 A revolution in February results in the formation of a Russian provisional government and the abdication of the tsar; in a second revolution eight months later, the Bolshevik Party led by Vladimir Ilyich Ulyanov (Lenin) establishes a Communist government that would eventually become the Soviet Union. [**Russian Federation**]

1918 The adoption of the Constitution of the Russian Soviet Federated Socialist Republic severs the centuries-old relationship between the Orthodox Church and the Russian state, thereby removing the church's legal position of privilege and power, denying its clergy the right to vote or to hold office in the state, and depriving them of the right to food rations and education for their children. [**Russian Federation**]

1927 Soviet authorities release Metropolitan Sergii Stragorodskii from prison, whereupon he seeks to find accommodation with the state by issuing a declaration accepting its recognition of the Russian Orthodox Church; this declaration causes sharp dissent within the Orthodox Church, those still in prison for their resistance to the government seeing it as a "sellout" to the atheistic state. [**Russian Federation**]

1927 Under the leadership of Canadian Anglican missionary bishop Charles H. Brent, more than four hundred delegates from the Anglican, Baptist, Congregationalist, Lutheran, Methodist, Presbyterian, and Quaker Churches meet at Lausanne to form the Faith and Order Movement (together with the complementary Life and Work Movement) to examine the differences of belief, liturgical practice, polity, and ministry among the various Christian denominations with a view to understanding this diversity; these two movements are important precursors of the Ecumenical Movement. **[Switzerland]**

1929 The Lateran Pacts between Pope Pius XI and the Italian dictator Benito Mussolini establish the Vatican City State as an independent political entity. **[Holy See (Vatican City)]**

1934 Following the Synod of Barmen's theological declaration against Nazism in May 1934, the second Synod of Dahlem seven months later creates the *Bekennende Kirche* (Confessing Church) in opposition to the Nazi-dominated Reich Church. **[Germany]**

1936-1938 The Soviet government launches the Stalinist Great Purge; estimates place the total number of people killed at between 700,000 and 1.2 million, including many bishops and priests who are imprisoned and executed. **[Russian Federation]**

1938 Bernhard Lichtenberg, provost of St. Hedwig's Cathedral in Berlin, bravely protests the arrest of more than twenty thousand Jews and the destruction of nearly two hundred synagogues on *Kristallnacht* (the night of broken glass) on November 9-10, 1938; he is the only priest in the entire German Reich to speak out against this violence: "What happened here yesterday, we know; what will happen tomorrow, we do not know; but we are witnesses of what is happening today. Outside (this church), a synagogue is burning—and a synagogue, too, is a house of God."[8] **[Germany]**

1939 Germany invades Poland; consequently, Britain and France (who had guaranteed military support for Poland in the event of its being attacked) declare war on Germany, thus beginning the Second World War. **[Germany, Poland]**

---

8. Freidländer, *Pius XII*, 91.

1940 Swiss Protestant Roger Schütz founds the Taizé Community, an ecumenical religious order, in Taizé, Saône-et-Loire, France; the community includes more than one hundred brothers from many countries and from both Catholic and Protestant traditions, and has, since its founding, become a significant site of Christian pilgrimage. [**France**]

1943 George Bell, bishop of Chichester, condemns the saturation bombing of German cities such as Hamburg and Dresden, which had resulted in many deaths among their civilian populations. [**United Kingdom of Great Britain and Northern Ireland (England)**]

1945–1947 The installation of one-party Communist governments in most Eastern European countries and in the Balkan states leads to the oppression of the churches there to varying degrees, the closure of churches and church schools, the imprisonment of thousands of clergy, and the promotion of state atheism. [**Eastern Europe**]

1948 The first Assembly of the World Council of Churches takes place in Amsterdam, with 147 churches from different confessions and many countries coming together to commit themselves to the ecumenical movement. [**Netherlands**]

1950 Pope Pius XII issues the bull *Munificentissimus Deus*, proclaiming the dogma of the Virgin Mary's bodily assumption into heaven as an article of Catholic faith based on papal infallibility. [**Holy See (Vatican City)**]

1958 Elderly Italian Cardinal Angelo Giuseppe Roncalli becomes Pope John XXIII; although expected to be a short-term "caretaker pope" and only reigning for five years, he launches the *aggiornimento* (bringing up to date) of canon law and convenes the influential Second Vatican Council, which implements many of his concerns for reform. [**Holy See (Vatican City)**]

1958–1964 Premier Nikita Khrushchev launches an anti-religious campaign in the Soviet Union. This takes the form of mass closures of churches, monasteries, convents, and seminaries; the restriction of parental rights to teach religion to their children; a ban on the presence of children in church services; and other restrictions on church life. [**Russian Federation**]

1962–1965 The Second Vatican Council convenes, with more than 2800 bishops from 116 countries (together with thousands of observers and laypersons, both Catholic and Protestant) attending its four sessions between 1962 and 1965; church historians view the council as one of the most significant religious events of the twentieth century, since it attempted to take account of the world outside the church and to remove the "fortress mentality" that had characterized Catholicism since Vatican I in 1870. [**Holy See (Vatican City)**]

1966 Michael Ramsay, the archbishop of Canterbury, visits Pope Paul VI in Rome, the first such engagement of the leaders of the Anglican and Roman Catholic Churches since the Reformation; following their meeting, they issue a Common Declaration on the development of fraternal relations, the removal of the causes of conflict, and the reestablishment of unity. [**United Kingdom of Great Britain and Northern Ireland (England)**]

1967 Enver Hoxha's hard-line Communist regime closes all religious institutions, bans all religious practices, and declares Albania to be the world's first and only "atheist state"; this severe persecution virtually destroys the Albanian Church. [**Albania**]

1968 The papal encyclical *Humanae Vitae*, affirming the church's moral teaching on the sanctity of life (and reiterating its ban on artificial methods of birth control), creates dissent in Catholic circles, with its opponents seeing it as abrogating efforts to limit population growth worldwide. [**Holy See (Vatican City)**]

1978 The College of Cardinals elects Polish Cardinal Karol Wojtyla as the first non-Italian pope for more than 450 years; as Pope John Paul II, he becomes a significant influence in the fall of Communism in Eastern Europe, especially in Poland. [**Poland**]

1989 In Poland, the Catholic Church becomes a focal point of anti-Communist activism and its pressure for reform a powerful element in the emergence of the Solidarity movement; this develops into a mass campaign for political change, winning a majority in the Polish elections, and inspiring popular resistance to Communist regimes in Eastern Europe later that year. [**Poland**]

1989 Soviet premier Mikhail Gorbachev visits Pope John Paul II at the Vatican; the two leaders agree to establish diplomatic relations, and Gorbachev promises to allow greater religious freedom within the Soviet Union. [**Holy See (Vatican City)**]

1989 Communism collapses in Eastern Europe with the holding of free democratic elections in Poland and Czechoslovakia, the opening of the borders with the West by Hungary and East Germany, and the removal of longtime Communist leaders in Bulgaria and Romania; the most symbolic moment is the dismantling of the Berlin Wall, which had kept East Berlin and West Berlin physically divided for twenty-eight years. [**Bulgaria, Czechia (Czech Republic), Germany, Hungary, Poland, Romania, Slovakia**]

1990 During the annual May Day parade celebrating the end of World War II, Russian Christians participate in the first ever anti-government demonstrations against the Kremlin rulers in Red Square, Moscow; during these demonstrations, an Orthodox priest with a life-size cardboard crucifix directly addresses Premier Gorbachev: "Christ is risen, Mikhail Sergeyevich!"[9] [**Russian Federation**]

2015 A major refugee crisis emerges in Europe; by the end of 2016, nearly 5.2 million refugees had arrived across the Mediterranean from Syria, Iraq, Afghanistan, and Africa, and many thousands more had lost their lives or gone missing while attempting to reach safety. [**France, Greece, Italy**]

2018 *Europe's Young Adults and Religion*, a report based on the 2014–16 European Social Survey, finds that a majority of young adults aged sixteen to twenty-nine years old in twenty-two European countries have no religious faith (Czechia, Estonia, and Sweden being the most irreligious at 91 percent, 80 percent, and 75 percent, respectively); by contrast, Poland has the highest religious adherence at 83 percent, followed by Lithuania at 75 percent.[10] [**Czechia (Czech Republic), Estonia, Lithuania, Poland, Sweden**]

Bibliography

Bainton, Roland. *Here I Stand*. Tring, UK: Lion, 1984.
Boniface VIII, Pope. *Unam sanctam*. New Advent, Nov. 18, 1302. Transcribed by Bob Van Cleef and published by CUA Press in 1927. https://www.newadvent.org/library/docs_b008us.htm.

9. Schodolski and Chicago Tribune, "Gorbachev Jeered in Red Square."
10. Bullivant, *Europe's Young Adults*.

Bullivant, Stephen. *Europe's Young Adults and Religion: Findings from the European Social Survey (2014–16) to Inform the 2018 Synod of Bishops*. St Marys University, 2018. https://www.stmarys.ac.uk/research/centres/benedict-xvi/docs/2018-mar-europe-young-people-report-eng.pdf.

Burleigh, J .H. S. *A Church History of Scotland*. London: Oxford University Press, 1961.

Davidson, Ivor. *The Birth of the Church: From Jesus to Constantine, AD 30–312*. Edited by John D. Woodbridge et al. Monarch History of the Church 1. Oxford: Monarch, 2005.

———. *A Public Faith: From Constantine to the Medieval World, AD 312–600*. Edited by John D. Woodbridge et al. Monarch History of the Church 2. Oxford: Monarch, 2005.

Friedländer, Saul. *Pius XII and the Third Reich: A Documentation*. Translated by Charles Fullmann. London: Chatto & Windus, 1966.

Fuller, Thomas. *The Church History of Britain, from the Birth of Jesus Christ until the Year 1648*. 3rd ed. 3 vols. London: Tegg, 1842.

Hill, Jonathan, ed. *Zondervan Handbook to the History of Christianity*. Oxford: Lion, 2006.

Hollister, C. Warren. *Medieval Europe: A Short History*. 7th ed. New York: McGraw-Hill, 1994.

Jenkins, Philip. *The Next Christendom: The Coming of Global Christianity*. 3rd ed. Oxford: Oxford University Press, 2011.

Johnson, Todd M. "Christianity in Global Context: Trends and Statistics." Pew Research, May 2005. https://www.pewresearch.org/wp-content/uploads/sites/7/2005/05/051805-global-christianity.pdf.

Lamport, Mark A., ed. *Encyclopedia of Christianity in the Global South*. 2 vols. Blue Ridge Summit, PA: Rowman & Littlefield, 2018.

Marty, Martin E. *The Christian World: A Global History*. New York: Modern Library, 2007.

———. "Introduction: Religion in America 1935–1985." In *Altered Landscapes: Christianity in America 1935–1985*, edited by David W. Lotz et al., 1–16. Grand Rapids: Eerdmans, 1989.

McManners, John, ed. *The Oxford Illustrated History of Christianity*. Oxford: Oxford University Press, 1995.

Neill, Stephen. *A History of Christian Missions*. Pelican History of the Church 6. 2nd ed. Edited by Owen Chadwick. Harmondsworth, UK: Penguin, 1986.

Quasten, Johannes. *Patrology*. 4 vols. Westminster, MD: Christian Classics, 1983.

Roberts, J. M. *The Penguin History of the World*. Rev. ed. Harmondsworth, UK: Penguin, 1995.

Schodolski, Vincent J., and *Chicago Tribune*. "Gorbachev Jeered in Red Square." *Chicago Tribune*, May 2, 1990. https://www.chicagotribune.com/news/ct-xpm-1990-05-02-9002050412-story.html.

Stevenson, J., ed. *Creeds, Councils and Controversies: Documents Illustrating the History of the Church to AD 337–461*. Revised by W. H. C. Frend. London: SPCK, 1991.

———. *A New Eusebius: Documents Illustrating the History of the Church to AD 337*. Rev. ed. Revised by W. H. C. Frend. London: SPCK, 1992.

Toland, John. *Christianity Not Mysterious, or, A Treatise Shewing That There Is Nothing in the Gospel Contrary to Reason, nor above It and That No Christian Doctrine Can Be Properly Call'd a Mystery*. Orig. London: Buckley, 1696. Ann Arbor, MI: Text Creation Partnership, 2011. http://name.umdl.umich.edu/A62844.0001.001.

Index

Abelard, Peter, 26
Act of Succession (1810), 105
Act of Supremacy (1534), 106
Act of Toleration (1689), 108–09, 120
Act of Union (1707), 106, 108
Action Française, 85
Acts of Uniformity, 106–07
Adcock, Rachel, 118
Adenauer, Konrad, 92
adversos Judaeos, 142
Aeterni Patris, 83
"Against the Heresies," 4
aggiornamento, 89, 91
Agobard (Saint), 135
Alaric, 11
Alban (Saint), 131
Albertus Magnus, 139
Albrecht of Brandenburg, 99
Alcuin, 20
Alexander I, Tsar, 55
Alleine, Joseph, 123
Allgemeines Landrecht für die Preußischen Staaten, 101
Ambrose of Milan, Bishop, 10, 13, 141
Anabaptist, 119
   as dissenters from Zwingli's reforms, 170
Anglican Church Mission Society, 59
Anglo-Irish War (1919–1921), 186
anti-Bolshevism, Christian,186
anti-communism, 85
Antoninus Pius, 133
Apocalypse of Peter, 4
apocalyptic Jews, 4
Aquinas, Thomas, 25–26, 29
"Architectonic Critique" of the Social Order, 159–60
Aristotle, 138

Arius, 8
Articles of Confederation *(Bundesakte),* 102
asceticism, 9
Athanasius, 8–9
Athenagoras, 132
Augustine of Hippo, 11, 15–16
   Augustinians, 171
Austrian Succession (1740–48), 183
Averroes (Ibn Rushd), 138, 139, 140
Avicenna (Ibn Sina), 138, 139, 140

Balkan Wars (1912–1913), 185
Baptiste-Joseph Gobel, Jean, 53
Bardaisan, 4
Batavian Revolution, 111
Battle of Phoenix (674), 137
Battle of Tours (Poitiers), 137
Battle of Waterloo (1815), 184
Baxter, Richard, 122, 123
Bays, Daniel, 177
Bell, Bishop George of Chichester, 182
Benedict XV, Pope, 84
Benedict XVI, Pope, 89, 92–94, 189
Berger, Maurits, 136
Bergoglio, Jorge Mario, 94
Bernard of Clairvaux, 142–43
Bethel Foundation, 158
Bill of Rights in 1776, 198
Billot, Louis, 85
birth control (artificial), 91–92
Births and Deaths Registration Act, 109
Bishops and Priests Measure (2014), 109
Blake, William, 153
Bodelschwingh (von), Friedrich, 158
Bodenstein von Karlstadt, Andreas, 103
Boehm, William, 122

Bojaxhiu, Anjezë Gonxhe (Mother Teresa), 92
Bolshevik Revolution of October 1917, 185, 202
Boniface (Saint), 135
Book of Common Prayer, 106, 108
Book of Healing, 139
Book of Order (1560), 107
Booth, William, 158
Boris, Khan of Bulgaria, 72
Brethren of the Common Life, 35
Brewer, John, 125
Bridget of Sweden, 29
Brown, Callum, 215
Brown, Sylvia, 118
Brunner, Daniel, 122
Brüsewitz, Oskar, 208
Bubonic plague, 11
Bund der Evangelischen Kirchen in der DDR (BEK), 103
Bunyan, John, 123
Butler, Josephine (1828–1906), 218
Byzantine liturgy, 69

Caecilian. 7–8
Caliph Mu'awiya I, 137
Caliph Uthman, 137
Calvin, John,
Calvin, John, 44, 115, 136, 169
    Institutes of the Christian Religion,169; Calvinism, 44
Cambridge Seven, 176
Campbell, Ted, 121
Canon Episcopi, 135
Canon of Medicine, 139
Carey, William, 173
Carolingian Empire, 230
Casaubon, Méric, 117
Cathars, 135
Cathedrals, 24
Catherine of Siena, 28
Catherine the Great, 51–52
Catholic Action (CA), 216
Catholic Action, 84, 86
Catholic Emancipation Act (1829), 52, 109
Catholic women becoming nuns, increase of, 217

Catholic Women's Suffrage Society (CWSS), 221
Chalcedon, 13
Chalmers, Thomas, 154, 157
Charles I, 108, 117
Charles II, 108
Charles V, Emperor, 15, 19–20, 37, 98, 110, 169, 230
    innovation of a "supranational Western unity," 169
    also Charles the Great, Charlemagne
Chemin de fer—chemin l'enfer (road to hell), 155
Christadelphians, 191
Christendom, 241
Christian Committee for the Defense of the Rights of Believers in the USSR, 209
Christian Democratic parties, 160
Christian II, 103
Christian III, 104
Christianity and Social Order, 161
Christina (Queen) of Sweden, 105
Christlich Demokratische Union, 92–93
church and state, marriage between, 169
Church in Iceland, 104
Church of Christ the Savior in Moscow, 202
Church of Denmark and Norway (and Iceland), 104
Church of England, 106–10
Church of Scotland, 106–10
Church of Sweden, 105–06
Church of Wales, 109
Church, synodal structure, 67
Churchill, Winston, 186; as deist, 186
Civil Constitution of the Clergy, 53
Clare of Assisi, 26
Clarke, Elizabeth, 121
Clement of Alexandria, 4
Clement XIV, 50
Cleves, 99–100
Clovis, 15
Cluny, 21–22
Code of Canon Law (1917), 84–85
Coffey, John, 114, 119, 122, 124
Cohn-Sherbok, Dan, 143
Cold War (1947–1991), 187

Collinson, Patrick, 114
Colloquium, 130
Coltman, Constance (1889–1969), 224
Columbus, Christopher, 170
Comblin, José, 92
Communism and European Christianity, 196ff., 207ff.
  legacy of, 210
  risings in Berlin and Munich (1918–1919), 185
Conciliarism, 81–2, 92
Concordat (Lateran Treaty), 85
Concordat of Bologna, 98
concordat, in 1801, 54–55
Confessio Augustana, 101, 105
Congar, Yves, 89
Congress of Vienna, 55
Constans II, 137
Constantine VI, 70
Constantine, 8, 10, 66, 72, 131
  Constantinople, 77, 137
Contagious Diseases Acts (suspended, 1883; repealed, 1886), 218
"Continental Sunday," 193
corpus Christianum vs. *civitas Dei*, 130
Council for Religious Affairs, 204
Council of Carthage (418), 11
Council of Chalcedon in 451, 12–13, 77
Council of Constantinople, 9
Council of Ephesus, 13
Council of Europe, 243
Council of Nicaea, 8–10
Council of Trent, 44
Counter-Reformation, 33, 44
Crimean War (1853–56), 185, 193
Cromwell, Oliver, 117, 183
Crusade, First, 23–24
cuius regio, eius religio, 101, 111
Cyril of Alexandria, 12

da Gama, Vasco, 170
Daly, Mary, 135
Damascene, John, 70
Daniel, Robert, 121
Danish Church Ordinance of 1537, 104
Dante, 139
de Chardin, Pierre Teilhard, 189
De Gaulle, General Charles, 186

Declaration of the Rights of the Peoples of Russia, 202
Decree on Freedom of Conscience, Ecclesiastical and Religious Communities" of 1918, 202
DeGaulle, Charles, 92
Degollado, Marcial Maciel, 93
Dei Verbum, 90
Delanty, Gerard and "kino-politics," 241
Democrazia Cristiana, 93
Devout Exercises of the Heart, 124
diaspora and European Christianity, 230ff.; and Christian communities, 236; re-presencing, 245
Dickens, Charles, 142
Didascalia apostolorum, 4
Diderot, Denis, 50
Diet of Augsburg, 101
Diet of Speyer, 100
Diet of Worms, 104
Diggers, 117
Dignitatis Humanae, 90
Diocletian, 7, 131, 186
Discourses on the Love of God, 124
Dix, Gregory, 134
Dobrotolyubie, 76
Doddridge, Philip, 124
Doerfer, Maia, 141
Dominicans, 26, 171
Donatus, 9. 11
Dostoevsky, Fyodor, 56
Dupuis, Jacques, 92
Dutch Reformed Church (*Nederlandse Hervormde Kerk*), 111
Dutch Republic, 110
Dworkin, Andrea, 135

Eastern Orthodox Church, 14
Eck, Johann, 42
École Biblique, 89
Edict of Milan (313), 132
Edict of Nantes, 51
Edict of Serdica, 8
Edict of Thessolanica (380), 132
Edict of Worms, 100
Edward VI, 106
Edwards, Mark, 131

Eire, Carlos, 115
Electoral Saxony, 100
Eliade, Mircea, 134
Elizabeth I, 107, 120
emperor and the pope as earthly leaders, 168
empire and European Christianity, 166ff.
    critique of, 166
    Great Commission and, 167
Enchiridion, 35
encyclicals, 83
Engels, Friedrich, 199
English Reformation, 106–10
"enthusiasm," 116–18
Erasmus, Desiderius, 35, 38–39
Esposito, John, 136
European Christian history, 238
    Reformation, 230
    reformations of the sixteenth century, 169
European Values Survey (EVS), 2017, 232
Evagrius of Pontus, 12
Evangelical Alliance of the UK, 240
Expositio evangelii secundum Lucam, 141

faeries (and elvish folk), 133
Faith on the Move, Pew report, 2012, 231
Fascist, 85–86
Faverches de, Richeldis, 27
Feast of Christ the King, 85
Feast of Corpus Christi, 27
Felix, Minucius, 4
feminist Catholic theology, 93
Ferretti, Giovanni Maria Mastai *see* Pius IX, Pope, 58
Ferry, Jules, 60
Feuerbach, Anselm, 199
Fifth Monarchists, 117
Finnish Civil War (1918), 185
First Council of Ephesus in 431, 12
First Estate and Second Estate of the society, 197
First Vatican Council (Vatican I), 59, 82, 94
First World War and European Christianity, 178; effect on German missions, 178
Fisher, Mary, 118

Flavian, Bishop of Constantinople, 12
    Flavian Dynasty, 132
Flett, John, 130
Florensky, Pavel, 203
Fourth Crusade, 74
Fox, Robin Lane, 131
Francis of Assisi, 26, 197
    Franciscans, 171
Francis, Pope, 83, 94, 95
Francke, August Hermann, 171
Franks, 15, 16. 19
Frederick II, 142
Frederick III, Elector, 37
Frederick IV, king of Denmark, 169, 172
Frederick of Saxony, 100
Frederick the Great, king of Prussia, 51, 183
Free Church of Scotland, 108
free or charity schools, 172
French invasion of Egypt (1798), 184
French Protestants, 198
French Revolution, 52–54, 183
Friedrich Engels, 157
Frykenberg, Robert Eric, 167
"full-fledged labor market," 151–52

Gabler, Matthias, 103
Galerius, 8, 9
Gassendi, Pierre, 139
Gaudium et Spes, 90
General Federation for the Abolition of State Regulation of Prostitution in 1875, 218
General Law Code of 1794 (Prussia), 101
George I (England), 101
George III, King, 184
German Old Catholic Church, 103
German Peasants' War, 42
German Protestant Church (*Deutsche Evangelische Kirche*), 103
German wars against Catholic Austria (1866) and the France of Napoleon III (1870–71), 185
Giacomo della Chiesa, 84
Global Christianity, xi; entanglement in, xvi
Glorious Revolution of 1688–89, 52, 169
"gnostic" Christians, 4

Goldhagen, Daniel, 143
"Gospel City," 157
Goths, 11
Graham, Billy, 187, 194
Grand Prince of Moscow, 75
Great Bible, 106
"great idea," 77
Great Terror of 1937, 203
Greek Orthodox Church, 56–57
Green Richard Firth, 133
Green, Thomas, 175
Gregory the Great, bishop of Rome, 15, 132, 141
Gregory V, Pope, 56
Gregory VII, Pope, 22–23
Gregory X, Pope, 142
Gregory XVI, Pope, 59, 155
Grmič, Vekoslav, Catholic Slovenian bishop, 208
Gutenberg, Johannes, 35

Hague Convention of 1899, 190
Handbook of the Militant Christian, 35
Hasidic Jews, 121
heart religion/vital religion, 121–25
Helsinki Final Act of 1975, 209
Henry III, 25
Henry IV, 22, 142
Henry VIII, King and reform agenda, 106, 169
Hermann von Wied, 99
Hildegard of Bingen, 28
Hill, Christopher, 114
Hindmarsh, Bruce, 123, 124
historical amnesia of European Christians, 242
Hitler, Adolf, 86
Hitler's war against the Jews, 187ff.
Hochstifte, 99
Holocaust. *See* Shoah
Holy Roman Empire, 168, 230, 238
Holy Synod, 76
hostility to non-Christian migrants, 233
Hotson, Howard, 125
Hromádka, Josef L, 205, 208
Hughes, Anne, 122
Hughes, Pennethorne, 135
Humanae Vitae, 91

Humani Generis, 87
Humbert, Cardinal, 74
Hungarian Soviet Republic (1919), 185
Hurtado, Larry, 132
Hypatia, 13
Hypostaseis, 12

Icons, 15, 32, 55, 69–71, 73
 Iconoclasm, 69–70
 Iconography, 73
Ignatius of Antioch, 6
Imitation of Christ, 123, 124
Immaculate Conception, 29, 81
Imperial Christianity, 166
Imperialism: A Study, J. A. Hobson, 166
indulgence, 30
Industrial Revolution, 149–54
Innocent IV, Pope, 142
"integralist" Catholic, 84–5
International Pauline Society, 208
Irenaeus, 4
Islam, 136–40
Istanbul. *See* Constantinople

Jacobites (Catholic) versus Williamites (Protestant) during Nine Years War (1688–97), 183
James II, 108
James VI, 107
Janeway, James, 123
Jansenism, 49
 Jansenist, 121
Javorová, Ludmila (1932–), 224
Jehovah's Witnesses, 191
Jenkins, Philip, 172, 238
Jerome, 11
Jesuits, 50, 171
Jesuits, 84
Jewishness, 141
Jews, apocalyptic, 3
JoachimI of Brandenburg, 99
Joan of Arc, 28
John Chrysostom, 10, 13
John Knox, 107
John of Saxony, 100
John Paul I, Pope 91, 209
John Paul II, Pope, 91–94, 191, 194
John XII, Pope, 230

John XXIII, Pope, 87, 88, 89, 91
Johnson, Paul, 142
Jones, David Ceri, 121
Jones, George, 134
Jovinian, 11
Jugendweihe, youth ceremony, 205
Julian II, Pope, 99
Julian of Norwich, 28
Juliana, 27
Jülich-Berg, 99
justification by faith. *See* Luther, Martin
Justin Martyr, 132
Justinian, 67–68

Kaiserswerther Diakonie, 217
Káldy, Zoltán, Hungarian Lutheran bishop, 208
Kautsky, Karl and *Christian communism*, 196
Kennan, George F., 192
Kennedy, G. A. Studdert, 189
Ketteler (von), Wilhelm Emmanuel, 158, 159
Khrushchev, Nikita, 88
Kirill, Patriarch, 77
Komnenos, Alexios I, 74
Kulturkampf (culture war), 82, 102
Kuyper, Abraham, 159–60
Kyushu, island of, 170

L'Avenir, 58
La France, pays de mission?, 88
Laborer Question and Christianity, The, 158
Landesherrliches Kirchenregiment, 101, 102
Late Antique Little Ice Age, 11
Lateran Council, 27
Latourette, Kenneth Scott, *History of the Expansion of Christianity* (1937–1945), 238
Laud, William, 108
Lavigerie, Cardinal, 60
Law on Religious Associations, of 1929, 203
Leagues of the Sacred Heart, 216

Lecky, William, *History of the Rise and Influence of the Spirit of Rationalism in Europe* (1865), 183
Legionaries of Christ, 93
Lenin, Vladimir Ilyich and the Russian Communist Party, 200, 202
Leo I, Bishop of Rome, 12
Leo III, Emperor, 70
Leo III, Pope, 82, 230
Leo IX, Pope, 22
Leo X, Pope, 98
Leo XIII, Pope, 83, 149, 150, 155, 159
    and *Rerum Novarum*, 201
Leopold II, King, 174
Lewis, C. S., *Chronicles of Narnia*, 190
Liberal Catholicism, 58
Life of God in the Soul of Man, 124
Livingston, David, 174
Loisy, Alfred, 83
Louis IX, 25
Louis XIV, 51
Loyola, Ignatius de, 50
Luciani, Albino, 91
Lumen Gentium, 90
Luther, Martin, 33, 35–47, 54, 97, 100–106, 111–117, 126, 128, 168
    justication by faith, 38–39, 41, 45
    Scripture alone, 40–41
Lutheran, 44
    Lutheran Swedish and Finnish deaconesses, 217

Machovec, Milan, 208
Mack, Phyllis, 118
MacKinnon, Donald, 189
Madame Guyon, 122
Makarios, St., 76
Mani, 4
Manning, Henry Edward, 82
Mapping Migration (2008, 2016, 2020), 232
Marcion of Sinope, 4
Maritain, Jacques and Raïssa, 88, 91
Martin, Greg, 139
martyrs of Cordoba, 137
Marx, Karl, 157, 196
Mary. *See* Virgin Mary
Mary I, Queen, 107

Mary, Queen of Scots, 107
Mater et Magistra, 88
Maurras, Charles, 85
Maximum Illud, 85
Mayr-Harting, Henry, 133
Mazowiecki, Tadeusz, 209
McLeod, Hugh, 193
medieval times, unified Christian social and political order in *(corpus Christianum)*, 168
Megas, Abraham ibn, 32
Mehmed IV, 118
Mehmet, Sultan, 75
Mellitus, 133
Methodios, 72
Methodist, 123
Metz, Johann Baptist, 208
Miaphysite, 13
Michael Keroularios, Patriarch, 74
migrant, 234
   age of, 242
   Christian arrival and presence in Europe, 237ff.
   Christian communities committed to welcome migrants and refugees, 233
   economic migrants, 235
   influx influence on majority world Christians, 240
   population growth of, 235
   refugees, 235
   seasonal workers, 235
   transnational, 235
Milan, Council at (390), 11
militarism, Christian, 194
Milton, John, 123
"mirrors for princes," 99
missionaries from Europe introduce Christianity to East Asia, 170
missions not a product between empire and religion, 173
Mit brennender Sorge (with burning anxiety), 86
modernism, 83, 86
Molchus, Johannes, 142
Moltmann, Jürgen, 189
monasteries, 9–10, 20–21;
   monasticism, 67

Monophysite Christians, 137
Montalembert, Charles Forbes René (de Montalembert), 82
Montini, Giovanni Battista, 91
Moody, D. L., 176
Moore, Henry, 117
Moravian influence, 172
More, Thomas, *Utopia*, 197
Mother of God, 81
Mother Theresa, 92; *see also* Bojaxhiu, Anjezë Gonxhe
Mouvement Républicain Populaire, 93
Muggletonians, 117
Muhammad, 16, 137, 139
Münster, 43
Murray, Courtney, 90
"muscular Christianity," 194, 215
Muslims, 16
Mussolini, Benito, 85–86

Nagy, Dorottya, 242
Nail, Thomas and "place-bound social membership," 241
Napoleon, 53, 101–02
   Napoleonic Wars, 55
National Union of Women's Suffrage Societies, Britain, 222
Nelson, Horatio, 184
neo-Gothic, 81
neo-scholasticism, 83
Neryllinus (cult), 132
Nestorius of Constantinople, 12
New Dissent, 119, 120, 121
New Rome, 66
Newman, John Henry, 82, 83, 90
Nicene Creed, 74
Nicholas II, Tsar, 201
Nikodimos, Saint, of the Holy Mountain, 76
Nonconformists, 52, 120, 121–22
Norwegian Law of 1687, 104
Nostra Aetate, 91

Odo of Cluny, 134
Odoacer, 11
Old Dissent, 119, 120, 123
Olofinjana, Israel, 242
"On the Apparel of Women," 4

Order of Poor Clares, 26
ordination of woman, 222
　anti-ordination:
　　Church in Finland (1988), 223
　　Church in Iceland (1974), 223
　　Church of Norway (1961), 223
　　Church of Sweden (1960), 223
　　Congregational Union in Scotland (1929), 224
　　Congregational Union of England and Wales (1929), 224
　　English Presbyterian Church (1921), 224
　　Evangelical Lutheran Church of Denmark (1948), 224
　pro-ordination: Baptist Union of Great Britain (1918), 224
　　Reformed Church (1966), 224
　　We Are Church (Rome, 1996), 223
　　Women's Ordination Worldwide (Austria, 1996), 223
ordination of female bishops:
　Norway (1993), 223
　Denmark (1995), 223
　Sweden (1996), 223
　Finland (2010), 223
　Iceland (2012), 223
Origen, 12
Orthodox Church of Ukraine, 187
Otto, Emperor, 230
Ottoman Empire (1828–29, 1853–56, and 1877–78), 185
Oxford History of Protestant Dissenting Traditions, 114

Pacelli, Eugenio, 86
Page, Anthony, 125
Papal infallibility, 81–82
Papal rejection of Communism, 200ff.
　And Pope Leo XIII, Quod Apostolici Muneris, 200
Papalization of Catholicism, 81–84
Paris, Matthew, 142
Parito Populare, 86
Paul VI, Pope, 83, 91
"Pauline" or "proto-orthodox" Christians, 4
Peace of Westphalia, 101, 136

Pelagius, 11
Peninsula War of 1808–14, 184
Pentecostal Movement, 177; Azusa Street Revival, 177
Pepin III, 15, 19
Perceval, Spencer, Archbishop, 193
Peregrinus Proteus (cult), 132
Peter the Venerable, 140
Peter, Tsar, 76
Philip II, 110
Photios, 74
Pietist movement, 171
Pietist/Pietism, 121, 123
Pirenne, 68
Pius IV, Pope, 44
Pius IX, Pope, 58–59, 81–82, 90
Pius VI, Pope, 52–53, 82
Pius VII, Pope, 53, 55, 184
Pius X, Pope, 83–84, 90
Pius XI, Pope, 85–86, 160
Pius XII, Pope, 86, 89
plague, 29–30
Pliny, 5
Plütschau, Heinrich, 172
Pocock, J. G. A., 118
Polanyi, Karl, 151, 152
Porter, Andrew, 167
Porter, Roy, 125
post-conciliar Catholicism, 91–2
Pragmatic Sanction of Bourges (1438), 98
Price, Richard, 124
Priestley Riots, 125
Priestley, Joseph, 124
Protestants, 43, 100
　missionary work in the nineteenth century as a new form of Protestant piety, 175
　revitalized by separation from European empires, 179
　revolts against Catholic Bourbon and Habsburg rule during the War of the Spanish Succession (1701–15), 183
　Seven Years War (1756–63), 183
　use of laity for mission, 174
Protestant Church

in Germany (*Evangelische Kirche in Deutschland*, EKD), 103
in the Netherlands (*Protestantse Kerk in Nederland*), 111
Prudentius Clemens, 142
purgatory, 29–30
Puritan, 120–23

Quadragesimo Anno, 160
Quakers, 117, 118, 119
Quas Primas, 85
Quietist, 121, 122

Rahner, Karl, 208
ralliement, 82
Ranters, 117
rational Dissenters, 124
Ratzinger, Joseph, 89, 92–94
Reform synod of 1917/18, 77
Reformed, 44
Regnum Christi, 93
Reichsbischof (imperial bishop), 103
Reichskonkordat, 86
Reinhardt, Martin, 103
relativism, 92
relics, 10, 24
religion as a "drug," 199
Religionsgesellschaften (religious societies), 103
Rerum Novarum, 83, 149–50, 153, 159–60
ressourcement, 89, 90, 92
Ricci, Matteo, 170
Richard the Lionheart, 185
Richard von Greiffenklau zu Vollrads, 99
Rise and Progress of Religion of the Soul, 124
Risorgimento, 82
Rivers, Isabel, 118
Robert, Dana, 174
Roberts, Alexandre, 138
Roman Catholic Church, 14, 168
into the fabric of Latin American life, 170
religious orders to establish and maintain overseas missions, 174
Roncalli, Angelo, 87
Rosenfeld, Alvin, 140

Rossi, Pellegrino, 59
Rostislav, Prince of Moravia, 72
Rowe, Elizabeth Singer, 124
Rowe, Thomas, 123
Royden, Maude (1876–1956), chair of
Anglican Church League for Women's Suffrage (CLWS), 222, 225
Congregational City Temple in Holborn, UK, 225
Guildhouse Fellowship, London, 225
Rublev, Andrey, 73
Ruggeri, Michele, 170
Rule of Benedict, 20–21
Runcie, Robert, Archbishop,190
Russell, James, 130, 135
Russian Orthodox Church, 204;
revolution and, 201ff.
Russian Social Democratic Labor Party, 202
Russo-Polish War (1918–1921), 185

Sacred Heart of Jesus, 81
Sacrosanctum Concilium, 90
Sághy, Marianne, 132
Saint Hedwig's Cathedral, 51
Sainte-Chapelle, 25
Salvation Army, 158
satanism, 135–36
Schmidt, Elizabeth (1908–1986), 224
Schmitt, Carl, 141–42
scholasticism, 25–26
Schoolmen, Edward M., 132
Schwärmerei, 117
Schwartz, Christian Fredrick, 172
Schwartz, Hillel, 117
Scougal, Henry, 124
Scripture alone. *See* Luther, Martin
Second Council of Constantinople (381), 14; in (553), 12–13
Second Council of Ephesus (449), 12
Second Council of Nicaea (787), 14
Second Ecumenical Synod of Nicaea, 70
Second Lateran Council, 21–22
Second Reformation, 47
Second Vatican Council (Vatican II), 87–95
Second World War, 178

Seed, John, 124
Senghor, Léopold, 89
separation of church and state, 48
Sergii, St., 73
Servetus, Michael, 125
Shaftesbury, William, 153
Shelley, Percy Bysshe, 142
Shenoute, 13
Shoah (Holocaust), 140, 143
siege of Vienna, 137, 138
Simpson, David, 123, 124
Sobrino, Jon, 92
Social Catholicism, 57–58
social conscience informed by evangelical activism for mission, 174
social motherhood, 216
Society of Jesus. *See,* Jesuit Order
sola scriptura, 116
Sorkin, David, 47
Soskice, Janet, 93
Spanish Civil War (1936–1939), 185
Spener, Philipp Jakob, 171
Spiritual Regulation, 76
St. Joan's International Alliance, 221; St. Joan's Social and Political Alliance, 221
St. Martin's Cathedral, Ypres, Belgium, 190
Stalin, Joseph, 202
Standesämter (register offices), 102
Stanley, Brian, 167, 173
and *global diffusion,* 240
Stark, Rodney, 135, 136
Stephen, Saint, 14
Stilicho, 11
storytelling components, xi, xvi
history, contexts, and communities, xii
migration and global diaspora, xvii
movement, xvii
public theologies, xvii
translation, xvii
Sturzio, Luigi, 86
Suger, Abbot, 24
Summa theologiae, 25
Superstitio, 4
survival of European Christianity, 243

Swedish Church Law of 1686, 106
Syllabus of Errors, 81, 90
Symphonia, 67
synodality, 94, 95
Synodikon of Orthodoxy, 70–71

Taylor, Hudson and China Inland Mission, 177
Temple, Archbishop William, 161, 194
Tertullian of Carthage, 4, 131, 134
Test and Corporation Act, 52, 109
The Communist Manifesto, 199
The Manifesto of the Communist Party, 198
The Nun, 50
"The Social Question," 155–62
Theodore the Studite, 71
Theodosius, 9; Theodosian Code, 13
Theologia Christiana, 25
theologies for political power, especially in Africa and the Americas, xviii
influence of evangelicalism, liberation theologies, and Pentecostal practices for, xviii
theotokos, 29
Third Council of Constantinople (680–81), 14
Third Council of Toledo (589), 14
Third Republic, France's secular, 189
Thirty Years' War (1618–48), 101, 171
Thomas à Becket, 22
Thomas a Kempis, 123
Thomas Aquinas, 139
Thomism, 83
Thompson E. P., 114
Tillich, Paul, 189
Tiridates, King III of Armenia, 8
Tolkien, J.R.R., *Lord of the Rings,* 190
Tolstoy, Leo, 55
Tourkokratia, 75
Treatise Concerning Enthusiasme, 117
Treaty of Munster, 110
Treaty of Vienna, 101, 102
Treaty of Westphalia (1648), 183, 243
Trotsky, Leon, 183

"ultramontane," 57
Ultramontanism, 81–82, 94, 95

Ummayad Caliphate, 137
Union of Brest, 75
Union of Utrecht, 110
Union Sacrée, bound Catholics, Protestants, Jews, and secularists, 188
United Kingdom of the Netherlands, 111
United Presbyterian Church of Scotland, 109
United Prussian Church, 102
Universal Christian Conference on Life and Work, Stockholm, August 1925, 219
Universal Declaration of Human and Civil Rights in 1789, 112, 198
University of Halle, 171
University of Leiden, 110
University of Tübingen, 99
university students take up the cause of missions, 176
Urban II, Pope, 23
Vasa, Gustav, 103, 105

Velichkovsky, St. Paisy, 76
vernacular languages, development of written, 176; translation of scripture, 176
Veuillot, Louis, 81
via media, 107
Virgin Mary, 29
  Marian devotion, 81
Vita sancti Geraldi, 134
volkskerk, 111

Waldensians, 135
Walls, Andrew, 173, 176, 238
Walsh, John, 123
war and European Christianity, 182ff.
  pacificism, 182
  role of the British churches in the First and Second World Wars, 182
War of Liberation of 1813, 184
Warsaw Pact, 187
Watts, Isaac, 124
Watts, Michael, 116
Watts, Ruth, 125
Weber, Max, 119

Weimar Republic, Article 137, 102
welfare state, 162
Wesley, John, 123
Westminster Abbey, 25
Whitefield, George, 123
Wightman, Edward, 125
William (of Orange) and Mary, 108, 110
William I, 111
Williams, George Hunstron, 115
Winter War (1939–1940), 186
witchcraft, 135–36
Wittenberg University, 33, 37, 100, 103
Wittgenstein, Ludwig, 189
Wodan, 134
Wojtyla, Karol, 91–94
Wolsey, Thomas, 98
women and gender studies, Europe, 213
  Christian institutions contribute to, 213
  "feminization of Christianity," 214ff., 220ff.
  middle-class ideology of "separate spheres, 214
  women and missions, 175
  Pandita Ramabai in India, 176
  women's voting rights, 220
  in France, *Action Sociale de la Femme* and *Union Nationale pour le vote des Femmes,* 221
  in Germany, *Deutsch-Evangelischer Frauenbund,* 220
"Worker Priest" movement, 86–87
World Christian Database (*WCD*), 231
world Christianity versus global Christianity, xiii; expansion of and the development of the ecumenical movement, 175
World Council of Churches, 161, 191
World Missionary Conference, 1910, 177
World Student Christian Federation, 177
World Youth Day, 93
Wykes, David, 125

Zentrum Party, 86
Ziegenbalg, Bartholomaüs, 172
Zwickau prophets, 116, 117
Zwingli, Ulrich, 44, 169

www.ingramcontent.com/pod-product-compliance
Lightning Source LLC
Chambersburg PA
CBHW031434230426
43668CB00007B/527